THE NEW BASIC READERS

CURRICULUM FOUNDATION SERIES

REG. U. S. PAT. OFF.

Guidebook

MORE ROADS TO FOLLOW

Helen M. Robinson

Marion Monroe

A. Sterl Artley

Charlotte S. Huck

Linguistic Advisor, W. Cabell Greet

Scott, Foresman and Company

Chicago   Atlanta   Dallas   Palo Alto   Fair Lawn, N. J.

Contents

The New Basic Reading Materials 4

Increasing Competence 7

ROADS HERE AND THERE 17

Introducing the Book and Unit One........................ 18
Open Range 18
Billy and Thunderbolt.................................... 20
When Is a Horse a Pony?.................................. 27
Out of Her Shell... 33
The World of Hogback Mountain........................... 40
Green Hill Neighbors..................................... 48
How to Tell the Top of a Hill............................. 48
Charley Brave 52
New Mexico 59
Louella 61
Soo-Pung Measures Up.................................... 67
It's a Wolf.. 74
Horse-Chestnut Time 81
May Day and Lei Day..................................... 83
Maile's Lei 88
Manaluk's Gold Rush..................................... 95

INTERESTING PEOPLE ALONG THE WAY 101

Introducing Unit Two..................................... 102
Greatness 102
"The Babe" 104
Get 'Em While They're Hot............................... 110
Wilbur Wright and Orville Wright......................... 116
Audubon's Birds 118
Spring Song 125
Sequoyah's Talking Leaves................................ 127
Sequoyah's Honors 133
Abe Lincoln 138
Nancy Hanks 144
A Reply to Nancy Hanks.................................. 144

Captain Smith of Jamestown............................... 146
The Girl with Three Names................................ 151

ROADS TO MAKE-BELIEVE 157

Introducing Unit Three.................................... 158
Roads 158
Puss-in-Boots 159
The Three Wishes... 165
Rapunzel 171
The Dog in the Manger.................................... 177
The Ant and the Grasshopper.............................. 177
The Dove and the Ant..................................... 177
The Boy and the Wolf..................................... 177
The Plate of Pancakes 183
Ridiculous People 187
    There was an Old Man with a beard...................... 187
    A tutor who tooted a flute 187
    There was a Young Lady whose chin 187
    Mrs. Snipkin and Mrs. Wobblechin 187
Pippi Is a Thing-Finder................................... 190
Ridiculous Animals 195
    When a goose meets a moose 195
    Way down South where bananas grow 195
    A fly and a flea flew up in a flue 195
    The Ostrich Is a Silly Bird 195
    A Centipede Was Happy Quite 195
    Only My Opinion..................................... 195
    The Panther.. 195
    Glowworm... 195
    The Duel 195
Pooh Goes Visiting....................................... 200
Us Two 204
Joji and the Fog.. 206
Looking Back 212

Special Articles and Reference Materials 213
A Firm Foundation for Middle Grades—Helen M. Robinson .. 214
Bibliography 227
Methods of Analysis Used to Identify Starred Words...... 231
Index.. 243
Cumulative Word List 252

The New Basic

Reading Materials

The core materials for the second half of the third-grade reading program include the basic reader *More Roads to Follow* (Book Three, Part Two) and the accompanying *Guidebook* and *Think-and-Do Book*.

The selections in *More Roads to Follow* are grouped into three units. Appreciation and understanding of the variety of cultures that contribute to the American way of life are fostered by stories in the first unit, "Roads Here and There," which have settings that span our nation from Hawaii to Vermont and from New Mexico to Alaska. The second unit, "Interesting People along the Way," introduces pupils to biography and highlights qualities displayed by men and women who have played a part, great or small, in America's past. Rollicking and quiet humor, adventure, and wisdom await readers of the third unit, "Roads to Make-Believe."

Articles in the first two units extend ideas and understandings related to the stories that precede or follow them. Poems that enhance the unit themes and at the same time appeal to the universal feelings of childhood stimulate imaginations and promote appreciation of poetic expression.

4

A glossary is included in the basic reader to encourage the development of independence in the effective use of a glossary or dictionary to determine the meanings and pronunciations of unfamiliar words encountered in reading.

In *More Roads to Follow* 735 new words and 30 new forms of known words are introduced. Pupils who have mastered the word-analysis program through Book Three, Part One level can be expected to identify independently 561 of these new words. The application of skills taught in *More Roads to Follow* will enable children to analyze successfully 34 other new words. Most of the words that were introduced at previous levels are repeated in this book.

The Teacher's Edition includes *More Roads to Follow* and its accompanying *Guidebook,* which suggests procedures for establishing background for the reading of the selections, for guiding the interpretation of each, and for developing competence in word perception and in the interpretation of printed language. Suggestions are also made for encouraging personal reading and for extending interests through reading aloud to children.

The *Think-and-Do Book* for use with *More Roads to Follow* reinforces and extends in new context the skills that have been developed and maintained through procedures suggested in the *Guidebook.* The Teacher's Edition of the *Think-and-Do Book* gives brief procedures for guiding the use of each exercise and indicates correct responses. Unfamiliar printed words that boys and girls can be expected to identify independently by combining context clues with word-analysis skills are starred on the page where they first appear.

The *Basic Reading Test* to be used immediately upon completion of *More Roads to Follow* provides an objective measure of each child's mastery of the skills emphasized at this level.

Time for Poetry, a Teacher's Anthology, Revised Edition, compiled by May Hill Arbuthnot, includes most of the poems recommended in this *Guidebook.*

The new *Tall Tales, Part Two,* Revised Edition, is the fifth of the Reading for Independence books that accompany The New Basic Readers. Designed for use immediately after completion of *More Roads to Follow,* this book gives pupils an opportunity to apply interpretive and word-analysis skills independently while they read new content that contains many new words. The questions that follow each story can be used to check children's proficiency in interpretation and their skill in word analysis.

The *Thorndike-Barnhart Beginning Dictionary,* Fifth Edition, which is to be introduced at third-grade level, includes over 20,500 entries with 33,500 meanings. The lessons that appear at the front of the *Beginning Dictionary,* like the dictionary itself, are planned for children who are learning to use a dictionary. These lessons are organized in four sections—the first designed to help pupils locate words in a dictionary, the second to help them find and use definitions, the third to help them interpret pronunciations, and the fourth to help them use a dictionary for spelling and writing.

Many youngsters, of course, will continue to turn to *My Second Pictionary,* which contains over 3800 words. The list of words includes most of the ones used in The Language Arts Program as well as in other programs in the Curriculum Foundation Series through the third grade. The second part of the book, "Words and Pictures," with its grouping of words according to their meaning and function, is especially helpful to children for independent writing.

Increasing Competence

In The New Basic Reading Program pupils progress through planned stages of difficulty to steadily rising levels of competence in reading. With *More Roads to Follow* (Book Three, Part Two), children enter upon the last level of the primary-grade sequence. As at previous levels, not all youngsters will have achieved the same degree of competence; despite the many individual differences apparent in any classroom, however, the teacher has the responsibility of helping all children move successfully toward independence in reading.

Evaluating competence

To help determine which understandings and skills may need special emphasis at this level, either for an individual or for a group, the results of the *Basic Reading Test* for *Roads to Follow* may be assessed. If youngsters have used the new *Tall Tales, Part One*, Revised Edition, the fourth of the Reading for Independence Books, the teacher will have another means of evaluating pupils' strengths and weaknesses before they begin *More Roads to Follow*. Children's answers to the questions at the end of each story in the new *Tall Tales, Part One* and their responses to the exercises at the back of the book will indicate their ability to interpret new stories independently and to use word analysis and context clues in identifying unfamiliar words as they read.

To these objective measures of children's competence the teacher will want to add her own observations. For a check list of the skills, abilities, and understandings that have been developed and applied through Book Two, Part Two level in The New Basic Reading Program, she can refer to pages 12-17 in the *Guidebook* for *Roads to Follow*. To this summary in three sections (word perception, interpretation, and attitudes and habits) should be added, of course, the skills, abilities, and understandings developed at Book Three, Part One level, discussed on pages 18-24 of the same *Guidebook*.

What's ahead

The selections in *More Roads to Follow*, the teaching procedures suggested in the *Guidebook*, and the accompanying exercises in the *Think-and-Do Book* are carefully planned to reinforce and extend the understandings, skills, abilities, and attitudes that pupils need for rapid progress in reading increasingly difficult material. This progress will be made in three directions—in strengthening and extending word-perception skills, in broadening and sharpening interpretive skills, and in building and reinforcing important habits and attitudes related to reading. The most important of the new aspects of growth are described in the following paragraphs.

Word perception

At Book Three, Part Two level children draw on knowledge gained at previous levels as they learn to apply word-analysis skills to multisyllabic words and strengthen their ability to use a glossary (or dictionary) for the meaning and pronunciation of words.

With the first word-perception exercises children reinforce and extend their ability to use phonetic analysis in identifying one- and two-syllable root words. Mastery of various skills and understandings is checked as they review what they have learned about consonants, vowels, syllables, and accent and apply this knowledge in identifying unfamiliar printed words. Among the basic concepts reviewed are the following

8

understandings: (1) different consonant letters may represent the same consonant sound; (2) different spellings may represent the same vowel sound; (3) spelling patterns provide visual clues to vowel sounds in one- and two-syllable words.

As youngsters review and reinforce learnings, they also extend their knowledge. For example, when children review the relationship of spelling patterns to vowel and consonant sounds in two-syllable words, they note that a single vowel letter followed by a consonant blend (as in *April*, *secret*, and *cyclone*) often stands for a long vowel sound. They learn that in words like *science* and *lion*, in which two vowel letters together represent two vowel sounds, the first syllable is usually accented and the first vowel letter often stands for a long vowel sound.

By comparing patterned groups of two-syllable words accented on the first syllable (groups like *harbor*, *carrot*, *carol* and *person*, *merry*, *very*), pupils note that the vowel letter *a* or *e* followed by two *r*'s or by a single letter *r* and a vowel letter does not represent the vowel of *car* or the vowel of *her*. In the discussion of such words as *also*, *Alvin*, *gallop*, *balance*, *corral* children learn that in words of more than one syllable the letter *a* followed by *l* in an accented syllable is more likely to stand for the vowel of *hat* than the vowel of *all*.

Next <u>pupils learn to use phonetic analysis in identifying words of three or more syllables.</u> Their attention is first called to accent patterns in three-syllable words and to spelling patterns that help determine the number of syllables in words. After generalizing that three-syllable words are usually accented on either the first or second syllable, they compare two- and three-syllable words and note, for example, that final *e* does not represent a separate syllable (*engine*, *medicine*) and that some vowel letters together indicate only one syllable (*agree*, *committee; station, attention; jealous, enormous*).

As children identify vowel sounds in accented syllables of multisyllabic words, they apply what they learned about vowel-consonant spelling patterns as clues to vowel sounds in one-syllable words and the accented syllables of two-syllable words. Youngsters recall that in an initial accented syllable of a two-syllable word a single vowel letter followed by two consonant letters, as in a word like *silver*, usually stands for a short vowel sound and that a single letter followed by one consonant letter, as in *pity* and *pilot*, may stand for either a short or long vowel sound. Then they learn that the same patterns apply to accented syllables in three-syllable words like *battery*, *president*, and *stadium*.

9

In their study of the spelling of such words as *carpenter, barrier* and *permanent, terrible*, pupils find that they can apply their previous learnings about similar spelling patterns in two-syllable words. (If an *a* or *e* is followed by two *r*'s together or by a single *r* and a vowel letter, the *a* or *e* does not represent the vowel of *car* or the vowel of *her*.) When children review the understanding that some words have two accents —primary and secondary—their ability to attack unfamiliar words is extended as they learn that clues to vowel sounds in accented syllables apply to syllables with secondary accents.

Youngsters' ability to use structural analysis is strengthened and extended at this level as they are introduced to the prefixes *fore-* and *re-* and the suffixes *-teen, -ty, -th, -ward, -able,* and *-ship*. They also note the differences between the numerical suffixes *-ty* and *-th* (used to form such words as *twenty* and *fourth*) and the noun-forming suffixes *-ty* and *-th* (used to form words like *cruelty* and *warmth*).

At Book Three, Part Two level boys and girls continue to combine structural and phonetic analysis to identify inflected and derived forms of unfamiliar root words—roots to which they can apply what they have learned about clues to vowel sounds in accented syllables (*divided, astonished, remarkable,* for example).

Just as at earlier levels, whenever structural- and phonetic-analysis skills are introduced or refined, children are given the opportunity to apply them immediately in identifying new words in context. These skills and understandings are strengthened further as youngsters use them to identify words independently in the *Think-and-Do Book,* in the selections in *More Roads to Follow,* and in the books and stories they choose to read on their own.

Children take another step toward mastering an important aid to independence in reading as they review and extend their knowledge of how to use a glossary (or dictionary) for the meanings and pronunciations of words. The glossary in *More Roads to Follow* provides the opportunity to call pupils' attention to the following types of entries: words with two pronunciations, words with alternate plurals or with plural forms that are the same as the singular forms, words with alternate spellings, homographs, cross references, words and phrases with special meanings, prefixes and suffixes, biographical entries, place names, compounds, two-word entries, abbreviations, entries for pronunciation only. In applying these understandings independently, children become increasingly familiar with the use of a glossary or dictionary and learn to recognize and appreciate the many helps and kinds of information that can be gleaned from them.

Boys and girls continue to strengthen ability to use a pronunciation key to interpret dictionary pronunciations. A variety of suggestions is given to strengthen competence in the use of pronunciation symbols, for as children develop facility with this tool, it becomes an important aid in independent reading.

Suggestions are also given to help strengthen youngsters' ability to select the appropriate meaning for a word to fit a given context. They then learn to adapt the definition to fit it smoothly into the context in which the word is used. In doing this they discover that it is sometimes sufficient to substitute the definition for the word in the sentence, but that in other instances it is necessary to add inflectional endings to root forms in the definition, to transpose words in the definition and/or in the sentence, or even to restate both the definition and the sentence in their own words.

Children may already have begun, at the preceding level, to use the *Thorndike-Barnhart Beginning Dictionary* in addition to the glossary at the back of *Roads to Follow*. (See the special article "Children Are Ready for the Dictionary," by A. Sterl Artley, in the *Guidebook* for *Roads to Follow*.) The *Beginning Dictionary* is especially geared to the needs of pupils at this level. The front section, "How to use this dictionary," provides step-by-step instruction that children may follow independently to strengthen their ability to use necessary dictionary skills. With the emphasis placed on personal reading, the dictionary becomes increasingly important as an independent way of learning the meaning and pronunciation of unfamiliar printed words. If youngsters have access to a dictionary, they should be encouraged to turn to it frequently for answers to their questions about words.

Interpretation

In *More Roads to Follow* children encounter subject matter that becomes progressively more varied and complex. At the previous level reading material branched out from the purely fictional to include factual articles, historical fiction, and poetry. At this level pupils are introduced to biographical writing and the pure fable form typified by Aesop's fables. Poetry selections are abundant, with lyrical poetry supplemented by narrative verse, nonsense rhymes, and limericks.

Story plots, settings, and style continue to grow in sophistication and in their demands upon youngsters' interpretive powers—for example, perceiving relationships, making inferences, grasping implied ideas, making judgments, forming sensory images. The ability to perceive relationships is among those particularly stressed, for children need to synthesize all facets of the setting that influence the characters in a selection: social forces, geographical factors, community and neighborhood environment, and the historical period in which the events take place. Young readers interpret the behavior of the persons in the stories, bearing in mind all the dimensions of the setting in understanding motives, in sensing mood and emotion, and in anticipating and reacting to events. Through application to more mature selections and to a greater variety of literary forms, children's basic interpretive skills are continually extended and refined.

The title of the first unit, "Roads Here and There," heralds the broadening trend that children will find in the stories. The settings, the characters, and the situations reflect the variety of people and places to be found in the United States. "Billy and Thunderbolt" (pages 9-17), for example, takes place in open-range country in the West, while "Maile's Lei" (pages 80-87) has a backdrop of Hawaiian waterfalls and ginger blossoms. Because many of the settings may be unfamiliar to some pupils, imaginations must be stretched to form vivid sensory images.

The diversity of cultures represented by the stories in this unit provides opportunity for youngsters to note that despite cultural differences people are basically alike and to relate their own personal experiences to those of the characters in the stories. For example, the story problem in "Soo-Pung Measures Up" (pages 58-65) stems from the desire of a Chinese-American boy to be big enough to help carry the symbolic dragon in the New Year's parade through the streets of San Francisco's Chinatown. The longing to be big enough to participate in some activity is one that most young readers will have shared at one time or another, rendering Soo-Pung's emotional reactions completely understandable even though the particular aspect of his problem may be entirely unfamiliar to them.

Biography is introduced in the second unit, "Interesting People along the Way." Both prose and poetry have been chosen with care to help children associate the subjects of the selections with information that they already have. Their own baseball experiences and stories in *Roads to Follow* will have supplied background for the biographical sketch of Babe Ruth (pages 102-110). "Get 'Em While They're Hot" (pages 111-114) gives one version of the origin of the hot dog, a popular food to which children need no introduction. Pupils should find a similar basis for interest in the subject of each selection and for understanding it.

With Book Three, Part Two the concepts of time and place are more complicated than those youngsters have encountered at earlier levels. This is especially evident in the biographical unit. For the historical unit in *Roads to Follow* boys and girls were required to gear their thinking to a distant time and place, but the stories themselves were sequential and the geographical area remained constant. As they read *More Roads to Follow*, pupils must adjust to different times in history—from the relatively recent day of Babe Ruth to the much more distant time of Captain John Smith and the Jamestown settlement—and to changes in locale from one selection to the next.

Time spans of individual stories also vary. Some selections present brief episodes in persons' lives, like the boyhood prank reported in "Abe Lincoln" (pages 140-153). Others cover extended periods, the most comprehensive being "The Girl with Three Names" (pages 163-171), which is a narrative summation of Pocahontas' life.

Building upon interests awakened by the unit on the Plymouth settlement in Book Three, Part One, pupils add to their appreciation of the past and develop a lively curiosity about people and events of former times. As they draw upon both past and present reading, they begin to realize how information gained from several sources can be organized to develop a more complete understanding of a time, place, person, or event.

New and old fanciful tales and poems are presented in the third unit, "Roads to Make-Believe." Some of these selections—"Pippi Is a Thing-Finder" (pages 217-231), "Pooh Goes Visiting" (pages 238-250), and "Us Two" (pages 251-252), for example—are modern classics while others are thousands of years old. A group of these ancient stories (pages 202-206) introduces pupils to the fable in its classic form.

Throughout their use of *More Roads to Follow* boys and girls develop sensitivity to clues that indicate character, mood, and plot development. These clues may be found in a character's speech, in his behavior, in his environment, and in his reactions to that environment. The sparse, terse dialogue in "The World of Hogback Mountain" (pages 27-34), for example, helps establish the mood of the story as it reveals the intensity of feeling of the main character. Similarly the conversation in "Abe Lincoln" (pages 140-153) gives expression to the sense of humor usually associated with Lincoln, provides a glimpse of the youth's ambition, and establishes a feeling for a particular place and time. Even in fanciful stories like "Rapunzel" (pages 193-201) speech, behavior, and environment combine to achieve the atmosphere of fantasy and the crystalline characterizations of fairy tales. The music of the refrain "Rapunzel! Rapunzel! Let down your golden hair," the rascality of the old witch, and the tower surrounded by a thorny thicket all belong to the world of make-believe. The overall effect of these elements does not result from the use of specific adjectives and statements, but it becomes evident as children draw inferences, grasp implied ideas, and make judgments. A variety of exercises in the *Think-and-Do Book* helps strengthen these skills.

Through careful guidance children are encouraged to respond to different types of poetry more varied in both form and subject matter at this level than at the preceding level. In order to appreciate a poem's message, it is sometimes necessary to understand implied ideas. One often needs to be aware of an emotion or mood, be it poignant or hilarious. Suggestions in the lesson plan for each poem point up specific skills that are important in interpreting each poem, making youngsters aware of the sensory imagery, alliteration, rhythm—or any combination of these—which distinguishes that poem.

In addition to the poems presented in the text, others are suggested that may help cultivate children's taste for poetry, eventually adding another source of enjoyment to personal reading.

Preparation for effective oral reading helps strengthen other reading skills as pupils, both readers and listeners, foster a creative approach when selections are interpreted orally. In combining pantomime and dialogue in scenes that build to a climax, children develop an appreciation for the structure of a story and for the ways an author reveals character

14

or mood. In reading narrative passages to discover whose thoughts are revealed or whose point of view is expressed, they develop habits that will aid in critical reading.

Especially important at this level is the interpretation of dialogue. Readers and listeners are helped to understand the characters and to experience vicariously the happenings of the story before oral reading begins. Listeners continue to identify with these story characters while their classmates read aloud, for they know they may soon have a chance to take a reader's place. Through such identification word-by-word reading is replaced with appropriate rate, pitch, and volume; the reader's quality of voice, facial expressions, and bodily movements become more flexible, approximating children's real-life conversations.

Pantomime continues to take an important place in oral interpretation. Through pantomime pupils visualize the characters in action and become thoroughly familiar with the sequence of events before long scenes are interpreted orally.

A variety of oral reading skills is emphasized so that children may be given help in that skill which most needs it. Pupils are challenged to use their imaginations so that even the slowest reader can find satisfaction in reading short passages.

Attitudes and habits

The variety of literary forms in *More Roads to Follow* lends added dimension to the meaning of the book's title and the titles of its units. For not only do the selections themselves lead young readers across America and to many periods in time, but the increased variety of prose and poetic forms continues to point up the idea that reading roads may take many different routes, all of which can be interesting and informative. Children are made increasingly aware that they may turn to factual as well as to fictional books, to poetry as well as to prose, and that they can benefit by considering the type of material appropriate for specific needs or interests.

Reading habits that aid in competent word perception and effective interpretation are strengthened and expanded to include more complicated language. The habit of turning to a glossary (or dictionary) for meaning and pronunciation of words is reinforced by consistent use as boys and girls discover that incidental and helpful information may also be procured from this source.

At this level, as at the Book Three, Part One level, children are continually encouraged to assume greater responsibility for understanding what they read—setting their own purposes for reading, adopting an inquiring attitude, evaluating what they read, and relating story situations and character reactions to their own experiences. Many self-directing pages of the *Think-and-Do Book* strengthen this attitude of responsibility, requiring boys and girls to read, understand, and follow printed instructions.

Particular emphasis is placed on developing the ability to grasp implied ideas and make generalizations and judgments so that children cultivate the habit of thinking beyond the literal meaning of what they have read. The development of critical reading is fostered as youngsters use the text to verify their own ideas and as they distinguish between facts and opinions presented by authors. Children who grow accustomed to bringing as much of themselves to reading as they can will receive the most from reading. This increasing sense of responsibility and greater discipline of thought are evidence of growing competence, hence independence, in reading.

The procedures suggested in the lesson plans that follow in this *Guidebook* point up the important aspects of each skill in proper sequence and in proper relation to other skills. The teacher will find these procedures effective if she bears in mind children's individual reading abilities and limitations and adapts the lesson plans accordingly. Adjustments in light of individual differences, coupled with adherence to the sequential development of these skills, will assure youngsters' progress on the road to independence in reading—the goal of The New Basic Reading Program.

ROADS HERE AND THERE

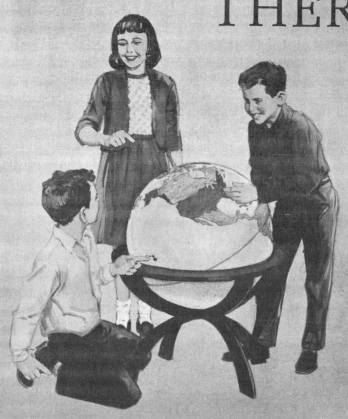

Introducing the Book and Unit One

A new book is welcomed by pupils as an indication of achievement and an appealing invitation to new adventures. To introduce *More Roads to Follow,* you might begin by reading aloud Kathryn and Byron Jackson's poem "Open Range," which appears on page 6. Suggest that as boys and girls listen, they try to see the picture the poets describe.

Children listen to the poem "Open Range"...

When children have heard the poem, invite them to tell what they saw and felt as they listened. Then ask: "Why do you suppose this poem is called 'Open Range'? Have you ever been on an open range, or have you seen open-range country on TV? In what part of the United States would you find this kind of land?" Stimulate imaginations by asking pupils what kinds of places they might find beyond the distant hills and mountains the poets described.

discuss their reactions...

At this point suggest that books can serve as roads to take us on journeys to many places and introduce us to many people. Can youngsters remember some of the roads they traveled as they read *Roads to Follow?* Who were some of the people they met along the way? Continue: "The name of our new book is *More Roads to Follow*. Let's find out about some of the new roads we'll travel and people we'll meet."

in new book note continuation of theme from Roads to Follow...

Next distribute copies of the book, and encourage boys and girls to comment on the picture on the cover. If no one recognizes the boy in the picture, comment that he is Eddie Wilson, whom they met in *Roads to Follow*. Do they remember what happened when Eddie decided to bring a pet goat home? Then inquire: "Do you suppose all the luggage in this picture belongs to Eddie? What makes you think it doesn't? Where do you think Eddie is? What do you suppose he's doing?"

discuss cover and title page of More Roads to Follow...

Suggest that youngsters turn to the title page to see whether Eddie found what he was looking for. When they have had a chance to speculate about what he might be doing with a parrot, comment that they will find out more about Eddie and the parrot as they read *More Roads to Follow*. (It is possible that some pupils have read about Eddie and Louella. You might suggest that these youngsters keep what they know a secret until everyone has had a chance to read the story.)

Invite children to look at the table of contents. Lead them to note the three groups of stories and to infer from the unit titles what kinds of stories they will be reading.

make inferences from table of contents . . .

When pupils have had an opportunity to leaf through their books and to chat informally about what they found, call attention to pages 6 and 7, the opening pages of the first unit. Reread the poem on page 6, this time suggesting that youngsters follow along in their own books as you read. Then point out that as children read the stories in this unit, they will visit boys and girls not only in the open-range country described by the poets but in many other places as well. Help pupils identify some of the other story settings in the first unit, using the clues in the illustration on page 7. Verify the idea that the stories take place in many different parts of the United States, making sure children note the location of Alaska and Hawaii.

and from unit title page.

Finally comment: "By the time you've finished these stories, you will have visited boys and girls in the states of Alaska and Hawaii, in New York City and in San Francisco, in the mountains of the eastern part of the United States, and in the vast open country of the West. You'll find that the characters in these stories are alike in many ways, just as were many of the story characters you met in *Roads to Follow*. As you read you may also notice how the place where a person lives influences his interests and activities. Now let's find out where the road in our first story takes us."

In this story patience and gentleness prove more effective in capturing and breaking a wild horse than fast mounts and lariats. Children who share Billy's pride in winning Thunderbolt's confidence will be quick to sense why his way of handling animals was a good one.

Time relationships are emphasized as children note clues that indicate the passing of time in this selection and in a story in the *Think-and-Do Book*. Pupils will also have an opportunity to reinforce their understanding of the types of help that can be found in a glossary or dictionary and to review dictionary skills they have learned at previous levels.

New words: *corral,* carrots, sugar, usually, afterwards, disappointed, *anxious,* understand (Thunderbolt*, ranch*, west*, bought*, *trailer*, enjoyed*, cattle*, arrived*, stretch*, saddle*, *bridle*, wore*, eager*, gaily*, *herd*, twice*, *ledge*, *whinnied*, harm*, moment*, shade*, lonely*, except*, advice*, distance*, mine*, bother*, became*, gentle*, unless*, *buck*, *rear*, trembled*, bareback*, trusted*)

Think-and-Do Book: Pages 1, 2, 3, and 4

Establishing background

Present some of the new words as you set the stage for the story. Comment: "In today's story you'll meet a boy named Billy who was going with his parents to spend the summer away from home. When Billy went away, he *usually* had to leave his pony behind, but this time he was taking the pony along. On the day they left, Billy made sure his boots and new cowboy outfit were packed. *Afterwards* he put a *bag of carrots* in the car and some *pieces of sugar* in his pocket. Why

Pupils identify new words . . .

do you suppose he did that? Do you have any idea where Billy might be going?" The words *corral, disappointed,* and *anxious* may be presented during the guided interpretation of the story, but youngsters should be encouraged to identify the word *understand* independently from context and spelling clues.

speculate about setting of story . . .

In this Guidebook *the verb* present *means that you are to write the italicized words, phrases, or sentences on the board as you use them in meaningful oral context. After each presentation have pupils read the words silently and orally. In this way children learn to associate sound, form, and meaning with each new word. (All italicized words in this section should be presented unless other suggestions are given.)*

The words that are printed in black at the beginning of each lesson plan are to be presented. Words printed in black and starred are ones youngsters should identify independently by combining context clues with methods of word analysis introduced at this level. Words printed in blue and starred are ones that pupils can identify by using methods of word analysis developed at preceding levels. Italic type indicates that the root or a form of the root word appears in the glossary. The particular type of word analysis children may use to identify each starred word is indicated at the back of this Guidebook *in the section "Methods of Analysis Used to Identify Starred Words."*

To encourage pupils to use the glossary, write the words *trailer, bridle, herd, ledge, whinnied, buck, rear, crop, scrub.* Comment that you are sure children can identify these words by themselves, but if, as they are reading the story, they have difficulty pronouncing them or understanding their meaning, they should use the glossary. Although the last two words are not new, they convey meanings that may be unfamiliar.

note words they may want to find in the glossary as they read . . .

Boys and girls should not be given the impression that it is necessary or even desirable to look up lists of isolated words in a glossary or a dictionary. Rather it is important that youngsters regard a glossary or a dictionary as a functional tool for checking pronunciations and meanings of unfamiliar words that they encounter in context.

Guiding interpretation

As pupils talk about the first illustration, call attention to the wide expanse of land, the hills, and the sparse clumps of grass —all of which will provide children with a basis for visualizing the setting and action as they read the story. During the conversation lead youngsters to infer that Billy's pony is in the trailer, and bring out that when Billy and his family arrive at their destination, he will probably *keep the pony in a corral* (present the phrase). Pupils might also turn with you to the glossary to check the meaning of *corral*.

Then call attention to the title and ask children who or what they think Thunderbolt is. Invite them to read the first three pages to find out.

Following silent reading, encourage youngsters to explain who Thunderbolt is and how Billy happened to see him. Have pupils seen Thunderbolt in an illustration yet? Lead them to note that Blaze, Billy's pony, is shown in the picture on page 10 and that Jim and his horse appear on page 8.

To focus attention on Billy's feelings about Thunderbolt, ask:
—Why do you suppose Billy didn't want the cowboys to catch the wild horse? Do you agree with Billy? Why [or why not]?
—Do you think he'll want to see Thunderbolt again? Would you, if you were Billy?

PAGES 12-13

Discussion of the following questions will highlight important events in this part of the story:
—How many times did Billy see Thunderbolt in this part of the story? How did he know where to look for Thunderbolt? What happened after Billy left Jim?
—Was Billy satisfied when he had seen Thunderbolt a second time? How do you know he wasn't? [As pupils describe Billy's daily trips to the hills, make sure they understand the meaning of *let the pony crop grass*.]

To present the words *anxious* and *disappointed*, lead children to point out that *Billy was anxious to see Thunderbolt again*.

Marginal notes:

form visual images . . .

identify new word corral . . .

read to find out who Thunderbolt is . . .

report on their findings . . .

infer Billy's interest in the wild horse . . .

recall details of subsequent trips to see Thunderbolt . . .

identify new words . . .

Comment that youngsters can probably understand *how disappointed he was* when he did not catch sight of the horse for several days. (You might add the word *anxious* to the list of words that can be found in the glossary.)

Then ask: "Do you think Billy will see Thunderbolt again? Why? Will Billy be satisfied with seeing the horse from a distance? What might he try to do?"

speculate about
development of plot . . .

PAGES 14-17

As children discuss Billy's success in taming Thunderbolt, check understanding of the important ideas and lead pupils to evaluate the actions of the main character.

—What were some of the important things Billy did to win Thunderbolt's confidence?

—Do you think Billy could have tamed the wild horse without Blaze? How did Blaze help in taming Thunderbolt?

recognize both Billy's
and Blaze's rôles in
taming Thunderbolt . . .

—Were you surprised when Billy was able to ride Thunderbolt? Why not? What happened that led Billy to try to ride the horse? Why wasn't he afraid? How did he calm the horse?

—What did he have to teach Thunderbolt before he rode him outside the corral?

make inferences . . .

—Do you think Jim had reason to be proud of the way Billy had trained Thunderbolt? What makes you think he did?

judge Billy's actions . . .

WHOLE STORY

Draw children's attention to the traits of character that helped Billy win Thunderbolt's confidence, and lead them to note what can be learned from his experience by asking:

—What do you know about the kind of person Billy was? What gave you these impressions?

make judgments . . .

—If Billy had been impatient and rough with Thunderbolt, do you think he would have been able to tame him? Why not?

—What do you think Billy learned from his experience with Thunderbolt? What can we learn?

link story events
to their own lives . . .

Their understanding of Billy's character will determine how well pupils can judge what Billy might do if faced with the situations described on page 1 of the *Think-and-Do Book.*

Foster an awareness of time relationships by encouraging youngsters to speculate about how much time was covered by the story. Was Billy able to tame Thunderbolt in just a few days, or did it take several weeks or even months? What makes children think as they do? Did the author tell exactly how long it took? How did he make the reader aware of the passing of time? (Suggest that pupils note time phrases used in the story.) Did the author tell about everything Billy saw and did during the summer? Why not? (Children's ability to note relationships of time will be strengthened as they use pages 2-3 of the *Think-and-Do Book*.)

note clues to time span of story...

discuss author's purpose...

Point out that when we have shared the experiences of story characters, we often wonder what might have happened after the end of the story. Do youngsters feel this way about Billy and Thunderbolt? Although they may never know for sure, they might make some interesting speculations. Lead boys and girls to consider what might be done with Thunderbolt when Billy and Blaze go home, how Thunderbolt might react, and whether Jim might be able to ride him. Ask: "If you were Billy, what would you do about Thunderbolt? Why?"

form and share opinions about future action...

make judgments...

Finally give pupils an opportunity to discuss visual images they formed as they read the story. Ask: "If you had never seen the western part of our country, what could you have learned about it from this story? [Encourage reference to both written and pictured clues.] Do you think the picture on pages 8-9 is typical of the West? What might Billy have seen in the West besides cowboys, ranches, cattle, and horses?"

clarify visual images of the West.

Extending competence

● Lead children to recall how surprised Billy was, and why, when he found Thunderbolt in the corral with Blaze. Recall also how he must have felt when he first rode Thunderbolt and later when Jim complimented him. Then introduce page 4 of the *Think-and-Do Book,* which tells of another boy's experience with a pet. After reading the story, youngsters must decide how the boy felt, and why, at various points in the episode.

Children sense emotional reactions in Think-and-Do Book exercise.

● As they begin to read *More Roads to Follow,* it would be well to <u>remind pupils of some of the things they have already learned</u> <u>about using a glossary or dictionary.</u>

Begin by commenting: "I'm sure you'll turn to the glossary many times while you're reading *More Roads to Follow.* So let's take a few minutes to talk about some of the words in today's story [point to the list you wrote on the board earlier] that are entries in the glossary." Then ask:

—Which of these words are found in the middle part of the glossary? in the first part? in the last part? [Recall the *a* through *g, h* through *p,* and *q* through *z* divisions as an aid in noting general position in an alphabetical listing.]

Pupils review general alphabetical position and sequence . . .

—Which would you expect to find first in an alphabetical list, *corral* or *buck?* Why? Would you find *bridle* before or after *buck?* Why?

—Is the word *bridle* on page 268? Is *corral* on this page? How can you tell without reading the entries? [Observe whether boys and girls recall the function of guide words.]

—In what ways does the glossary make the meaning of *bridle* clear? [If necessary, clarify the function of the picture caption.] What other entries from this story had one of the definitions pictured? [*corral, scrub, trailer*]

recall glossary aids to understanding meaning of words . . .

—Find the entry word *buck.* In what other way does the glossary help clarify the meaning of this word? [illustrative sentences]

—Who can tell us why *bridled* and *bridling,* but not *bucked* and *bucking,* are shown in heavy black type following the definitions of the entry word?

note purpose of run-ons . . .

—If you want to find the meaning of *whinnied,* what entry word will you look for? How can you be sure you've found the right entry word?

—Are there one or two *l*'s in the word *corralled?* Use the glossary to see whether you're right.

—Would you call twenty ducks and chickens a *herd?* Why not?

select homograph and definition to fit specific context.

—What does the word *reared* mean in the sentence *When he saw the cowboy, Thunderbolt reared and whinnied?* Which glossary entry fits this sentence? Which definition? What does a small number after an entry word tell you to do? [to look for other words spelled the same way] What other entry word from today's story has a small number after it? [*scrub*]

For page references to procedures that could be used with children who need additional help, see the heading "Developing dictionary skills and understandings" in the Index of Skills, Abilities, and Understandings at the back of the *Guidebook* for *Roads to Follow*. Appropriate exercises in the section "How to Use Your Dictionary" at the front of the *Thorndike-Barnhart Beginning Dictionary* could also be used.

● If some children have difficulty discriminating between words that are similar in form, you might make frequent use of such procedures as these to <u>call attention to individual letters or arrangement of letters that distinguish one word from another.</u> Begin by writing the following pairs of known words on the board:

buck	bought	there	quite	except	corral
back	brought	three	quiet	expect	carol

Pronounce one word from each pair, and ask pupils to tell whether you pronounced the first or the second word. Then have children look carefully at the words in each pair and note what differentiates one word from the other. A child might then point to a word, pronounce it, and use it in a sentence.

Pupils compare pairs of printed words that may be confused in reading.

Encouraging personal reading

As the term personal reading suggests, there is much that is truly personal about the reading a child does on his own. His attitudes and his experiences play a very important rôle in his choice of reading material and his enjoyment of a story. Although third-graders are usually avid readers of horse stories, for example, there will be some pupils for whom these hold little appeal. Even among horse enthusiasts, some will reach repeatedly for stories about horses while others search for more informative material on the subject.

The library table, then, should attract pupils with different interests because of its variety of reading material. Stories of mystery, adventure, historical fiction, fun and nonsense, the real and the unreal—all have a place on the library table when they have a place among the interests of young readers.

pages 18·19 | When Is a Horse a Pony?

As boys and girls discover the answer to the question posed by the title of this article, they will become acquainted with a method of measurement known to horsemen throughout the world. Children will also have an opportunity to note some of the characteristics that distinguish an article from a story.

Competence in word analysis is increased as boys and girls discuss the numerical suffixes *-teen, -ty,* and *-th* and note how the noun-forming suffixes *-ty* and *-th* function in such words as *safety* and *warmth.*

New words: **average, height,** fourteen (*breeds**, less*, inches*, measured*, twenty*, world*, Shetland*, size*)

Think-and-Do Book: **Pages 5 and 6**

Establishing background

Arouse interest in the article by relating it to the first story. Display the illustration on page 10 and the one on page 13 as you lead pupils to recall that in this story Blaze was called a pony and Thunderbolt a horse.

Children recall use of the terms horse and pony . . .

Next write the question *When is a horse a pony?* for pupils to read and try to answer. Then comment that as they read today's selection, an article that gives some interesting information about ponies and horses, they will find the answer. As you add that they will also find answers to other questions, write the following questions under the first one. Present the words *height* and *average,* but let children identify *measured* and *breeds* independently as the questions are read aloud.

speculate about meaning of terms . . .

identify new words as they note purposes for reading . . .

How is the height of horses and ponies measured?

What is the best-known breed or kind of pony?

What is the average, or most common, height for the smallest breed of pony?

Since pupils should be able to use context and spelling clues to identify the word *fourteen,* it is not presented here. You might also underline the words *height, average,* and *breed* to remind children that these words are entries in the glossary.

Interpreting the article

In the discussion following silent reading, <u>bring out the main ideas in the article.</u> As children discuss each of the questions on the board, encourage them to refer to the two illustrations.

discuss answers to questions on board . . .

    (When youngsters read the article on pages 5-6 of the *Think-and-Do Book,* they will learn more about the three ponies shown in the illustration on page 19 and will have an opportunity to compare and contrast them on the basis of size and class.) Then lead boys and girls to consider any of the following ideas that they did not mention earlier:

—In what ways are the six animals alike in the illustration on page 19? How are they different? What is a pony? [When a child points out that the average height of a pony is less than fourteen hands and two inches, commend him for figuring out the new word *fourteen.* Make sure, too, that children understand it is not correct to use the word *pony* when referring to a young horse that will be more than 14:2 hands when fully grown, but that the word *colt* ("young horse," "a male horse until it is four or five years old") or *filly* ("female colt") should be used.]

compare and contrast details . . .

—How does measuring the height of a horse or pony differ from measuring the height of a person?

—What is the difference between the length of a hand and the length of a foot as used for measuring?

—How many different breeds of ponies are there in the world? Why are the Shetland ponies the best known?

    To <u>help pupils summarize the information given in the article,</u> have them reread the first paragraph on page 18. Ask, "Who can tell in a few words what this paragraph is about?" As pupils respond, write the most concisely worded sentence on the board. Similarly guide youngsters in formulating one-sentence

state main idea of each paragraph . . .

summaries of the second and third paragraphs on page 18 and the first and second paragraphs on page 19. Point out that summarizing the article will help them remember what information was given. They may even want to use the summary in explaining to parents or to younger brothers and sisters what they learned from the article. The completed summary might look something like this:

1. A pony is a horse of a small breed.
2. Horses and ponies are measured from the highest part of the back to the ground.
3. Horses and ponies are measured in hands and inches.
4. Ponies are breeds of horses that average less than 14:2 hands.
5. Of the more than twenty breeds of ponies, Shetland ponies are the best known.

To help youngsters summarize the central theme of the entire selection, ask: "What was the most important idea the author explained in the article? Who can tell in one sentence what this article is about?"

state main idea of entire article . . .

Next lead pupils to point out that in the first story Blaze and Thunderbolt were never pictured together. Ask: "If you were to draw a picture of Blaze and Thunderbolt standing side by side, would you draw them about the same size? Why not? Which would be smaller?"

make judgment based on facts in article . . .

You may want to call attention to the parentheses and the colon that appear on page 19 for the first time in The New Basic Readers. Explain that parentheses are often used to enclose added explanations or comments that the author does not want to stand out in a sentence.

To illustrate, ask someone to read aloud the third sentence in the second paragraph on page 19, stopping after the word *hands*. Lead children to observe that the sentence is complete (makes sense) without the information shown in parentheses but that the parenthetical information is helpful to the reader who may be more familiar with measurements that are given in inches. Likewise point out that a colon is often used between numbers that are closely related; for example, hands and inches or hours and minutes.

discuss purpose of parentheses . . .

note one use of colon.

Extending competence

● Encourage youngsters to <u>compare and contrast the first two selections in this unit in light of each author's purpose.</u> To begin, recall that the selection just read is an article rather than a story. Point out that the article and the story are different in many ways. Can youngsters think of one way in which they are alike? (Both are about horses.)

Then ask: "If a friend wanted information about ponies, would you suggest that he read 'Billy and Thunderbolt' or 'When Is a Horse a Pony?' Why?" Help children conclude that the author of the article wanted to give factual information about ponies, while the author of "Billy and Thunderbolt" wanted to tell a good story. Emphasize that although stories may be based on facts and often contain explanations that help us understand story events, they are not written specifically to inform.

Children contrast purpose of story and article.

● These procedures <u>introduce the numerical suffixes -teen, -ty, and -th and call attention to the noun-forming suffixes -ty and -th in such words as safety and warmth.</u>

1. Write *fourteen;* have it pronounced and used in a sentence. What is the root word in *fourteen?* When pupils reply, underline *four* and ask what suffix is added to *four* to form *fourteen.*

Then suggest that children find the suffix *-teen* in their glossaries and read the definition. How many other number words ending in the suffix *-teen* can they think of? As they respond, write the number words *thirteen* through *nineteen* and ask what each means. Discuss briefly the change in the root in the derived forms *thirteen* and *fifteen.*

Pupils note how the numerical suffix -teen is used . . .

2. Next write the word *seventy.* Pronounce it, ask what suffix is added to *seven* to make *seventy,* and have pupils find the suffix *-ty* in their glossaries. When they have noted that there are two suffixes spelled *-ty* and read the definition for each one, ask which suffix, $-ty^1$ or $-ty^2$, is added to *seven* to make *seventy.* What does *seventy* mean?

How many other number words ending in the suffix *-ty* can youngsters think of? As the group responds, write *twenty,*

how the numerical suffix -ty is used . . .

she might have in a new school? Might coming from another country add to her problems? In what way? When you read the first part of the story, you'll find out how she felt about living *among people in a new land* and why she felt as she did."

anticipate problem of story character . . .

To encourage children to form the habit of using the glossary entries when necessary to check meaning and pronunciation, again list the glossary words on the board. As you write the words *Kirsten* and *Lacour*, explain that pupils will find these names and their pronunciations included in the glossary. Also list *difficulty, Denmark, booth, gasped, hastily, extra, excuse, envy, withdraw.* The remaining new words may be presented during the guided interpretation of pages 20-22.

Guiding interpretation

PAGES 20-22

After children note the rather unusual title, check to see whether they are familiar with the phrase *out of her shell.* Do they think it might be hard for someone like Kirsten to understand this expression? Why? Suggest that as they read, they keep their eyes open for other expressions that might puzzle someone who is not too familiar with the English language.

When pupils have read these pages silently, guide a discussion of Kirsten's problem with such questions as these:

—How did Kirsten feel about her new school? What made it especially hard for her to make friends? [As children discuss Kirsten's problem, note whether they referred to the entry *Denmark* in their glossaries.]

consider Kirsten's reactions . . .

—Why do you suppose Debbie decided to join another group? What do you think of the way Debbie acted?

evaluate Debbie's actions . . .

—Do you think perhaps Kirsten will make a new friend? What makes you think so?

—What will Kirsten and Amy have to do now?

As children answer, present the words *customers* and *holidays* by commenting that the girls had to think of an idea that would *bring customers* to their booth at the fun fair. Then ask whether pupils have planned programs for school events or for *special holidays,* and whether they can think of any ideas that Kirsten and Amy might use.

identify new words customers and holidays . . .

thirty, forty, fifty, and so on. Then encourage discussion of the meaning of each (*twenty,* for example, means "two tens"). Call attention also to the change in the root or base word in *twenty, thirty, forty,* and *fifty.*

3. To introduce the numerical suffix *-th,* write these sentences and have them read:

and how the numerical suffix -th is used . . .

Ten boys were at the party.
Tom was the tenth boy to arrive.

Ask, "What suffix is added to *ten* to form the word *tenth* in the second sentence?" Then have pupils find this suffix in their glossaries. Is it *-th¹* or *-th²?* What is the definition of *-th²?* What other number words ending in this suffix can the group think of? As words like *fourth, fifth,* and *twelfth* are mentioned, write them on the board and have each used in a sentence. Lead children to note also how the root or base word changes in some of these forms. If no one mentions it, comment that the suffix *-th* is not added to the number words *one, two,* and *three;* instead, these forms are *first, second,* and *third.*

Write such words as *fourteenth* and *sixtieth* on the board, and invite pupils to pronounce them. Ask: "What two suffixes are added to *four* to form *fourteenth?* to *six* to form *sixtieth?*" Then lead children to note that the letter *y* in the suffix *-ty* is changed to *ie* before the suffix *-th* is added.

note that two numerical suffixes may be added to a number word . . .

4. To call attention to the noun-forming suffixes *-ty²* and *-th¹,* write the words *cruelty* and *warmth* and ask pupils to pronounce them. Suggest that they use their glossaries to tell which suffix is added to *cruel* to form *cruelty* and to *warm* to form *warmth.* To bring out the meaning and function of these suffixes, have *cruel* and *cruelty, warm* and *warmth* used in sentences. Continue with *safe* and *safety, certain* and *certainty, grow* and *growth, true* and *truth.*

observe how the noun-forming suffixes -ty and -th are used . . .

In conclusion comment that just as some number words change form and pronunciation before the suffix *-th²* (the root *five* in *fifth,* for example), so do other root words to which *-th¹* is added. To illustrate, write the sentences shown on the next page. As pupils read each pair, ask, "Which word in the second sentence is a form of a word in the first sentence?" Then lead

identify derived forms in which spelling and pronunciation of root change before -th.

the group to note how the spelling and pronunciation of the root word change when the suffix -*th* is added.

> The river near our town is very wide.
> The river is about a mile in width.
>
> The water in the pool is not very deep.
> The depth of the water is fine for swimming.
>
> We have a long hall in our house.
> The length of the hall is twenty feet.

Extending interests

Third-graders who thrill to a good horse story will not be disappointed in those written by C. W. Anderson, Marguerite Henry, Will James, and Glen Rounds, many of whose works have been acclaimed as children's classics.

The full-page realistic drawings, brief text, and simple plot of the series of books about Blaze hold special appeal for reluctant young readers. As you <u>display C. W. Anderson's *Blaze Finds the Trail* and *Blaze and the Forest Fire,*</u> comment that in each of these adventures Blaze again helps his friend.

Children read about other adventures of Billy and Blaze ...

For a gentle story in which boy and prairie dog tame each other, patiently observing the proper rites, <u>suggest that pupils read *Amigo,* by Byrd Baylor Schweitzer.</u>

and about taming wild friends ...

To acquaint youngsters with another well-known author of books about horses, <u>read aloud Chapters 7 and 8 of *Justin Morgan Had a Horse,* by Marguerite Henry.</u> Afterwards encourage pupils to talk about Joel's intensity of feeling as he shared Little Bub's straining efforts and to tell how the author helped them share Joel's feelings as they listened. (This selection is also in *The Arbuthnot Anthology of Children's Literature,* Revised Edition, compiled by May Hill Arbuthnot.)

share character's reactions as they listen to a story ...

Then, for horse enthusiasts eager to learn more about their favorite animal, <u>select a few chapters from Marguerite Henry's *All about Horses.*</u> You might read the parts that tell about particular breeds of horses, that explain the color terminology used in describing horses, or that share the fascinating "secret language" of the horseman's world.

enjoy factual book about horses.

---

pages 20·26 | Out of Her Shell

Kirsten's problems in a new school will strike a familiar chord with many children. By viewing the situation through the eyes of the newcomer, young readers may gain insight into her feelings and into the nature of their own language.

Since at this level children encounter more and more words that are divided at the end of a printed line, an exercise in this lesson explains one function of the hyphen. In another exercise children review what they have learned about consonant sounds and the letters that represent them.

New words: **Kirsten, Lacour, difficulty,** convenient, course, favorites, holidays, customers, among (shell*, groups*, desk*, *Denmark**, classes*, divided*, *booth**, Larsen*, shyly*, sort*, sell*, *gasped**, *hastily**, insisted*, pity*, manage*, frowned*, *extra**, sandwiches*, giggle*, added*, stupid*, *excuse**, costumes*, punch*, *envy**, joy*, heart*)

Think-and-Do Book: **Pages 7, 8, 9, and 10**

Establishing background

<u>Highlight the theme of today's story</u> by asking: "How many of you have moved to a new neighborhood and entered a new school? How did you feel about making the change? Did your new home seem at first to be *as convenient* as the old one? *Of course,* we all have *a little difficulty* getting accustomed to new places and new faces. But even though we make new friends, we often miss our *old favorites.*

Children talk about moving ...

identify new words

"The story today is about these three girls. [Present the names *Kirsten* (kir′stən) and *Lacour* (lä kür′) as you write *Kirsten Larsen, Amy Lacour, Debbie Kilpatrick.*] Kirsten had just come to live in America. What are some of the problems

When they have finished the story to find out how Amy and Kirsten fared with their plans, <u>lead children to observe that by helping solve her group's problem, Kirsten has started to solve her own.</u>

—Why was it fortunate for both girls that Kirsten had invited Amy to come home with her?

—Do you think Amy might have gotten the idea without Kirsten? Why not?

—What other problems did Kirsten's invitation help solve?

—Do you think it may be easier for Kirsten to make friends from now on? Why?

note Kirsten's contribution . . .

and consider its long-range effects . . .

<u>Help pupils link the story to their own experience</u> by asking:

—Do you think anyone jumped to a conclusion in this story? Who? What might Debbie have learned from this experience?

—What do you think Kirsten discovered as she started to work on the booth for the fun fair?

—Do you think we could learn something from this story too? What would be a good thing to remember if we were in Debbie's shoes? in Kirsten's?

make judgments . . .

relate situation to personal experience . . .

Children who come from homes where customs of other countries are observed may have a wealth of experience to share with the class. <u>Draw upon pupils' own knowledge of foreign customs</u> by asking why people at the fun fair might be especially interested in Kirsten and Amy's booth. Point out that although the cookies and the sandwiches are often served in Denmark, they might be new to many people in America. Then ask whether children's parents or grandparents ever serve foods of other lands. Encourage pupils to describe these foods and tell where they originated. To start the ball rolling, you might point out that such common items as chili, sauerkraut, spaghetti all originated in other lands.

recognize novelty of the girls' idea . . .

talk about foods of other lands . . .

Many boys and girls may not realize that a second language spoken in their homes or customs kept alive by their families are a heritage to be treasured. Encouraging these youngsters to share what they know about the customs of other countries can foster an awareness and an appreciation of the values that other cultures offer.

<u>Encourage children to scrutinize the text for clues to the characters' thoughts, feelings, and reactions</u> by asking the questions suggested below. As pupils reply, watch for expressions, gestures, and tones of voice that suggest their identification with Kirsten's unhappiness, Debbie's disdain, and Amy's amused but genuine sympathy.

—How did Kirsten feel about joining the group? How do you know how she felt? Why did she offer to leave?

—Why do you think Debbie at first ignored Kirsten and later left the group?

—When Amy laughed, was she making fun of Kirsten? How do you know she wasn't?

Then help youngsters get the feel of a character by letting them pantomime Kirsten's actions as she joined the group. When they show her timidity and embarrassment, let them add the dialogue, *I am with you?* Next have pupils decide what Kirsten might have said when she offered to withdraw. Point out that they can substitute these words for the line *Hastily Kirsten offered to withdraw from the group* when they read the scene. Then choose three of the most responsive children to read pages 21 and 22.

Young readers can gain additional insight into the feelings of the characters they portray by listening and reacting to what the others say. Comment: "You have already noticed that in different parts of the story Kirsten is shy, puzzled, enthusiastic, and happy. But does she have these feelings only while she is talking?" Lead children to conclude that in each instance she feels and reacts while listening to others and then puts her reactions into words. Encourage listeners as well as readers to view the scene from the standpoint of one of the characters. When their turns come to read, they will be able to interpret the printed page more effectively.

discuss characters' thoughts and reactions...

pantomime Kirsten's actions...

supply dialogue...

read episode aloud...

listen and react to other characters...

After several groups have read and the characterizations have become definite, continue with the remaining episodes.

Personal traits and emotional reactions are also emphasized on pages 7 and 8-9 of the *Think-and-Do Book*. On page 7 children choose the word that best describes the main character in each episode. After reading the story on pages 8-9 they must indicate whether each of several statements applies to Kirsten or Juanito or to both children.

Extending competence

● Many of the expressions that puzzled Kirsten are idioms that children use and hear in everyday speech. <u>Call attention to some of the idioms used in the story</u> by asking children whether they think the phrase *come out of your shell* is a good way to describe someone who is becoming more friendly and less shy. Why?

Continue: "What made it hard for Kirsten to understand what this phrase meant? What were some of the other expressions that baffled her? Who can tell us what they mean?" If the phrases *white elephant, thinking cap*, and *on the house* are new to children, you may want to have them find the place in the story where each is defined. Then comment: "Our language is full of expressions that do not mean exactly what the words say. We call these expressions *idioms*. Just think how strange they must sound to someone who has never heard them."

Then invite children to think of other idioms they may have heard and to tell what they mean. You can start the discussion going with such examples as *kill time, break a record, apple-pie order, a piece of my mind, catch cold.*

● To <u>point up the use of a hyphen in dividing words at the end of a printed line,</u> call attention to the second sentence on page 25, and note the hyphenated word *thinking.* Explain to children that when a word of two or more syllables is too long to fit at the end of a line, a hyphen may be used to show that part of the word is printed on the next line.

read scenes aloud.

Children explain meaning of idioms used in story . . .

interpret similar figurative expressions.

Pupils note significance of hyphen after word or syllable at end of line . . .

Next suggest that pupils find the entry word *anxious* in their glossaries. Help them recall that the spaces between syllables in the spelling of an entry word indicate the places where the word may be divided with a hyphen at the end of a line of print or writing. Continue with the word *body*, leading children to note that although it is a two-syllable word, it may not be divided at the end of a line. Also use the entry words *height* and *cliff* to emphasize the idea that one-syllable words are not divided at the end of a line.

and how possible syllable divisions are indicated in glossary.

● This exercise and page 10 of the *Think-and-Do Book* review the concept that different consonant letters may represent the same consonant sound and check pupils' ability to associate consonant sounds with the letters that represent them in printed words.

1. First write the known word *keep* and ask with what sound this word begins. When the *k* sound is identified, ask, "What letter stands for the *k* sound in *keep?*"

Under *keep* write *car*, *rock*, *Christmas*. As each word is pronounced, ask pupils to tell where they hear the *k* sound in it and to notice the spellings that stand for the *k* sound. Continue with these consonant sounds and known words:

Pupils associate same consonant sound with different letters . . .

> *s* sound: safe, circle, science, grass, else, twice
> *z* sound: zoo, buzz, does, please
> *j* sound: join, gentle, huge, hedge
> *ch* sound: chin, catch, picture
> *sh* sound: shake, sugar, machine, motion, tension, ocean
> *g* sound: give, guess, egg
> *h* sound: hill, whole
> *f* sound: fat, off, elephant, enough
> *ng* sound: hung, tongue, trunk

2. To review briefly the idea that a consonant letter (or letters) may represent no sound in a printed word, write the known word *knob* and have it pronounced. Then ask:
—With what letter does the word *knob* begin?
—Do you hear a *k* sound at the beginning of *knob?* With what sound does *knob* begin?

recall that a consonant letter may represent no sound . . .

Continue with the letter *w* in the word *wrong*, the letter *h* in the word *hour*, the letter *l* in the word *talk*, the letter *t* in the word *whistle*, the letter *b* in the word *climb*, and the letters *gh* in the word *high*.

3. To conclude, write the known word *chin* and have it pronounced and used in a sentence. Erase the letters *ch* and substitute the letters *th* to make *thin*. Have *thin* pronounced and used in a sentence. Then change *thin* to *thing*, *thing* to *think*, *think* to *thick*, *thick* to *quick*, *quick* to *sick*, and *sick* to *six*.

identify words formed by changing initial or final consonants.

Use similar procedures with each italicized word below, forming in succession the words shown after it:

    went—bent, cent, scent, sent, sense
    hide—side, slide, stride, guide, glide
    cap—cash, catch, camp, lamp, lamb
    pen—when, wren, wrench, bench, bend
    rock—knock, knot, slot, blot, block
    his—hiss, miss, mist, wrist, list
    cage—age, ache, ape, shape, shake

Extending interests

In connection with today's story you will want to read "The Hundred Dresses," by Eleanor Estes (in *The Arbuthnot Anthology of Children's Literature*). Afterwards let children discuss it freely—the unfriendly little girls and whether they meant to be cruel, why Wanda told the story of the hundred dresses, how the girls must have felt when the teacher read Mr. Petronski's letter, the surprise of the hundred dresses. What might—and should—the children in Wanda's school have done about Wanda long before she moved away? Invite youngsters to compare Wanda and Kirsten—each girl's loneliness, her reaction to it, and its ultimate solution. What prevented Kirsten from experiencing the unhappiness that Wanda did?

Children listen to two stories with similar themes . . .

discuss reason for different endings.

Then introduce Ursula Nordstrom's *The Secret Language* by reading aloud the first three chapters. The foregoing discussion might also be applied to Vicky and Martha and their different attitudes at boarding school.

The World of Hogback Mountain

Young readers will respond with sympathetic admiration to the realistic portrayal of the heartaches and struggles that result from Rufe Kaller's intense desire to make his crippled friend's wish come true. Discussion of the story problem will deepen appreciation of skillful characterization and eloquent language even as it leads children to an ethical evaluation of motives and conduct.

One exercise in this lesson emphasizes the importance of context clues in comprehending sentence meaning. Others focus attention on the interpretation of dictionary pronunciations and on familiar spelling patterns that serve as visual clues to vowel sounds in one-syllable words.

New words: Kaller, *examine,* though, months, precious*, *business* (mountain*, Rufe*, doctor*, sighed*, costs*, dollars*, chairbound*, *cliff**, leafy*, *whittling**, sharp*, figure*, sea*, forty*, fellow*, mind*, halfway*, smoke*, breath*, *pines**, rod*, wandered*, present*, snatched*, carved*, startled*, stuck*, trade*, speechless*, forward*, stared*, worth*, *ruffling**, moon*, tears*, swallowed*)

Think-and-Do Book: Pages 11 and 12

Establishing background

Conversation about the title and first illustration will help establish the setting of the story and heighten interest in reading. First write the title on the board for children to read, and clarify the meaning of *world* in this context through a discussion of such phrases as the world of books, the world of sports, and *the world of business.* Then ask youngsters what they think the world of Hogback Mountain might be like.

Pupils discuss meaning of world in title ...

thirty, forty, fifty, and so on. Then encourage discussion of the meaning of each (*twenty,* for example, means "two tens"). Call attention also to the change in the root or base word in *twenty, thirty, forty,* and *fifty.*

3. To introduce the numerical suffix *-th,* write these sentences and have them read:

> Ten boys were at the party.
> Tom was the tenth boy to arrive.

and how the numerical suffix -th is used . . .

Ask, "What suffix is added to *ten* to form the word *tenth* in the second sentence?" Then have pupils find this suffix in their glossaries. Is it *-th¹* or *-th²?* What is the definition of *-th²?* What other number words ending in this suffix can the group think of? As words like *fourth, fifth,* and *twelfth* are mentioned, write them on the board and have each used in a sentence. Lead children to note also how the root or base word changes in some of these forms. If no one mentions it, comment that the suffix *-th* is not added to the number words *one, two,* and *three;* instead, these forms are *first, second,* and *third.*

Write such words as *fourteenth* and *sixtieth* on the board, and invite pupils to pronounce them. Ask: "What two suffixes are added to *four* to form *fourteenth?* to *six* to form *sixtieth?*" Then lead children to note that the letter *y* in the suffix *-ty* is changed to *ie* before the suffix *-th* is added.

note that two numerical suffixes may be added to a number word . . .

4. To call attention to the noun-forming suffixes *-ty²* and *-th¹,* write the words *cruelty* and *warmth* and ask pupils to pronounce them. Suggest that they use their glossaries to tell which suffix is added to *cruel* to form *cruelty* and to *warm* to form *warmth.* To bring out the meaning and function of these suffixes, have *cruel* and *cruelty, warm* and *warmth* used in sentences. Continue with *safe* and *safety, certain* and *certainty, grow* and *growth, true* and *truth.*

observe how the noun-forming suffixes -ty and -th are used . . .

In conclusion comment that just as some number words change form and pronunciation before the suffix *-th²* (the root *five* in *fifth,* for example), so do other root words to which *-th¹* is added. To illustrate, write the sentences shown on the next page. As pupils read each pair, ask, "Which word in the second sentence is a form of a word in the first sentence?" Then lead

identify derived forms in which spelling and pronunciation of root change before -th.

the group to note how the spelling and pronunciation of the root word change when the suffix -th is added.

The river near our town is very wide.
The river is about a mile in width.

The water in the pool is not very deep.
The depth of the water is fine for swimming.

We have a long hall in our house.
The length of the hall is twenty feet.

Extending interests

Third-graders who thrill to a good horse story will not be disappointed in those written by C. W. Anderson, Marguerite Henry, Will James, and Glen Rounds, many of whose works have been acclaimed as children's classics.

The full-page realistic drawings, brief text, and simple plot of the series of books about Blaze hold special appeal for reluctant young readers. As you display C. W. Anderson's *Blaze Finds the Trail* and *Blaze and the Forest Fire*, comment that in each of these adventures Blaze again helps his friend.

Children read about other adventures of Billy and Blaze . . .

For a gentle story in which boy and prairie dog tame each other, patiently observing the proper rites, suggest that pupils read *Amigo*, by Byrd Baylor Schweitzer.

and about taming wild friends . . .

To acquaint youngsters with another well-known author of books about horses, read aloud Chapters 7 and 8 of *Justin Morgan Had a Horse*, by Marguerite Henry. Afterwards encourage pupils to talk about Joel's intensity of feeling as he shared Little Bub's straining efforts and to tell how the author helped them share Joel's feelings as they listened. (This selection is also in *The Arbuthnot Anthology of Children's Literature*, Revised Edition, compiled by May Hill Arbuthnot.)

share character's reactions as they listen to a story . . .

Then, for horse enthusiasts eager to learn more about their favorite animal, select a few chapters from Marguerite Henry's *All about Horses*. You might read the parts that tell about particular breeds of horses, that explain the color terminology used in describing horses, or that share the fascinating "secret language" of the horseman's world.

enjoy factual book about horses.

| Out of Her Shell

Kirsten's problems in a new school will strike a familiar chord with many children. By viewing the situation through the eyes of the newcomer, young readers may gain insight into her feelings and into the nature of their own language.

Since at this level children encounter more and more words that are divided at the end of a printed line, an exercise in this lesson explains one function of the hyphen. In another exercise children review what they have learned about consonant sounds and the letters that represent them.

New words: **Kirsten, Lacour, difficulty,** convenient, course, favorites, holidays, customers, among (shell*, groups*, desk*, *Denmark**, classes*, divided*, *booth**, Larsen*, shyly*, sort*, sell*, *gasped**, *hastily**, insisted*, pity*, manage*, frowned*, *extra**, sandwiches*, giggle*, added*, stupid*, *excuse**, costumes*, punch*, *envy**, joy*, heart*)

Think-and-Do Book: **Pages 7, 8, 9, and 10**

Establishing background

Highlight the theme of today's story by asking: "How many of you have moved to a new neighborhood and entered a new school? How did you feel about making the change? Did your new home seem at first to be *as convenient* as the old one? *Of course,* we all have *a little difficulty* getting accustomed to new places and new faces. But even though we make new friends, we often miss our *old favorites.*

"The story today is about these three girls. [Present the names *Kirsten* (kir'stən) and *Lacour* (lä kür') as you write *Kirsten Larsen, Amy Lacour, Debbie Kilpatrick.*] Kirsten had just come to live in America. What are some of the problems

Children talk about moving . . .

identify new words . . .

she might have in a new school? Might coming from another country add to her problems? In what way? When you read the first part of the story, you'll find out how she felt about living *among people in a new land* and why she felt as she did."

anticipate problem of story character . . .

To encourage children to form the habit of using the glossary entries when necessary to check meaning and pronunciation, again list the glossary words on the board. As you write the words *Kirsten* and *Lacour*, explain that pupils will find these names and their pronunciations included in the glossary. Also list *difficulty, Denmark, booth, gasped, hastily, extra, excuse, envy, withdraw*. The remaining new words may be presented during the guided interpretation of pages 20-22.

Guiding interpretation

PAGES 20-22

After children note the rather unusual title, check to see whether they are familiar with the phrase *out of her shell*. Do they think it might be hard for someone like Kirsten to understand this expression? Why? Suggest that as they read, they keep their eyes open for other expressions that might puzzle someone who is not too familiar with the English language.

When pupils have read these pages silently, guide a discussion of Kirsten's problem with such questions as these:

—How did Kirsten feel about her new school? What made it especially hard for her to make friends? [As children discuss Kirsten's problem, note whether they referred to the entry *Denmark* in their glossaries.]

consider Kirsten's reactions . . .

—Why do you suppose Debbie decided to join another group? What do you think of the way Debbie acted?

evaluate Debbie's actions . . .

—Do you think perhaps Kirsten will make a new friend? What makes you think so?

—What will Kirsten and Amy have to do now?

As children answer, present the words *customers* and *holidays* by commenting that the girls had to think of an idea that would *bring customers* to their booth at the fun fair. Then ask whether pupils have planned programs for school events or for *special holidays,* and whether they can think of any ideas that Kirsten and Amy might use.

identify new words customers and holidays . . .

34 | MORE ROADS TO FOLLOW

When they have finished the story to find out how Amy and Kirsten fared with their plans, <u>lead children to observe that by helping solve her group's problem, Kirsten has started to solve her own.</u>

—Why was it fortunate for both girls that Kirsten had invited Amy to come home with her?

—Do you think Amy might have gotten the idea without Kirsten? Why not?

—What other problems did Kirsten's invitation help solve?

—Do you think it may be easier for Kirsten to make friends from now on? Why?

note Kirsten's contribution . . .

and consider its long-range effects . . .

WHOLE STORY

<u>Help pupils link the story to their own experience</u> by asking:

—Do you think anyone jumped to a conclusion in this story? Who? What might Debbie have learned from this experience?

—What do you think Kirsten discovered as she started to work on the booth for the fun fair?

—Do you think we could learn something from this story too? What would be a good thing to remember if we were in Debbie's shoes? in Kirsten's?

make judgments . . .

relate situation to personal experience . . .

Children who come from homes where customs of other countries are observed may have a wealth of experience to share with the class. <u>Draw upon pupils' own knowledge of foreign customs</u> by asking why people at the fun fair might be especially interested in Kirsten and Amy's booth. Point out that although the cookies and the sandwiches are often served in Denmark, they might be new to many people in America. Then ask whether children's parents or grandparents ever serve foods of other lands. Encourage pupils to describe these foods and tell where they originated. To start the ball rolling, you might point out that such common items as chili, sauerkraut, spaghetti all originated in other lands.

recognize novelty of the girls' idea . . .

talk about foods of other lands . . .

Many boys and girls may not realize that a second language spoken in their homes or customs kept alive by their families are a heritage to be treasured. Encouraging these youngsters to share what they know about the customs of other countries can foster an awareness and an appreciation of the values that other cultures offer.

Encourage children to scrutinize the text for clues to the characters' thoughts, feelings, and reactions by asking the questions suggested below. As pupils reply, watch for expressions, gestures, and tones of voice that suggest their identification with Kirsten's unhappiness, Debbie's disdain, and Amy's amused but genuine sympathy.

—How did Kirsten feel about joining the group? How do you know how she felt? Why did she offer to leave?

—Why do you think Debbie at first ignored Kirsten and later left the group?

—When Amy laughed, was she making fun of Kirsten? How do you know she wasn't?

Then help youngsters get the feel of a character by letting them pantomime Kirsten's actions as she joined the group. When they show her timidity and embarrassment, let them add the dialogue, *I am with you?* Next have pupils decide what Kirsten might have said when she offered to withdraw. Point out that they can substitute these words for the line *Hastily Kirsten offered to withdraw from the group* when they read the scene. Then choose three of the most responsive children to read pages 21 and 22.

Young readers can gain additional insight into the feelings of the characters they portray by listening and reacting to what the others say. Comment: "You have already noticed that in different parts of the story Kirsten is shy, puzzled, enthusiastic, and happy. But does she have these feelings only while she is talking?" Lead children to conclude that in each instance she feels and reacts while listening to others and then puts her reactions into words. Encourage listeners as well as readers to view the scene from the standpoint of one of the characters. When their turns come to read, they will be able to interpret the printed page more effectively.

discuss characters' thoughts and reactions . . .

pantomime Kirsten's actions . . .

supply dialogue . . .

read episode aloud . . .

listen and react to other characters . . .

After several groups have read and the characterizations have become definite, continue with the remaining episodes.

Personal traits and emotional reactions are also emphasized on pages 7 and 8-9 of the *Think-and-Do Book*. On page 7 children choose the word that best describes the main character in each episode. After reading the story on pages 8-9 they must indicate whether each of several statements applies to Kirsten or Juanito or to both children.

Extending competence

● Many of the expressions that puzzled Kirsten are idioms that children use and hear in everyday speech. Call attention to some of the idioms used in the story by asking children whether they think the phrase *come out of your shell* is a good way to describe someone who is becoming more friendly and less shy. Why?

Continue: "What made it hard for Kirsten to understand what this phrase meant? What were some of the other expressions that baffled her? Who can tell us what they mean?" If the phrases *white elephant, thinking cap,* and *on the house* are new to children, you may want to have them find the place in the story where each is defined. Then comment: "Our language is full of expressions that do not mean exactly what the words say. We call these expressions *idioms.* Just think how strange they must sound to someone who has never heard them."

Then invite children to think of other idioms they may have heard and to tell what they mean. You can start the discussion going with such examples as *kill time, break a record, apple-pie order, a piece of my mind, catch cold.*

● To point up the use of a hyphen in dividing words at the end of a printed line, call attention to the second sentence on page 25, and note the hyphenated word *thinking.* Explain to children that when a word of two or more syllables is too long to fit at the end of a line, a hyphen may be used to show that part of the word is printed on the next line.

read scenes aloud.

Children explain meaning of idioms used in story . . .

interpret similar figurative expressions.

Pupils note significance of hyphen after word or syllable at end of line . . .

Next suggest that pupils find the entry word *anxious* in their glossaries. Help them recall that the spaces between syllables in the spelling of an entry word indicate the places where the word may be divided with a hyphen at the end of a line of print or writing. Continue with the word *body*, leading children to note that although it is a two-syllable word, it may not be divided at the end of a line. Also use the entry words *height* and *cliff* to emphasize the idea that one-syllable words are not divided at the end of a line.

and how possible syllable divisions are indicated in glossary.

● This exercise and page 10 of the *Think-and-Do Book* review the concept that different consonant letters may represent the same consonant sound and check pupils' ability to associate consonant sounds with the letters that represent them in printed words.

1. First write the known word *keep* and ask with what sound this word begins. When the *k* sound is identified, ask, "What letter stands for the *k* sound in *keep?*"

Pupils associate same consonant sound with different letters . . .

Under *keep* write *car, rock, Christmas.* As each word is pronounced, ask pupils to tell where they hear the *k* sound in it and to notice the spellings that stand for the *k* sound. Continue with these consonant sounds and known words:

   s sound: safe, circle, science, grass, else, twice
   z sound: zoo, buzz, does, please
   j sound: join, gentle, huge, hedge
   ch sound: chin, catch, picture
   sh sound: shake, sugar, machine, motion, tension, ocean
   g sound: give, guess, egg
   h sound: hill, whole
   f sound: fat, off, elephant, enough
   ng sound: hung, tongue, trunk

2. To review briefly the idea that a consonant letter (or letters) may represent no sound in a printed word, write the known word *knob* and have it pronounced. Then ask:
—With what letter does the word *knob* begin?
—Do you hear a *k* sound at the beginning of *knob?* With what sound does *knob* begin?

recall that a consonant letter may represent no sound . . .

Continue with the letter *w* in the word *wrong*, the letter *h* in the word *hour*, the letter *l* in the word *talk*, the letter *t* in the word *whistle*, the letter *b* in the word *climb*, and the letters *gh* in the word *high*.

3. To conclude, write the known word *chin* and have it pronounced and used in a sentence. Erase the letters *ch* and substitute the letters *th* to make *thin*. Have *thin* pronounced and used in a sentence. Then change *thin* to *thing*, *thing* to *think*, *think* to *thick*, *thick* to *quick*, *quick* to *sick*, and *sick* to *six*.

identify words formed by changing initial or final consonants.

Use similar procedures with each italicized word below, forming in succession the words shown after it:

> *went*—bent, cent, scent, sent, sense
> *hide*—side, slide, stride, guide, glide
> *cap*—cash, catch, camp, lamp, lamb
> *pen*—when, wren, wrench, bench, bend
> *rock*—knock, knot, slot, blot, block
> *his*—hiss, miss, mist, wrist, list
> *cage*—age, ache, ape, shape, shake

Extending interests

In connection with today's story you will want to read "The Hundred Dresses," by Eleanor Estes (in *The Arbuthnot Anthology of Children's Literature*). Afterwards let children discuss it freely—the unfriendly little girls and whether they meant to be cruel, why Wanda told the story of the hundred dresses, how the girls must have felt when the teacher read Mr. Petronski's letter, the surprise of the hundred dresses. What might—and should—the children in Wanda's school have done about Wanda long before she moved away? Invite youngsters to compare Wanda and Kirsten—each girl's loneliness, her reaction to it, and its ultimate solution. What prevented Kirsten from experiencing the unhappiness that Wanda did?

Children listen to two stories with similar themes ...

Then introduce Ursula Nordstrom's *The Secret Language* by reading aloud the first three chapters. The foregoing discussion might also be applied to Vicky and Martha and their different attitudes at boarding school.

discuss reason for different endings.

The World of Hogback Mountain

Young readers will respond with sympathetic admiration to the realistic portrayal of the heartaches and struggles that result from Rufe Kaller's intense desire to make his crippled friend's wish come true. Discussion of the story problem will deepen appreciation of skillful characterization and eloquent language even as it leads children to an ethical evaluation of motives and conduct.

One exercise in this lesson emphasizes the importance of context clues in comprehending sentence meaning. Others focus attention on the interpretation of dictionary pronunciations and on familiar spelling patterns that serve as visual clues to vowel sounds in one-syllable words.

New words: Kaller, *examine,* though, months, precious*, *business* (mountain*, Rufe*, doctor*, sighed*, costs*, dollars*, chairbound*, *cliff**, leafy*, *whittling**, sharp*, figure*, sea*, forty*, fellow*, mind*, halfway*, smoke*, breath*, *pines**, rod*, wandered*, present*, snatched*, carved*, startled*, stuck*, trade*, speechless*, forward*, stared*, worth*, *ruffling**, moon*, tears*, swallowed*)

Think-and-Do Book: Pages 11 and 12

Establishing background

Conversation about the title and first illustration will help establish the setting of the story and heighten interest in reading. First write the title on the board for children to read, and clarify the meaning of *world* in this context through a discussion of such phrases as the world of books, the world of sports, and *the world of business.* Then ask youngsters what they think the world of Hogback Mountain might be like.

Pupils discuss meaning of world in title . . .

In what ways might it be different from (or similar to) the area in which they themselves live?

As the illustration on page 27 is discussed, bring out details that might escape the cursory glance. Comment: "*Rufe Kaller* [(kal′ər)], the boy standing on the porch, is visiting his friend Dan Steel. Who else is visiting Dan? Why do you suppose the doctor has come to Dan's home *to examine his leg?* Do you think Dan has just injured it? What makes you think as you do? [If necessary, draw attention to the wheels on the chair.] If Dan is chairbound *for weeks or months or even longer,* what can he do to entertain himself? Right now he is telling the doctor about something he would like to do *even though he cannot walk.* As you read the first two pages and find out about Dan's wish, notice how Rufe feels about Dan."

Write the words *examine, cliff, whittling, pines, business,* and *ruffling* on the board, too, and remind pupils to use the glossary to check the meaning or pronunciation if necessary.

In succeeding lesson plans it will be assumed, unless other suggestions are made, that the words which are to be found in the glossary will be written on the board and attention called to them before pupils read the selection.

talk about setting and identify new words ...

make inferences based on details in picture ...

Guiding interpretation

PAGES 27-28

When children have compared the information on these pages with their own surmises about the story, point up the problem and the intense feelings of the characters.
—What problem do the story characters face? Did Dan think it would be easy to solve? Why not? [Make sure pupils understand the second paragraph on page 28 and recognize lack of money as a significant aspect of the problem.]
—Why did Rufe leave Dan's home so quickly? What made his eyes sting? What thoughts were probably going through his mind as he looked at the mountain?
—As Rufe went home, he was wondering how he could get the telescope Dan wanted. Do you suppose anyone at home can help him answer that question?

discuss opening scene and check inferences ...

identify problem ..

grasp implied ideas ...

Emphasize Rufe's sensitivity to the thoughts and feelings of others and his realization that they, too, have unfulfilled desires.
—What made Rufe realize that most people long for something?
—How did Rufe show that he understood his uncle's longings?
—Why did Rufe start walking toward the mountain?
—Why did he frown at the sight of smoke?
—Did Rufe really get away from his thoughts? What brought his thoughts back to Dan? [If necessary, clarify the phrase *caught his breath sharply.*]

interpret motives and inner drives of characters...

Then call attention to the picture on page 31, encouraging pupils to tell how they imagine Rufe feels and what he may be thinking as he watches the boy. Suggest that they read this page to check their opinions.

Since youngsters will be eager to continue reading, pause only long enough after silent reading to make sure children understand the struggle in Rufe's mind.
—What was Rufe tempted to do? Could he have taken the telescope without being seen by the campers? When?
—Why didn't he take it?
—What does the author mean by the words *an idea struck him?* What do you think Rufe plans to do now?

understand reason for Rufe's conflicting emotions...

anticipate action...

After discussion of the solution to the "telescope" problem, guide pupils in evaluating the actions of the characters.
—Why do you suppose George was willing to trade something as valuable as his telescope for the ship Rufe had carved?
—Why did Rufe show Mr. Williams the carving of Mary Kate? Did he have the same right to trade that as he did the ship?
—How many people were helped by Rufe's trading his ship for the telescope? In what way was Mr. Williams helped? Uncle Case? Dan? Rufe?
—Why was Rufe close to tears as he took the telescope and hurried away? What do you think he was most happy about?

discuss how problem was resolved...

make judgments...

perceive implied reason for Rufe's reaction...

To help boys and girls recognize and appreciate the author's skillful characterization, ask: "Which character in this story do you feel you know best? How does the author help you become well acquainted with Rufe in a short time?" Guide pupils in locating on each page the conversation and explanations the author uses to develop the character of Rufe so realistically. (The author's choice of language as one means of effective characterization should not be overlooked, and any regional expressions that are unfamiliar to children in the group should be clarified during this discussion.) Such points as the following may be brought out:

> Page 27—Rufe's concern for Dan (paragraph 1)
>
> Page 28—his understanding of Dan's desire to explore the mountain (paragraphs 3, 4, 5)
>
> Page 29—his strong desire to fulfill Dan's wish and his patience and care in carving (paragraphs 2 and 6)
>
> Page 30—his understanding of his uncle and his realization that most people want something (paragraphs 2 and 3)
>
> Page 31—his inner struggle and refusal to yield to temptation as well as his resourcefulness in solving the problem (paragraphs 2 and 3)
>
> Pages 32-33—his determination to help another that overcomes his shyness and makes him willing to sacrifice the ship he carved with such great care

locate passages that reveal Rufe's character . . .

ORAL INTERPRETATION

This story provides excellent opportunities to help readers interpret thoughts and feelings that are stated indirectly without the signaling words *he thought,* which children are accustomed to seeing. If pupils are to convey the significance of these passages to listeners, they need to read them from Rufe's viewpoint. To emphasize identification with Rufe, then, call attention to the first sentence of the fourth paragraph on page 30. Ask youngsters to tell what thoughts Rufe was trying to get away from, and have them read the third paragraph aloud.

Next remind children of Rufe's inner struggle as he peered at the telescope from behind the trees when the entire family

state Rufe's thoughts before reading passages aloud.

had wandered off. Suggest that they think his thoughts, and then let different pupils put them into words. They may say, for example: "Look at that telescope! I could take it so easily. No one would see me. And Dan would like it so much. But I just couldn't face Uncle Case if I took it. And Mary Kate would throw a stolen present back at me!"

When youngsters are identifying with Rufe and expressing his thoughts, let different ones read aloud the exact words of this portion of the story, beginning with the last sentence in the first paragraph on page 31.

Similar procedures can be used to help oral readers enliven their reading of other passages that reveal thoughts (the last sentence on page 32, the sixth paragraph on page 33, and the first three sentences of the last paragraph in the story).

Extending competence

● One aspect of the realistic and appealing style of this story is the natural manner in which the author records conversations and explains a character's thoughts. Many of these remarks and thoughts convey meaning only when the surrounding context is known. To strengthen ability to comprehend sentence meaning in the light of total context, write the following statements:

> Probably never would, the doctor thought. (page 27)
> "Twenty, maybe twenty-five dollars." (page 28)
> But twenty dollars! (pages 28)
> "Can't say as I do." (page 29)
> "Down the mountain." (page 32)
> "Took me six months to make it." (page 32)
> "My uncle did." (page 33)

Explain that we might not understand these remarks at all unless we had read the story. As pupils read each one silently, see whether they can remember who said or thought it and at what point in the story. Next let them find the statement and explain its full meaning in light of the context in which it occurs (for example, Dan probably never would be able to walk). Then ask someone to show the meaning and feeling of the character by reading aloud the part in which the statement appears.

Children interpret ideas in light of context.

● Use of page 11 of the *Think-and-Do Book* will strengthen ability to visualize and to perceive relationships of place. Comment that youngsters will find out about some of the things George did and saw during the rest of his vacation as they read each part of this page and decide where George was.

In Think-and-Do Book pupils note place relationships.

● This exercise may be used whenever time permits to reinforce pupils' understanding of dictionary pronunciations and check their ability to interpret them. Ask youngsters to open their books to the Full Pronunciation Key on page 266, and lead them to recall the purpose of such a key. Then suggest that they use it as a reference for a pronunciation game.

To begin, write the pronunciation (yel′ō) and (yō′dl), and ask which one of these is a color. As children respond, write *yellow* beside the appropriate pronunciation. Then let pupils determine what the second word is and write that word beside its pronunciation.

Children interpret dictionary pronunciations.

Which means "very clean"? (spot′līt′) (spot′lis)
Which keeps a boat from drifting? (ang′kər) (ang′gər)
Which is a shellfish? (ois′tər) (ēs′tər)
Which is an animal? (al′fə bet) (el′ə fənt)
Which means "at this time"? (nou) (nô)
Which is something to wear? (kēp) (kāp)
Which is a place to park a car? (gär′bij) (gə räzh′)
Which can you swim in? (pül) (pül)
Which is a vegetable? (kū′kum bər) (hun′ē kōm′)
Which means "more smooth"? (smuᴛʜ′ər) (smuᴛʜ′ər)
Which is a fruit? (pãr) (pėr)
Which is a short way to say *that is?* (thach) (ᴛʜats)
Which is a month of the year? (ok tō′bər) (ok′tə pəs)
Which means "not tight"? (lüz) (lüs)
Which is a metal? (sliv′ər) (sil′vər)

● The use of the procedures that follow and page 12 of the *Think-and-Do Book* will provide a review of some of the spelling patterns that children have learned to use as visual clues to vowel sound in one-syllable printed words.

Begin by writing the following columns of words on the board:

(1)	(2)	(3)	(4)
ranch	shade	chance	me
west	Steve	twelve	go
inch	size	since	hi
job	rope	lodge	by
shut	huge	plunge	
harm	bare	carve	
herd	here	verse	
thirst	wore	horse	
sort		nurse	
churn			

(5)	(6)	(7)	(8)	(9)
grain	least	sheep	road	day
wait	cream	breed	coax	sea
faint	reach	week	soap	bee
				toe
chair	near	queer	roar	die
hair	bear	cheer	board	
	learn			

After the first five words in Column 1 have been pronounced, ask these questions:

—Do you hear long vowel sounds or short vowel sounds in these words?

—What do you see in the spelling of each word that would lead you to expect a short vowel sound? [The single vowel letter followed by one or more consonant letters.]

Use the remaining words in the first column to help pupils recall that if the consonant letter following the single vowel letter is *r,* the vowel sound is usually *r*-controlled.

Continue similarly with the other columns of words, giving pupils an opportunity to recall and state in their own words the following generalizations about spellings and vowel sounds:

> Column 2: In words that pattern like *shade, Steve,* and *size,* a single vowel letter followed by one consonant letter and final *e* usually stands for a long vowel sound. If the consonant letter is *r,* the vowel sound may be *r*-controlled.

Pupils recall visual clue to short vowel sound...

note effect of r on this clue...

recall other clues to long and short vowel sounds and note effect of r...

Column 3: In words that pattern like *chance, twelve,* and *since,* a single vowel letter followed by two consonants and final *e* usually stands for a short vowel sound. If the vowel letter is followed by *r,* the vowel sound is usually *r*-controlled.

Column 4: In words that pattern like *me, go,* and *by,* a single vowel letter at the end of a word usually stands for a long vowel sound.

Columns 5, 6, 7, 8: The letters *ai, ea, ee, oa* together in a word followed by one or more consonants usually stand for long vowel sounds. If the consonant letter that follows these vowel letters is *r,* the vowel sound is probably *r*-controlled.

Column 9: In words that pattern like *day, sea, bee, toe,* and *die,* the two vowel letters together at the end of a word usually stand for a long vowel sound.

Finally write the following sentences, underlining the italicized words. Note pupils' ability to identify the underlined words.

use context and
spelling patterns to
identify printed words.

Is the *spare* tire in the car? The *stray* cat was hungry.

Jim saw fish in the *stream.* *Scrape* the dry paint loose.

Rinse the dish with hot water. I like *crisp* cookies.

Who will *serve* the ice cream? Dan hurt his *knee.*

Ann wears her hair in *braids.* Our dog *guards* the house.

Extending interests

Commenting that Rufe and Dan would have felt right at home with the Tatum family in their mountain home, read Ruth and Latrobe Carroll's *Tough Enough and Sassy.* Comparison of this book and "The World of Hogback Mountain" will provide a springboard for discussing traits the characters displayed in their reactions to their problems and the ways they set out to solve them. What might have been Beanie's reaction to Dan's (and Rufe's) problem? How might he have tried to solve it? What might Beanie's mother have suggested?

Children listen to
a story with similar
theme and setting...

compare traits
and reactions
in both stories.

If pupils have not heard or read *Beanie,* the first in the series of stories about the Tatums, they might enjoy it now.

Green Hill Neighbors
and
How to Tell the Top of a Hill

The sounds of poetry enliven its imagery and bring its message to the reader's heart. This can be made evident to youngsters as they hear and read lyrical verses about the small animals that inhabit one hill and about the exact location of another hill's top. After becoming familiar with the poems, pupils may look at hills through different eyes—with new feelings and interests —and the sight of hills may, in turn, remind children of things they found most enjoyable in the poems.

Establishing background

Recall the title of the last story, and review its meaning with pupils. Who were the inhabitants of Hogback Mountain? After rereading the last paragraph on page 28, stimulate youngsters' imaginations by asking: "Do you suppose there sometimes were animals close to Rufe that he didn't realize were there? Where might they have been? [Make sure children note the possibility that some animals were inside their homes in trees, ground, or rocky caverns.]"

Children recall animal world of Hogback Mountain...

Guiding interpretation

PAGE 35

As you relate Frances Frost's poem to the story, alert youngsters to the delightful images in "Green Hill Neighbors." Comment: "Today I'm going to read you a poem written by someone who has her own neighboring world of wildlife. If you use your imaginations as you listen, you'll be able to catch a glimpse of each of her little wild friends."

Immediately after they have heard the poem, let children tell what they saw as they listened. Then invite them to open their

and relate it to poem...

anticipate imagery...

listen to poem and describe imagery...

books to page 35 and see what kind of picture an artist was inspired to paint. When pupils have discussed the illustration, talk about the general meaning of the poem, encouraging them to tell why they think the poet enjoyed living near the hill and what she meant by her friends *inside* the hill. Do boys and girls believe that Rufe might have had similar feelings when he looked at Hogback Mountain? What about pupils themselves—when they see a hill or mountain, or a picture of one, will they think only about how it looks? What things might they wonder about after hearing this poem?

expand personal outlooks . . .

Next <u>direct youngsters' attention to two of the poet's tools—rhythm and alliteration.</u> To keep discussion on children's level, touch upon these devices lightly, emphasizing the resultant imagery. You might begin by observing that a poem not only may make pictures come alive in people's minds but may also be musical. A good poet makes the music suit what he or she is saying. One of the ways a poet creates music with words is by repeating certain sounds, just as a musician repeats chords in a piece of music.

anticipate discovery of poem's lyric quality . . .

To illustrate, draw attention to the last line in the first stanza and ask pupils what sound they notice in three of the words. Since the appeal of alliteration is aural, say the line aloud and invite youngsters to do the same. When they have noted the alliteration, remark: "Doesn't the *c-h* sound go well with a small, stumpy, cuddly animal? Listen as I say the line again: *The woodchuck's chubby child*." You may wish to introduce the word *alliteration*, telling children that it means the repetition of the first sound in a group of words or in a line of poetry.

note use of alliteration . . .

and its effect . . .

Continue by reading the next two lines and asking, "What does *busy whiskered faces* mean?" There is some alliteration in these two lines also, but it is perhaps not so obvious. If alliteration seems to catch pupils' fancy, point out the initial sound in *Rabbits* and *rocks*. The *r* sounds in *whiskered* and *Peering* may also be brought to their attention. Then emphasize the musical effect of the words and the rhythm by repeating *Rabbits with busy whiskered faces/Peering out of rocks*.

enjoy rhythm of poem . . .

When children hear the phrase *The big-eared meadow mouse*, they should immediately spot the alliteration. Then bring out the charm of the last animal description by telling youngsters that sometimes the rhythm of poetry forces a reader to linger over the word that makes the picture one sees very vivid. You might note with pupils, for example, how the rhythm of the words *the dainty/Gold-eyed baby fox* draws attention to the color of the baby fox' eyes.

After boys and girls hear the whole poem once more, ask, "Has the poet made you feel as though you've really been introduced to these little creatures?" Then let youngsters read the poem independently.

PAGE 36

In introducing John Ciardi's "How to Tell the Top of a Hill," use the illustration as a topic of discussion. Make the observation that the artist has shown another hill, and ask: "Where is the boy? Can he climb any higher? What does he seem to be looking at?" Bring the poem's title to children's attention, and ask them how they would describe the top of a hill. How do boys and girls know when they have reached a hill's top? Comment that the poet John Ciardi explains it in a way that may never have occurred to them. Then read Ciardi's humorous, lilting poem aloud.

Though the words of the poem have a childish, nonsensical air, they are actually extremely logical. Draw attention to this fact, as it enhances the poem's drollness. Is everything that John Ciardi has said true? Does what he has said make sense? Suggest that pupils reread the poem to themselves before making a definite decision.

Before you invite youngsters to read the poem aloud, see whether they realize that *UP* is written in capital letters and that *most* is italicized to indicate that more stress is to be given to these two words. Also, see whether they recognize that the two colons and the dash signal a change of pace in reading. Then remind pupils not to pause at the ends of lines when doing so will break the train of thought. Having absorbed this information, good readers should have little difficulty in letting the melody of the poem carry them along.

read poem aloud . . .

discuss illustration . . .

listen to poem . . .

consider poem's droll logic . . .

note punctuation and style of type as clues to stress and pace . . .

read poem aloud.

Extending interests

Most youngsters have learned by this time that if they have enjoyed one story by a certain author, they are likely to be interested in other stories by the same person. By occasionally reading to children other poems written by poets whom they have met on these pages, you may <u>lead pupils to the understanding that one may find his favorite poets as easily as his favorite story writers.</u> An excellent poem to read at this time is Frances Frost's "Night of Wind," in which her sympathetic intimacy with wildlife is again beautifully revealed. Other poems of hers that can be found in the same book (*Time for Poetry*) and that children may particularly enjoy hearing are "Beach Fire," "Dandelion," and "The Little Whistler."

Boys and girls who have been amused by John Ciardi's humor will be pleased to find that he has written many other poems in the same vein, some of them in his book *The Reason for the Pelican* (from which "How to Tell the Top of a Hill" was taken). For example, "Samuel Silvernose Slipperyside," "Lucifer Leverett Lightningbug," "The Principal Part of a Python," and "Why Nobody Pets the Lion at the Zoo," are all delightfully zany.

The Arbuthnot Anthology of Children's Literature includes verse-choir suggestions for two of Ciardi's poems, "Halloween" and "The River Is a Piece of the Sky," which pupils might add to their repertoire. (Boys and girls who have used the *Learn to Listen, Speak, and Write* series may already have had the fun of interpreting the latter poem in a verse choir.)

Pupils hear more of Frances Frost's nature poems . . .

and John Ciardi's humorous poetry.

A homemade car and the interest it provokes help solve a problem for Charley. Children will find food for thought as they discuss the initial misunderstanding and the common ground that is established between two ways of life.

In one exercise in this lesson attention is focused on words whose pronunciation is determined by meaning and function. In another pupils review the understanding that different spellings may represent the same vowel sound.

New words: reservation, California, hospital, *valley*, impatiently*, *Sioux*, satisfied, exercise, questioned, none, attention, curious, sew, *English*, eleven (Charley*, dust*, mad*, Jean*, nurse*, Jerome*, dumb*, panting*, boiling-hot*, drove*, mistaken*, lawn*, mower*, cocoa*, pay*, granny*, suggested*, cloth*, Friday*, aloud*, song*, meant*, stuff*, honey*, fact*)

Think-and-Do Book: **Pages 13, 14, 15, 16, and 17**

Establishing background

After recalling how Kirsten felt about living in a new land, discuss the change in scene that confronts Charley Brave. Comment: "The boy in today's story had a problem that may remind you of Kirsten's. He and his family had just moved from a big city to *a reservation where the Sioux Indians lived.* A school and *a small hospital* were near his new home, but there were no big buildings or busy streets. Although he got *plenty of exercise exploring the hills and valleys* by himself, he *was not satisfied* to be alone. What else might he want to do?"

Continue: "Yes, Charley wanted to make friends with other boys on the reservation. But *none of them would pay attention*

Children identify new words . . .

to him. They were *very curious* about something he had brought *from California*, but they never *questioned him about it.* In fact they didn't even *speak English to him.* What do you suppose the trouble was?" Then suggest that children read the first five pages to discover what caused the difficulty and how Charley tried to overcome it. (The remaining words may be presented before pupils read pages 42-45.)

and begin to think about problem of main character . . .

Guiding interpretation

PAGES 37-41

Encourage pupils to consider the reasons for Charley's difficulty and to anticipate a possible solution by asking:

—Why was it hard for Charley to make friends with the boys on the reservation?

discuss Charley's problem . . .

—In what way did Charley think his sister was more fortunate than he?

—What happened that gave Charley another chance to try to make friends? Why was it important to round up the goats and drive them back into the pen?

—How successful was Charley's effort to make friends? How successful was Dr. Brave's effort to persuade the people to try goat's milk?

—Do you think Jean's idea might help solve either of these problems? How?

and consider possible solutions . . .

On page 13 of the *Think-and-Do Book* children are again asked to identify the problem in each of two episodes and to consider how the main character might solve it.

PAGES 42-45

Present the words *eleven* and *sew* by commenting: "Jean and Mary soon thought of some party fun that would interest the girls. They gathered some bright scraps of cloth, needles, and *eleven* spools of thread. What do you think they planned to do? [Present the word *sew* when this activity is mentioned.] Do you think their plan would interest the boys as well? As you finish the story, you'll find out what Charley thought of the idea and how well the plan worked."

identify new words eleven and sew . . .

After silent reading <u>focus attention on the factors that con-</u><u>tributed to the solution of the two main problems.</u>

evaluate outcome of the plan . . .

—Would you say the party was a success? In what ways?

—Why do you suppose no one on the reservation had been will-ing to try goat's milk before?

—Had Charley thought the party would help him very much? Did it help him? How?

—Do you think Charley and the boys learned something about each other? What do you think they found out?

—Do you think Charley's life on the reservation will be different or much the same from now on? Why?

WHOLE STORY

<u>Point up the parallel between Charley's experience and</u> <u>Kirsten's</u> by leading boys and girls to note that both children had the same kind of problem, although their feelings about it were different. Then ask pupils why they think the boys on the reservation acted the way they did. Do their actions re-mind youngsters of Debbie's actions toward Kirsten? In what way? When children have observed that the boys, as well as Debbie, jumped to conclusions before they really understood the newcomer, ask why this would make it hard for Charley or Kirsten to get acquainted with the other children.

compare actions of characters in two stories.

Then let pupils tell what both Charley and Kirsten did that helped them make friends. How might the stories be different if neither had given the other children a chance to be friendly?

Extending competence

● For many readers the setting of today's story will be as new as it was for Charley. <u>Help children realize what they have</u> <u>learned from story details</u> by asking:

Pupils note details included in story . . .

—Did you find some new and interesting words in today's story? What were they? What do the Indian words *hoksila cheecha* and *wa-ste* mean?

—What made it difficult to keep cows on the reservation? Why might goats be easier to raise?

—How do you suppose Granny Yellow Bird got her name?

—Do you think the author could have told about Charley's problem without using Indian words, without mentioning Granny Yellow Bird, and without telling why goats were raised on the reservation? Why do you think this information was included?

Invite children who speak a second language to share their knowledge with others by teaching them some common words and expressions. Using the story as a starting point, these pupils might volunteer words for *boy*, *girl*, *good*, and *bad*. Other words that children will enjoy knowing and using are *hello*, *good-by*, *yes*, *no*, *please*, and *thank you*.

Pages 14-16 of the *Think-and-Do Book* provide another glimpse of life on an Indian reservation. To complete the exercise, youngsters must visualize city life and ranch life and recall the differences between them.

● Check pupils' ability to interpret and use dictionary pronunciations by calling attention to words whose pronunciation depends upon their meaning and function in context. To begin, write these sentences and underline the italicized words:

Everyone wanted to be in the *contest*.
Both teams decided to *contest* the new rules.

Please *excuse* Ann from school early.
They had no *excuse* for being late.

Have children listen carefully to the underlined word as you read each sentence in the first pair. Was the underlined word pronounced the same way in each sentence?

Next have pupils find *contest* in their glossaries. After they note how many definitions and pronunciations are given, lead them to recall that the number after each pronunciation indicates with which definition that pronunciation is used. Ask what the underlined word means in each sentence and how it is pronounced. Then have the sentences read.

Continue similarly with the second pair of sentences, leading children to conclude that the pronunciation of words like *contest* and *excuse* is determined by their meaning in a sentence.

infer reasons for their inclusion . . .

compare and contrast ways of life in Think-and Do Book exercise.

Children hear contest pronounced in different contexts . . .

note that meaning and function of words may determine pronunciation.

GUIDANCE FOR PAGES 37·45 | 55

● In this exercise children review the concept that different spellings may represent the same vowel sound. The procedures check ability to associate vowel sounds with spellings that represent them both in known one-syllable words and in those that pupils have not encountered in The New Basic Readers.

1. Write the following key word and groups of words:

vowel of bed

check	else	breath
test	ledge	thread
spell	fence	meant

Pupils note different spellings for a given vowel sound . . .

Have children pronounce the key word *bed* and each group of words. Lead them to note that they hear the vowel of *bed* in each group. Then call attention to the spellings that stand for the vowel of *bed* in each group (the letter *e* followed by consonant letters, the letter *e* followed by two consonant letters and final *e*, the letters *ea* followed by consonant letters).

Ask pupils to think of other words in which they hear the vowel of *bed* and, as they respond, write each word under the appropriate group and have it used in a sentence. If a child suggests a word like *friend* or *said*, which represents an uncommon spelling for the vowel of *bed,* write it and note the spelling.

Continue similarly with each of the following key words and groupings. (The pronunciation of words marked with an asterisk varies regionally and hence may not always represent the vowel sound of the key word.)

vowel of eat

Pete	seat	need	tree	chief
Steve	steam	cheek	free	field
eve	please	queen	glee	piece

vowel of ice

twice	pie	sly	sigh	find	wild
strike	tie	sky	fight	kind	child
prize	die	fry	slight	grind	mild

vowel of go

code	boast	toe	snow	cold	most
hose	float	Joe	own	roll	post
smoke	loan	hoe	blown	bolt	ghost

vowel of <u>all</u>

small	straw	brought	caught	lost*
salt	crawl	thought	pause	dog*
talk	lawn	ought	fault	cross*
				long*

vowel of <u>out</u>

found	frown
south	growl
mouse	crowd

vowel of <u>book</u>

shook	pull	could
foot	push	should

vowel of <u>boot</u>

cool	flew	blue	rule	group	fruit
noon	grew	true	tune*	soup	suit
droop	stew*	glue	flute	rouge	juice

vowel of <u>care</u>

scare	fair	wear	where
dare	stairs	bear	there
share	pair	pear	

vowel of <u>bird</u>

dirt	her	curb	earth	word
whirl	jerk	fur	heard	worth
squirm	serve	urge	earn	worm

2. Write these sentences, underlining the italicized words, and note pupils' ability to identify these words in context.

use word analysis to identify printed words in context . . .

The heavy rains were a *threat* to the old bridge.
We had time only for a *brief* visit.
Grandmother gave me a *pearl* ring.
The last snowstorm was the *worst* one this year.
Those bright lights *blind* me.
We like to *count* the cars as they pass by.
He began to *scoop* up water with his hand.
I *drew* a picture of a fishing boat.
The roar of the machines will *drown* the music.
The woman's ring was made of *gold*.

On page 17 of the *Think-and-Do Book* children are to choose from among several key words the one that has the same vowel sound as the underlined word in each sentence.

identify vowel sounds in Think-and-Do Book.

Extending interests

Boys and girls who shared Charley's loneliness and his pleasure at the outcome of the party will want to read the rest of Charley's story. Place the book *Charley Brave*, by Edna Walker Chandler, on the library table with the suggestion that pupils find out how a sun dance, the rescue of a friend, and a lonely hunting trip help Charley win his heart's desire.

Children enjoy the book from which today's story was taken . . .

When several children have read the book, you might provide an opportunity for them to talk about what it added to their understanding of Charley Brave. Was Charley the same at the end of the story as he was in the part that youngsters read in *More Roads to Follow?* How did he change? What do pupils think he learned? What did Charley want—was it really the warbonnet? Why was the warbonnet important to him?

discuss development of main character in story and book . . .

You might also recommend Lois Lenski's *Little Sioux Girl,* another story of life on a Sioux Indian reservation in the Dakotas, as one that will appeal especially to the girls.

read another story about life on a Sioux reservation.

Encouraging personal reading

The wide variety of settings in "Roads Here and There" provides excellent opportunity to help children note how the place where a person lives can affect his interests, activities, and desires. Youngsters who have observed this influence in the stories read thus far should be encouraged to watch for similar evidence of it in books and stories they are reading on their own. Then, when they gather to share their enjoyment of certain favorites, you might pose a question or two about influence of story setting to stimulate conversation along this line. A single question will often lead children to look at a story in a new light and send them back to it with a different purpose for reading.

Any child who has ever seen the moonlight transform a familiar object into something strange and mysterious will appreciate the change in mood in this poem.

Establishing background

Turn pupils' thoughts to western settings of stories they have recently read in *More Roads to Follow,* touching upon the fact that not all of the West is "open range." First ask them where Charley Brave lived before he went to the Indian reservation. Through your questions bring out that California is on the western coast of the United States and has many large cities. Then ask: "When people say 'out west,' what part of the West are they usually speaking of? In what kind of country is a 'western' story or movie usually laid? Have you read a story or poem in this book that took place in ranch country? What are some things that Billy might have seen as he rode Blaze across the open range?"

Children contrast different areas in the West...

Guiding interpretation

Call attention to the title of Polly Chase Boyden's poem, and invite pupils to listen to the way this poet describes "out west."

listen to poem...

When the poem has been read, guide discussion in a way that will make the imagery more vivid for children who fail to pick up indirect meanings or do not apply what they already know to new material. Include such questions as these:

—Why does the open range tend to be windier than many cities? Why can it be called wide?

discuss stated and implied meanings...

—Does anyone know what a prairie dog looks like? Have you ever seen a jack rabbit?

—Was Charley Brave a Pueblo Indian? The Pueblo Indians were so named because they lived in *pueblos,* a Spanish word meaning 'village.' [If pupils are not familiar with pueblos, explain that they are something like large apartment buildings and they are made of dried clay and mud. One story of a pueblo is often built on top of another like steps so that the roof of one story forms a porch for the one above it.] Can you see the silhouette of a pueblo in the illustration?

—Do you think this part of the West may be near Mexico? What makes you think perhaps it is?

—What does the poet mean when she says *I pass . . . sunsets?* Might sunsets on the open range and in a large city look different? Why?

—Do you think the poet liked living out west? Why?

Then see whether boys and girls have caught the shift in mood and time in the third stanza, and make its meaning clear. How is the third stanza different from the first two? What does the poet mean when she says *when the moon comes sliding?* How would sagebrush turn to foam? Did the moonlight ever make something with which pupils were familiar look mysterious and different? Where did the poet want to be at night? Why? (If youngsters are uncertain of the reason, suggest that they think about the poet's possible reaction to "seeing" the sagebrush become foam.) How do children think the last two lines of the poem should be read?

note poem's change in mood . . .

Encourage pupils to read along silently with you as the poem is reread. Then suggest that they take turns reading it, boys reading the first two stanzas and girls the last.

read poem aloud . . .

Invite children to try their hands as poets, writing poems about their own areas. Not only will the natural surroundings in which pupils live affect the images they think of, but the types of communities will also be revealed. Some poems will reflect the hustle and bustle of large cities, while others will speak of the tranquillity of smaller towns and the country. Youngsters may find themselves unexpectedly delighted by the beauty that can be evoked by descriptive detail.

compose poems that reflect environment.

Here again is Eddie Wilson, that likable friend of all animals, whom youngsters will certainly remember from *Roads to Follow*. The plot turns on a revolving door and Eddie's difficulties in extricating himself and his companions. Children will find that the basic ingredients of this funny tale are amusing characters and situations.

Discussion of the elements that contribute to the humor of the story increases awareness of the author's style and purpose. Skill in identifying new words is extended as pupils review known suffixes and learn the meaning of the suffix *-ward*.

New words: **Louella,** *committee,* **decorations, shrieked***, **hey, discovered, impossible, outward,** *naturally,* **become** (stray*, rewards*, changed*, parrot*, jealous*, scream*, themselves*, hated*, appeared*, Texas*, dance*, borrow*, south*, hotel*, drew*, paid*, revolving*, refused*, enter*, allowed*, pardon*, declared*, lady*, sputtered*, wailed*, loaned*, written*, tag*, spilled*, wagging*, collar*)

Think-and-Do Book: **Pages 18, 19, and 20**

Establishing background

In introducing the story, capitalize on children's familiarity with Eddie Wilson. Ask who remembers the name of the boy on the cover of their books, encouraging pupils to recall the kind of person Eddie was. Then have them turn to the title page. When children have identified the bird Eddie is carrying as a parrot, present *Her name is Louella,* and explain: *"Eddie soon discovered that Louella was jealous of his other pets. She squawked and shrieked and it was almost impossible to keep her quiet."*

Pupils relate story
to pictures and
to past reading . . .

identify new words . . .

Suggest that pupils read pages 48-50 to find out more about Louella and to learn how she was supposed to help a *committee* in their plans for *party decorations.* If there is doubt about what a committee is, discuss the glossary definition with children. The remaining words may be introduced before pupils read pages 51-57.

Guiding interpretation

PAGES 48-50

When silent reading is finished, <u>let youngsters contribute freely to a character sketch of Louella.</u> Sharing their enjoyment with one another will spark boys and girls' delight in the humor of these pages.

enjoy humor of Louella's actions . . .

Pupils will appreciate, too, the naturalness with which the humorous touches evolve throughout the story. This feature may be pointed up in concluding the discussion with such questions as the following to <u>bring the author's implied ideas to children's attention:</u>

—Why was Louella accustomed to seeing a great many other pets? Why didn't she get to know any of them very well?

observe cause-effect basis of humor . . .

—What were some of the phrases Louella would say? Why do you suppose each of these phrases was a part of her vocabulary? [Discuss each of these individually: *Cats! Cats! Texas is better! Eddie is best! No funny business!*]

—What were Eddie's reactions to the committee's request to borrow Louella? Why do you suppose he first thought the committee wanted Louella to dance? Why would Eddie get the idea that Louella might be hung on a tree?

As they complete page 18 of the *Think-and-Do Book,* boys and girls have other opportunities to state in their own words ideas that are implied in two different episodes.

To <u>prepare children for the delightful imagery that is of prime importance to their appreciation of the rest of the story</u> and to present the remaining words, comment: "In delivering Louella to the hotel ballroom, Eddie ran into a problem. You'll hear him yelling *Hey! Go away!* You'll also find that a revolving door is part of the problem. Do you know how a revolving door

acquire background for visual imagery . . .

and identify new words . . .

turns in a circle, a section facing inward and then *outward?* [If some youngsters are unfamiliar with the operation of a revolving door, have others explain this.] *Naturally* you *may become* a little dizzy as you finish the story!"

PAGES 51-57

While pupils are talking about Eddie's predicament with the parrot, the dog, the revolving door, and the doorman, ask children to describe their visual images in detail. How did the problem begin? Why did Eddie fail to step inside the hotel on each go-around? How many times did Eddie and Louella go around? Suggest that youngsters refer to the text for the answer or to verify their opinions. (The use of page 19 in the *Think-and-Do Book* will help in assessing each pupil's ability to form sensory images.)

reveal clarity of visual imagery . . .

Then bring out how Eddie remains in character to the end.
—When the problem of getting Louella into the hotel had been solved, why was Eddie faced with a new problem? [Make sure children understand that the single quotation marks used in the third paragraph on page 57 indicate that Mrs. Wilson was quoting the exact words Eddie's father has said.]

note quotation within quotation . . .

—In trying to adopt the dog, how did Eddie show right away that he had learned something from his experience with Gardenia the goat? What 'diplomatic' things did he say to his mother? What else had Eddie learned since the time he talked with Mr. Kilpatrick about the goat?

evaluate actions in light of past reading about Eddie . . .

—How do you think Eddie said the last line in this story? What does this tell you that Eddie was hoping? Would you have expected Eddie to say something like this? Why?

ORAL INTERPRETATION

Call upon youngsters' imagination and perceptive responses to the visual and kinesthetic images of the story by asking pupils to create with pantomime the illusion of Eddie's experience in the revolving door.

Suggest that children set the scene of action, designating the place in the classroom for the wall between the interior and exterior of the hotel. Also establish the location of the revolving door and the direction in which it turns. Then say: "Who would like to be someone who goes from outside into the lobby of the hotel? Remember that you will have to push the door and always circle in the same direction."

visualize setting and characters' movements . . .

When several have experienced the feeling of going around in the revolving door, challenge youngsters to use their imaginations to create the characters who enter and leave the hotel while Eddie is trying to deliver Louella to the ballroom— story characters mentioned only as someone, a man, a man with a suitcase, a lady.

Next ask who would like to be Eddie. Hand a volunteer an imaginary cage and send him on his way. As other Eddies succeed him, stimulate them to enrich the characterizations by asking: "How do you feel when you find the strange dog is going around with you and Louella? when you can't get out of the door? when the doorman begins to scold and threaten?"

enrich characterization of Eddie with emotional reactions . . .

The rôle of the doorman will be a popular one. To be convincing, children will have to appreciate how the doorman feels about his job and about such intruders as stray dogs, noisy parrots, and boys who make a game of going around and around in the door. You may also need to ask questions to get pupils to understand his attitude toward what Eddie is doing. After a brief discussion of how he looks, stands, acts, and feels, let several children take turns pantomiming his actions. Similar procedures can be used in developing the characterization of Eddie's mother.

try characterization of antagonistic adult . . .

and sympathetic adult . . .

When the characterizations are convincing, suggest that pupils pantomime the various episodes in succession. To avoid confusion, make certain that everybody understands which characters appear in each scene, in what order, and in what places they enter and exit from the door. Once youngsters can pantomime the action without losing their characterizations, let them add the dialogue, scene by scene.

pantomime entire scene . . .

add dialogue . . .

Occasionally children may feel the need of rereading the story to check dialogue and the sequence of events. If this is necessary, one child could read the pertinent passages while others listen for the points in question.

The last episode of the story, the one in which Eddie uses diplomacy with his mother, is excellent for oral reading. As groups take the rôles of these characters, encourage them to read exactly as if they were talking to one another.

read last scene aloud.

When pupils read three accounts of the revolving door episode on page 20 of the *Think-and-Do Book*, those who identified with the story characters during oral interpretation will readily recognize each character's point of view.

Extending competence

● To draw attention to the elements of the story that heighten the humorous effect, comment that much of the impact of an enjoyable story comes from the characters the author creates and the situations in which he places them. In this case both lend humor to the tale. Invite pupils to point out parts of the story they thought especially funny and, keeping discussion on a light and enjoyable plane, draw attention to the contributions of various characters and props to the comic effect. What was added to the humor of these incidents by Louella, the dog, the doorman, the revolving door, the cage, and Eddie? What would the story have been like without any one of them?

Children react to ideas in light of author's purpose . . .

You may also wish to highlight the author's use of language —refreshing ways of saying things in place of more familiar phrases. Children may recall some examples of this, and you can add such expressions as *ever since he was old enough to go around the block* and *added much to the weight of Eddie's bank* (page 48). Ask pupils to supply the ordinary ways these things could have been said and to contrast their reactions to the two ways of expressing the same thoughts. The comic effect of word selection can be illustrated by Eddie's "reason" for being friends with the dog: *Why, on all those trips we had together* (page 57).

and discuss use of picturesque language.

● Use the procedures given on the next page to introduce the suffix *-ward* and strengthen children's ability to identify derivatives ending in known suffixes.

1. Write the known word *outward*, and have it pronounced and used in a sentence. Ask what the root word is in *outward*, and underline *out*. Continue similarly with the derived forms *upward*, *backward*, and *homeward*. Then ask what suffix is added to *out*, *up*, *back*, *home*, and suggest that pupils find *-ward* in their glossaries and read the definition.

Pupils use derivatives ending with suffix <u>-ward</u> in sentences . . .

read definition of <u>-ward</u> in glossary . . .

2. To review known suffixes, write the following sentences and underline the italicized words, which are derived forms of known roots. After each sentence is read, have pupils tell with what suffix (or suffixes) each underlined word ends, what the root word is, and what each underlined word means.

identify in context derivatives ending in known suffixes.

> You should use *gentleness* in training a pet.
> The ring **Tom** found was *worthless*.
> The tables and chairs are *dusty*.
> The pioneers kept moving *westward*.
> The little girl said *tearfully* that her dog was lost.
> We need another *actor* and a *dancer* for the school play.
> The troll spoke to the goats in a *thunderous* voice.
> I helped Mother *tighten* the rope around the big box.
> My sister has *reddish*-brown hair.
> "You'll need the heavy coat for *warmth*," said Mother.
> Rules about crossing the street are for our *safety*.
> Dad said his trip was a *disappointment* to him.

Extending interests

To introduce Carolyn Haywood's *Eddie and Louella*, ask youngsters the name of the book that today's story comes from, and let them tell how they know this. (If necessary, call attention to the copyright line at the bottom of page 48 in their books.) Place the book on the library table so children can continue the adventure begun in "Louella." You might also add this author's *Eddie and Gardenia* for those who have not yet read it.

Then read "The Doughnuts," by Robert McCloskey (in *The Arbuthnot Anthology of Children's Literature*). Pupils might enjoy comparing and contrasting the two boys, Homer and Eddie, and the distinctive elements of humor in each situation.

Children follow the adventures of Eddie and Louella . . .

enjoy another humorous story.

pages 58·65 | Soo-Pung Measures ·Up

As children share the last day of the Chinese New Year with Soo-Pung, they will sympathize with his desire to be "big enough" and admire his cleverness in achieving it. Then through comparison and contrast pupils reach the generalization that in spite of differences people are basically alike.

Included in this lesson plan are suggestions for discussing definitions in a glossary or dictionary that require reference to another entry word. Procedures are also given for reviewing vowel-consonant patterns that are clues to vowel sounds in accented first syllables of two-syllable words.

New words: *Soo-Pung, San Francisco's, spirits, Wei,* touching, *Li,* although, *Confucius, ancestors* (Chinese*, excitement*, awakened*, *Chinatown**, rice*, eagerness*, dragon*, goodness*, soles*, dissatisfied*, beans*, *sprouts**, pound*, 'silk*, teeth*, Ping*, Lin*, burst*, pairs*, trousers*, shiny*, wall*, marked*, measurement*, *despair**, ills*, possibly*, shaped*, thick*, *wisdom**, *wedges**, swung*, *mid**, person*, switching*)

Think-and-Do Book: **Pages 21, 22, 23, and 24**

Establishing background

In presenting the word *ancestors,* let pupils mull over the fact that most Americans have family roots in other countries. Write *Most of us have ancestors who came from other lands,* and ask youngsters whether they can read it and explain its meaning. Suggest that they refer to their glossaries for help with one of the words (indicate *ancestors*). Having read recently about the Pilgrims in *Roads to Follow,* pupils should be able to tell why this statement is true.

Pupils identify new words . . .

use prior reading to justify generalization . . .

GUIDANCE FOR PAGES 58·65 | **67**

Then call attention to the illustration of a city street on page 58. When children have guessed from what country the ancestors of the people in this area probably came, explain that the picture shows part of a street in *San Francisco's* Chinatown. (If pupils do not know where San Francisco is, suggest that they turn to that entry in their glossaries.)

Next list these names on the board as you pronounce them for children: *Soo-Pung* (sü′pung′), *Wei* (wā), *Mr. Li* (lē). Explain that these are the names of the boy in the story, his brother, and his father, all of whom live in Chinatown. Remind boys and girls that if they should forget how to say these names, they can find the pronunciations in their glossaries. Then write the name *Confucius* and inquire whether anyone has ever heard this name. If no one has, take a moment to find and discuss this glossary entry with them.

Continue: "*Although they are Americans,* Soo-Pung's family still celebrates the Chinese New Year. At that time they observe many Chinese customs, or ways of doing things. One of these customs has to do with *keeping bad spirits away*."

Before reading begins, set pupils to thinking about personal experiences that will help them understand Soo-Pung's feelings. Have they ever wanted very much to do something but could not because they were too young or too small—for example, wanting to ride a bike when their legs were *too short to touch* (present the phrase) the pedals? What have children wanted to do? Then suggest that they read the story to see what Soo-Pung's ambition was and whether he managed to achieve it.

Interpreting the story

Immediately following silent reading, ask youngsters to explain Soo-Pung's problem and to describe his solution. During discussion bring out salient points of the plot with these questions:
—How did you know that it was very important to Soo-Pung that he be tall enough to help carry the dragon?
—What do you suppose gave him the idea of making wooden blocks for his feet? [Pupils should note Wei Li's suggestion

make inference from illustration . . .

anticipate content of today's story . . .

relate story problem to their own experience . . .

recall relevant details . . .

that Soo-Pung carve a dragon, Mr. Li's quotation, and Soo-Pung's thought about the quotation.]

—What did Mr. Li think of Soo-Pung's idea? How do you know?

grasp implied meanings and evaluate actions . . .

—Do you think it was a good idea? Why [or why not]? Can you think of another way he might have solved his problem?

—In your opinion what sort of person was Soo-Pung?

—Do you think 'Soo-Pung Measures Up' is a good title? Why? In what ways did Soo-Pung measure up?

On page 21 of the *Think-and-Do Book* pupils compare and contrast suggested titles in order to select the one that best expresses the main idea of each of four brief episodes.

To emphasize the idea that all peoples are basically alike, begin by having children cite Chinese-American New Year's customs mentioned in the story. (Suggest that they refer to their books when necessary.) Then ask whether all people in the United States celebrate New Year's Day on the same day and in the same way. Let pupils describe New Year's customs that they or people they know may observe. Did any of these customs originate in other lands? Encourage youngsters whose families observe customs of other countries to share what they know about these ways of doing things.

reread for specific information . . .

compare and contrast ways of celebrating New Year's Day . . .

Boys and girls may also compare and contrast familiar ways of saying things with unusual phraseology in the story.

—Did you notice any expressions that were probably Chinese ways of saying things? [*I wish you joy; May joy be yours; By my ancestors!*] How would you express these ideas?

as well as expressions and attitudes . . .

—Can you think of any expressions you use that might seem unusual to people in other parts of our country?

—Do you suppose others besides Chinese-Americans quote Confucius? Why?

—What was the wise saying of Confucius that Mr. Li quoted? What does this mean? Who remembers a person in *Roads to Follow* who said much the same thing? [Help pupils recall Johnny's disappointment in 'Johnny Three Eyes' and Uncle Bill's remark, *Things we don't like happen to us all. But it doesn't help to be unhappy about them.*]

and recall analogous idea from story in Roads to Follow . . .

—Do you think people are alike even though their customs and expressions differ? What makes you think as you do?

make generalization . . .

Analogous relationships are also emphasized on pages 22-23 of the *Think-and-Do Book*. On these pages pupils read more about the Chinese-American New Year and compare it with the New Year's observance with which they are familiar.

Help children learn to look at illustrations with more perceptive eyes by occasionally asking them to consider pictures from the artist's viewpoint. This can be presented with the challenge and fun of a puzzle by saying: "An artist has different reasons for what he pictures. His purpose may be to arouse curiosity, get you in the mood of the story, acquaint you with the characters, or help you know what an unfamiliar place or object looks like. Let's think how the illustrator helps us understand and enjoy the story about Soo-Pung." Then ask such questions as the following:

—Which pictures make you feel that something interesting and unusual may happen? How does the artist do this?

—Why do you think the artist chose the street scene on page 58 even though many of San Francisco's streets look like those in most American cities?

—What do you learn about the Li home from the picture at the bottom of page 59? about the Li shop from the picture on page 62?

—How do you feel when you look at the picture on pages 64-65? Does it help you understand Soo-Pung's desire to be a part of the parade? What other purpose may the artist have had?

interpret artist's purpose.

Extending competence

● Use these procedures to review the use of cross references in a glossary or dictionary. After calling attention to the last sentence on page 64, suggest that pupils turn to the entry *mid* in the glossary. Ask:

—How many entries do you see that are spelled *m-i-d*?

—Which entry for *mid* fits the sentence in our book? Would it be correct to say 'That evening the beautiful dragon swung through the streets of San Francisco middle the loud pop, pop, pop of firecrackers'?

—How can you be sure that the meaning for *mid²* fits? What does the word *amid* mean? [Have children turn to the entry *amid* and read the definition.]

—Who will read the sentence on page 64 and use other words instead of the word *mid?*

You might also point out that a word may have two correct spellings by inquiring whether *'mid* could be used in the sentence just read. Reference to the two entries for *mid* will show youngsters that *mid²* and *'mid* are identical in meaning and that either spelling may be used to mean "in the middle of."

Next write *Her hair is naturally curly,* and have children turn to the glossary to determine the meaning of *naturally* in this context. When they have decided that the second definition of *naturally* is the correct meaning for this sentence, ask what the phrase *by nature* means. After they have studied the definitions of *nature,* lead pupils to conclude that *curly* describes the regular or normal condition of the hair.

● This exercise and the one on page 24 of the *Think-and-Do Book* review vowel-consonant patterns that are clues to vowel sounds in accented first syllables of two-syllable words.

1. Write the following groups of known words on the board, and have the words pronounced and used in sentences:

fancy	paper	garden
better	Peter	certain
pilgrim	final	squirrel
doctor	moment	corner
bucket	music	turkey

Have pupils tell how many syllables they hear in each word and which syllable is accented. Then ask these questions:

—In which group of words do you hear short vowel sounds in the accented syllables? How many consonant letters follow the first vowel letter in these words?

—In which group of words do you hear long vowel sounds in the accented syllables? How many consonant letters follow the first vowel letter in these words?

—Would you expect short vowel sounds in the accented syllables of the third group of words? Why not?

Children use cross references in glossary.

Pupils identify accented first syllable in two-syllable words . . .

recall that two consonant letters after first vowel letter are a clue to a short vowel sound . . .

and one consonant is often a clue to long vowel sound . . .

Then write these sentences, underlining the italicized words, and note pupils' ability to read each underlined word in context:

use these clues to identify words in context...

The farmer will plant *barley* next year.

Mother says I am a *lazy* boy.

Please put some *mustard* on this hot dog.

She tied a *ribbon* around her hair.

2. Next write the following groups of known words and have them pronounced. Lead children to note that these are also two-syllable words accented on the first syllable.

baby	cabin
even	seven
pilot	pity
pony	promise

Guide discussion of the words with the following questions:

—If you didn't know how to say these words, would you try a long or a short vowel sound first in the accented syllables? Why?

recall that one consonant letter after first vowel letter may be a clue to a short vowel sound...

—In which group do you hear long vowel sounds in the accented syllables?

—If a long vowel sound doesn't make a word that sounds right, what vowel sound would you try?

—In which group do you hear short vowel sounds?

Continue as suggested in the last part of Step 1 with the italicized words in these sentences:

identify such words in context...

Will you do me a *favor?*

The man was sent to *prison.*

There was a strange *silence* before the storm.

It's our *duty* to obey the rules.

3. To help pupils recall that the number of consonant letters after the first vowel letter and before *le* provides a clue to vowel sound, use similar procedures with these groups of words and the italicized words in the sentences:

review clues to vowel sound in words ending in le ...

saddle	table	startle
whittle	bridle	circle

We always *chuckle* when Tom tells a joke.

What is the *title* of that book?

Let's watch the *hurdle* race.

identify such words in context.

Extending interests

Today's story of a boy with big hopes and the resourcefulness to attain them presents a good opportunity to introduce *The Singing Hill,* by Meindert DeJong, a story that captures the whole range of a child's thoughts and emotions.

The first four chapters will acquaint children with Ray and his family. When you have read this far, encourage pupils to share impressions of each story character individually and in relation to the other members of the family.

Children evaluate characters' traits in The Singing Hill . . .

Because The Singing Hill *is a book that children should not miss, you will want to plan your reading of it in short sessions over a period of several days. Suggestions are given here and in subsequent lesson plans to guide pupils in evaluating the traits and reactions of the main character and relating them to those of story characters in "Roads Here and There." As a result youngsters' understanding of the story characters and the problems they encounter will be deepened. For example, lonely, timid Ray, new to the mysteries of country living, may remind pupils of Kirsten Larsen and Charley Brave, who also felt uncertain in new surroundings. The small boy who learns to feel not quite so small may call to mind Soo-Pung. Ray's gentleness toward creatures is reminiscent of young Billy's way with Thunderbolt. As the story unfolds, boys and girls will note other comparisons that they will want to talk over as time permits.*

If the 1964 edition of *Childcraft: The* How and Why *Library* is available, display Volume 5, *Holidays and Customs,* commenting that in this book youngsters will find information about many holidays and some of the ways they are observed in various countries. After showing a few of its illustrations (particularly that of the dragon in the Chinese New Year's parade), place the book on the library table. On succeeding days, if time permits, you might invite a child to describe one of the holidays he found especially interesting, telling why he chose it and illustrating his description with pictures in the book.

read and talk about other holidays.

| It's a Wolf

The vivid imagery, the ingenious development of suspense, and the humorous climax of this story will appeal to children and heighten awareness of such characteristics in good writing.

Procedures are suggested for helping pupils adapt glossary definitions to context by substituting a definition for a word in the context or by transposing words to fit a definition smoothly into a sentence. In another exercise children recall that visual clues to vowel sounds in one-syllable words also apply in the accented syllables of two-syllable words.

New words: potato, backwards*, *island,* lose, peculiar, *vicious*,* enormous, continued, *cautiously*,* relieved*, difference (delighted*, bunk*, spent*, *mist*,* *stag*,* shone*, *antlers*,* plainly*, *doe*,* *paused*,* bent*, lump*, ceiling*, fairy*, lying*, growl*, stiffly*, apart*, fearfully*, sniffing*, gun*, lick*, *chops*,* choked*, peered*, fur*, rubbed*, toasty*, scamp*, chuckled*)

Think-and-Do Book: **Pages 25 and 26**

Establishing background

Relate this story to an earlier one in the unit as you lead pupils to describe the mountainous area in which Rufe lived. After youngsters have talked about Hogback Mountain or similar regions with which they may be familiar, comment: *"There is a difference between the area where Rufe lived and the one you'll visit today. The family in today's story was vacationing near a lake with an island in it.* Do you know what an island is? [If there is any uncertainty, let pupils find *island* in the glossary.] Soon after they reached the cabin, it was time to eat. This is one of the things they ate. [Write *potato soup,* and give chil-

Children recall mountainous setting of earlier story...

identify new words...

dren an opportunity to attack the word *potato* by using context and spelling clues.]" The remaining words may be introduced after discussion of the first part of the story.

Continue: "The boys went to bed early, but in the middle of the night Penny woke up. As you read, pretend that you are right there with him. When you reach the bottom of page 67, close your eyes and try to see, smell, and hear everything that Penny did. Then turn the page and read to the bottom of page 69. When you have read that far, try to picture the area around the cabin."

form sensory images as they read . . .

Guiding interpretation

After silent reading guide boys and girls in summarizing what they have learned about the setting of the story.
—Do you think this cabin would be a pleasant place to spend a weekend? Why?
—What could be seen around the cabin? What did the boys see from the island that they couldn't see from the cabin?
—Who will describe what Penny heard, saw, and smelled when he woke up in the middle of the night?
—Which part of the story is illustrated by the picture on page 68? Why do you think the artist painted a picture like this?

describe cabin and its surroundings . . .

infer purpose of the artist . . .

Arouse interest in the rest of the story as you present the remaining words. Remark: "At lunchtime the two boys asked whether they might take a walk in the woods. Their father told them they might investigate the woods if they *continued to keep the lake in sight* so they would not *lose their way*. During their excursion the boys had a frightening encounter with *a peculiar gray animal* that had *enormous teeth* and looked vicious. What do you suppose it was? Let's finish the story."

identify other new words . . .

anticipate change in mood and action in story . . .

PAGES 70-74

Since most children will be bursting to tell about the encounter with the "wolf," let them relate the main points and enjoy the humor of the ending.

grasp main ideas . . .

GUIDANCE FOR PAGES 66·74 | 75

Then focus attention on the author's skillful development of suspense and Peter's and Penny's reactions to their adventure.

—When did the boys first suspect that the animal was a dog? When did you first realize this?

—Do you suppose the author wanted you to think the animal was a wolf? What words did she use that led you to believe the dog was a wolf? [Encourage pupils to locate phrases and similes that create this impression. The sixth paragraph on page 70 and several paragraphs (sixth, seventh, eleventh, and fourteenth) on page 72 will be especially productive.]

talk about author's purpose ...

—Why do you suppose the author wanted us to believe that this animal was a wolf?

—How did the author and artist change our mental picture of a vicious wolf into one of a friendly pet? [Have boys and girls read the phrases that describe the friendly actions of the dog and contrast the illustrations on pages 71 and 74. You may also wish to point up the humor implied in the dog's name.]

note how author and artist transform "wolf" into a dog ...

—Why do you think the dog growled and followed the boys when he first saw them?

—How do you think Peter and Penny felt when Toasty's master said that some people thought his dog looked like a wolf? In what way does the picture help you know what Peter is thinking as he says *nearly anyone would know that he is a dog?*

identify emotional reactions ...

—Does this story remind you of one of the Pilgrim stories in *Roads to Follow?* How is it like 'A Terrible Fright'?

WHOLE STORY

Time and place relationships may be used to help pupils organize the sensory images aroused by the story and recognize the artful use of language that stimulates these images. Have children locate phrases in the story that tell when and where each episode took place. Write these as pupils respond:

note time and place relationships ...

>Friday evening in the cabin
>Friday night outside the cabin window
>Saturday morning on the lake and island
>Saturday afternoon in the woods

Then suggest that youngsters describe the sensory images in each part of the story. To start them off and encourage them to think of images not specifically mentioned in the text, you might say: "On Friday evening in the cabin I could see a blazing fire. I could hear the crackle of the fire, feel its warmth, and smell the smoke from the burning logs. What else could you see, hear, feel, smell, or taste?" Questions similar to those below will heighten awareness of the descriptive language used to create vivid mental impressions.

—What words did the author use to tell us how bright the fire was? Penny's real name was William. Why do you suppose he was nicknamed Penny?

—What simile helped you know the boys were very hungry?

—What did Father mean when he said that the boys were *like monkeys on a stick?*

Use similar procedures in discussing Penny's experience during the night. Stimulate thought about the author's choice of words by asking, for example, what word tells that Penny thought the smell of wood smoke and pine trees was pleasant. What words did the author use to show how quiet everything was as Penny looked out the window? How did she tell the reader that what Penny saw seemed almost unreal?

As children talk about the boys' trip to the island, draw out descriptions of the lapping water, the dipping oars, and the cool breeze in addition to the more obvious images.

Conversation about the final episode might center around the second and third paragraphs on page 70, with special emphasis on sounds the boys heard as they walked through the woods.

While attention is focused on descriptive language, you may wish to have pupils turn to page 25 of the *Think-and-Do Book*. In each group of sentences on this page children are to select the ones that use the most colorful language.

describe sensory images . . .

observe author's use of language to create vivid images . . .

react to vivid language in Think-and-Do Book exercise . . .

ORAL INTERPRETATION

The tense scene between Peter and Penny while they were treed by the "wolf" will give oral readers an opportunity to differentiate the reactions of two characters to the same threat. Although both boys were genuinely frightened, their dialogue reveals two distinct personalities reacting differently to the same problem.

Assign each of Penny's seven speeches on page 72 to a different reader, asking pupils to prepare to read Penny's speeches by imagining where he is, how he feels when he utters the speech, and why he feels that way. After Penny's speeches have been read in succession without the intervening ones of Peter, lead children to observe that Penny's mind is set on the viciousness of the wolf and that he becomes more frightened and miserable each time he speaks.

concentrate on reactions of a single character...

When several groups of seven have read Penny's remarks, let groups of five concentrate in the same manner on Peter's speeches on this same page. As soon as the first group of five has read, ask pupils in which of his speeches Peter sounds most like Penny. Then bring out the fact that, unlike Penny, Peter seems to be trying to find a solution to the problem.

contrast reactions of second character...

To stimulate children's imaginations, let them decide on the location of the trees and pretend they are sitting in them as groups of two read the scene. Suggest that readers try to reveal to listeners the difference between the excitable Penny, who can think of nothing but the terrible wolf, and the more thoughtful and optimistic Peter, who keeps trying to think of a way out of the trouble.

visualize setting as they read aloud...

concentrate on staying in character...

When pupils are able to stay in character, depict the mood of the story, and build this scene to a climax, add a narrator and a man and let groups of four read to the end of the story.

read scene with contrasting mood.

Extending competence

● Children have had much experience in selecting the appropriate meaning of a word for a specific context. The next step is to develop ability in fitting definitions into specific context. In this exercise youngsters substitute glossary definitions for words in context and change the order of words to fit a definition smoothly into context.

1. Write the sentence *He was in serious difficulty*, and ask: "How would you explain this sentence to someone who does not know what the word *difficulty* means? Which glossary definition fits this context? Who will reread the sentence on the board, using the definition in place of the word *difficulty*?"

Pupils substitute glossary definitions for words in context...

Continue similarly with the sentence *That stag has large antlers* and the glossary definition for the word *stag*.

2. Next write the sentence *Peter wanted to examine the animal's neck*, and ask pupils to find the entry *examine* in the glossary. Which definition of *examine* fits this sentence? Would children say "Peter wanted to look at closely and carefully the animal's neck"? Lead them to see that to make the statement read smoothly, they must change the order of the words and say "Peter wanted to look closely and carefully at the animal's neck."

transpose words in definition and sentence . . .

3. In conclusion write the following sentences and underline the italicized words. Children are to decide which definition of the underlined word is used and then reread the sentence, using that definition instead of the word. (The words *brief, enchant,* and *terrify* have not yet appeared in The New Basic Readers; the others are known words.)

> He read a *brief* story to the class.
> She was sure the story would *enchant* her friends.
> The men did not *despair* of being rescued.
> The fierce storm did not *terrify* the sailors.
> *Scrub* that dirty shirt with soap and water.

tune definitions into sentences on board . . .

Youngsters also adapt definitions to context by simple substitution or by making necessary changes in word order as they complete page 26 of the *Think-and-Do Book*.

and in Think-and-Do Book exercise.

● Take time now to review the concept that visual clues to vowel sounds which pupils have learned to use in identifying one-syllable words also apply to the accented syllables of two-syllable words. After writing the following words, have them pronounced and used in sentences:

eager	enjoy
measure	divide
awful	approach
mountain	exclaim
trousers	around
power	declare

Then have youngsters pronounce the words in the first column again and tell which syllable is accented in all these words. When children have noted that the first syllable is accented, lead them to identify the clue to vowel sound in the accented syllable of each word.

Children identify clues to vowel sounds in accented syllables ...

Use similar procedures with the words in the second column, all of which are accented on the second syllable.

To conclude, write the following sentences, underlining the italicized words, which have not yet appeared in The New Basic Readers. Note pupils' ability to identify the underlined words.

identify two-syllable words in context.

I like *sausage* and eggs for breakfast.

Too much sun *destroys* some plants.

No one likes to be called a *coward*.

My dog is *jealous* when I pet another dog.

I think Tom's picture *deserves* a prize.

Extending interests

Be sure to <u>recommend Carolyn Haywood's *Penny and Peter*</u> (a chapter of which served as the basis of today's story) so that youngsters can read more about these two adventurers—and a basketful of crabs, some blue paint, an enormous dog named Tootsie, and a very special gift.

Pupils turn to other exploits of Penny and Peter ...

Then, after commenting that Penny and Peter's fear of an animal that turned out to be friendly would have helped them understand young Ray's fear in a very similar circumstance, <u>continue reading Meindert DeJong's *The Singing Hill*.</u> When children have heard Chapters 5, 6, and 7, allow for spontaneous reactions to Ray's emotions as he stood alone at the skunk hole, as he faced the "charge" of the big white horse at the end of the lane, and as he suddenly found himself on the horse's back. Can pupils explain how Ray felt—and why—as he ran down the lane to home and Mother?

hear about case of mistaken identity in The Singing Hill ...

Guide the conversation to Ray's feelings at other times by asking children how he reacted to Martin and Shirley's ill-humored teasing, to Mother's uneasiness about mice, to playing alone in the lane, and above all to his new friend, Thee-Rim. What do these reactions reveal about Ray?

make inferences about Ray's personal traits in light of his emotional reactions.

| Horse-Chestnut Time

If children are encouraged to build upon their own imagery of the fall season before this poem is read, they will find more enjoyment in the experiences of the poet.

Establishing background

Start youngsters talking about the autumn countryside and about things they see and like to do at that time of year. Guide discussion so that each of the poet's images will be either directly or indirectly included. As the children speak of falling leaves, encourage them to think, too, of apples falling from apple trees, acorns from oak trees, and so on. If corn and milkweed are not familiar to pupils, acquaint them with the appearance of these plants in autumn. When boys and girls mention the southward flight of birds, bring out that migratory flocks often rest along their routes.

Pupils build their own imagery of autumn scenes ...

In pursuing children's favorite fall pastimes, such activities as raking leaves, watching bonfires, picking apples or grapes, and gathering bittersweet might be discussed. If your area has no season like that described in the poem, you will need to supplement pupils' knowledge.

and activities ...

Guiding interpretation

After reading the title aloud, suggest that youngsters find some horse chestnuts in the illustration on page 76. Draw attention to the prickly burrs that cover the nuts and that often burst as the nuts ripen and fall to the ground.

note details in illustration ...

Then invite pupils to listen to Kaye Starbird's description of fall in her part of the country. When they have heard the poem, let them describe her autumn.

listen to poem ...

To strengthen children's impressions of the poem's imagery, suggest that youngsters find word pictures that Kaye Starbird has painted for them. There are a variety of images that should have struck pupils' fancies; someone, for instance, should have been delighted by the simile *birds, like clothespins, . . . clipped to the telegraph wire.* Do they recognize *I feel like a king with treasure* as another simile? Children could also be asked to look for an example of exaggeration and to think about why *Where millions of chestnuts grow* helps create a vivid image.

look for vivid
word pictures . . .

identify similes
and exaggeration . . .

Finally ask questions similar to the following to relate the poet's experience to those that youngsters may have had.
—Why did the poet like to gather horse chestnuts? Is there
   something that means or symbolizes fall to you? What is it?
—Does anything else symbolize a season of the year for you?
   What is it?
   Ask pupils whether they recall a fall poem in *Roads to Follow*. How did Carl Sandburg picture autumn in "Theme in Yellow"? Could pumpkins symbolize fall for some people? Why?

allow poet's thought
to carry their own
thoughts afield.

Extending interests

By introducing children to other poems that catch the spirit of fall and that are rich in imagery, you can help pupils realize the infinite variety of ways in which the same season can be described, each way lovely in its own right. Many such poems can be found in *Time for Poetry:* "September," by Helen Hunt Jackson; "Autumn Fires," by Robert Louis Stevenson; "Autumn Woods," by James S. Tippett; "October," by Rose Fyleman.
   If boys and girls have been using the *Learn to Listen, Speak, and Write* books, they already have experience in comparing poetic images. Fall and the beauties of nature are major themes of pages 6-7 and 11-14 in Book 3[1], for example. Poetic impressions already formed may be enriched as pupils review these pages; for, as W. Cabell Greet states in his article "What Is Beautiful Language?" in the Teacher's Edition of the same book, "Language is not less beautiful because we know what makes it so."

Children hear
other poets'
portrayals of fall . . .

and note the
variety of imagery.

The colorful way in which Hawaii celebrates the first day of May is the subject of this article. Comparison of the article with other selections reinforces awareness of the characteristics of fictional and nonfictional writing.

Knowledge of spelling patterns that function as clues to vowels sounds in two-syllable words is extended to printed words which contain consonant blends, as in *April,* and to words in which two vowel letters represent two vowels sounds, as in *lion.*

New words: **lei,** celebrated, *Hawaii,* whose (states*, united*)
Think-and-Do Book: **Pages 27, 28, and 29**

Establishing background

Tie in the article's title and first illustration with a discussion of local May Day customs. After reading the title, ask youngsters whether they celebrate May Day. If so, what do they do? What is the boy pictured on page 77 doing?

Pupils talk about May Day . . .

Then ask whether pupils know what a *lei* is, and have them turn to the glossary to verify their definitions. In what state are leis often seen? (Write *Hawaii* and suggest that the pronunciation of this word be checked in the glossary.) Do children think May Day and Lei Day might be alike in some way? Why?

identify new words . . .

Finally suggest that as youngsters read this article, they will find answers to the questions below. As you write them on the board, present the word *celebrated.*

read to learn specific information . . .

> How are May Day and Lei Day alike?
> What are some ways in which May Day is celebrated?
> What do school children in Hawaii do on Lei Day?
> Why should the celebrating of Lei Day be beautiful to see?

Since pupils know the word *who,* they should have no difficulty recognizing the word *whose* in context.

Interpreting the article

Answers to the questions should be discussed immediately following silent reading. While children are talking about the second one, make sure they know what a Maypole is and how a Maypole dance is performed if this custom is unfamiliar to them.

discuss main ideas . . .

Then talk over with youngsters the ways in which an article and a story may differ.
—What other holiday have you read about in this book? How is the way the author told you about the Chinese New Year in 'Soo-Pung Measures Up' different from the way this author told you about May Day and Lei Day? [If this question proves too abstract, follow it with these questions: What was the author's purpose in 'Soo-Pung Measures Up'—to tell a story or to give information? in 'May Day and Lei Day'?]
—What is one way that an article can be different from a story?
Youngsters' understanding of the characteristics of nonfictional writing may be broadened by reminding them of "The Whirlybird and Me" in *Roads to Follow*. They may remember that in this article the author told about his feelings and opinions.

compare authors' presentation of information . . .

Then encourage pupils to think about the difference between facts and opinions by having them find examples of both in today's article. You may need to help children understand that, with the exception of the last sentence, the information given on page 79 is opinion.
Ability to distinguish between fact and opinion will be strengthened further as pupils complete pages 27-28 of the *Think-and-Do Book*. After reading another article about Hawaii, they are to indicate which of several statements from the selection are judgments or opinions rather than facts.

make judgments . . .

Finally lead children to generalize that holiday customs in our country vary. What have pupils learned from reading and from personal observation about the celebration of holidays in the United States? Draw out the facts that not all people celebrate the same holidays and that ways of observing a specific holiday may differ from place to place.

make generalization about American holiday customs.

Extending competence

● Forming accurate and vivid imagery enriches reading enjoyment. To develop this skill, pupils must be able to grasp details and transform them into mental images. A great aid to the visual imagery suggested by the text is that provided by illustrations.

To begin, suggest that children think about what the pictures on pages 78-79 add to the article. Do they show things the article tells about? What? Do they show other things the article does not tell about? What?

Pupils note function of pictures ...

As you pronounce the name of each country, have youngsters locate the appropriate drawing, look carefully at the costume, and think what, if anything, can be told about the dance. Then, to check pupils' alertness in noting pictorial detail, ask them to close their books and to make up riddles to see whether others can guess which country's representative is being described. Encourage riddle makers to include as much detail as they can in their descriptions, and as they talk, note the degree of accuracy and detail in their observations.

scrutinize illustrations ...

use sensory imagery as aid to memory.

Similar exercises might be provided at other times for youngsters who are weak in noting visual details. In addition to making use of story illustrations, you might clip pictures from papers and magazines. These pupils could then work in a group, checking each other's descriptions.

● Use this exercise and page 29 of the *Think-and-Do Book* to extend understandings of the relationship between spelling patterns and vowel and consonant sounds in two-syllable words.

1. Write the following words, pronounce them, and then have pupils say them and use them in sentences:

April	cyclone
secret	program

When boys and girls have pronounced the words again, ask:
—How many syllables do you hear in each word?
—Which syllable is accented in all the words?
—Do you hear a long or a short vowel sound in the accented syllable? How many consonant letters follow the first vowel letter in each word?

Pupils identify accent in words accented on first syllable ...

Lead children to note that the two consonant letters following the first vowel letter in each word represent a consonant blend. Explain that, as in these words, a single vowel letter followed by a consonant blend often stands for a long vowel sound.

note that a vowel letter followed by consonant blend may stand for a long vowel sound . . .

To provide practice in identifying words of this kind in context, write these sentences and invite pupils to read them:

Many flowers are very *fragrant*.

A *zebra* looks something like a horse.

Mother wears an *apron* when she cooks.

identify words of this kind in context . . .

2. Next write these words in a column, pronounce them, and then have children pronounce them and use them in sentences.

science   fuel

lion   poet

diet   Leo

Bring out that there are two vowel letters together (underline them) in each word. After each word is pronounced again, ask:

—How many syllables do you hear in each word? Which syllable is accented?

note that two vowel letters together may represent two syllables . . .

—In which words do you hear the vowel of *ice* in the accented syllable? In which do you hear the vowel of *use?* the vowel of *go?* the vowel of *me?*

Explain that in words like those on the board, in which two vowel letters together represent two vowel sounds, the first syllable is usually accented and the first vowel letter often stands for a long vowel sound.

Then write the following sentences and note pupils' ability to identify the italicized words:

identify words of this kind in context . . .

The *giant* in the story was friendly to the children.

There are many *neon* signs on this street.

The flowers made a *riot* of color in our yard.

Too much rain will *ruin* the crops.

3. Write the following words, and comment that this time children are to listen to the vowel sound in the unaccented syllable of each word as you use it in a sentence.

appear   moment

connect   turnip

suggest   parrot

86 | MORE ROADS TO FOLLOW

Then have pupils pronounce each word in the first list, leading them to note that the first syllable is unaccented in these words and that the same vowel sound—the schwa sound—is heard in the unstressed syllable. Continue with the words in the second list, in which the schwa sound is heard in the second syllable. Call attention to the vowel letter in each unaccented syllable to review the concept that any vowel letter may represent the schwa sound in an unstressed syllable.

identify schwa sound in unaccented syllables . . .

Use similar procedures with the words in each of the following lists to review the concept that more than one vowel letter may represent the schwa sound in an unstressed syllable. (The schwa sound is heard in the second syllable of each word.)

recall that one or more than one vowel letter may represent schwa sound . . .

captain	jealous	fashion	million
patient	cautious	tension	onion
ocean	anxious	motion	question
special	precious	station	region

Next suggest that children look carefully at the spelling of each word and listen to the consonant sound heard before the schwa sound in it as you pronounce the words in each list again. Ask:
—In which three words in the first list do you hear the *sh* sound before the schwa sound? in which three in the second list?
—What consonant sound is heard before the schwa in *captain?* in *jealous?*
—In which list of words is the *sh* sound heard before the schwa in all the words?
—In which words in the fourth list do you hear the *y* sound before the schwa sound? In which word is the *ch* sound heard before the schwa? the *j* sound?

note spellings for consonant sounds before schwa sound . . .

In conclusion write these sentences and note pupils' ability to identify the italicized words:

identify words in context.

> There is no *mention* of the accident in the paper.
> This chair needs a new *cushion.*
> My sister was in the Christmas *pageant.*
> It takes *patience* to work this puzzle.
> A large house may be called a *mansion.*
> America is a great *nation.*

pages 80·87 | Maile's Lei

Maile sets a fine example for readers when, in deciding to help a friend, she cheerfully gives up her own chance to win a contest at the fair. Youngsters will find that many of Maile's actions can be aptly described by well-known proverbs.

As children contrast vowel sounds in accented syllables of words like *harbor* and *carrot, walnut* and *valley,* understanding of visual clues to vowel sounds in accented syllables is extended. Suggestions are also given for introducing the prefix *fore-.*

New words: Maile's, Tutu, poured, forenoon, giant*, honorable, mention*, familiar (alive*, blossoms*, *contest*, two-toned*, win*, prize*, nets*, dead*, beneath*, *shaved*, syrup*, coconut*, mix*, glanced*, disappointment*, aboard*, needle*, thread*, dew*, grumbled*, judging*, reminded*, *Japan*, ribbon*, mayor*)
Think-and-Do Book: Pages 30 and 31

Establishing background

With the help of the illustration on pages 80-81, set the scene for the opening of the story. Comment: "The girl you see is named *Maile* (mä′ē le). She was walking up a mountain path in Hawaii *in the forenoon.* When would that be? If you were with Maile, you might hear her mention *a friend she called Tutu* (tü′tü). Tutu is a name that is *familiar to people in Hawaii* because to them it means 'grandmother.' Maile was going to *a place where water poured over a cliff.* What do we call a place like that? Why do you suppose Maile was going there?" As children reply, note whether they use the title as an aid in making inferences. (Since *hasten, ginger,* and *fashion* are used in this story with meanings that may be unfamiliar, add them to the glossary list.)

Pupils identify new words . . .

learn something about setting of story . . .

conjecture about Maile's plans . . .

Then suggest that children read the first two pages to see what else they find out about Maile and her plans. (The word *honorable* may be presented after discussion of these pages.)

Guiding interpretation

PAGES 80-81

When all have read silently, let boys and girls tell what they have learned about Maile and her plans.

Then, before they finish reading the story, help pupils visualize the setting and atmosphere of a fair by calling upon several volunteers for descriptive contributions. (No detailed description of a fairgrounds is given in the story.) When contests are discussed, ask how many prizes are usually given in a single competition and what may happen to an entry that is not quite good enough to take third place. When honorable mention is suggested, present *honorable*. You may also have this sentence read independently: *It may win honorable mention.*

Comment that after Maile left the mountain, she had several surprises. Pupils may finish the story to see what they were.

discuss additional details of story background . . .

draw on personal experience in imaging background . . .

identify new word honorable . . .

PAGES 82-87

Start off with children's observations on the outcome of the story. After asking what Maile's first surprise was, invite pupils to describe Tutu's problem and to tell how Maile helped her. As they talk about each surprise in turn, challenge youngsters to think beyond the literal meaning of the text by asking:
— Why do you think Maile helped Tutu instead of making her own lei? What does this tell you about the kind of person Maile is? What else showed that Maile is unselfish?
— Why hadn't Maile started making her lei earlier in the day?
— Do you think winning a prize was more important to Maile or Tutu? Why? Which person probably had a better chance of winning? What makes you think so?
— What did the bus driver ask everyone to do when the tire went flat? Why did he do this?
— How do you suppose the mix-up in bags occurred?
— Why was the Mayor's voice both familiar and unfamiliar?

discuss main events of story . . .

make inferences and judgments involving cause-effect relationships . . .

In the concluding discussion develop pupils' concept of Maile as a cheerful, considerate, unselfish person. Ask:

—Why wasn't Maile disappointed for very long when she thought she wouldn't have a lei to enter in the contest?

—When the bus broke down, how did Maile's reactions differ from those of some of the other passengers?

—Did Maile expect her lei to win a prize? Why not? Did she let this bother her? How do you know she didn't?

—Was Maile more concerned with Tutu's cake or with her own lei? How do you know this?

—Why wasn't Maile sad at not having won any prize money? How did she happen to earn some money anyway? What did she plan to do with the money?

—How would you describe the sort of person Maile is?

note Maile's character-revealing thoughts and acts ...

draw conclusions about them ...

WHOLE STORY

In a reference to "Soo-Pung Measures Up" remind children of Confucius and give them a chance to apply one of his proverbs to new situations. If they cannot remember the wise saying that Soo-Pung's father quoted (*Despair only adds to man's ills*), suggest that they find it in their books. Then ask, "Can you think of any times in this story when Maile might have had the same thought?" Have pupils cite specific instances and refer to the pages on which the incidents took place.

Other sayings that may be used to set children on similar searches for appropriate examples are listed below. Before they try to find examples for each proverb, make sure that they understand its meaning.

think about wise saying in earlier story ...

and relate it to Maile's attitude ...

apply generalizations to specific situations in story ...

> Be thankful for small pleasures.
> Don't count your chickens before they're hatched.
> A friend in need is a friend indeed.
> It is better to give than to receive.

Further practice in applying proverbs to specific situations is provided on page 30 of the *Think-and-Do Book.*

and in Think-and-Do Book.

Old sayings, when understood, give young minds something to grow on. This kind of exercise also gives pupils an opportunity to interpret figurative language in light of story content.

Extending competence

● To give youngsters a variety of activities that will draw upon their abilities to conjure up mental pictures, suggest that as you read sentences from the story, pupils listen carefully and be ready to describe the story situation that each one calls to mind. Follow the reading of each sentence with pertinent questions, varying them to suit the situation. For example, you might ask: (1) Where was Maile? (2) What was happening? (3) How did Maile feel? (4) What made her feel that way? Such sentences as the following could be discussed:

Children image story incidents and tie in Maile's emotional reactions . . .

> Her heart pounded with excitement as she raced to the booth. (page 86)
>
> And just then there was another giant sigh outside. (page 84)
>
> Tears of disappointment choked her for a second. (page 83)
>
> The flowers were as cool and fresh as the dew. (page 84)

Volunteers may read sentences of their own choosing and alter the questions as they wish. Some may want to ask: "How did Tutu feel? the Mayor? the bus riders?"

Next focus pupils' thinking on the locale of each part of the story by asking: "If you were planning a play based on this story, how many scenes would it have? Where would each scene take place?" When children's answers are listed on the board, they should be similar to the following:

organize story's major settings in sequence . . .

1. mountain path
2. Tutu's house
3. roadway that the bus traveled
4. fairgrounds

Encourage boys and girls to describe how they think each scene appeared. Then have them use the four major settings of the story as an outline for retelling events.

and use them in retelling story.

● The following procedures introduce the prefix *fore-* and check ability to identify words to which known prefixes are added.

1. To begin, write the sentence *Maile did not have time to pick the flowers in the forenoon.* As you point to the word *forenoon,* ask: "What prefix is added to *noon* to make the word *fore-*

Pupils tell what prefix fore- means in forenoon . . .

noon? What does *forenoon* mean?" Suggest that pupils find the prefix *fore-* in their glossaries and read the definitions. Which definition of *fore-* is used in the word *forenoon?*

Then write the sentences below, underlining the italicized words. After children have read each sentence, have them tell what the underlined word means.

read definitions of fore- in glossary ...

discuss meaning of derivatives formed with prefix fore- ...

> My dog hurt one of his *forepaws.*
> We cannot *foretell* what will happen next year.

Comment that *fore* is a word as well as a suffix, and have pupils find the definitions of the word *fore* in their dictionaries.

note that fore is also a word ...

2. For a review of known prefixes, write the following sentences, underlining the italicized words. As each sentence is read, ask with what prefix the underlined word begins. To what word is the prefix added? Then have children tell in their own words what each underlined word means in the sentence.

identify in context derivatives beginning with known prefixes ...

> John left his breakfast *untouched.*
> It is *improbable* that it will rain tonight.
> I *disagreed* with what he said.
> *Unhook* the door and let the dog out.
> Tim fell and bumped his *forehead.*
> We discovered our boat *adrift* on the lake.

Pupils' responses on page 31 of the *Think-and-Do Book* will give you a means of ascertaining how well each child has grasped the meanings of various affixes.

apply knowledge of affixes in Think-and-Do Book.

● To extend pupils' understanding of visual clues to vowel sounds in accented syllables, begin by writing the following three groups of words on the board:

(1)

harbor	carrot	carol
market	arrow	parent
pardon	carry	Sarah

(2)

person	merry	very
certain	errand	sheriff
Herman	terror	merit

(3)

also	gallop	balance	corral
walnut	valley	palace	canal
always	Alvin	salad	

GROUP 1: As you indicate the words in the first group, comment that they are all two-syllable words accented on the first syllable. Then ask pupils to listen to the vowel sound in the accented syllable of each word as you pronounce it.

Children compare patterned groups of two-syllable words—

Next have children say the words. In which three words do they hear the vowel of *car* in the accented syllable? Lead pupils to notice that in the words *harbor, market,* and *pardon* the letter *a* is followed by the letter *r* and another consonant letter; whereas in the remaining six words the letter *a* is followed by two *r*'s or by one *r* and a vowel letter.

in which the letter a
is followed by two r's
or a single r . . .

Pupils are not asked to identify the vowel sound in the accented syllables of words like carrot, arrow, carol, *and* parent *because it varies regionally. This sound may approximate the vowel of* let, *the vowel of* hat, *or in some regions the vowel of* age.

To provide practice in applying what youngsters have just noted, write the following sentences (underlining the italicized words) and invite pupils to read them. Then ask: "In which underlined word do you hear the vowel of *car* in the accented syllable? Why would you expect to hear the vowel of *car*? Why would you not expect to hear it in the other underlined words?"

The dress Jane bought was a good *burgain.*

In this story the prince asks the girl to *marry* him.

My uncle took a trip to *Paris* last year.

GROUP 2: Use similar procedures with the words in the second group and the sentences below. Guide children in noting that in these words the letter *e* followed by two consonant letters, the first of which is *r*, represents the vowel of *her;* whereas the letter *e* followed by two *r*'s or by one *r* and a vowel letter represents the vowel of *let.*

in which the letter e
is followed by two r's
or a single r . . .

The king had many *servants.*

Tom did not make any *errors* in the ball game.

A *heron* is a very large bird with long legs.

GROUP 3: After you and then children have pronounced the words in the third group, ask: "In which three words is the vowel of *all* heard in the accented syllable? What vowel sound is heard in the accented syllable of the remaining words?" (the vowel of *hat*) Lead pupils to note that in each accented syllable the letter *a* is followed by one or two *l*'s. Comment that in words of more than one syllable the letter *a* followed by one or two *l*'s in an accented syllable is more likely to stand for the vowel of *hat* than the vowel of *all*.

in which the letter a is followed by l.

Next write the following sentences, underlining the italicized words, and invite children to read them. Ask: "In which underlined word does the letter *a* in the accented syllable stand for the vowel of *all*? What sound does the letter *a* stand for in the other underlined words?"

There were flowers on the *altar* in the church.

The man at the station put ten *gallons* of gas in our car.

My brother's name is *Albert,* but we call him Al.

Extending interests

Youngsters whose interest in Hawaii has been quickened by to-day's story will enjoy another that presents an authentic picture of life and customs in a small Hawaiian village. Read *Faraway Friends,* by Vivian L. Thompson, and afterwards let pupils tell what this story added to their understanding of a way of life that might well have been Maile's.

Guide boys and girls in pointing up the similarity between *Faraway Friends* and stories they have read in *More Roads to Follow.* What might Kirsten Larsen and Charley Brave have learned from Lani and Mary Jane? What did Lani and Mary Jane learn from their friendship with each other? Then place the book on the library table for those who wish to read it for themselves and look at the engaging illustrations.

You might also recommend Meindert DeJong's *The Last Little Cat* to young readers who are enjoying his book *The Singing Hill.* As you make it available, comment that this is the story of how the last little cat found a home—not just any kind of home, but the perfect home.

Pupils gain better understanding of Hawaiian customs . . .

relate story to two others with similar themes . . .

read another story by author of The Singing Hill.

| Manaluk's Gold Rush

In their interpretation of this story with a familiar theme—
everyone longs for something—youngsters are encouraged to
delve beneath surface desires to perceive how environment
influences one's goals.

The wealth of incidental information about Alaska presented
in the story is utilized as pupils locate details, organize them,
and recognize their significance. The suffix *-able* is introduced
and children are given practice in combining structural and
phonetic analysis to identify printed words. Included, too, are
suggestions for evaluating progress in interpretive and word-
analysis skills.

New words: **Manaluk's, Alaska, comfortable,** medicine, vegetables, shoulder (gold*, post*, crayons*, peaches*,
loaded*, sled*, lie*, rescued*, whiskers*, pencil*,
pack*, *flushed**, hid*, melted*, mud*, *chores**,
rich*, weeds*, scooped*, pebbles*, till*, single*,
sick*, sickness*, castor*, bottle*, sky*, threw*,
waist*, striking*, squishy*)

Think-and-Do Book: **Pages 32, 33, and 34**

Establishing background

Explain that today's story is about a boy with this name (write
Manaluk on the board) who lived in this state (write *Alaska*).
After they have used the glossary to determine the pronunciation
of *Manaluk* (man′ə lük) and the location of Alaska, encourage
pupils to share their impressions of life in Alaska. The word
comfortable may be presented as homes are discussed, and the
word *vegetables* may be introduced into the conversation about
food. You will want to mention, too, that children's ideas about
Alaska may be changed as they read the story.

Pupils identify
new words . . .

share their knowledge
of Alaska . . .

With the comment that there were some things Manaluk wanted very much, encourage boys and girls to speculate about what he might long for and how he might get them. Then write the title on the board and let pupils read and discuss it. Do they know what a gold rush is? Do they suppose Manaluk might be more interested in having gold itself or in the things it would buy? Send children to the story to verify their ideas and to discover what started Manaluk hunting for gold.

consider implications of title . . .

read to verify opinions . . .

The words *shoulder* and *medicine* may be presented before the last part of the story is read. The words *snowshoes, pan,* and *overhear* should also be included in the list of glossary entries that you write on the board.

Guiding interpretation

PAGES 88-92

When everyone has had a chance to read these pages silently, lead boys and girls to observe the reasons underlying the thoughts and actions of the story characters.
—Why do you think Manaluk and the old man became friends?
—How did the old man happen to be in Manaluk's home?
—What was Manaluk thinking about when he spied the stranger on the river?
—What did Manaluk want for himself? for his mother?
—Why did he think there was no hope of getting these things?
—Which of the old man's gifts do you suppose Manaluk appreciated most? Why?
—Do you think Manaluk will be eager to pan for gold? [If necessary, clarify the meaning of the expression *pan for gold.*] Why? What do we call someone who pans for gold?

discuss cause-effect relationships . . .

note implied reason for statement . . .

To present the words *medicine* and *shoulder,* comment: "After the old man had gone, Manaluk's parents became worried about their son. Because Manaluk neglected his chores, his father thought he *needed medicine.* His mother wasn't sure medicine would help, for every time she glanced *over her shoulder* at him, Manaluk seemed to be daydreaming. What do you suppose he was thinking about? As you finish the story, you'll want to see whether his dreams come true."

anticipate thoughts of main character . . .

Youngsters will be eager to discuss the meaning of the title and Manaluk's good fortune. Such humorous touches as the effect of the mention of castor oil, the loss of some vegetables because of vigorous weeding, and Manaluk's decision to eat the whole can of peaches first of all should certainly find their way into the conversation too.

After they have shared their enjoyment of the story incidents, guide pupils in evaluating Manaluk's difficult decision and the factors that influenced him in making it.

—Why did Manaluk want his father to search for gold?

—How did his father feel about this idea?

—When did Manaluk first begin to doubt that he should be a prospector? Was this a good reason for changing his mind?

—Why did he finally decide to become a trapper and hunter? Do you think this was a wise decision? Why [or why not]?

observe humorous elements in story...

make judgments...

WHOLE STORY

To help children understand the relationship of environmental factors to needs and desires, ask what Manaluk wanted to buy for himself and for his parents. Then, after leading pupils to recall what Maile planned to buy, bring out the reasons for each child's choices. Would shaved ice be a treat for Manaluk? Why might this not appeal to him as much as it did to Maile? Why would Maile prefer the ice to canned peaches? (If necessary, remind youngsters of the rows of canned goods Maile saw at the fair.) Why might a new hat seem more important to Maile's aunt than to Manaluk's mother? Why would window glass be more important in Alaska than in Hawaii?

In a similar manner ask questions that will point up the way in which the area where each child lived determined or limited the methods by which money could be secured.

Next help children relate the discussion to their own situations. Can they think of something they want (or have wanted) very much? Why do (or did) they want this particular item? Would Manaluk or Maile be more likely to want the same thing? In what ways do youngsters secure money for things they want?

compare two stories...

note how location influences desires...

relate story to their own experience...

Finally let pupils apply their understandings about environmental influences to situations not mentioned in the stories.

—Which child would prefer ice skates, Maile or Manaluk?

—Who would be happier with a new swimming suit? [Pupils may recall that even in summer the water into which Manaluk fell was icy. Can anyone figure out why?]

—Who might appreciate a jacket with a fur collar and hood?

—Would Manaluk or Maile feel more at home where you live? Why? What things could be strange to both of them?

make inferences on basis of facts in two stories.

Extending competence

● To point up how much one can sometimes learn about a place through reading a story, ask children whether any of their impressions about Alaska were changed as they read this selection. What new knowledge did they acquire? Then encourage youngsters to look back through the story and study the illustrations again to discover details about *homes*, *work*, *food, travel*, *clothing*, and *climate* in the part of Alaska where Manaluk lived. (You may wish to write these headings on the board to guide pupils' thinking and discussion.)

Children compare information in story with earlier ideas about Alaska . . .

Next recall the title of this unit, and lead children to discuss new ideas they acquired as they read about other places. Which selections in the unit—poems, articles, or stories—contained especially appealing descriptions of places? (Youngsters may wish to read or hear favorite poems again.) Which place mentioned would they most like to visit? Why?

recall settings of other stories and poems in unit.

The last question might well lead into a conversation about some of the story characters and provide the opportunity again for pointing up the interesting diversities and the fundamental similarities among people.

● These procedures introduce the suffix -able and give children practice in combining structural and phonetic analysis.

1. To begin, write the following sentences on the board:
   Did you enjoy the play last night?
   I thought it was very enjoyable.

After youngsters have read the sentences, ask: "What word in the second sentence is formed from a word in the first sentence? What suffix has been added to *enjoy* to make the word *enjoyable*? What is *an enjoyable play?*" Then suggest that the children find the suffix *-able* (use the letter names) in their glossaries and read the definitions.

Pupils note that *-able* is a suffix . . .

read definitions of -able in glossary . . .

Next write the following sentences, underlining the italicized words. Ask pupils to read each one and to tell in their own words what the underlined word means in the sentence.

discuss meaning of derivatives ending in *-able* . . .

> Tom was *agreeable* to the plan.
> She always wears *fashionable* clothes.
> The spot on your coat is not *noticeable*.

2. To provide practice in combining structural and phonetic analysis, write the following sentences and underline the italicized words, which are derivatives of words not yet introduced in The New Basic Readers. As each sentence is read, have children tell in their own words what the underlined word means.

combine structural and phonetic analysis to identify written words.

> John has pictures of many *famous* baseball players.
> The people promised *loyalty* to their king.
> I like the *arrangement* of the rooms in your new house.
> Have you read the story about the *cowardly* lion?
> Ann was *unaware* that the guests had arrived.
> The policeman said the accident was *unavoidable*.

Extending interests

Introduce the last three chapters of *The Singing Hill* by commenting that, like Manaluk, Ray cherished a very special secret —his friendship with Thee-Rim.

Children listen to concluding chapters of The Singing Hill . . .

When children have savored the story's satisfying conclusion, lead them to discuss the qualities Ray displayed in saving his friend despite dangers that to him were terrifying. Is this the way pupils described him before they listened to his rescue of Thee-Rim? In what way had Ray changed? What led him to act as he did in this last part of the story? Then let youngsters point out other instances, perhaps not so dramatic, in which Ray displayed the same traits.

consider again Ray's personal traits . . .

The characterization of Ray is only one of many aspects of *The Singing Hill* that could be discussed. You might, for example, challenge more perceptive pupils to tell a few of the ways the author helped them know Ray and understand how he felt, or point up examples of the companionship and understanding of Ray's parents.

and their development by the author.

Evaluating progress

The use of pages 32 and 33-34 of the *Think-and-Do Book* will help you evaluate individual progress in word analysis and in interpretation. Pupils' responses on page 32 provide some measure of their understanding of visual clues to vowel sounds in accented syllables and their recognition that different spellings may represent the same sound.

In Think-and-Do Book pupils take informal tests.

As children read the selection on page 33 and answer the questions on page 34, many interpretive abilities are called upon. Among the skills emphasized are perceiving relationships of place and of cause and effect, visualizing details, and making inferences.

An evaluation of each pupil's responses on the test pages, coupled with your observations of his daily performance, will enable you to answer such questions as the following:

—Does the child associate the sound and meaning of a word with its printed form?

—Does he use word analysis and context clues in identifying unfamiliar printed words as he reads?

—Is he using the glossary [and dictionary] as an aid in determining pronunciation and meaning?

—Does he form vivid sensory images as he reads?

—Can he recognize motives and emotional reactions of characters and use these as aids in interpreting the story?

—Does he perceive various kinds of relationships?

—Can he grasp the main idea of a story and see how it relates to his own experience?

When you have summarized your observations about each child, you will be better prepared to judge the type of guidance needed as youngsters proceed in the next unit.

INTERESTING PEOPLE ALONG THE WAY

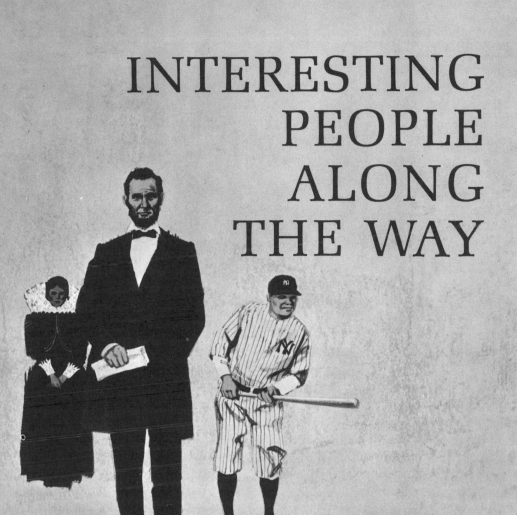

Introducing Unit Two

This unit explores a new area of interest in The New Basic Reading Program—biography. Boys and girls will have much to ponder and to grow on as they begin to develop an awareness that interesting people of the past are more than just "names" whose birthdays are celebrated, more than pictures in a book or statues in a park. As pupils discover interesting and sometimes amusing events in the lives of these men and women, they will have an opportunity to note some of the personal qualities and accomplishments for which these people are remembered.

Lead into a discussion of biography—what it is and why it is fun to read—by writing the unit title on the board. Emphasize the idea that reading is a road that not only lets us travel to many different times and places but introduces us to many people who actually lived.

Then invite children to mention interesting or famous persons they have read or heard about, their achievements, and some anecdotes about them. Comment: "Sometimes stories of the lives of real people and real happenings are more exciting than stories in which the characters and perhaps the events are created by an author. Why do you suppose this is so?" Explain that the written story of the life of a person who really lived is called a *biography*. (Write the term on the board.) With some groups you may want to distinguish between biography and historical fiction. For example, point out that in historical fiction the author attempts to reconstruct life as it was during a period of time other than the present. Historical fiction then is usually centered around an event or series of events and may or may not involve real people, while biography is centered on the life of a person who actually lived.

Continue by encouraging pupils to consider what we mean when we say that someone was a great person. What qualities might a great person possess? Then, before they read the selec-

Children discuss the lives of men and women they have read about...

identify this type of writing as biography...

tions in this unit, help children understand the words written by Phillips Brooks that are quoted on page 100 in their books. When pupils have turned to this page, read the quotation aloud to them and bring out its main idea—that greatness is not size or being well known or written about, but something fine or special about certain men and women or about what they have done. To clarify further the meaning of this quotation, you might read and discuss with children the definitions of *great* in the *Beginning Dictionary*. Then ask: "Is there someone living today whom you would consider great? In what way?" As you reread the quotation, invite boys and girls to read it with you.

talk about meaning of quotation about greatness ...

Next center attention on the unit title page. Explain that each of the people pictured on this page really lived and that in the selections in this unit pupils will read about some interesting events in the lives of these people. Do youngsters recognize any of them? Which one was once President of the United States? When children have identified Abraham Lincoln, comment that they will read about a funny incident that happened when he was a boy. Suggest that the baseball player was a member of the New York Yankees team many years ago and that youngsters will probably recognize his name. Mention, too, that children will read about the entire life of the woman shown in the picture. Do they have any idea who she might be?

examine and discuss unit title page ...

Before directing attention to the first selection, suggest that boys and girls turn to the table of contents and look over the titles of the selections in the second unit. Then invite them to leaf through the pages of this unit to discover some of the other famous people they are going to read about. Encourage youngsters to tell what they already know about the ones they recognize. Why might these people be considered great? Through this informal discussion stimulate a curiosity about these individuals, their lives, and their accomplishments—a curiosity that children will satisfy as they read the selections.

and table of contents.

Most young readers will warm to the subject of this biographical sketch, a baseball hero who delighted children and adults alike. In considering what baseball did for the Babe as well as what the Babe did for baseball, pupils note the flashback used by the author of this selection and consider his purpose in using it.

In this lesson new emphasis is given to the use of context clues in determining the meanings of words. Attention is also focused on accent patterns in three-syllable words and visual clues to the number of syllables in a word.

New words: **Ruth,** *stadium,* **Ruthville,** *Baltimore, orphanage,* **Matthias,** *terrific,* **orioles, stomach, discouraged** (babe*, Herman*, New York*, Yankees*, fan*, *bleachers*, chant*,* mischief*, *tailor*,* earn*, problems*, fifteen*, aware*, lanky*, hundred*, famous*, *lathered*,* mustard*, ache*, happiness*, illness*, tip*)

Think-and-Do Book: **Pages 35, 36, and 37**

Establishing background

Use the title and the illustration on pages 102-103 to stimulate interest in the subject of this selection. Ask whether children know who "the Babe" was and what his real name was. As you write his last name on the board, suggest that pupils check their information by finding the entry *Ruth* in the glossary.

When children have found and discussed the entry, point out that as well as being a home-run king, Babe Ruth had *a terrific throwing arm.* Then continue: "Although the Babe *grew up in Baltimore* and started his career as a pitcher *with the Baltimore Orioles,* he was best known when he played right field for the New York Yankees. In fact he was so well known that *one*

Children identify new words ...

part of the stadium was called Ruthville when he played there. When you read the first part of this selection, you'll find out where Ruthville was and how the Babe's fans felt about him."

Comment that pupils may use their glossaries to check the meanings of the words *terrific* and *stadium,* and that they may want to look up *Baltimore* if they do not know the name of the state it is in. In listing the other glossary words, you will want to include *wedge* and *promising.*

The remaining words may be presented after the guided interpretation of pages 102-104. Children should also have the opportunity to identify the word *stomach* from context and clues in the spelling as they read page 109.

Guiding interpretation

PAGES 102-104

After silent reading <u>encourage boys and girls to tell what they have found out about the Babe and his fans</u> and to conjecture why he was such a favorite.

discuss relevant details . . .

Then <u>help pupils anticipate what the author will discuss next</u> by asking: "Had Babe Ruth always been a great favorite with the people who knew him? How do you know? What do you think the author will tell about next?" From the last paragraph on page 104 and the illustration on page 105 children may infer that they will learn something about the Babe's childhood.

anticipate flashback to Babe Ruth's childhood . . .

Present *orphanage, Matthias,* and *discouraged* as you add: "One thing you'll find out is that *nothing ever discouraged the Babe* from playing baseball. You'll also meet *Brother Matthias* [(mə thī′əs)], a man who *taught school at an orphanage* and who helped the Babe. But first let's find out what the author meant when he pointed out that Babe Ruth had not always been loved as he was by his friends in Ruthville."

identify new words . . .

PAGES 105-108

When children have told what part of Babe Ruth's life the author's statement referred to, <u>initiate a discussion of the events that started young George on the road to baseball fame.</u>
—Why had George spent most of his time on the streets?

GUIDANCE FOR PAGES 102·110 | **105**

—How did he feel at first about living at the orphanage? What helped him change his mind?

—Why do you think George admired Brother Matthias so much? What do we know about the way he taught the boys?

—Why didn't George become a tailor after all?

—How did he get his nickname?

PAGES 109-110

Before they finish the selection, suggest that children read the first paragraph on page 109 to find out what the author will tell about next. Then ask whether they think the section about Babe Ruth's childhood might be important in understanding this final part of the selection. Why? What things will they want to keep in mind as they read?

After silent reading help pupils summarize their impressions of the Babe and consider possible reasons for his appeal.

—What did the author mean when he said that Babe Ruth had broken training rules *with a bang*? What were the results of his big snack? [Let pupils tell how they figured out the new word *stomach*.]

—Why did the author think the Babe might have developed such a big appetite? Do you agree? Why [or why not]?

—Why do you think the Babe was especially fond of children? Why do you suppose they were especially fond of him?

Finally encourage children to recall Phillips Brooks' thought about greatness and to tell what qualities they believe made Babe Ruth such a favorite in the world of baseball.

WHOLE STORY

Explain that in most stories pupils have read, the events were told in sequence. Point up the flashback in this selection and lead children to consider the author's purpose in using it by asking whether the author told about the major events in Babe Ruth's life in the order in which they happened. If he had put these events in order, which part of the story would have come first? Comment that the section on pages 105-108 is called a

consider cause-effect relationships . . .

sense importance of flashback . . .

evaluate author's opinion . . .

evaluate Ruth's qualities . . .

note reversal of time sequence . . .

flashback (write the word on the board) and ask why pupils think the author used a flashback in telling about Babe Ruth's life. Lead children to conclude that perhaps the author wanted to capture the reader's interest by mentioning at the beginning that Babe Ruth was a famous baseball player, and that once readers knew who the Babe was, they would be interested in hearing about his childhood.

On pages 35-36 of the *Think-and-Do Book* children will read and interpret another article that employs the flashback.

recognize story structure . . .

consider author's purpose in using flashback . . .

ORAL INTERPRETATION

Encourage children to read exposition and narration in the same lively manner they use to make explanations in everyday conversation. After pupils recall what interested them most about Babe Ruth, let them share their interest with classmates by finding and reading the portion of the selection that told about it.

Begin by calling on volunteers who show a special interest in Babe Ruth. On succeeding days urge other children to find and read interesting items about other characters in the selections that follow or in books of their own choosing. Given the opportunity to select topics that interest them, reluctant oral readers may respond with more enthusiasm.

Baseball enthusiasts may want to share their interest in Babe Ruth with parents or brothers and sisters at home. To help children organize what they have learned, suggest that they look back over the selection and pick out two or three points that they would want to remember if they were telling the story to someone. As they summarize the selection, encourage them to mention what kind of person the author showed Babe Ruth to be as well as what he told about the events in his life.

choose parts of selection to read aloud . . .

summarize what they have learned about Babe Ruth.

Extending competence

● Point up the ways in which context clues can help readers determine the meanings of words. Begin by calling attention to the second sentence on page 106 and asking how children could figure out the meaning of the word *trade* if they did not know what it meant. When they note the phrase *way of making a living* in the following sentence, comment that the sentences preceding or following a word often give clues that help to make the meaning of the word clear. What clues in the paragraph helped children figure out the meaning of the word *tailor?*

Pupils note clues to word meaning in printed text . . .

Continue by letting pupils point out textual clues to the meaning of *chant* (fourth paragraph, page 104) and *orphanage* (first paragraph, page 106) and the picture clue to the meaning of *tip* (second paragraph, page 110).

and in picture . . .

Responses on page 37 of the *Think-and-Do Book* will help you evaluate each child's ability to use context clues as an aid in determining word meanings.

determine meaning from context in Think-and-Do Book.

● Use of these procedures will <u>call attention to accent patterns</u> <u>in three-syllable words</u> and to <u>spelling patterns that help deter-</u> <u>mine the number of syllables.</u>

1. Write the following columns of known words on the board:

accident	Alaska
elephant	important
animal	electric
hospital	remember
customer	potato
terrible	examine
possible	committee
probable	attention
radio	position
medicine	enormous

Explain that all words in the first column have the same number of syllables and are accented on the same syllable. Then comment that you will pronounce the words and invite pupils to say them after you. Ask:

Children say groups of three-syllable words . . .

—How many syllables do you hear in all these words? [three]
—Which syllable is accented in all of them? [first]

Continue with the second column of words, all of which are three-syllable words accented on the second syllable. Then lead children to generalize in their own words that a three-syllable word is accented on the first or on the second syllable.

note that either the first or second syllable is accented . . .

2. Next ask: "If you had never seen these words before, do you think you could tell by looking at them that they are three-syllable words? Let's look at each word to see how the spelling helps us know that it is a three-syllable word. How many vowel letters do you see in the word *accident?* How many vowel sounds do you hear?" Continue with the remaining words in the first column, leading pupils to note that the final *e* in *medicine* does not represent a separate syllable any more than the final *e* in the word *fine* or *engine* does.

note clues in spelling to the number of syllables . . .

Use similar procedures with the words in the second list. Help pupils note that the final *e* in *examine,* like the final *e* in *medicine,* does not represent a separate syllable. Bring out, too, that the two *e*'s together in the final syllable of *committee* represent one vowel sound (as in *tree* and *agree*); that one vowel sound—the schwa sound—is heard in the final syllable of *attention, position, enormous* and two vowel letters together stand for the schwa sound in the spelling (as in *station* and *jealous*).

3. Write the following and explain that there is one three-syllable word and one two-syllable word in each sentence. Let pupils read each sentence and identify these words.

discriminate between known two- and three-syllable words in context.

> Saturday is Joe's birthday.
> Put your picture in this envelope.
> Ann had no idea what a lion looked like.
> We certainly liked the old sea captain.
> George saw a new invention at the science fair.

Extending interests

To give children a better appreciation of the handicaps Babe Ruth overcame in his rise to fame, read *Babe Ruth, Baseball Boy,* by Guernsey Van Riper, Jr. After reading a chapter or two, place the book on the library table for pupils to read.

From a book pupils learn more about Babe Ruth . . .

If you have access to the 1964 edition, you might recommend *People to Know,* Volume 13 of *Childcraft,* for children's perusal. Comment that in this book pupils will find interesting—and true —stories about famous people, including one about Babe Ruth's promise to a young boy.

read true incidents in lives of other great men and women.

Get 'Em While They're Hot

As boys and girls read this version of the origin of the hot dog, they will enjoy meeting Charlie Feltman, the man who has been credited by many as the first to make sandwiches out of sausages and rolls.

An exercise gives pupils experience in locating specific information in the article to verify an opinion or prove a point. In another exercise youngsters note that vowel-consonant spelling patterns which are clues to vowel sound in initial accented syllables of two-syllable words also apply to accented syllables of three-syllable words.

New words: failure, frankfurters, popular, president, *England* (heat*, *Coney*, Charlie*, *inns*, *obliged*, sausage*, wrapping*, served*, picnics*, laid*, queen*, royal*)

Think-and-Do Book: **Pages 38 and 39**

Establishing background

Introduce the subject of this article by leading youngsters to recall from the preceding selection about Babe Ruth the episode involving hot dogs. Then ask: "Would you say that hot dogs are *a popular food in America* today? Do you think they were as well known a hundred years ago? By what other names is the hot dog known?

"The article you'll read today tells several things about *hot dogs or frankfurters* that you may not have known before. You'll probably even be surprised when you read about a special event attended by the *President of the United States* and some royal visitors *from England.*" (Since most pupils will be able to identify the new word *failure* on page 112 from its spelling and from context clues, it is not presented here.)

Pupils identify new words . . .

Interpreting the article

As soon as they have turned to page 111, give youngsters a few moments to comment on the illustration. When someone mentions the old-fashioned clothing, call attention to the year 1868 in the first sentence, and ask children to tell about how long ago this was. Then introduce Charlie Feltman (the man standing inside the pie wagon) with the remark that youngsters will find out more about him as they read the article.

note relationship of time . . .

To help pupils organize the main ideas as they read, write the following questions on the board, and comment that when youngsters have finished reading the article, they will be able to answer each of them.

read to learn about specific facts . . .

>Who was Charlie Feltman?
>What problem did he have?
>How did he solve it?
>How did a favorite American food become popular in England?

During the discussion of the first two questions following silent reading, make sure that everyone knows where Coney Island is located, and check to see whether pupils used their glossaries to find out. While boys and girls are talking about the answer to the third question, ask whether they can think of a saying that could be used to explain why this new kind of sandwich was made. If no one recalls the saying "Necessity is the mother of invention," you might remind children of the story "The Mother of Invention," which they read in *Roads to Follow,* and ask how this proverb can be applied to Mr. Feltman's problem. As pupils bring out the need that led Charlie Feltman to create a new kind of sandwich, note whether or not they identified the word *failure* correctly.

discuss main ideas in article . . .

When children discuss the fourth question, encourage them to cite information in the article that tells why the hot dog became popular in England as well as in America. Also call attention to the English, French, and Spanish headlines shown in the illustration on page 114. Pupils will find it interesting to note that the American term *Hot Dog* was used not only in the English headline but also in the French and Spanish ones.

Youngsters will enjoy considering the different words that are used today to designate the sandwich Charlie Feltman sold from his pie wagon. Invite pupils to point out the words the author used in place of *hot dog.* Can they think of any other words besides *frankfurter in a roll* and *sausage in a sandwich* that might be used either for the sandwich or for the meat in the sandwich? Such terms as *wiener, blimp, frank,* and *Coney Island red hot* may be among those that are familiar to many boys and girls in the class.

suggest other names used for the hot dog...

Finally ask: "Have you ever heard someone call out 'Get 'em while they're hot!' at an amusement park or a ball game? Do you think this phrase is a good title for the article? Why?"

note appropriateness of title.

Extending competence

● This exercise gives pupils experience in locating specific information that will verify an opinion or prove a point. Read each of the following statements and ask children to decide which ones are true and which are false. Suggest, too, that they look through the article and justify their answers by reading aloud passages from it.

Children consider validity of statements about information in the article...

1. In America today more hot dogs are eaten than any other food.
2. Charlie Feltman invented sausages and bread.
3. Mr. Feltman thought of a new way to serve sausages and bread.
4. He created the new sandwich because he wanted something fancy to serve at his pie wagon.
5. Mr. Feltman started selling frankfurters in buns because all the inns were selling them.
6. Hot dogs were popular in England at the time the Pilgrims came to America.

This type of exercise is valuable in developing abilities that will become increasingly important in an expanding curriculum. It requires children to identify specific information that is relevant to a general statement, to interpret accurately what has been read, and to determine on the basis of given facts the validity of the conclusions drawn. At later levels youngsters will apply these same principles of critical reading or thinking in judging whether an author's or speaker's conclusions are supported by the facts cited.

Awareness of the structure or organization of an article is essential for locating pertinent information that supports or invalidates a statement. The guidance in perceiving various types of relationships that was provided at earlier levels has laid a foundation for this skill. Mature readers at this level may be able to turn quickly to relevant information in the text because they have sensed the structure of the article during their first reading of it. Other boys and girls will need repeated practice and guidance with this type of exercise which requires them to decide in which part of an article they should look for facts related to a particular idea.

On page 38 of the *Think-and-Do Book* children are given another exercise in evaluating statements as they decide which are possible and which are exaggerations.

make judgments in Think-and-Do Book.

● The following procedures should be used to introduce the understanding that vowel-consonant spelling patterns that are clues to vowel sound in initial accented syllables of two-syllable words apply to accented syllables of three-syllable words.

1. To begin, write the known words *silver, pity, pilot;* have them pronounced and the accented syllable identified. Then ask pupils to look at the spellings. If they did not know how to pronounce these words, what do they see in the spellings that would help them know what vowel sound to try in the first syllables? Lead children to recall that in an initial accented syllable a single vowel letter followed by two consonant letters usually stands for a short vowel sound (*silver*), and a single vowel letter followed by one consonant letter may stand for a short or a long vowel sound (*pity, pilot*).

Pupils identify accented first syllable in two-syllable words . . .

review clues to short and long vowel sounds in these accented syllables . . .

2. Next comment that these clues to vowel sounds apply in accented syllables of three-syllable words. Write the lists of words given at the top of the next page:

battery	amateur	favorite
yesterday	telephone	radio
Indian	president	stadium
possible	popular	curious
customer	holiday	vitamin

Pronounce the first list of words and have pupils say them. Bring out that these three-syllable words are accented on the first syllable. Then, as pupils look at each word, ask:
—How many consonant letters follow the first vowel letter?
—What vowel sound do you hear in the first syllable?

apply understandings to accented first syllable of three-syllable words . . .

When you and then children have pronounced the second and third lists of words and pupils have noted that these are three-syllable words accented on the first syllable, ask: "In which list of words do you hear long vowel sounds in the accented syllables? short vowel sounds? How many consonant letters follow the first vowel letter in each list of words?"

As children pronounce each word in the second and third lists again, ask them to look at the spelling and think about the vowel sound in the accented syllable of each.

To give pupils a chance to apply what they have just learned, write the following sentences, underlining the italicized words. Note their ability to identify each underlined word.

identify in context three-syllable words accented on first syllable . . .

> Many words have more than one *syllable*.
> We spent our vacation in *Canada*.
> John and his family are going to *Mexico*.
> Bears *hibernate* in winter.
> That book is not *difficult* to read.
> Dad's *telegram* said he had arrived safely.
> Tom is a very *sociable* person.

3. Next write these lists of known words on the board:

Alaska	examine	potato
electric	eleven	convenient
committee	terrific	peculiar

Pronounce the words in the first list and have pupils say them. Bring out that these are three-syllable words accented on the second syllable. Underline the second *a* in *Alaska* and ask how many consonant letters follow the *a*. Does it stand for the short or the long *a* sound? Continue with *electric* and *committee*.

apply understandings to accented second syllable of three-syllable words . . .

Use similar procedures with the second and third lists of words, bringing out that a single vowel letter followed by one consonant letter may represent a short vowel sound (second list) or a long vowel sound (third list).

In conclusion write the following sentences, underlining the italicized words, and note pupils' ability to identify each underlined word in context.

identify in context three-syllable words accented on the second syllable . . .

> Last winter we rode on a *toboggan.*
> The ending of the story will *astonish* you.
> We need a new *antenna* for our TV set.
> I like *molasses* on pancakes.
> The *horizon* is the line where earth and sky seem to meet.
> John has his *diploma* from a business school.
> We used *enamel* to paint the kitchen walls.
> I ate a *banana* after school.

As children use page 39 in the *Think-and-Do Book,* they will have further practice in applying the understandings developed in this exercise.

identify three-syllable words in Think-and-Do Book exercise.

Extending interests

Boys and girls who have never experienced the excitement, color, and concert of sounds at a fair or an amusement park can enjoy them vicariously as you read Eleanor Farjeon's "Jill Came from the Fair" (in *Time for Poetry*). When youngsters have heard the poem, encourage them to describe what they saw, heard, and felt as they listened.

Children enjoy vicarious experience as they respond to imagery of poem . . .

If it is available, place *Scientists and Inventors,* Volume 11 of *Childcraft,* on the library table, inviting children to read about other "firsts" similar to Charlie Feltman's. To pique their curiosity, you might ask whether pupils know (or can guess) why doughnuts have holes. Who made the first sandwich—and why? Have youngsters ever eaten ice cream with a waffle wrapped around it? or popcorn with sugar and cream? What do they think gave someone the idea of putting erasers on pencils? Pupils who accept this invitation should be given an opportunity later to tell what they found out about these and other things taken for granted today.

read stories of other "firsts."

Wilbur Wright and Orville Wright

In this light-hearted poem children encounter a biographical narrative in poetic form. They should relish the touches of nonsense mixed with fact as they would frosting on a cake.

Establishing background

Ask boys and girls to tell what they know about Wilbur and Orville Wright. Provide any of the following information that youngsters fail to mention: Wilbur and Orville were brothers who were running a bicycle shop at the time they began their flying experiments. They worked with gliders and later made the first successful airplane. Their earliest flights were made at Kitty Hawk, a town in North Carolina.

Children draw upon personal knowledge of Wright brothers . . .

Guiding interpretation

Remind pupils that the selections about Babe Ruth and Charlie Feltman told of events in the lives of real people. Then inform children that today's poem also tells a story about real people. Continue: "But the poet has told his tale all in the spirit of fun. Listen to what Stephen Vincent Benét has to say about Wilbur Wright and Orville Wright."

anticipate poem's subject matter . . .

listen to poem . . .

When they have heard the poem, provide an opportunity for pupils to savor many of the poet's light-hearted touches by encouraging them to tell what makes the poem fun to hear. During the discussion ask youngsters to explain why Wilbur refers to his brother as *O* while Orville calls Wilbur *W,* what *a bed of roses* means, and what the abbreviation *bro.* stands for. Benét's playful presentation of facts should also be pointed up. Do pupils think Wilbur and Orville Wright really talked this

cite poet's whimsy . . .

and his purpose . . .

way to each other? Did they do things exactly as the poet describes? Why do children think Benét told the story this way?

After the amusing aspects of the poem have been explored, clarify words and expressions that may have proved troublesome—for example, the meaning of *trying* and *grant* in the first stanza and the significance of the last four lines of the poem. Draw attention also to the dates beneath Wilbur's and Orville's names in the title, and see whether pupils realize that these give the years of each brother's birth and death.

grasp unfamiliar meanings . . .

Reread the poem to children, and then invite volunteers to read the poem aloud. Suggest that they take turns reading stanzas or that a group of three take the parts of Wilbur, Orville, and narrator. If the latter course is chosen, encourage readers to scan their parts first so that they can read at the proper times without hesitation. Remind pupils that they do not drop their voices or stop at the end of a line of poetry unless the thought ends, and suggest that they familiarize themselves also with this aspect of the poem. To help youngsters think of more than a single line as a unit of thought, you might have them answer such questions as the following: "What did Orville Wright find so trying about birds? What did the brothers do while they were building their gliders?"

read poem aloud.

Extending interests

Underlying the humor of this poem is a recognition of the ingenuity, perseverance, and courage of these two brothers who proved that man could fly. To give youngsters insight into the early development of qualities that made for greatness in the lives of Orville and Wilbur Wright, read the selection from Quentin Reynold's *The Wright Brothers* in *The Arbuthnot Anthology of Children's Literature.*

When children have heard and commented on the selection, invite them to consider the mother's influence upon her sons, bringing out some of the qualities she encouraged in them. How was "getting it right on paper" to help them later at Kitty Hawk?

Pupils hear about childhood incidents in the lives of the Wright brothers . . .

and discuss early influences on later success.

pages 117·126 | Audubon's Birds

Audubon's attempt to verify his theories about phoebes and his determination to test his conclusions by experimentation provide good examples for young readers to follow.

Procedures suggested in the exercises will strengthen ability to distinguish between opinion and fact, call attention to ways in which a glossary or dictionary indicates the size of objects, and introduce the suffix *-ship*.

New words: **Audubon's**, **Pennsylvania**, *museum*, *friendship*, **upward***, *phoebes*, **proved**, **already**, *gratefully*, **marry***, **marriage** (*Frenchman**, *Lucy**, **cave***, **nest***, *underbrush**, **graceful***, **gazed***, **dipped***, **distant***, **protested***, **born***, **urged***, **discussing***, **rust***, **bracelet***, **indeed***, **James***, **wasting***, *fate**, **healthy***)

Think-and-Do Book: **Pages 40, 41, and 42**

Establishing background

Discover what knowledge boys and girls may have about John James Audubon by inquiring whether they have ever heard of a famous man named *Audubon*. If response is limited, suggest that pupils turn to the glossary to discover when this man lived and why he is remembered.

Continue: "Audubon's pictures of the birds of our country *have proved helpful* to many people. Among the ones that he painted were some *birds called phoebes.* Perhaps *you already know something* about these birds." Let children tell what they know and check their information in the glossary.

Then direct attention to the story title and picture on page 117, explaining that Audubon (shown at the left) had just moved to *the state of Pennsylvania* and that the other two men

Children use glossary to find facts about Audubon . . .

identify new words . . .

were neighbors of his. Continue: "At first many of Audubon's neighbors thought some of the things he did were odd and that *his house looked like a museum.* Can you imagine what made them think that? [The title and the definition of *museum* may suggest possibilities.] As you read the first part of the story, you'll find out whether Audubon made friends with these neighbors. You'll also be interested in an experiment he thought of to test one of his ideas about birds."

make inference . . .

When you list the glossary words on the board, you might include *natural* and *France.* The word *marriage* may be presented before pages 123-126 are read. Most children should be able to identify independently *friendship* and *gratefully* by using context and spelling clues as they read, but you may wish to check their recognition of these words during discussion.

Guiding interpretation

PAGES 117-122

After silent reading point up motives and cause-effect relationships underlying the conversation and actions of the characters.

—Why was John the talk of the countryside? Which of his ways did his neighbors wonder about?

note attitude toward stranger . . .

—What did John want to show Tom and Lucy in the cave?

—Why did he think the phoebes that came to the cave had been there before?

—Why wasn't Tom satisfied with John's statement that the birds had come back to their old nest? What questions did he raise?

discuss reasons for Tom's doubts . . .

—Do you think John himself was satisfied that his idea was correct? How do you know? What plan does he have in mind to test his opinion? Do you think it will work?

describe John's plan to verify idea and read to determine outcome of plan . . .

Then comment, "As you finish the story to see how that plan turns out, you'll also learn about John and Lucy's *plans for marriage* [present this phrase]."

PAGES 123-126

To focus attention on Audubon's attitude toward his experiment and bring out the distinction between fact and opinion, ask questions like those on the next page.

—What made John think that the birds in the cave were the mother and father birds he had watched there a year ago? Could he be sure that they were? Why not?

—What did John prove by his experiment?

—Was John discouraged because he hadn't proved that the mother and father birds had come back to their old nest? Why not?

—What do you think may be some of the things Audubon had in mind when he said *There are so many things to do?*

—What child or children in the first part of our book might especially enjoy reading about Audubon and his work? Why? [Pupils will probably recall Rufe and Dan's interest in nature in the story 'The World of Hogback Mountain.']

identify basis for John's opinion . . .

recognize verified fact . . .

grasp implied idea . . .

WHOLE STORY

To help children appreciate the significance of Audubon's accomplishments, explain that for many years he traveled throughout the United States studying birds. Point out that he found many different kinds of birds in our country and drew life-sized pictures of them. If his book *The Birds of America* is available, give pupils an opportunity to see and enjoy some of the pictures. Comment that Audubon also learned and wrote a great deal about the habits of birds.

Then lead boys and girls to discuss the importance of Audubon's pictures and of the information he gathered about the habitats, habits, and migrations of birds. Explain that he was the first to think of a way to identify birds in order to study their migratory habits. Do children know what this way of identifying birds is called? Are they aware that Audubon's work led other people to become interested in bird banding as well as in protecting birds because of their beauty and usefulness?

consider importance of Audubon's work . . .

Encourage children to consider whether Audubon approached his work scientifically. (Pupils who have been using The Basic Science Program of the Curriculum Foundation Series will be familiar with the scientific method of studying a problem.) The fact that much of the information about birds in science books today was unknown before Aubudon began his study will also interest children.

note his scientific approach in gathering information . . .

Youngsters will learn additional facts about Audubon's life and work as they read the article on pages 40-41 of the *Think-and-Do Book*. As they answer the questions following the article, they strengthen their ability to reread to locate specific information and to grasp main ideas.

Develop awareness of the various kinds of information found in biographical materials as you lead pupils to compare and contrast the style and purpose of the first four selections in this unit. First have them turn to the table of contents (page 3), look at the titles of the biographical selections they have read, and tell what types of information they found in each. Then stimulate further thought by asking:

discuss various kinds of information found in biographical materials ...

—Which selection tells more about a man's idea than about the man himself? ['Get 'Em While They're Hot'] Why do you think this selection was written like this?
—Which one do you think was written mostly to amuse or entertain the reader? ['Wilbur Wright and Orville Wright']

think about purposes of authors ...

—Which selection gives the most information about a person's life? ['The Babe']
—In which selection did the author choose one important event from a person's life as the basis for an interesting story and add to it conversation and other things that might have happened? ['Audubon's Birds']

ORAL INTERPRETATION

Prepare children for reading aloud with appropriate variations in volume by encouraging them to reconstruct story scenes and sense the feelings of each character.

Call attention to the first scene in the cave (beginning with the second paragraph on page 118), and suggest that pupils try to see the scenery, the characters, and the action as if they were on TV. Then bring the scene into the classroom by inviting three volunteers to pantomime it. To clarify images and to help youngsters use more detailed action, ask: "Where is the nest? How did the three characters exit from the cave? Where did they hide? In which direction did the birds fly when they left their nest?"

visualize setting, characters, and action ...

pantomime scene ...

Lead pupils to consider the volume of the speakers' voices by asking: "When Lucy gave a sudden cry, did she cry out loudly or quietly? How do you think John spoke when he suggested that they give the birds a chance to come into the cave? Do you think their voices showed excitement and enthusiasm even though they spoke softly? After the birds had flown away, do you suppose the characters continued to talk so quietly? Why not?"

sense feelings and appropriate volume for speakers . . .

When children have read the fifth paragraph on page 120, lead them to express the ideas of the paragraph in direct discourse. Then suggest that this dialogue be used instead of the narration as different groups of three read aloud the conversation through the third paragraph on page 121.

put Tom's thoughts into direct discourse . . .

After a narrator has read the link that introduces the next episode at the cave, suggest that each child imagine he is holding the baby bird as John and Lucy read the conversation on pages 122 and 123. If the readers do not adjust their voices to avoid frightening the bird, call attention to the key words *whispered* and *quietly*.

observe words that give clues to volume . . .

Continue with the remaining scenes of the story, reminding pupils to think about what is happening and decide whether the characters would talk quietly or not. Children who are envisioning the entire scene will sense the crescendo in Audubon's final speech (page 126), which expresses his optimistic enthusiasm about future endeavors.

read other scenes aloud.

Extending competence

● The wealth of information about phoebes in this story can be used to strengthen ability to make valid inferences and judgments on the basis of given facts. This exercise, like the story itself, points up the importance of verifying opinions. Begin by writing the statement *All birds build their nests in trees.* Is this sentence true? Have pupils find and read passages in the story that prove their opinions (page 118, paragraph 2; page 125, paragraph 6). Continue in the same manner with the sentences that follow. (The page references shown after each statement are for your convenience only.)

Pupils reread to locate evidence that supports or disproves opinions . . .

1. Some birds' eggs hatch in two weeks. (page 121, paragraphs 5 and 6)
2. It is difficult to get a close look at phoebes because they are easily frightened. (page 121, paragraphs 4 and 6; page 125, paragraphs 3 and 6)
3. All birds build new nests each spring. (page 119, paragraph 2; page 125, paragraph 6)
4. Watching how a bird flies may help one decide what kind of bird it is. (page 118, paragraph 5)

After children have located information that confirms or denies each of the preceding statements, ask:
—If we said *All birds' eggs hatch in two weeks*, would the sentence be correct? How could we find out if it is true?
—Might the statement *Some birds build new nests each spring* be true? Would you expect to find that information in this story? Why not?
—If we changed the words *may help* in the last sentence to *always helps*, would the statement still be true? Why not?

observe fallacy of generalizing on basis of limited information.

● Use these procedures and page 42 of the *Think-and-Do Book* to emphasize ways in which a glossary or dictionary indicates size. After asking how big a full-grown phoebe is, have pupils turn again to the entry *phoebe* and the accompanying illustration to discover how the size of the bird is explained.

Children discuss how glossary indicates size of things.

Suggest that children use the glossary to find answers to the following questions. As you pronounce each italicized word that pupils are to find in the glossary, write it on the board.
—Is a *dove* bigger than a phoebe? How can you tell? What does the small number after the word *dove* under the picture indicate? [Lead youngsters to note the two entries for *dove* and to conclude that the first entry is the one illustrated.]
—Which is bigger, a *stag* or a *doe*? About how much bigger than the doe is the stag shown in the picture?
—Is the picture of a *mite* smaller or larger than a real mite? Which definition of *mite* is illustrated?
—How does the glossary help you know the size of *snowshoes*? [Comparison with the boots gives an idea of size.]

● To introduce the suffix *-ship,* write the known word *friendship* and ask what the root word is. What suffix has been added to *friend* to form *friendship?* Invite someone to use *friendship* in a sentence. Then have pupils find the suffix *-ship* in their glossaries and read the definitions.

Pupils note that -ship is a suffix and read glossary definitions . . .

As you say each of the following sentences, omit the italicized word and write it on the board for children to read. (The root words *champion* and *member* in *championship* and *membership* give pupils an opportunity to apply what they have learned about clues to vowel sound in accented syllables.) Pupils should also explain the meaning of each sentence.

identify derivatives ending in -ship.

Last year our team won the state *championship.*

The science club hopes to increase its *membership.*

If a piece of furniture is made well, we might say that it shows good *workmanship.*

Extending interests

Boys and girls may enjoy hearing how Chuck, an accident-prone young man, and Chen, an accident-prone wild goose, coöperate to illustrate the theory John Audubon proposed and tested in today's story. Read *A Wild Goose Tale,* by Wilson Gage, and in the ensuing discussion let youngsters talk about what Chuck learned—not only about wild geese. Then encourage them to point up the touches of humor and keen interest in nature the author displays in this story.

Children listen to A Wild Goose Tale . . .

discern and interpret elements of humor and nature lore . . .

You might also recommend *Pierre Pidgeon,* by Lee Kingman, a story about another boy whose enthusiasm shattered—though only temporarily—his heart's desire. (If the book is not available for pupils to read, you might read it to them from *The Arbuthnot Anthology of Children's Literature.*)

read a story about another discovery . . .

Conclude on a light note by reading Robert Frost's "The Last Word of a Bluebird" (in *Time for Poetry*), offering the comment that although the birds Audubon observed told him much that he wanted to know, none was so obliging as the unusual bird in this poem. (Children who have used *Learn to Listen, Speak, and Write,* Book 3[1], will be familiar with the poem.)

enjoy poet's conversational flight of fancy.

page 127 | Spring Song

A joyous welcome to the first signs of spring is an emotion that is probably shared by everyone where seasons change. When Aileen Fisher describes the harbinger, a meadow lark that flutters about looking for a lost song, pupils should find it easy to appreciate the figurative language of poetry.

Establishing background

Draw upon children's own experiences and reactions in discovering spring in their neighborhood. Begin by asking them what signs of spring they usually notice first. When several examples have been given, encourage pupils to think about their reactions to these signs. For example, ask: "How do you feel when you take your roller skates out of the closet for the first time after winter? when new leaves give trees a lacy look? when you see a gay tulip in someone's yard? when the wind turns into a fragrant breeze?"

In some areas of the country, spring changes are more striking than in others. If your pupils live in a fairly even climate, ask what they know of changes that take place when spring comes in other parts of the United States.

Pupils relate poem's theme to personal experience . . .

Guiding interpretation

Read aloud the title of Aileen Fisher's "Spring Song," and ask children what they think the poem will be about. After making sure pupils know that a *cleft* is a crack or divided place, suggest that they listen to what the poet has to say.

To help children visualize the sights and sounds described and infer the emotion that these conveyed, ask such questions as those given on the next page.

listen to poem . . .

—How did the poet describe the landscape? [City youngsters may need help in imaging hay that has been bleached and flattened by wintry weather.]

—Can't you just see the meadow lark tossing the melody about? How would he look? How would he sound? How would you have felt if you'd heard him?

—Did his song sound as lovely as it had the previous summer? How did the poet tell you this?

By leading boys and girls to contrast the literal and figurative themes, you will help make the beauty of poetry's figurative language apparent. What do children think the poet actually saw and heard that inspired her to write this poem? What was the make-believe story she thought about as she watched and listened to the lark? Then invite youngsters to listen to the poem again.

Finally help children note how the punctuation marks and capitalization aid in understanding the poem. Point out that, unlike most poems, this one does not have a capital letter at the beginning of each line. The poet, by choosing to use capitals only at the beginnings of her sentences, has simplified the reading of "Spring Song" in meaningful phrases. If pupils read it aloud, you might also draw attention to how the rhythm of the poem changes the instant that the lark finds his song.

Extending interests

Children may find some of their own feelings about spring reflected in "Spring," a gay, rollicking poem by Karla Kuskin. Be prepared to read it more than once so that youngsters can savor the delightful imagery.

This poem is but one of several by Karla Kuskin in her collection *In the Middle of the Trees*. You will want to select a few poems to read aloud as the occasions arise, and be sure the book is made available to children so that they can enjoy the fun, freshness, and humor of the verses and the pictures.

enrich their sensory imagery...

recognize main idea...

contrast literal and figurative speech...

observe how capitalization and punctuation help in interpretation.

Children hear another poet's interpretation of the spring season.

pages 128·135 | Sequoyah's
Talking Leaves

This account tells about Sequoyah as a person and highlights his struggle to create a way to write the Cherokee language. As children consider the reactions of Sequoyah's fellow tribesmen toward his "talking leaves," they are led to sense the need for developing an open mind toward new ideas.

Skill in adapting definitions to context increases as pupils learn to make inflectional adaptations in fitting a definition into a sentence. Other procedures extend understanding about vowel-consonant spelling patterns that are clues to vowel sound in accented syllables of words of more than two syllables.

New words: *Sequoyah's, Cherokee,* relations, *brief**, consider, *alphabet, syllables* (lame*, magic*, destroy*, sheets*, tribe*, *spelling*, *threatened**, foolishness*, leaking*, anger*, hut*, peace*, daughter*, speech*, arranged*, printed*, *honors**)

Think-and-Do Book: **Pages 43, 44, and 45**

Establishing background

To help children appreciate the magnitude of the task that faced the subject of this biographical sketch, comment: "Have you ever written a letter to a friend or to *one of your relations?* What do you have to know in order to write a letter? to read one? Have you ever stopped to *consider what our lives would be like* if we didn't have an alphabet? How might they be different? Do you think it would be difficult to invent *an alphabet* or a way to write a language? Why [or why not]?"

Continue by telling youngsters that today they will read about a man named *Sequoyah* (si kwoi'ə). Does anyone know who he was or why he is remembered? Have boys and girls turn to the entry *Sequoyah* in the glossary. As they read the entry

Children identify new words . . .

bring out possible problems of an alphabet maker . . .

silently, note whether pupils use the glossary for help in pronouncing the word *Cherokee* and understanding its meaning. When youngsters have discussed the biographical information about Sequoyah, comment that today's selection will tell them more about the system of writing he invented.

Since most children will be familiar with both the form and meaning of the word *syllables,* give them an opportunity to identify it independently as they read page 134.

check words in
glossary . . .

Guiding interpretation

PAGES 128-132

When pupils have turned to page 128, direct attention to the title and illustration. Ask children whether they have any idea what might be meant by *talking leaves.* After introducing Sequoyah (shown sitting beside his cabin), invite pupils to conjecture what he is doing and why he is being watched. Then suggest that they read the first five pages to check their ideas and to find out what problems Sequoyah has.

read to satisfy
curiosity aroused by
title and illustration . . .

Following silent reading, guide a discussion of Sequoyah's "talking leaves" with such questions as these:

—What did Sequoyah mean by *talking leaves?* Why did he believe they were important to his people?

identify meaning of
talking leaves . . .

—What two ideas did Sequoyah experiment with first as he tried to find a way to write the Cherokee language? Why did he discard each of these?

—What did Sequoyah decide was the answer to his problem? What do we call the parts of words he was thinking about?

—In addition to the problem of figuring out a way to write the Cherokee language, what other problem did Sequoyah face? Why was his work destroyed the first time? the second time?

note dual nature of
Sequoyah's problem . . .

—What was Sequoyah's attitude toward the task he had set for himself? How do you know?

and sense his
dedication . . .

PAGES 133-135

Before children finish the selection, encourage them to tell what they want to find out as they read on. After silent reading talk about the Cherokee writing Sequoyah invented. Check identification of the word *syllables* as you bring out how his way of writing differs from our alphabet.

explain Sequoyah's method of writing . . .

Then discuss the acceptance of Sequoyah's alphabet by the Cherokee people. Ask:

—How did it come about that Sequoyah's system of writing was accepted by the Cherokee people?

discuss reactions to it . . .

—What was the Chief's first reaction? Why did he hesitate to accept the invention? What helped him change his mind?

—Who were the last to accept the writing? Were the old men and chiefs easy to convince? What makes you think not?

—Do you think that learning Sequoyah's method of writing was easy or difficult for most of the Cherokees? What makes you think as you do? Which was more difficult, inventing the system of writing or learning it? Why?

—How did Sequoyah's invention change the lives of his people? [In an exercise on page 43 of the *Think-and-Do Book* pupils consider how written language affects their own lives.]

and note its effect on the lives of the Cherokee people . . .

—Do you think he deserves to be honored? Why?

WHOLE STORY

Children will find it interesting to contrast the Indians' early attitude toward Sequoyah and his work with their attitude after they had learned to use his alphabet and to think of reasons for this change. To begin, recall with pupils that when Sequoyah was trying to devise a written language, the other Indians thought that he was practicing "bad magic" and calling on bad spirits to destroy the Cherokee people. Then ask:

—Why do you suppose the Indians thought as they did? Why wouldn't they have understood what Sequoyah was trying to do even if he had tried to explain his idea to them?

contrast reactions to idea before and after it was understood . . .

—How did the Indians finally feel about his invention? What made them change their minds? Do you think their opinion of Sequoyah changed also? In what way?

—What other inventions do you know about that people were afraid of or made fun of at first?

and link these reactions to other situations . . .

—Can you think of anything that might be invented during the next hundred years that seems impossible to us today?

Draw pupils into a discussion of the character traits that contributed to Sequoyah's success. Ask: "Why didn't Sequoyah give up trying to find a way to write his people's language? What kind of person was Sequoyah? How did the author help you know this—by telling what kind of man he was, or by telling what he did?" Then lead youngsters to recall Phillips Brooks' thought about greatness (page 100). Encourage them to bring out the personal qualities that helped Sequoyah succeed in his self-appointed task of writing the Cherokee language and in convincing his people of its value.

note qualities of greatness Sequoyah possessed.

Extending competence

● This exercise and the one on page 44 of the *Think-and-Do Book* will reinforce and extend children's ability to fit glossary definitions into specific context.

   1. Write these sentences, underlining the italicized words:

    Tom was *grateful* that he did not fall.

    Father asked Bill to *whitewash* the fence.

After children have read the first sentence and found the glossary definition for *grateful,* have them read the sentence, substituting "thankful" for the word *grateful.*

Pupils substitute a definition for a word in context . . .

Then have the second sentence read. Ask: "Is the word *whitewash* used as a word for a thing or as a word for what we do or did? It always helps to remember how a word is used in a sentence when you're deciding which definition fits." Then lead pupils to see that they must change the order of words to make the second definition fit smoothly into the sentence.

note function of word in a sentence . . .

transpose words in a definition . . .

   2. Next help pupils develop ability in adapting the grammatical form of a definition to fit into context. Write *He paused before going on.* How would children use the definition of *pause* to explain the meaning of *paused* in this sentence? Would they say "He wait before going on" or "He waited before going on"? Make sure youngsters understand that to make the sentence sound right, they must add *ed* to *wait* (or *stop*) in the definition.

make inflectional adaptation . . .

Continue with the sentence *The wind was ruffling the water.* Lead children to note that the first definition of *ruffle,* "make rough or uneven," fits this sentence, but that they must add *ing* to *make* in the definition and change the order of words when they use the definition in the sentence.

combine transposition and inflectional adaptation...

3. Conclude with the following sentences. Note pupils' ability to use substitution, inflectional adaptation, and transposition in adapting meanings of the italicized words to context.

tune definitions into sentences on board...

    John could not *spell* all the words.
    It was suggested that Sequoyah *withdraw* from the village.
    Today *Cherokees* are proud of Sequoyah.
    People *honored* Sequoyah in many ways after he died.
    The woman *scrubbed* the floor with a brush.

● These procedures extend the understanding that vowel-consonant spelling patterns that are clues to vowel sound in accented syllables of two-syllable words also apply to accented syllables of words of more than two syllables.

Children discuss patterned groups of three-syllable words—

1. To begin, write these lists of words, pronounce them, and then have pupils say them and use them in sentences:

carpenter	barrier	terrible
permanent	narrative	terrier
circumstance	character	Cherokee
furniture	parachute	heroine
ornament	charity	periscope

Bring out that the words in all three lists are three-syllable words accented on the first syllable. Then have the words in the first list pronounced again and ask:

—How many consonant letters follow the vowel letter in the accented syllable of each word?

in which one vowel is followed by r and another consonant...

—Do you hear a short vowel sound in any of the accented syllables? Why wouldn't you expect to hear a short vowel sound? [The first of the two consonant letters following the vowel letter is *r*, as in the accented syllables of the two-syllable words *market, person, circus, turkey,* and *corner*.]

in which a is followed by two r's or one r and a vowel letter...

After having the words in the second list pronounced again, ask whether youngsters hear the vowel of *car* in the accented syllable of any of these words. Why would they not expect to hear this vowel sound? Lead the group to recall that in an accented syllable the letter *a* followed by two *r*'s or by one *r* and a vowel letter usually represents the vowel sound heard in the first syllable of *parrot* and *carol*.

Continue similarly with the words in the third list, helping children recall that in an accented syllable the letter *e* followed by two *r*'s or by one *r* and a vowel letter often represents the vowel of *let*—the vowel sound heard in the first syllable of the words *merry* and *very*.

in which e is followed by two r̄'s or one r and a vowel letter ...

2. Next write and pronounce the following words. Then have pupils say them and use them in sentences:

   Baltimore   valentine
          allergy
          alphabet

When youngsters have noted that the first syllable is accented in these three-syllable words, ask:

—What vowel letter do you see in the accented syllable of all these words?

in which a is followed by l ...

—What consonant letter follows the letter *a* in the accented syllables of these words?

—In which word do you hear the vowel of *all* in the accented syllable? What vowel sound do you hear in the accented syllable of the other three words?

Then lead children to recall that in accented syllables the letter *a* followed by *l* is more likely to stand for the vowel of *hat* than for the vowel of *all*, as in *balance*, *valley*, and *Alvin*.

3. To give pupils practice in using the clues to vowel sound they have been discussing, write these sentences and note pupils' ability to identify the italicized three-syllable words.

use these clues to identify three-syllable words on board ...

  Tom's pet *parakeet* can say quite a few words.
  This watch was made in *Germany*.
  Linda says that snakes *terrify* her.
  Look at the *calendar* and tell me what the date is.
  Do you like peanut butter or *marmalade* on your toast?

Conclude by having children turn to page 45 of the *Think-and-Do Book*. There they will have another opportunity to use context and phonetic analysis in identifying unfamiliar words of more than two syllables.

and in Think-and-Do Book exercise.

This article, with a photograph of a letter written in the syllabary which Sequoyah invented, will reinforce pupils' appreciation of his contribution and give them additional insight into this man's lifework.

Children's understanding of the growth of language is enriched through a discussion of the origin of some of the place names in our country. In addition attention is called to entry words in the glossary for which two correct pronunciations are given.

New words: **Washington, D.C.,** statue*, **Oklahoma,** *Mexico*
(amazing*)
Think-and-Do Book: **Pages 46 and 47**

Establishing background

Help pupils relate the previous selection to the one they are about to read by inviting someone to read aloud the last paragraph on page 135. Then ask, "What are some of the ways we honor great men and women?" Comment that if boys and girls were to visit *Washington, D.C.,* or the *state of Oklahoma,* they could see some of the ways in which Sequoyah has been honored. (For youngsters who live in these areas, ask whether they know where a visitor might go to see one of the honors given to Sequoyah. Suggest, too, that they will find it especially interesting to learn about some of the other honors Sequoyah has been given.)

If children are not familiar with the location and importance of Washington, D.C., suggest that they find the entry *Washington* in the glossary and decide which meaning fits this context. If they are not sure what the initials *D.C.* stand for, have them turn to the entry *D.C.* in the glossary. Then ask: "In

Pupils identify new words . . .

what part of the glossary would you expect to find the entry *District of Columbia?* Would you look for it before or after the initials *D.C.?*" Bring out that such words as *District of Columbia* that are used together are often entries in a glossary or dictionary and are listed in alphabetical order as if they were one word. When pupils have found the entry, discuss the information given.

Write the words *redwood* and *fitting* on the board with the suggestion that children can find these words in the glossary if the meaning seems unclear as they read the article. The word *Mexico* will be presented before pupils read page 139.

Guiding interpretation

PAGES 136-137

Send pupils to the first two pages of the article to find out about the ways in which Sequoyah has been honored. During the ensuing discussion bring out the author's opinion of Sequoyah's invention and why she thinks Sequoyah's accomplishment is so amazing. As children talk about the honors he received, be sure to give those who have visited the places mentioned a chance to describe what they saw.

read for specific information . . .

discuss main ideas . . .

The bas-relief sculptures on the bronze doors of the east and west entrances of the Annex Building of the Library of Congress in Washington, D.C., represent those who are credited with developing the written languages of some of the great civilizations of the world. With the exception of Sequoyah all are legendary or mythological characters, because the origins of many forms of written communication are obscure. Sequoyah is honored along with such figures as Cadmus, who was revered in Greek legend for having invented the alphabet, and Odin, who in Norse mythology was the originator of the science of written communication. It is significant that Sequoyah, who lived in relatively modern times, should be honored in this manner. Youngsters might be interested in knowing that even today there are men working to develop alphabets for people in some parts of the world who speak languages that have not yet been written.

If anyone should mention that a particular kind of tree named after this man is spelled *S-e-q-u-o-i-a*, point out that there are several ways of spelling the sounds of Sequoyah's name and that the trees named after him represent one way. You might add that his name is sometimes spelled *S-e-q-u-o-y-a*.

Continue by commenting: "When Sequoyah was quite old, *he went to Mexico* to look for a part of the Cherokee tribe. [Present the italicized phrase.] After he had been gone for quite some time, some of his friends in the United States received a letter. On the next page you'll find a photograph of this letter. Although it was not written by Sequoyah, it was written in the Cherokee writing that he had invented."

identify new word Mexico . . .

PAGES 138-139

When children have commented on the writing, suggest that they read page 139 to find out why the letter was written and what part of it said.

Following silent reading, let pupils discuss Wind's letter:
—Why was the letter written? Who was Wind?
—What did the letter tell you about Sequoyah? about his son? [As pupils note the son's reason for not returning to the Cherokee Nation, clarify the meaning of *the late Sequoyah*.]
—Why do you suppose Sequoyah wanted to find the Cherokee Indians who had moved to Mexico? What does this tell you about how he felt toward his people? How must they have felt toward him?

identify author and purpose of letter . . .

note implied ideas.

Extending competence

● To enrich children's understanding of the growth of language, initiate a discussion of the origin of some of the place names in our country. You might begin by commenting that it is from the big trees named after Sequoyah that Sequoia National Park in California takes its name. Point out also that although the name *Sequoyah* was not given to the state where most of the Cherokee Indians now live, this state was eventually named Oklahoma, from an Indian word meaning "red people."

Pupils note origin of some place names in United States . . .

Then comment that a great number of words have been borrowed from the American Indians and that many have been used in naming cities and states in our country. For example, *Kentucky* comes from an Indian word meaning "level land," *Alabama* has an Indian origin meaning "thicket-clearers" or "vegetable gatherers," *Utah* takes its name from the Ute Indians and means "the hill dwellers" or "those who dwell up high." The names of many cities (*Minneapolis, Chicago, Tallahassee,* and so on) also have Indian origins.

Do youngsters know of any place near them that was given a name borrowed from an Indian word or named after an Indian or Indian tribe? Let children tell what they already know, and then suggest that they ask their parents, grandparents, or other adults in the neighborhood for additional information. Later set aside a discussion period for them to present their findings to the group.

discuss place names in their own area . . .

If your area has no place names of Indian origin, you might encourage boys and girls to find out some of the sources of place names in your locality. Be sure to mention that because it is sometimes very hard or even impossible to learn the true origin of a place name, there may be some disagreement about its origin.

Youngsters' understanding of the growth of language will be enriched further as they read an article about the development of the alphabet we use and complete the exercise on pages 46-47 of the *Think-and-Do Book*.

grasp main ideas in Think-and-Do Book exercise.

● To heighten awareness that there may be more than one correct pronunciation for some words, write the word *Washington* and have it pronounced. Ask how many syllables are heard in this word and which syllable is accented. Do youngsters hear the vowel of *hot* or *all* (write the words) in the accented syllable? Then have them turn to the glossary entry *Washington*. Ask: "How many pronunciations are given for *Washington?* What are they? Which pronunciation of the word do you use?"

Children note that glossary indicates two pronunciations for some words . . .

Continue with the word *booth*. Lead children to note that only one pronunciation is given for *booth* in the glossary, but that two ways of pronouncing the plural are shown. What are they? How do boys and girls pronounce the word *booths?*

Reëmphasize the idea that many words may be pronounced correctly in more than one way and that when two pronunciations are given in the glossary or dictionary, as for the two words just discussed, it does not matter which one youngsters choose. Comment that youngsters will probably want to pronounce these words in the way they are pronounced by most people in the part of the country where they live.

and that either
is acceptable.

Encouraging personal reading

Biographical selections give young minds much to ponder and to grow on. As children read about the trials and triumphs of a famous person, they gain some insight into the kind of person he was, meet some of the people who influenced him, and share a part of his life. They become, to some extent, acquainted with him—and they find this acquaintance exciting. In informal discussions invite boys and girls to share this excitement, this personal knowledge of famous men and women they have gained from independent reading. Encourage them to exchange ideas about people they are especially interested in, recommend books about these persons to one another, and suggest why someone else might enjoy reading these books. If several youngsters have read about the same person, let them specialize a bit, talking over what they learned about him, the qualities of greatness evidenced in his life, and perhaps even the personal hopes and ambitions his example quickened in them as they read.

pages 140·153 | Abe Lincoln

Children will enjoy the humor of this episode from young Lincoln's life and will discover in it some of the qualities that set him on the road to greatness. The informal conversational style of the story points up one means of achieving realistic characterization, leads to a consideration of the effect of time and place upon language, and provides opportunity for adapting the story to dramatic form for oral interpretation.

Competence in using a glossary or dictionary is extended as pupils discuss plural forms and variant spelling of entries.

New words: Mathilda, pa, ma, *trough,* Sarah, *gourdful,* mamma, truth*, interrupted, apron* (Abe*, *Lincoln**, Crawford*, Johnston*, bonnet*, Dennis*, *loft**, *ain't**, *meekly**, rinse*, wiped*, damp*, *blessing**, Lord*, *Thee**, stool*, sternly*, wicked*, *didos**, *reckon**, spanked*, towering*, cheeks*, *mite**, tub*, *dander**, hug*, breathlessly*)

Think-and-Do Book: Pages 48 and 49

Establishing background

When they have read the title of today's selection, encourage children to share their knowledge and impressions of Lincoln. Why do they think a story about Abraham Lincoln is included in this unit? How long ago did Lincoln live? (The glossary entry *Lincoln* will help establish the time of this episode as more than one hundred years ago.) What do pupils know about Lincoln as a boy and a young man?

Children talk about Abraham Lincoln . . .

Next call attention to the picture on page 140, and introduce Abe's stepsisters, Betsy and *Mathilda* (mə til′də) Johnston. (If necessary, clarify relationships in the Lincoln family by referring to the entries *stepsister, stepbrother, stepfather,* and *stepmother* that are included in the glossary.) Then continue: "The girls have *interrupted their talking* just long enough to say something to Abe. They and their mother, *Sarah Lincoln,* were going to visit a new neighbor. Before they left, Mrs. Lincoln gave Abe a *gourdful of soap* and told him to go down to the *horse trough* to wash his hair. [You might have pupils turn to the glossary at this time for the meaning of the words *gourd* and *trough.*] Abe *obeyed his mamma,* and while he was following her orders, he had a wonderful idea for a practical joke.

and identify new words . . .

"As you read about his joke, you'll notice that young Abe's life was different from yours in many ways. Even the language his family used was somewhat different from that used in many parts of our country today. For example, most children called their parents *ma and pa.* The glossary will help you with some words that may be unfamiliar to you." As you list glossary entries, include the words *body, oblige, threat, whitewash.*

anticipate language differences in the story . . .

Interpreting the story

The pictures and direct conversation will enable most youngsters to read this story easily as a unit. If you wish to divide the story for a particular group, however, suggest that pupils stop reading when they reach the sentence *Come on, we're going to play a joke on Mamma* (top of page 144). After speculating about the possible nature of the joke, they can read to the bottom of page 149, evaluate the proposed discipline, and then finish the story to discover how Abe felt about his punishment.

Immediately after silent reading encourage children to express their reactions to the story. Also give them a chance to discuss elements of humor that appealed to them.

share main points of episode . . .

Then use the questions that follow to point up the characterization of the Lincolns, particularly of Abe and Mrs. Lincoln.
—Which of Lincoln's traits that you already knew about are brought out in this story?
—What qualities does Lincoln display in this story that you did not know he possessed?

—What characteristics did Lincoln show as a youth that helped him become a great man? [Responses should include his eagerness for knowledge, his sense of humor, his willingness to admit that his joke was a mistake and to make amends for it, and his understanding of the other members of his family. On page 48 of the *Think-and-Do Book* children are to identify words that might describe both Abe and Sarah Lincoln.]

—Do you think Abe was fortunate in having a stepmother like Sarah Lincoln? Why? How do you know that she was an understanding person? that she had a sense of humor?

make inferences on basis of incidents in story ...

—Do you think that whitewashing the cabin was a fair punishment for Abe's prank? Why [or why not]?

—Think about the way in which this story is written. How does the author make you feel that you know the Lincoln family?

discuss author's style of writing ...

Responses to the last question in the preceding section will provide opportunity to point up the influence of time as well as place upon language usage. Write on the board or read aloud the following sentence: *Take a gourdful of soap, go down to the horse trough, and wash your head.* Then inquire:

—How might your mother give you the same instructions? [She might say, 'Take this bottle (tube, jar) of shampoo, go into the bathroom, and wash your hair.'] Why should your mother's instructions be different from Mrs. Lincoln's?

note how language changes with passage of time ...

—What word or words do people today often use instead of the word *bonnet?* [Similarly discuss the use of *ain't* on pages 142 and 143, *That ought to learn him* on page 149, and *Now you be acting like a young one again* on page 153.]

—What do you call a paper or cloth container for carrying things? Do you know what it is called in other parts of our country? [bag, poke, sack]

and how it varies from place to place ...

—When it is raining, do you wear *overshoes, rubbers, galoshes, boots,* or *gumshoes?*

—What other words might be used instead of *right tasty* [page 141]? *How come* [page 141]? *didos* [page 148]?

—What other expressions in the story were new to you? How would you express the same ideas?

—Do you think there is any one way of expressing an idea that is best for all places and all times? Why not?

Page 49 of the *Think-and-Do Book* is designed to strengthen awareness of time relationships and ability to make comparisons. After reading about activities in the nineteenth century, pupils explain how the same actions might be carried on today.

ORAL INTERPRETATION

Today's story is an excellent one for informal play reading. This can be done quite simply by having pupils read from their books without making major movements around the stage. A table and a few chairs will suffice for properties.

To prepare for oral reading, let children examine the story for clues that suggest how and why the persons act and speak as they do. In working out each episode, readers need time to concentrate on the dialogue they will read aloud and to study narrative links that explain how the characters talked.

look for clues to character traits...

study the dialogue...

When pupils are familiar with dialogue and characterizations, teach them to pick up cues in reading conversation. Suggest that each character listen carefully, react as others read, and then answer as he would in real life.

read conversations in a natural manner...

Since interrupted speeches require special attention if readers are to achieve the rhythm and intonations of everyday conversations, emphasize that the first speaker think to the end of his idea and that the interrupting speaker prepare to speak immediately upon hearing a specific word cue. With Sarah's speech on page 141 (*Before you put the potatoes on——*), for example, suggest that Sarah think the entire sentence she would have said if Abe had not interrupted. While she speaks, Abe should be thinking how much he wants to read his book and be ready to say *I can read?* when Sarah says *on*.

practice reading interrupted speeches...

A narrator can introduce the first scene, reading to the point of Sarah's first speech. Sarah and Abe should then continue without interruption through the third paragraph on page 142.

convert story to play form...

In preparing the episode at the watering trough, ask listeners and readers to make vivid mental pictures as the narrator, Abe, and Johnny read. After the first reading let several pairs pantomime simultaneously the action they visualized. Then, while another group reads, have everyone listen for details he may have missed the first time. As others pantomime the scene,

pantomime scene as pictured mentally while listening.

encourage Abe and Johnny to feel the emotions and sensations suggested in the story. This preparation should precipitate an animated reading by the narrator, an exuberant shout from Johnny, and a mischievous reply from Abe in the oral reading.

In the scene at the supper table the narrator will read only the second and third paragraphs on page 144 and the third paragraph on page 150. Remind the seven characters that they must tell the rest of this part of the story with their pantomimed reactions and their reading of the lines.

The last scene between Sarah and Abe can be developed in much the same way as the preceding ones, with a narrator reading the fourth and fifth paragraphs on page 150, the last paragraph on page 151, the first one on page 152, and the first on page 153.

Extending competence

● Call attention to plural forms and variant spellings of words that are shown in the glossary. First write the word *stadium*, and ask pupils how they would spell the plural form or the word that means "more than one stadium." After they have turned to the glossary to check their opinions, point out that there are two correct ways to form the plural of a few words. Two other entries with alternate plurals are *dido* and *Cherokee*.

Next suggest that children use the glossary to find the plural of the word *Sioux*. If necessary, explain that the letters *pl.* are the abbreviation for *plural*. When pupils have noted that the plural and singular forms are identical, see whether they can think of other words in this category. (*Sheep* and *deer* may be familiar.) Draw out the fact that context clues indicate whether such words mean "one" or "more than one."

By calling attention to the entries *snowshoes, sprout, stag*, lead pupils to conclude that the plural form is shown in the glossary only when it differs from the usual plural form.

In a similar manner use the glossary entries *good-by, mid²*, and *syrup* to illustrate that there are some words in the English language that can be spelled correctly in more than one way and to show how two spellings are indicated.

Pupils observe that some words have alternate plural forms ...

discuss words with same plural and singular form ...

note when plural form is found in glossary ...

talk about variant spellings of words.

● To increase pupils' awareness of their growing skill in word analysis, comment that in today's story they identified independently twenty-four words that had not been used previously in their basic readers. Calling attention to the story title, ask children what clues helped them identify the first word (*Abe*) and the second (*Lincoln*). As youngsters discuss the other starred words, lead them to point out context clues and understandings about word analysis that aided in determining pronunciation and meaning of words. You might also inquire whether they used the glossary to check the meaning or the pronunciation of some of these words.

If the discussion reveals that some pupils failed to distinguish between words that are similar in form, you might use the procedure suggested on page 26 of this *Guidebook*. As boys and girls explain how they identified words, notice which children need more help in mastering skills in word analysis and the use of context clues. Observations of individual problems might serve as a basis for regrouping pupils for additional practice on specific skills.

Children explain how they identified new words in story.

Extending interests

Introduce the book from which today's story was taken, Frances Cavanah's *Abe Lincoln Gets His Chance,* by pointing up its theme—that courage can turn handicaps into opportunities. When several children have read it, they might discuss the development of this theme. Pupils who have also read Ingri and Parin d'Aulaire's *Abraham Lincoln* will, by their contributions to the discussion, stimulate interest in this biography as well.

Pupils read biographies of Abraham Lincoln . . .

Then read *Martin and Abraham Lincoln,* a story based on a true incident, by Catherine Cate Coblentz. Afterwards encourage youngsters to bring out some of the ways Abe helped Martin and how young Martin, in turn, gave comfort to his President. (If the book is not available, you can find the story in *The Arbuthnot Anthology of Children's Literature.*)

listen to true incident in Lincoln's life . . .

talk about implied ideas . . .

You might want to recommend *Clara Barton, Soldier of Mercy,* by Mary Catherine Rose, a biography of a young woman who also talked over her troubles with President Lincoln.

enjoy a biography of Clara Barton.

pages 154•156 | Nancy Hanks
and
A Reply to Nancy Hanks

The moving poem "Nancy Hanks" arouses a desire to respond to the mother's wistful inquiry about a son known and loved by millions. This wish to comfort Abe's mother is fulfilled as children read one boy's reply to her questions.

Establishing background

To supply information necessary for understanding the poem, lead children to recall that Sarah Lincoln was Abe's stepmother, and explain that Lincoln's mother, Nancy Hanks Lincoln, died when Abe was nine years old.

Then comment: "Rosemary Carr Benét has written a poem in which she imagines that Abe's own mother is asking questions about her son. As you listen to the poem, notice what the author thinks Nancy Hanks would want to know."

Pupils learn theme of poem . . .

Guiding interpretation

PAGES 154-155

Read "Nancy Hanks" aloud to children, and afterwards let them share their spontaneous reactions. Encourage youngsters to discuss what the poem suggests about Nancy Hanks' feelings toward her son and the reasons for her concern. Pupils should recall from the preceding story that Tom was Abe's father. Although they may have received the impression that the family was poor, you may need to clarify the meaning of *rolling stone, pinching times, get on.*

After boys and girls have had an opportunity to examine the illustration on pages 154-155 and to express their thoughts about it, suggest that they think about possible answers to Nancy Hanks' questions as you read the poem once again.

listen to and discuss poem . . .

To <u>introduce the theme of the second poem</u>, ask: "Which of Nancy Hanks' questions were answered in the story about Abe's prank? How would you answer some of her other questions?"

discuss answers to questions Nancy Hanks asked in first poem ...

Continue: "One boy who heard the poem 'Nancy Hanks' responded to her questions by writing another poem. You'll want to read his answer, which is called 'A Reply to Nancy Hanks.' " Although the words *whom* and *heart* may be new to some children, they should be easily identified.

read silently one child's reply to these questions ...

When boys and girls have read Julius Silberger's reply, let them tell how they think it would have made Lincoln's mother feel. You might also ask whether they are familiar with the statue pictured. If no one can identify it, explain that it is in the Lincoln Memorial in Washington, D.C. Can pupils think why this is an appropriate illustration for this poem? How does it support the statement that Lincoln *lives in the heart/Of everyone?*

relate illustration to poem ...

<u>Pupils will also enjoy reading aloud "A Reply to Nancy Hanks."</u> After they have sensed the tempo and rhythm of the poem by listening to you read it, let groups of three read it aloud. One child could read the first four lines, another the next two, and a third the final lines.

read the poem aloud.

When youngsters can read the poem smoothly without interruption, suggest that the two poems be read in sequence, with you reading "Nancy Hanks" and three children responding with "A Reply to Nancy Hanks."

Perhaps the knowledge that "A Reply to Nancy Hanks" was written by a young boy will inspire some individuals or groups to write their own answers to Nancy Hanks' questions. If so, their efforts should be encouraged. You should not, however, expect results comparable to the poem in the text, which was written by a somewhat older student.

This account of Jamestown and one of its leaders provides an interesting parallel to the stories of Pilgrim Plymouth that children read in *Roads to Follow*. As pupils discuss the difficulties encountered by the Virginia settlers and John Smith's efforts to keep the community alive, they are led to note the different purposes of the two settlements.

In group discussion and in the *Think-and-Do Book* children are encouraged to make comparisons based on information they have gained through reading. The prefix *re-* is introduced in another exercise.

New words: **Virginia, terror*, captured*, warriors, Powhatan, rebuilt** (*Smith**, tents*, protected*, beads*, pale*, prisoner*, clubs*, *spared**)
Think-and-Do Book: **Pages 50 and 51**

Establishing background

Cue children to the time and setting of the selection that they are about to read by leading them to recall that the Pilgrims settled over three hundred years ago in what is now called Massachusetts and by asking whether they were the first people to come from Europe and settle in the New World. Then explain: "Several years before the Pilgrims arrived, a group of people had come to America and settled farther south. Like the Pilgrims these people faced many difficulties, and they were not sure that the Indians would be friendly. Some thought that there was little danger of being captured, while others thought that *Indian warriors might attack* at any minute.

"As you read about this group of settlers and about one of their leaders, Captain Smith, you may want to use your glossaries to find out about another important person, *Powhatan*

Pupils relate
Jamestown settlement
to early Plymouth ...

identify new words ...

[(pou'ə tan')], and to learn something about these places [list *Virginia* and *Jamestown* on the board]." The new word *rebuilt* may be introduced before children read pages 159-162.

Guiding interpretation

PAGES 157-159

To help youngsters organize factual materials as they read, ask what they would like to find out about these early settlers. As they reply, list these or similar questions on the board:

Who were the settlers?

Why did they come to America?

Where did they settle?

When did they arrive?

What problems did they face in a strange land?

Then suggest that when pupils have read to the third paragraph on page 159, they stop and think about answers to the questions on the board.

read to find specific details . . .

After silent reading lead pupils to summarize the information they have found in brief answers to each question. (Leave the questions on the board for later discussion.)

Then ask: "What did Captain Smith do that tells you he was concerned for the safety of the settlers? Was he successful? Why not? As you finish the article, you'll discover what happened to Captain Smith and the colony at Jamestown. You'll also find out whether the settlement was ever *rebuilt* [present the word] as Plymouth was."

organize findings . . .

read for further information . . .

PAGES 159-162

Initiate a discussion of John Smith's capture and the friendship that resulted by asking:

—What was the story that Captain Smith told about his capture? How many of you have heard or read about his adventure with the Indians before?

—How did the Indian girl's friendship help the other settlers?

—How did the colony change after the first year? Why do you think the women and children had been left behind at first?

discuss a well-known incident . . .

and consider its effects . . .

—What finally happened to the Jamestown colony? Why do you suppose the settlers decided not to rebuild their homes?

—What would you find if you were to visit Jamestown today?

make inference.

Extending competence

● To help youngsters compare and contrast early Plymouth and the Jamestown settlement, review the answers to questions that were previously written on the board, and lead children to consider the points listed below under each one. The questions are repeated here for your convenience.

Who were the settlers?

—What did the settlers of Jamestown and Plymouth have in common?

—In what way were the two groups different? [Point out that whole families settled in Plymouth but that only men and boys founded Jamestown.]

Children discuss differences in two expeditions . . .

Why did they come to America?

—Why had the Jamestown settlers crossed the ocean?

—Did the Pilgrims come for the same reason? What made them decide to settle in a new land?

—Can you think of a reason why only men and boys went to Jamestown? why the Pilgrims brought their families?

and reasons for the differences . . .

Where did they settle?

—Which group of settlers sailed up a river to land? Which group stayed near the ocean?

—Which group could step from ship to shore? Why?

—Which group of settlers probably found the land muddy and squishy underfoot?

talk about details of place and time . . .

When did they arrive?

—Did the group at Plymouth or at Jamestown settle first?

—About how long was it until the other settlers came?

What problems did they face in a strange land?

—What did both groups of settlers need for their new homes in America? Which group took greater care to provide homes? food? protection?

consider settlers' common problems and their solution . . .

—Which group do you think found it easier to work together? Why do you think this may have been true? [Lead children to recall that the Pilgrims had signed an agreement to work together and had chosen a leader before they landed.]

—In which settlement was there greater danger of Indian attacks? Why?

—Which settlement faced a greater problem in providing the things its people needed? Why might it have been harder to provide for a group that included women and children than for a group of men and boys?

Finally encourage pupils to examine the picture of the recon- structed settlement on page 162 and to compare the buildings with the house shown in the picture on pages 144-145 of *Roads to Follow*. Do the Jamestown houses look like the ones at Plymouth? In what ways? In what ways are they different?

contrast details of illustrations . . .

The exercise on pages 50-51 of the *Think-and-Do Book* will provide further opportunity for children to compare the settle- ments at Jamestown and Plymouth.

make comparisons in Think-and-Do Book exercise.

This lesson introduces the prefix *re-* and checks pupils' ability to identify derivatives formed with this prefix.

To begin, write the sentence *Jamestown was not rebuilt after the fire* and have it read. Pointing to the word *rebuilt,* ask: "What prefix is added to the word *built* to make the word *re- built?* What does *rebuilt* mean in the sentence?" Suggest that pupils find the prefix *re-* in their glossaries and read the defini- tions. Then have the group tell which definition explains the meaning of the prefix *re-* in the word *rebuilt*.

Pupils tell what prefix re- means in rebuilt . . .

read definitions of re- in glossary . . .

Next write the following sentences on the board, underlining the italicized words. As each one is read aloud, have boys and girls explain in their own words what the underlined word means in the sentence.

identify in context derivatives beginning with prefix re-.

I *rewrote* the letter because I had made some mistakes.
The truck had to be *reloaded* after the accident.
The man *repaid* the money he had borrowed.
Dad decided to *repaint* the fence.
Mother *rearranged* the chairs before the party began.
Sam *repacked* his suitcase because he couldn't shut it.

Extending interests

For the thoughts and impressions of a child who aspires to deeds like those of people who have gone before, read Mary Austin's "Song of Greatness" (in *Time for Poetry*). After children have heard the poem, ask whether they have ever dreamed that they, like Captain Smith, might someday make new discoveries or explore the unknown.

Then, for youngsters who have indicated particular interest in the early settlement of our country, introduce *The First Book of the Early Settlers,* by Louise Dickinson Rich. The first three chapters present a fine comparison of the settlements that third-graders have read about, Plymouth and Jamestown. When children have heard these chapters, let them enlarge upon their earlier comparison of the two settlements by discussing the new understandings they acquired as they listened.

Conclude by recommending two light-hearted stories centering upon the search for a new home—Le Grand's *How Space Rockets Began* and Munro Leaf's *Wee Gillis.* In the tongue-in-cheek style for which he is known, Le Grand tells how Wind-wagon Smith found the place he was looking for and hints that without the first "space rocket" there might not have been a wind wagon, railroads, or even a city named Chicago. Youngsters will also be delighted by the very satisfactory way Wee Gillis solved the problem of where he should live. After displaying the books, put them on the library table for children to read and enjoy at their leisure.

Children associate their feelings with those of a leader ...

listen to comparative accounts of two settlements ...

and contrast them on the basis of added information ...

enjoy imaginative touches in two stories with similar themes.

| The Girl
with Three Names

This biography, which includes almost all that is known about Pocahontas' life, offers an unusual opportunity for children to observe character development.

As pupils compare this selection with the preceding one, they recognize how contrasting points of view influence the way an incident is recounted. They also note how information gained from more than one source can be organized to develop a more complete understanding of a time, place, person, situation, or event. In addition children review ways the glossary can be used in determining pronunciation and meaning of words.

New words: Matoaka, Rebecca, *Pocahontas,* immediately, *palace** (*meal**, scrape*, arguing*, argument*, church*, *Rolfe**, Dale*, Thomas*, princess*)

Think-and-Do Book: Pages 52, 53, and 54

Establishing background

Introduce the selection by having children find and read the title in the table of contents (page 4). Then say: "Perhaps most of the girls you know have been given three names, but probably not in the same way or for the same reasons as the girl you'll read about today. *Immediately after* she was born, this girl was given the name of *Matoaka* [(mat′ō ä′kə)]. The other names by which she was known are *Rebecca* and *Pocahontas* [(pō′kə hon′təs)]. Do you recognize any of these names? What do you know about this girl?"

Then continue: "Do you think she might have known any of the other people we've read about in this unit? Read the first page of the selection to check your opinions about these questions. If you forget how to pronounce *Matoaka* or *Pocahontas,* you can find these names in the glossary."

Pupils identify new words ...

Guiding interpretation

PAGE 163

When youngsters comment that the three names were given at different times, encourage them to explain the meaning of the name Pocahontas. Did they recognize Powhatan as the name of the Indian chief mentioned in connection with Captain John Smith? If it is not suggested, point up the relationship between this selection and the previous one by asking whether Pocahontas might have known some of the settlers at Jamestown. What clue indicated that she might have? Suggest that as children finish the selection, they notice which part of it reminds them of the preceding one and also observe how much of Pocahontas' life is covered.

PAGES 164-171

Emphasize the reasons and motives underlying Pocahontas' actions as you guide a discussion of the events in her life.
—What words might be used to describe Pocahontas as a young girl? [*mischievous, athletic, intelligent, curious, friendly*]
—Why do you suppose she asked her father to spare Captain Smith's life?
—In what other ways did she help the settlers at Jamestown?
—Why was she a good person to settle an argument between the Indians and the settlers?
—Why wasn't she afraid in the woods at night as she took a message to Jamestown? How had her childhood prepared her for this task?
—What did the author mean when she wrote that in England the young Indian woman *looked more like a Rebecca than a little Pocahontas?* Do you think Captain Smith thought of her as Rebecca or as Pocahontas? Why?
—In what ways might Pocahontas be compared with Squanto, the Indian who helped the early settlers at Plymouth?

WHOLE STORY

Guide boys and girls in comparing the accounts of Captain Smith's capture and release, told from two points of view.

discuss meaning of title...

make inference from detail on first page...

note character traits of the young girl...

discuss relationship between childhood and later events...

First ask them to locate the parts of the last two stories that tell about the same event (page 159, paragraph 3 through page 161, paragraph 3; page 165, paragraph 3 through page 167, paragraph 4).

compare two accounts of same event...

Then guide children in an examination of the two accounts with such questions as the ones below. As answers are located in the text, have the pertinent sentences read. If the same idea is found in both reports, ask pupils to point out likenesses and differences. If only one story recounts a particular incident, encourage youngsters to think about why it was included in one and not in the other.

and note reasons for differences...

—Which account tells that John Smith was captured and taken to Powhatan? [page 159, paragraph 3; page 165, paragraph 3]

—Which one describes the room to which Captain Smith was taken and the position of the Indians? [page 159, paragraph 4]

—Which one describes Captain Smith's appearance? [page 165, paragraph 4]

—Which one describes the actions of the Indians and thoughts of Captain Smith? [page 160, paragraph 2 and paragraph 3, first sentence]

—Which one explains why Captain Smith's life was spared? [page 161, paragraph 2; page 167, paragraph 1]

—Which describes the friendship that developed between Captain Smith and Pocahontas? [page 161, paragraph 3; page 167, paragraphs 3 and 4]

Next point up the value of organizing information from various sources to obtain a more complete picture of an event or problem. Comment: "Each of the last two selections in this unit helps us understand the other one. Let's look at them carefully to discover how both of them together help us understand better some of the things that happened during the early years at Jamestown."

—In which story did we find out that Captain John Smith returned to England?

—What effect did his return to England have on Pocahontas' visits to Jamestown?

perceive relationships of time and cause-effect...

—In what way had Jamestown changed by the time Pocahontas returned to the settlement?

—How does this change in Jamestown clue us to the time that Captain Smith probably returned to England? Can you find a paragraph in the Jamestown story that covers this period of time? [page 161, paragraph 4] Why do you suppose the author didn't choose to tell about Captain Smith's departure from Jamestown? This title of the selection gives a clue.

—Read the first paragraph on page 159. Was this Indian attack the same one that is referred to in the fifth paragraph on page 167? How do you know it was not?

use information in one selection to interpret statements in another.

—Now read the fourth paragraph on page 167. What do we know about the importance of the gifts of food referred to here? [See page 161, paragraph 3.]

—Do you think Jamestown was still standing when Pocahontas' son returned to Virginia? What makes you think it wasn't? [See page 161, paragraph 5, and page 171, paragraph 4.]

Extending competence

● Bring out the difference between this biographical selection and others in the unit by focusing attention on the time span. Lead children to observe that the story begins with Pocahontas' infancy and tells about important events in her entire life. After they have looked through the story to learn how long she lived and have compared this with glossary information about her, point out that this selection includes most of the known facts about Pocahontas. Do pupils think this is true of any of the other selections in the unit? What reasons can they give for their opinions? Which of the other selections covered long periods of time? Which covered a short time?

Children compare selection with others in the unit.

Next draw attention to the final paragraphs of the selection about Pocahontas that tie the story to the present day. Were any of the other selections in this unit, "Interesting People along the Way," related to the present day? In what way? (Some youngsters may recall references to the current consumption of hot dogs and to the memorials to Sequoyah that can be visited today.)

● To provide an interesting review of dictionary skills, suggest that pupils turn to the glossary in *More Roads to Follow* and see how quickly they can answer the questions below. As you pronounce each italicized word, write its root form.

Pupils recall and use dictionary skills in locating entries . . .

—Would you expect to find the word *syllable* in the first, middle, or last part of the glossary? Where would you find *oblige? wedge? France?*

—Which would you expect to find first, *meal* or *meek?* Why?

—Is the word *fate* on page 272? Is the word *height* on this page? How can you tell without looking at all the entries?

—What word on page 273 is spelled correctly in two ways?

—Are there two *p*'s in the spelling of the word *chopped?* Why are *chopped* and *chopping,* but not *hastened* and *hastening,* shown following the definitions of the entry words?

—Why are there two words in heavy black type following the definition of the entry *dido* on page 270? Why isn't the plural form of the word *doe* shown?

in deriving meanings . . .

—If, when you read the definition for the entry *D.C.* on page 270, you did not know where the District of Columbia is located, how could you find out?

—Which entry word on page 271 has a special meaning included in the definitions?

—How would you say the sentence *The men were corralling the wild horses* [write the sentence], using a glossary definition in place of the word *corralling?*

—Could you buy a chair made of *pine?* Might you *pine* for someone? What does the small number after the entry word *pine* tell you to do? Which entry of *pine* is illustrated? which definition? In what three ways does the glossary help you understand the meanings of *pine?*

—Is Alaska larger than New York? How do you know? Should the word *Alaska* be divided at the end of a line? Between what two letters might it be divided?

—In what ways does the glossary indicate the size of things?

—Why is *Matoaka* an entry word in the glossary?

and in deriving pronunciations.

—Which word on page 274 can be pronounced correctly in two different ways? What are the two pronunciations for this word [write *loft*]? What are the two correct pronunciations for this word [write *syrup*]?

Extending interests

As an inducement for boys and girls who seldom visit the library table, you might recommend Augusta Stevenson's biography of the popular frontiersman, *Daniel Boone, Boy Hunter*.

Then, just for fun, select a few poems from Karla Kuskin's *In the Middle of the Trees*. Pupils will enjoy the personification in "The Tree and Me," the delightful last line of "The Hat," and the bit of nonsense called "Around and Around."

Pupils read biography of Daniel Boone . . .

and respond to poetry.

Encouraging personal reading

Because there will always be youngsters whose interests lead them to books bearing little relation to the theme of the unit, be sure to give these children a chance to share their enthusiasm for books they have read.

Children share independent reading interests.

As a child talks about one of his favorites, he might use the illustrations to tell just enough about the story to tease listeners' curiosity, explain the problem facing the main character (without, of course, giving away its solution), or compare a story character or problem with one youngsters have read about in *More Roads to Follow*.

Evaluating progress

The responses on pages 52-53 and 54 of the *Think-and-Do Book* will help you evaluate pupils' progress in using ideas gained through reading and in interpreting dictionary definitions and pronunciations. As children use pages 52-53, they must think about whether a particular individual evidenced a certain personal quality and decide which of the other people pictured had this same quality. The dictionary definitions of the qualities referred to are included on page 53.

Pupils take informal tests in Think-and-Do Book.

Page 54 provides a means of testing each child's competence in using a short pronunciation key to determine the pronunciations of words found in a glossary or dictionary.

ROADS
TO
MAKE-BELIEVE

Introducing Unit Three

For many children the world of make-believe is rounded by the words "once upon a time" and "happily ever after." In this unit boys and girls will find the fanciful element represented in several ways, including new and old fanciful tales, the fables of Aesop, and humorous verse.

Before pupils open their books, comment: "Not all the roads we follow in this book will lead us to people and places that could actually be visited today or long ago. When Rachel Field wrote the poem 'Roads,' she had some other ideas about where they might lead. As you listen, notice what other kinds of places she had in mind."

When children have heard the poem on page 172, let them tell which of these roads they would like to follow. Which ones might they find in real life? Which journeys would they have to make in their imaginations?

Pupils note element of fantasy in poem ...

Suggest that pupils follow along as you reread the poem, this time to enjoy the descriptive words the author uses in each two-line vignette. Then call attention to the unit title page, and ask where the roads in this unit will take them. What kinds of stories would they expect to find? Are any of the characters in the illustration familiar to them?

relate poem to unit theme ...

Invite children to examine the table of contents and leaf through the unit to find some familiar faces and to discover what other kinds of make-believe selections they will be reading. Lead pupils to note that the unit contains many humorous poems as well as fanciful stories. Then point out that although some stories—for example, "Pippi Is a Thing-Finder"—are comparatively new tales of make-believe, others—like "The Three Wishes"—have been told in many lands from generation to generation.

briefly examine the unit.

Conclude by commenting that children are probably familiar with the first story in this unit and may regard the main character as an old friend.

pages 175·186 | Puss-in-Boots

The hero of this story epitomizes the talking beasts who cleverly surmount all obstacles in order to assure the triumph of good over evil. Such tales help children satisfy vicariously their desires for achievement. As this story is contrasted with others, pupils become aware that different types of story development require various techniques of interpretation.

In an exercise suggestions are given for increasing pupils' awareness of context, pictures, and the glossary as aids in determining the meaning of new words.

New words: salad*, Willowonder, *courtyard*, *majesty**, cruel*, *ogre*, aha (puss-in-boots*, jacket*, master*, sack*, duke*, poked*, *butler**, wits*, throne*, accept*, *dine**, *coach**, rumbling*, drowning*, alas*, guard*, shivering*, cape*, *barley**, *hallo**, *castle**, greedy*, tiger*, split*, *larder**, *faithful**, favor*, clap*, cloud*, handsome*)

Think-and-Do Book: Pages 55, 56, and 57

Establishing background

Stimulate interest in the story by commenting: "On your first trip along the 'Roads to Make-Believe' you'll meet a remarkable cat and his master, the *Duke of Willowonder*. At one point you'll hear the word *Aha* roaring through a castle and *the courtyard outside*. This tells who shouted 'Aha.' [Write *an ogre*, and suggest use of the glossary if pupils need help with pronunciation and meaning.] Many of you have probably heard this story. As you read it, notice how it is different from and how it is like the story you may know."

The words *herdsmen, presently,* and *spell* should be included in the list of words that are to be found in the glossary.

Children identify new words...

Most youngsters will enjoy reading the entire story without interruption. If pupils are not familiar with the story, however, and you feel that it would be advisable for them to read it in two parts, suggest that they pause at the bottom of page 180. Discussion of the first part of the story could center around the development of the cat's plan up to this point and speculation about what else he might have in mind.

Interpreting the story

Ask children to think of one word that best describes Puss-in-Boots, and then give pupils time to tell which of his clever tricks and remarks they enjoyed most. During this conversation make sure all understand the motives for Puss' request that Jack hide his clothes and the cat's desire that the King think the fields, cattle, and castle belonged to the Duke.

infer motives for actions . . .

Then let boys and girls who are familiar with other versions compare them with this one. If a different name is mentioned for Jack, you could explain that the story came to us from France and that the French name, Marquis of Carabas (kär ä bä′), is often used when the story is retold.

compare different versions of story . . .

To point up the importance of reinterpreting the events of this story in the light of information disclosed at the end, guide pupils in comparing the structure of the selection with that of other stories. Comment that in many stories the author lets the reader know exactly what the characters are thinking and planning as each action takes place. To illustrate, have children turn to "Maile's Lei" on page 80 in their books. Ask why Maile was going up the mountain and why she was excited about the contest. Does the author explain the answers to these questions on the first pages of the story? Similarly lead pupils to note that on page 82 the specific reference to poor crops and Maile's recognition of Tutu's need explains why Maile decided to help Tutu.

note structure of familiar stories . . .

Continue: "In other stories the author may even give the reader information that some of the story characters don't have. Can you remember any stories in which this is so? [Pupils may recall the exchange of grocery lists in 'Betsy and Ellen Go to Market' or the story 'Funny Faces' in *Roads to Follow*.]

"Now let's look at 'Puss-in-Boots' and see how it differs from these other kinds of stories." Guide discussion of the first episode with such questions as the following:

contrast type of story development in "Puss-in-Boots" . . .

—As you read page 175, did you find out what plan the cat had when he asked for a jacket and boots? [If children attempt to explain his plan by using information revealed later in the story, challenge them to indicate where on page 175 the author tells this.]

—Was Puss interested in helping Jack make a living? What did you read on page 175 that suggests he was? [*you'll not be sorry*]

—Was making Jack rich the only thing Puss-in-Boots wanted? What makes you think as you do? At what point in the story did you find out that the cat had something else in mind?

Continue with the other parts of the cat's scheme: his gifts to the King (pages 176-178), his arrangement to present Jack to the King (pages 179-180), his instructions to the guards of the barley field and the herdsmen (page 181), his plan to get rid of the ogre (pages 181-183), his request that Jack kill him (page 185). In each instance have youngsters point out what Puss-in-Boots did, noting whether the author explains the motive for the actions at the time they take place. Then help them bring out that the reasons for everything the cat did are not made clear until the final page of the story.

note that the final episode clarifies motives for earlier actions . . .

Finally comment: "When we read a story in which the author doesn't tell us until the end what is going on in a character's mind, we should think back through the whole story after we finish reading it. Can someone explain why?" Help children conclude that we may need to do this in order to understand why the character acted as he did.

Responses on page 55 of the *Think-and-Do Book* will help you evaluate pupils' ability to interpret cause-effect relationships that can be fully understood only in light of the whole story.

As youngsters discuss the fanciful elements in this story and recall similar ones in other stories, develop awareness of characteristics that are common to many folk tales.

—What was the first clue that this was going to be a fanciful story?

—Can you think of other folk tales you've heard or read in which animals talk?

—Are there other things in this story that remind you of familiar fairy tales? [Children will probably recognize as common characteristics the idea of breaking a spell and the repetitive element in the way Puss-in-Boots announces his presence at the palace and castle.]

note repetition and other characteristics of folk tales . . .

ORAL INTERPRETATION

The episodes in which the cat takes presents to the King and outwits the ogre provide a good opportunity to encourage pupils to use appropriate variations in volume in reading aloud as they do in conversing. After observing that as we listen to people talk, we hear them speak loudly sometimes and quietly at other times, ask:

discuss causes for variations in volume . . .

—If you were speaking to someone at a great distance, would you whisper? Why not?

—In what situations in the story did Puss-in-Boots have to talk loudly?

—Did the ogre speak with the same volume all the time? Why didn't he?

Next focus attention on the episode in which the cat presents the rabbit to the King, beginning with the fourth paragraph on page 176. Suggest: "Before you read your part, think where you are in relation to the other characters, what you are doing, and how you feel. As you read, try to see the characters you are speaking to." Then, if a child who is reading the part of the cat does not use appropriate variations in volume, you might ask: "Where was the cat when he first called out? Where was he when he spoke next? Would he speak the same way in both places? Why not?" If a child speaks too softly, urge him to go across the room from the King before he reads the line in the courtyard.

visualize relative positions of characters . . .

sense that place relationships, character traits, and feelings affect volume . . .

To help a child who seems overly self-conscious while reading aloud, focus attention on the characterization by asking: "What kind of cat is Puss-in-Boots? Try walking up to the

King as the cat would, with the rabbit in the sack over your shoulder. Remember how confident he is that he can get the King interested in seeing Jack."

Since oral interpretation depends on familiarity with the text and an understanding of the characters, repetition of scenes by different casts is frequently helpful. You might suggest to pupils that listening to classmates read aloud helps them read well when their turn comes.

Continue with the scene in which the cat presents two ducks to the King. Before children read aloud the scene between the cat and the ogre, remind those who take the part of the ogre to think about what happens when he turns into a tiger.

interpret ogre's transformations by changes in speech.

Extending competence

● **Pages 56 and 57 of the *Think-and-Do Book* may be used at this time.** On page 56 pupils read another old tale, and then number in sequence the main ideas of the selection.

In Think-and-Do Book pupils note sequence of events . . .

Before introducing page 57 of the *Think-and-Do Book,* call attention to some of the expressions in "Puss-in-Boots" that are idiomatic or unusual in some way. After children have read the last sentence on page 177, let them tell what the last two lines mean. Continue with *caught the fancy of* (page 182, paragraph 3) and *I am off to my other lands* (page 186, paragraph 3). Then suggest that boys and girls turn to page 57 of the *Think-and-Do Book,* where they will interpret similar expressions in sentences.

and interpret expressions from "Puss-in-Boots."

● To **point up the ways in which pictures, context clues, and the glossary help in understanding the meaning of new words,** ask such questions as the following:
—What words in the second paragraph on page 175 tell you· that a *jacket* is something to wear? If you didn't know that a *jacket* is a short coat, could you tell by studying pages 174-175? How? [In the picture Puss is wearing a jacket.]

Children discuss text and picture clues to word meaning . . .

—Is a *butler* a servant? What clues on page 177 suggest this? What kind of work does a butler do? Could you tell this from reading today's story? How can you find out?

—What words on page 179 suggest that a *coach* is something to ride in? How does the illustration on page 180 give you a better mental picture of a coach than the words of the story alone? What other meanings for the word *coach* does the glossary give?

—What words on page 180 tell you that a *cape* is an article of clothing? Does a *cape* have sleeves? How do you know?

—What is *barley*? What on page 181 suggests that it is a crop? Is *barley* used for food? Where can you find this information?

—What is a *larder*? What did you read on page 184 that makes you think it might be a place where food is kept? Does the word *larder* always refer to a place? What other meaning is given in the glossary?

note how glossary extends understanding of word meaning.

Extending interests

For youngsters whose first acquaintance with Puss-in-Boots was made as they read today's story, read the traditional version of this folk tale in *Favorite Fairy Tales Told in France,* retold by Virginia Haviland. (If this book is not available, you can find the story in *The Arbuthnot Anthology of Children's Literature,* where it has the title "The Master Cat.")

Pupils enjoy traditional version of "Puss-in-Boots" . . .

Because this version, except for its ending, closely resembles the one pupils have just read, you might begin reading at the point where Puss approaches the ogre's castle. Invite children to compare and contrast the two versions of this folk tale. Which do they prefer, and why?

weigh merits of each version . . .

If youngsters wish to hear the entire story, suggest that as they listen, they mark the cat's impudence or his resourcefulness in profiting by circumstances. After pupils have discussed these traits, place *Favorite Fairy Tales Told in France* on the library table so they can read the other selections and enjoy the illustrations.

pick out evidence of particular traits.

pages 187·192 | The Three Wishes

Words spoken in haste, alas, cannot be recalled, though the man in this folk tale would probably rather have bitten his tongue than the succulent sausage on his dinner table. Even as they are amused by the story, pupils will observe how shortcomings in character can lead to unhappiness.

Children recall that some words have primary and secondary accents and note that clues to vowel sound in accented syllables apply to syllables with secondary accent.

New words: **fortunate***, **diamonds*** (*humble**, cottage*, granted*, *empire**, pearls*, prefer*, instant*, fault*, rather*, complaining*, towel*, slightest*)
Think-and-Do Book: **Pages 58, 59, and 60**

Establishing background

Lead youngsters into a lively consideration of their fondest desires. Imaginations can be sent soaring by prefacing a discussion about children's wishes with the reading of Annette Wynne's "I Keep Three Wishes Ready" (in both *The Arbuthnot Anthology of Children's Literature* and *Time for Poetry,* General Edition, Revised). Then ask, "If you should meet such a fairy, what would your three wishes be?" After boys and girls have had their say on the subject, suggest that they read today's tale. They can then read to find out what wishes are made in the story.

Pupils listen to poem about three wishes . . .

and decide on their own wishes . . .

Interpreting the story

After silent reading have children tell the important events and express opinions about the merit of the man's wishes.

evaluate wishes . . .

Then draw pupils' attention to the circumstances that bring about each of the three wishes by asking:

—Did the man and his wife agree upon the wishes they wanted to make? What wishes did each consider?

—Do you think the man intended to make any of the wishes he did make? Why do you think he made each one? [Have youngsters consider why the man wished for a sausage, what made him wish the sausage onto his wife's nose, and why he wished the sausage would disappear.]

—What did the man and woman have left? Do you think the man could have salvaged at least one wish? What might he have done?

Suggest that children think of features this folk tale has in common with many others. They should be able to cite the appearance of a fairy, the granting of wishes, and the fact that the number of wishes granted is three. You may have to remind pupils that some folk tales teach a lesson; then ask: "Does this story teach a lesson? What is it?"

To make it obvious to children that it might be easier than they think to make at least one such error as the man's, even though his was largely due to foolishness, ask boys and girls whether they have ever said "Oh, I wish——," and finished their sentences with statements that they did not really mean. Endings such as "that this day would never end," "that I could eat a hundred chocolate sodas," and "that I lived on a desert island" might remind youngsters of something they have said in a moment of emotion or during a flight of fancy.

On pages 58-59 of the *Think-and-Do Book* pupils will have a chance to provide useful wishes for a story character.

ORAL INTERPRETATION

Since the outcome of this story is determined by the character traits that prompt the man and woman to act and talk as they do, help children bring the characters to life. For example, you could say: "Imagine that you are the woodcutter. You have been in the forest all day chopping wood. You are very hungry because you have had almost nothing to eat. When

note initial disagreement of characters . . .

state implied reasons for actions . . .

think of alternate final wishes . . .

make generalization about story's indirect lesson . . .

gain tolerance for others' foibles by association with personal experience . . .

identify with woodcutter and fairy . . .

you feel like the tired, hungry, discouraged man, recall what he thought." Children may lean on imaginary ax handles or chop wearily as they think. When the mood of the woodcutter pervades the room, have a child read his soliloquy while the others listen as the understanding fairy. Then choose a woodcutter and a fairy to read the scene.

read scene aloud . . .

Preceding the reading of the episodes between the man and his wife, recall with children the reasons for each character's specific speeches. Let youngsters think, too, what the man may have intended to say when his wife interrupted him. Suggest that they think his complete thought when they read this speech aloud.

think of reasons
for actions . . .

Encourage concentration on characterizations by saying, "When you read the part of the woodcutter or his wife, listen to the person talking to you and then answer because of what you thought and felt as you listened." This suggestion will help children portray the characters and sense the mounting intensity of feelings that result from the disagreement, the faultfinding, and the complaining.

feel reactions
when listening . . .

sense rising tension
that builds to
story climax . . .

The last two paragraphs give narrators an excellent opportunity to conclude the story, not from a supercilious point of view but with understanding of the characters.

read conclusion
from viewpoint
of characters.

Extending competence

● To reinforce pupils' understanding that the same word may have different meanings in different contexts and provide practice in careful use of the glossary, have youngsters select the appropriate definitions for words in sentences on the board, given on the following page. For example, after children have read a sentence that has the word *humble* underlined, let them decide which of three definitions given in the glossary is most pertinent and place the number of the definition in the blank preceding the sentence. Suggest that in selecting the correct meaning it often helps to think about how the word is used in the sentence. Is it used as a word for a person, animal, place, or thing (a noun), as a word for what we do or did (a verb), as a word that tells what kind?

Children select
from various meanings
of words . . .

associate word's
meaning with
its function . . .

_____The man and his wife lived in a *humble* cottage.

_____"It was my fault," the man said in a *humble* way.

_____The herdsman *humbled* himself before the king.

_____Black horses pulled the king's *coach*.

_____Mr. Wilson will *coach* the girls' baseball team.

_____The train had twenty-one *coaches*.

_____This dog is *faithful* to his master.

_____The picture was a *faithful* copy of a great painting.

_____The man and his wife thought they were *fortunate*.

_____The cat was a *fortunate* gift for Jack.

Youngsters will have additional practice in selecting appropriate meanings of words used in different contexts as they do the exercise on page 60 of the *Think-and-Do Book*.

select meanings in Think-and-Do Book.

● Suggestions in this lesson will <u>help children review the understanding that many words have two accented syllables— one with primary accent and one with secondary.</u> (Primary and secondary accents were introduced at Book Three, Part One level, when pupils were learning to interpret glossary or dictionary pronunciations.) These procedures will also <u>develop the understanding that clues to vowel sound in accented syllables apply to syllables with secondary accent.</u>

1. Write the following words in columns and pronounce them. Then have pupils say the words.

Pupils say groups of multisyllabic words and note the following patterns of accent—

syllable	violin	Massachusetts
accident	interrupt	disappointment
customer	understand	education
fortunate	disappoint	reservation
radio	represent	invitation
president	entertain	automatic

Have the words in the first column pronounced again, and ask how many syllables pupils hear in each of them. (three) Then have the words pronounced once more, and ask which syllable is accented in all these words. (the first syllable)

three-syllable words accented on the first syllable . . .

When children have pronounced the words in the second column again, ask how many syllables each word has. (three)

Remind pupils that many words have two accented syllables, one syllable being accented a little more strongly than the other. As you say the words again, ask boys and girls to listen for the two accented syllables in each one. Then ask children to tell which syllable has the stronger, or primary, accent in each word. (the last syllable) Which syllable has the lighter, or secondary, accent? (the first)

three-syllable words with secondary accent on first syllable, primary on third . . .

Similarly have the words in the third column pronounced. How many syllables does each of these words have? (four) Which syllable in each word has the primary accent? (the third) Which has the secondary accent? (the first one)

four-syllable words with secondary accent on first syllable, primary on third . . .

Then suggest that children think about what they have noticed about these words. Lead them to summarize as follows:

summarize what has been noted about accent in these words . . .

(1) All the words have three or more syllables.
(2) All the words are accented on the first syllable (either a primary or secondary accent).
(3) The words in the first column have one accented syllable (a primary accent).
(4) The words in the second and third columns have two accented syllables (a secondary accent on the first syllable, a primary accent on the third).

Comment that although these patterns of accent are heard in many words of three or more syllables, there are other patterns, too, which pupils will discuss another day.

2. Next suggest that as children say each word in the first list, they listen to the vowel sound in the accented syllable and note the spelling clue to that vowel sound. Bring out these points in the discussion:

(1) One vowel letter followed by two consonant letters usually stands for a short vowel sound (as in *syllable, accident, customer*), unless the first of the consonant letters is *r* (as in *fortunate*).

note clues to vowel sound in accented syllables . . .

(2) One vowel letter followed by one consonant letter may stand for a long vowel sound (as in *radio*) or for a short vowel sound (as in *president*).

Continue similarly with clues to vowel sound in the two accented syllables of each word in the second and third lists.

The word *violin,* for example, presents an opportunity to review the following understandings:

(1) When two vowel letters together represent two syllables, the first vowel letter often stands for a long vowel sound in an accented syllable (as in the two-syllable words *lion* and *fuel*)

(2) A single vowel letter followed by a consonant letter other than *r* in the final accented syllable (as in *violin*) usually stands for a short vowel sound (as in *tin*).

3. To conclude, write the following sentences, underlining the italicized words. Explain that each underlined word has two accented syllables—secondary accent on the first syllable and primary accent on the third. Then note pupils' ability to identify the underlined words.

identify in context words of three or more syllables with two accents.

> I *recommend* that you read this good book.
> The man would not *guarantee* that the old car would run.
> The *Mississippi* is the longest river in the United States.
> Ed enjoyed watching the *kangaroo* at the zoo.
> One *locomotive* could not pull the long train.

Extending interests

For a story that points up the care with which a magic wish should be treated and, by contrast, the folly of the people in today's story, read *The Magic Fishbone,* by Charles Dickens. When youngsters have heard the story, let them talk about some of the ways it is like the one they have just read.

Children compare another story about a magic wish with story in text . . .

Because much of the charm of this fanciful tale lies in the author's use of language and in the extraordinary setting he provides for such traditional elements of folklore as a fairy godmother and a magic wish, encourage pupils to point up the humorous touches that distinguish Dickens' story. Among the incongruities that might be brought out are a king who eagerly awaits payday, a capable young princess who keeps house for the royal family (including eighteen younger brothers and sisters), and a fairy who promises the princess thirty-five children with naturally curly hair as a wedding gift.

discuss reasons for distinctive charm of The Magic Fishbone.

pages 193·201 | Rapunzel

Children will enjoy reading this old German tale and will long remember Rapunzel, who is rescued from a cruel witch to live, in traditional make-believe style, happily ever after.

Exercises that grow out of the interpretation of the story help boys and girls observe how an author's choice of words creates moods and images. In still another exercise pupils continue to note patterns of accent in multisyllabic words and clues to vowel sound in accented syllables.

New words: Rapunzel*, *rampion**, *comfort**, *remarkable**, *terrified**, *skein* (surrounded*, dared*, witch*, *content**, *dusk**, slipped*, *fetch**, neither*, nor*, proper*, child*, *thicket**, thorn*, scratch*, *bade**, braids*, sweetly*, crept*, *enchanted**, *kingdom**, learnt*, deceive*, rage*, seized*, snip*, sadness*, blinded*, wept*, sobbing*)

Think-and-Do Book: **Pages 61, 62, 63, 64, and 65**

Establishing background

Through a brief preview pique children's interest in today's story. Explain that as boys and girls begin reading, they will meet a woman who saw something so delicious in a neighbor's garden that she thought she would never be content without it. Explain: "This is what she longed for. [Write the word *rampion* for youngsters to identify independently.] Do you have any idea what rampion is?" Suggest that pupils find the entry word in the glossary and check their opinions.

Continue: "You'll also read about a beautiful girl with very, very long golden hair who lived in a tower in the woods and who spent many days braiding *skeins,* or small bundles, of silk thread into a ladder. Can you guess who she was?" If youngsters

Pupils learn what rampion is...

identify new word skein...

do not immediately identify her as Rapunzel, suggest that they look at the title of the story on page 193 for the answer. Although most children should be able to pronounce the name *Rapunzel* (rə pun′zl) independently, make sure everyone is saying it correctly. (As you list the glossary words, you will want to include *pine* and *spellbound*.)

Then comment that even though boys and girls may have heard this tale before, they will now enjoy reading the entire story for themselves. Mention also that in some ways this story may be different from the version they know.

Interpreting the story

When everyone has finished reading, give children a few moments to comment on the satisfying outcome of the story.

As they recount the events in the story, help pupils recognize some of the reasons for the actions of the characters.

—How did Rapunzel come to live in the tower in the woods? Why was she put there?

perceive cause-effect relationships . . .

—What kind of person was the witch? Why did the man agree to let her have the child? [Encourage children to cite specific examples from the story as they describe the witch. You might point out that vividly portrayed evil characters are typical of folk literature and that in fairy tales a wicked character often wants to take someone's child.]

infer motives for various actions . . .

—Why was Rapunzel taken to a hut in the forest? In what kind of place was it located?

—How did you feel when the witch let down the braids for the prince to climb up to the tower window? Why? What did the witch say to the prince? [Invite someone to read the first paragraph on page 201.] What did the witch mean? Who was the cat she referred to? the pretty bird?

react to events in story . . .

discuss figurative language . . .

—How did you feel when the prince fell from the tower? when he found Rapunzel?

Lead youngsters to note fanciful elements in this story and to recall other old tales with similar characteristics. Begin by asking: "Why do you suppose fairy tales are enjoyed by so many people? Does the story of Rapunzel remind you of other old tales you have read or heard? In what way?" Most children will mention that the wicked witch, the handsome prince, the beautiful girl who became a princess, the rhythmic refrain, and the beginning and ending of the story are common to this type of literature. Some may also recognize the familiar setting and the characteristic style and theme and recall examples of these characteristics in other folk stories.

relate fanciful elements in "Rapunzel" to characteristics of other familiar tales . . .

You may want to call attention to the colon at the end of each sentence preceding the refrain, explaining that a colon is often used to introduce a quotation. Can pupils recall another way in which a colon is used? (In "When Is a Horse a Pony?" children noted that a colon separated numbers which were closely related —14:2 hands, meaning fourteen hands and two inches.)

note another use of colon . . .

Finally encourage youngsters who are familiar with other versions of this story to mention points of difference. In some versions, for example, Rapunzel cuts her braids while the witch is climbing up. Then the prince takes the key and releases Rapunzel from the tower. Which version do children like best? Are they able to explain why?

compare different versions of story.

Extending competence

● Lead children to note the importance of the choice of words in creating a specific mood or image. Invite pupils to find sentences in the story that helped them see a vivid picture or hear certain sounds or feel a certain way. Suggest that they select the word (or words) in each sentence that did most to make them see or feel what the author meant. You might start by calling attention to the descriptive words in the sentences *It happened that a handsome prince was riding one day near the thorny thicket* (page 196) and *She took Rapunzel away from the tower to a hut in a wild and lonely spot at the very heart of the forest* (page 200). As children discuss these and other examples, bring out how these sentences lose their effect when the descriptive words are omitted or replaced by lackluster words.

Children discuss author's use of descriptive words in "Rapunzel" . . .

While attention is focused on descriptive language, you may wish to have pupils use pages 61 and 62-63 of the *Think-and-Do Book*. On page 61 youngsters underline the words and phrases that help them understand the actions and personal traits of the main character in each of two incidents. To complete the exercise on pages 62-63, children identify the paragraph that signals a change in mood and choose words that describe the emotions of a story character.

and in Think-and-Do Book exercises.

● In this exercise pupils note patterns of accent in multi-syllabic words and clues to vowel sound in accented syllables.

1. To begin, write the following lists and pronounce them. Then have pupils say the words.

Pupils say groups of multisyllabic words and note the following patterns of accent—

(1)	(2)
Oklahoma	helicopter
Alabama	kindergarten
decoration	dictionary
manufacture	television
artificial	alligator
locomotive	elevator

Comment: "The words in both lists are alike in two ways—they are all four-syllable words and they all have two accented syllables. But when you say the words again, you'll notice something quite different about the two lists." When pupils have pronounced the words in the first list again, ask on which syllable they hear the stronger, or primary, accent (the third syllable) and on which the lighter, or secondary, accent (the first).

four-syllable words with secondary accent on first syllable, primary on third . . .

Continue similarly with the words in the second list, leading the group to note that primary accent comes before secondary accent in all these words—the primary accent on the first syllable, the secondary accent on the third.

four-syllable words with primary accent on first syllable, secondary on third . . .

2. Next write the following lists of words, pronounce them, and have children say them:

(3)	(4)
imagination	refrigerator
apologetic	vocabulary
communication	accelerator

Have the words in the third list pronounced again, letting children point out that these are five-syllable words. On which syllable in each of these words do youngsters hear primary accent? (the fourth syllable) Which syllable has the secondary accent? (the second)

five-syllable words with secondary accent on second syllable, primary on fourth...

Repeat the procedures with the five-syllable words in the fourth list. Bring out that in these words primary accent comes before secondary accent—primary on the second syllable, secondary accent on the fourth.

five-syllable words with primary accent on second syllable, secondary on fourth...

3. On the basis of the words on the board and what children have learned in preceding exercises, help the group generalize as follows about accent:

generalize about accent in words having two accented syllables...

   (1) Many words have two accented syllables (one syllable with primary accent, one with secondary accent).
   (2) All words of three or more syllables are accented on the first or second syllable.
   (3) The accent on the first or second syllable may be a secondary accent, as in the words in lists 1 and 3, or it may be a primary accent, as in the words in lists 2 and 4.

Have the words in each list pronounced again, and suggest that pupils listen to the vowel sound in the accented syllable of each word. What clues in the spelling of each word do boys and girls see that would lead them to expect these vowel sounds in the accented syllables? (The first syllable of the word *Oklahoma*, for example, provides opportunity to recall that when a single vowel letter in an accented syllable is followed by consonant letters that represent a consonant blend, the vowel letter often stands for a long vowel sound, as in the first syllable of the word *cyclone* or *cobra*.)

note clues to vowel sound in syllables with primary and with secondary accent...

4. To conclude, write the following sentences, underlining the italicized words. Tell pupils that although you are sure they can read the underlined words, you will give them some hints about accent in these words. Begin by explaining that all the underlined words have two accented syllables and that the words in the first three sentences have primary accent before secondary accent. When children are ready to read the last

identify in context multisyllabic words with two accents...

three sentences, point out that these words have secondary accent before primary.

> My aunt's birthday is in *January.*
> We rode up to the third floor on an *escalator.*
> This book tells about an *imaginary* trip to the moon.
> We had *macaroni* and cheese for lunch.
> Our neighbors took a trip to *Arizona.*
> Jim likes stories that are full of *exaggeration.*

Responses on pages 64-65 of the *Think-and-Do Book* will help you evaluate pupils' ability to identify new words as they read. The procedures suggested on pages 186 and 193 of this *Guidebook* will prove especially helpful to youngsters who have difficulty applying word-analysis skills.

apply word-analysis skills in Think-and-Do Book exercise.

Extending interests

Introduce youngsters to Elizabeth Johnson's *The Three-in-One Prince*, a story that turns upon a riddle. After reading "Part One" to establish the riddle and its purpose, pause to let boys and girls give their interpretations of it. Continue with "Part Two," which presents three candidates for the Princess' hand. Then, as you place the book on the library table, suggest that children may be surprised to learn which of the brothers proves that he is indeed "three in one."

Children enjoy a fanciful story with an unusual ending.

Encouraging personal reading

Now that children are pursuing various reading interests stimulated by the wide variety of selections in *More Roads to Follow*, you might arrange a round-table discussion that will give each child an opportunity to communicate his enthusiasm for favorite books, whether fanciful or realistic, biographical or fictional. Encourage pupils to cite examples of story characters who displayed particular traits or learned lessons that remind them of characters in their basic readers. They might also compare stories on the basis of setting, plot, and even style. A discussion like this may lead others to read these books.

pages 202·206 | The Dog in the Manger
The Ant and the Grasshopper
The Dove and the Ant
The Boy and the Wolf

Although at an earlier level children read stories based on fables, this is their first experience in The New Basic Reading Program with the pure fable form attributed to Aesop. Each short, lively incident, given a light touch by the illustration, makes clear the universal truth that is summarized in the moral at the end of the fable. Youngsters also have an opportunity to enjoy one fable in verse form.

Children's attention is called to the general characteristics of fables, and procedures are suggested that will extend their ability to adapt definitions to context in instances which require rewording of the definitions.

New words: **manger, dove** (*ox**, nap*, muttering*, ant*, chat*, stream*, helplessly*, *fowler**, deserves**)
Think-and-Do Book: **Pages 66, 67, and 68**

Establishing background

To point up one of the distinguishing features of a fable, remind children of the saying "Necessity is the mother of invention." What does this saying mean? Have pupils any idea where it originated? If possible, read or tell "The Crow and the Pitcher," which in many versions ends with this saying as the statement of the moral. (The fable may be found in *The Arbuthnot Anthology of Children's Literature.*) Let boys and girls discuss what the crow did and why.

Then inquire whether pupils recall other wise sayings that are illustrated by stories. (They may be familiar with "Do not count your chickens before they are hatched," "It is easy to despise what you cannot get," and "Slow and steady wins the

Children note
form of fables ...

race.") Do children know what we call stories that end in this way? Introduce the word *fable* if it is not mentioned, and explain that many stories of this type were told about 2500 years ago, supposedly by a man named Aesop who lived in Greece.

Before introducing these selections to boys and girls you may want to look over the discussion of fables in Children and Books, *Revised Edition, or in* Time for Fairy Tales. *Both sources point up these essential elements of the Aesop form, which is now regarded as the pure fable type: it is a brief narrative that attempts to make concrete an abstract idea of good, bad, wise, or foolish behavior, in a manner striking enough to be understood and remembered; whether the characters are animals or men, they remain impersonal and engage in a single significant act that points up a moral.*

Encourage youngsters to look briefly at the selections on pages 202-206, and let them comment about pictures or about titles that are familiar. As you call attention to the statement in italic type at the end of each fable, explain that a saying that gives advice about how to live is called a moral. Suggest that after pupils read each fable, they make up their own moral before reading the one in their books.

learn meaning
of the word <u>moral</u> . . .

Although the selections are very short, it is suggested that pupils read and discuss them one at a time. Because fables are concerned with abstract ideas, children need time to discuss the incident that points up the moral, to restate the moral in their own words, and to decide how it applies to their everyday experiences. Keep the discussion light and brief—the simple, vivid form of the fables is appealing, and the moral is easily accepted when not belabored.

Guiding interpretation

PAGE 202

To introduce "The Dog in the Manger," read the title and ask: "What is *a manger*? [Present the italicized words.] Where is the manger in the picture? What is the large animal? How

identify new word
manger . . .

would you describe his expression? As you read the fable, you'll understand how the Ox felt, and why."

After silent reading have the moral of the fable read aloud, and let children tell how it applies to this episode. Then <u>clarify the main point of the fable</u> by asking:
—Would you like to be called 'a dog in a manger'? Why not?
—What words would you use to describe the Dog?
—Have you ever known people who acted like the Dog in the manger? In what way?

discuss moral of fable . . .

PAGE 203

When "The Ant and the Grasshopper" has been read, <u>discuss the illustration</u>. What time of year is pictured? How did the artist show the different attitudes of the Ant and the Grasshopper?

Then <u>help boys and girls apply the moral to their own lives.</u> Can they think of times when this advice would have helped them? Have they ever put off doing homework or some other task and later wished they had done it earlier?

apply moral to specific situations . . .

Page 66 of the *Think-and-Do Book* provides another opportunity for pupils to note general-specific relationships as they select appropriate morals for the situations described.

PAGE 204

Calling attention to the title "The Dove and the Ant," ask children to find *dove* in the glossary and decide which entry word and definition fit this context. Then write the word *fowler,* and let youngsters find its meaning and pronunciation also.

After boys and girls have finished reading, let them share their enjoyment of the humorous moment captured by the artist.

discuss humor in illustration . . .

Then <u>encourage pupils to think about the meaning of the fable and to relate it to actual situations.</u>
—How were the Dove and the Ant alike?
—Do you suppose the Dove thought the Ant would ever be able to help her in return for her good deed? Why?
—In what ways might our school be different if everyone were as thoughtful and helpful as the Dove and the Ant? How would our world be different if all people were like this?

relate main idea to personal experience . . .

GUIDANCE FOR PAGES 202·206 | 179

Comment that Louis Untermeyer has retold one of Aesop's fables in the form of a poem called "The Boy and the Wolf." If children are familiar with a prose version of the fable, let them recall the story and state the moral in their own words. (On page 67 of the *Think-and-Do Book* youngsters read the prose form of the fable and compare it with the poem.)

Then suggest that boys and girls follow in their books as you read the poem aloud. Afterwards point up the main idea of the selection by asking:

—Which parts of the fable did the artist illustrate?

—Can the villagers hear the boy's shouts in the second picture? Why aren't they paying attention?

—Why did the boy cry *Wolf! Wolf!* in the first part of the poem?

—What lesson does this fable teach?

Invite pupils to listen to the rhythm of the poem as you read it again. How does the swinging rhythm add an element of fun to the poem? When boys and girls have become acquainted with the verse, they might try reading it aloud.

listen to fable
told in poetry . . .

identify main ideas . . .

note rhythm
of poem . . .

ORAL INTERPRETATION

Children may find it fascinating to create for radio presentation the characters from fables. Before pupils approach a real or imaginary mike, you might ask: "If Grasshopper and Ant were talking on the radio, how could listeners tell them apart? What kind of character is Grasshopper? Ant? What kind of voice might Grasshopper have that would make him sound different from Ant?"

Give children time to work out their own ideas for projecting characters by voices that distinguish them. Different Ants and Grasshoppers might take turns conversing while classmates tune in. Grasshoppers may speak with a lively pace or an indolent one; they may sound more carefree than Ant, or the rhythm of their speech may suggest hopping.

If interest in this type of activity runs high, you might invite boys and girls to work out a variety of characterizations. Some youngsters in the group may want to present characters from other fables they have read or heard.

portray characters
by voice quality,
rhythm, pitch.

Extending competence

● Use the questions that follow to guide children in summarizing elements found in most fables.

—For what purpose are fables written?

—How would you describe a fable to someone who had never read one? [They are short, they are often about animals that talk, they teach a lesson, the lesson or moral may be stated at the end of the fable.] 'Puss-in-Boots' is a story about a talking animal. Why isn't it a fable?

—Do you think a fable is a good way to teach a lesson? Why? Why do you suppose Aesop's fables are usually about animals instead of people?

Pupils make generalizations about fables.

You may also wish to point out that longer stories are sometimes based on fables, even though they may be written very much like other stories and may not end with the statement of a moral. Recall with children the stories "A Foolish Rabbit," "The Turtle Who Talked Too Much," "City Mouse and Country Mouse," and "Gray Owl and the Rabbits" that they read in *More Friends Old and New* (Book Two, Part Two) as examples of this kind of story, and encourage them to formulate a moral for each one.

● The use of this exercise and page 68 of the *Think-and-Do Book* will help children adapt definitions to context by rewording the definition and sometimes the sentence in which the new word occurs. To begin, write the following sentences, underlining the italicized words:

> The dog would not let the ox come near the *manger*.
> That is an *English* ship.
> Susan looked with *envy* at Ann's new dress.
> The *height* of that building is one hundred feet.
> Some of his *ancestors* came from China.

Have the first sentence read, and ask: "How does the glossary define the word *manger*? If you wanted to reword the sentence without using the word *manger*, would you use the definition just as it appears in the glossary? Would changing the order of words help?"

Children study definition to obtain general idea of meaning...

Lead pupils to note that they must form a general idea about the meaning of *manger* and then state the definition in their own words. Encourage several children to try this, and let the group decide which recasting of the sentence best clarifies the meaning of the original. Perhaps they will agree that something like the following is satisfactory: *The dog would not let the ox come near the place where the ox' food was.*

Continue in much the same manner with the remaining sentences, emphasizing each time that boys and girls read the complete definition (or definitions) of the word in question to get a general idea of its meaning.

reword definition to explain meaning.

Extending interests

The most popular of the beautifully illustrated editions of individual fables for young readers are those with the greatest story appeal and an obvious bit of humor. From the many books that fit these qualifications you might select *A Camel in the Tent* and *The Man, the Boy, and the Donkey,* retold and illustrated by Katherine Evans, for children to read.

Pupils read fables in story form . . .

Share with boys and girls Boris Artzybasheff's beautifully illustrated edition of *Aesop's Fables* by suggesting, as you place it on the library table, that they see how this artist has pictured some of their favorite fables. Although advanced pupils may be able to read the fables for themselves, you will want to keep the book on hand also to read aloud from time to time fables requested by other youngsters.

enjoy interpretations by an artist . . .

Then read John Ciardi's *John J. Plenty and Fiddler Dan,* told in verse, in which Aesop's story of the earnest go-getter ant and the happy but improvident grasshopper is given fresh interpretation. When children have shared their enjoyment of the poem's understated humor and vivid imagery, let them point up its three sprightly morals (Ciardi's own) and contrast them with the moral of Aesop's fable. Which of the two interpretations do youngsters prefer, and why?

and by a poet . . .

discuss and choose between contrasting points of view.

The realistic and the fanciful are skillfully blended in this story. Fairies and goblins are mentioned but never seen, and references to voices heard by the little boy lend themselves to either a literal or figurative interpretation. These ambiguities stimulate interest and provoke critical thought as the plot and style of the story are discussed.

Suggestions are given for oral reading that will arouse the enthusiasm of pupils and provide an opportunity to evaluate their progress.

New words: astonished*, fourteenth*, fifteenth* (frying*, sawmill*, Karl*, selected*, crispest*, napkin*, goblins*, ripe*, lingered*, disagreed*, bid*, count*, tempt*, hindered*)

Think-and-Do Book: Pages 69, 70, and 71

Establishing background

To stimulate interest and relate today's story to children's experience, ask: "Did you ever beg for a chance to prove you were big enough or grown-up enough to do a particular thing and then discover, when you tried it, that you weren't grown-up enough after all? If you've had that experience, you'll sympathize with Karl in today's story."

Pupils recall experiences related to the story...

Interpreting the story

When all have finished reading silently, point up Karl's problem and help children evaluate his grandmother's advice.

—Do you think Karl's mother and grandmother were surprised when he returned with the pancakes? Why not [or why]?

—How did Karl's mother explain his second failure? Do you agree that goblins kept him from succeeding? Who or what tempted him to eat berries? to chase the rabbit?

identify Karl's problem . . .

—Why do you think his grandmother wanted to give him a third chance? Why was her advice helpful?

discuss grandmother's advice . . .

—Why do you suppose Karl was never again hindered by anything when he went through the woods?

—Can you think of an occasion when the advice of Karl's grandmother would have helped you? Tell us about it.

relate it to their own experience . . .

Next focus attention on the style of the story as the primary reason for its inclusion in a unit of fanciful tales rather than among a group of realistic stories.

—Do you think this story could have happened? What makes you think as you do? [While opinions will differ, pupils may recognize that the wood was merely called Enchanted, people thought goblins and fairies lived there, and a voice seemed to beckon Karl to stop and eat berries. Even the call of the rabbit and the bird can be interpreted as Karl's thoughts when he saw them.]

note that selection resembles realistic stories in content . . .

—In what ways does this story remind you of other folk tales you've read? [The three trials, the repetition of certain phrases, the suggestion of fairies and goblins, and the beginning and ending of the story are reminiscent of folk tales.]

and is similar to fanciful stories in style . . .

—How is this story like a fable? Can you think of a moral for it?

form a generalization.

Extending competence

● Introduce pages 69, 70, and 71 of the *Think-and-Do Book* at this time. On pages 69 and 70 pupils are asked to distinguish between realistic and fanciful situations. On page 71 they decipher words, using the number code suggested in the grandmother's advice to Karl, to complete a story.

In Think-and-Do Book children identify fanciful statements . . .

● To evaluate individual progress in oral reading and to give children the satisfaction that accompanies effective oral reading, suggest a "story parade" in which favorite characters

and use context clues.

appear. So that each child can participate, you might plan several presentations—a make-believe radio or TV broadcast, a story hour in the library, a sharing time with parents.

Invite youngsters to browse through the text in search of interesting episodes about favorite characters that they would like to interpret orally. Reluctant readers may have more success with short scenes from familiar stories, but able readers can be encouraged to interpret scenes from other books.

Children select favorite episodes from stories . . .

Stress bringing the characters to life for interested listeners as the purpose of each presentation and as motivation for careful preparation. One step in achieving this goal might be a comparison of storybook friends—for example, shy Kirsten, critical and snobbish Debbie, tolerant and friendly Amy, honest and resourceful Rufe, irrepressible Eddie.

make plans for interpreting story characters to an audience.

Encourage each child to visualize the character he has selected and to read his own interpretation. You might have an opportunity to point out that such characters as the witch in "Rapunzel" or the ogre in "Puss-in-Boots" may be read effectively in a variety of ways, depending upon the reader's conception of the character.

During the preparation you will want to note possibilities for strengthening each reader's ability to identify with the characters and to read aloud with the intonations and rhythms of conversation. Focusing attention on thinking, feeling, and talking for the characters they portray will help pupils—

1. group words in meaningful units, stressing important ideas and subordinating less important ones,
2. reflect changes in characters' positions and actions by adjusting volume and pace of reading,
3. convey the feelings of characters through appropriate voice quality, facial expression, and slight bodily tensions and movements,
4. show distinctions between types of characters—wicked, shy, complaining, mischievous,
5. think through interrupted speeches and read them as if conversing,
6. listen and respond to other characters in the story,
7. identify and convey in oral reading the point of view from which narrative passages are written.

● The following procedures review spelling patterns that are clues to vowel sounds in one-syllable words and in accented syllables of words of more than one syllable.

1. Write these known words and have them pronounced:

joy	fight	eager	below
thread	shriek	cautious	approach
earn	trade	coward	attack
wail	sack	feeble	prepare
hair	slow	leather	parade
south	her	trousers	reply
fault	near	royal	appear
down	sky	early	believe
peek	dare	tailor	prefer
meal	load	fairy	delight

Ask: "In which two lists are all the words one-syllable words? two-syllable words? In which list are all the two-syllable words accented on the first syllable? the second syllable?"

Next explain that for each one-syllable word there is a two-syllable word that has the same vowel sound in the accented syllable and the same spelling for that vowel sound (*joy, royal,* for example). Then have pupils say each one-syllable word and locate the two-syllable word.

Pupils review clues to vowel sounds in one- and two-syllable words.

Extending interests

Karl's remarkable experiences in the Enchanted Wood are reflected in the teasing dialogue of Eleanor Farjeon's "For a Mocking Voice" (in *Time for Poetry*). When children have heard this poem a few times and repeated it with you, read the rôle of the child yourself and let youngsters speak the taunting words of the elf, closing with his light, mocking laughter.

Imaginative boys and girls will sustain the mood of the story as they listen to poems about invisible people and things; for example, Robert Louis Stevenson's "Windy Nights," Christina Rossetti's "Who Has Seen the Wind?" and Rose Fyleman's "The Goblin." (Pupils using the *Learn to Listen, Speak, and Write* series might repeat their verse-choir renditions of these poems, which are also in *Time for Poetry*.)

Children listen to poet's dialogue with an elf...

project its mood in choral speaking...

enjoy other poems about the unseen.

pages 214·216 | Ridiculous People

The rollicking rhythm and rhyme of these limericks should tickle youngsters' tongues as well as their "funny bones," and the narrative nonsense verse lends itself to choral speaking.

Establishing background

Introduce children to the terms *nonsense verse* and *limerick*. Begin by reading aloud the title on page 214 and letting pupils infer the type of poetry they are about to read. Accept any description that suggests the wildly humorous, and explain that such poems are often called nonsense verse. When these are written in the short rhyming pattern of the verses on page 214, they are called limericks.

Children learn general characteristics of nonsense verse and limericks . . .

Guiding interpretation

PAGE 214

Because so much of the fun of limericks is in their sounds, let what is possibly children's first encounter with these three poems be an oral one. Before you read the second poem aloud, you will want to make clear the meaning of *tutor*.

listen to limericks . . .

Since they cannot help enjoying the gay, dancing tempo of these verses, youngsters will be eager to read the limericks aloud themselves. Suggest that they familiarize themselves with the lines first by reading the poems silently several times. Then encourage them to think of the meaning of each poem so that they will be less likely to stumble in reading aloud, for limericks can be tongue twisters.

read each poem silently and then orally . . .

Urge each reader of the first poem to think of himself as the Old Man and to see each bird he names. He might choose a classmate to whom he can explain the amazing state of his beard.

identify with the Old Man . . .

To emphasize the contrasts that occur in the second limerick, suggest that pupils read in groups of three, one child taking the first three lines and two "young tutors" reading the last two lines in unison. Thus children will tend to think of the meaning and to speak with natural pitch and stress.

make vocal contrasts with appropriate intonations . . .

Before the last limerick is read aloud, it is important to make children aware of the units of thought. For example, ask children to tell what the Young Lady's chin resembled, and then suggest that they read the first two lines in the same way that they answered your question.

observe continuity of thought . . .

After having read and heard these jingles several times, many pupils may have learned at least one by heart. Let volunteers say the limericks without depending on their texts.

quote limericks . . .

PAGES 215-216

When boys and girls have listened to "Mrs. Snipkin and Mrs. Wobblechin," prompt youngsters to let their imaginations delineate the comical characters. What characteristics might the two women have had? (During the conversation see whether children inferred the meaning of *pipkin* from the illustrations and text.)

contrast poem's two characters . . .

Prepare pupils for choral speaking by reading the poem several times until they can say it with you. Two choirs may then be used. The group that speaks for Mrs. Snipkin should speak with a kind of tight, prim biting-off of words, the "Wobblechin" choir should speak slowly and lazily, and the last line should be made to sound properly climactic. One of the three following patterns may be chosen:

interpret poem in verse choir.

1. High-medium voices say the first three lines of each verse, and low-medium voices the last three.
2. A narrative chorus of mixed but harmonious voices speaks the first and last verse; a high solo voice speaks the first three lines of the middle verse, and a low solo speaks the last three lines.
3. Pattern 1 is used, but a high solo voice speaks the words of Mrs. Snipkin and a low solo voice speaks the words of Mrs. Wobblechin.

Extending interests

Draw youngsters' attention to the names of the poets, explaining that these people have written many poems for children. Edward Lear is especially famous for his limericks. Do pupils know any of them? (*Story and Verse for Children*, Revised Edition, compiled by Miriam Blanton Huber, contains several.) Have they heard Edward Lear's nonsense poems "The Owl and the Pussy Cat" and "The Jumblies"? Have they heard Carolyn Wells' poem "How to Tell the Wild Animals"? Laura Richards' "Eletelephony" or "Jippy and Jimmy"? Let popular demand be your guide in reading any or all of these selections aloud. (These poems are in *Time for Poetry*.)

Pupils learn about other poems by these writers . . .

If they express an interest in writing their own limericks, you may want to acquaint youngsters further with the limerick form. In that case, point out that limericks have five lines. (The Lear verses are printed with lines 3 and 4 written as one line on page 214, so be sure to point this out.) Have children tap the accented beats on their desks as they listen to you read a limerick and then as they read one themselves. They will discover the traditional pattern of three accented beats for lines 1, 2, and 5 and two accented beats for lines 3 and 4.

tap out rhythm of limerick . . .

Pupils can then listen for the words that rhyme: the lines with the same number of accented beats also rhyme with each other—lines 1, 2, 5; lines 3, 4.

and determine rhyming pattern . . .

Keep these activities in the spirit of fun, for at this level children's attitudes toward hearing and reading nonsense verse are more important than their learning the structure. But when youngsters have enjoyed composing their own limericks, they will find further pleasure in sharing them with one another.

enjoy each other's limericks . . .

Finally acquaint youngsters with Kerby Maxwell, a boy who wrote limericks with the help of a friend. Read the first two chapters of Scott Corbett's *The Limerick Trick* to introduce the characters and Kerby's problem; then let children finish the story to find out how a magic chemistry set solves Kerby's immediate problem—and creates another. Later they might talk over what Kerby learned from Mrs. Graymalkin.

enjoy story about the problems of "instant poetry."

Intrepid Pippi, unawed by the biggest bully, is the superchild that almost every boy and girl would like to be. Children will savor the humor of the situations that arise when this unpredictable little girl takes matters into her capable hands.

New words: absolutely∗, *Villekulla, Annika* (Pippi∗, Longstocking∗, cradle∗, *villa*∗, playmate∗, dull∗, thin∗, gutter∗, silence∗, lazy∗, rats∗, candy∗, screws∗, knees∗, pickets∗, *utterly*∗, *hutch*∗, tin∗, jar∗, spool∗, bubbles∗, necklace∗, heels∗, Willie∗, Bengt∗, fight∗, cowards∗, hash∗, astonishment∗, *birch*∗, hollow∗, loop∗, stump∗, *coral*∗, tuck∗, slept∗, pillow∗, quilt∗)

Think-and-Do Book: **Pages 72 and 73**

Establishing background

Set the stage for this modern tale by commenting: "Today's story doesn't begin with the words 'Once upon a time.' It might have happened any time at all—even yesterday. In the story we'll meet a little girl named Pippi Longstocking, who came to live in a *villa* [write the word on the board for children to read] at the edge of a small town. What kind of place is a villa?" Suggest that boys and girls use their glossaries to check the meaning of this word.

Continue by explaining: "This villa had an unusual name. It was called *Villa Villekulla* [(vil′ə kul′ä)]. And *Tommy and Annika* [(än′i kä)], who lived next door, thought their new neighbor was a very unusual person. The first four pages of the story will give you some ideas about Pippi. When you've read these pages, be ready to tell what kind of person you think she is, and why you think so."

Children note modern setting of tale . . .

identify new words . . .

Guiding interpretation

PAGES 217-220

Help pupils note clues to Pippi's personality by asking:

—Does Pippi Longstocking seem like an ordinary person to you? Why not?

—Why was Pippi living alone at Villa Villekulla?

—How do you suppose Tommy and Annika felt when they first met her? How would you have felt? Why?

—We've already found out a great deal about Pippi, but there are some things the story hasn't explained yet. What else would you like to know about her?

When children have recalled the title and speculated about thing-finding, suggest that they finish the story to find out what a Thing-finder does and how successful a one Pippi is.

discuss impressions of Pippi . . .

anticipate plot development . . .

PAGES 221-231

After silent reading lead children to discuss Pippi's success at thing-finding and bully-taming.

—Why was Pippi a Thing-finder? Do you think she really expected the search to turn up lumps of gold? Why might she have been pretending?

—Did Pippi seem to think the things she found were useless? What did she intend to do with her discoveries?

—What happened that interrupted the hunt?

—Do you suppose the boys will ever bother Pippi or Willie again? Why not? What do you think of the way Pippi handled the situation?

—Why do you think Tommy and Annika were so successful as Thing-finders?

On page 72 of the *Think-and-Do Book* children have an opportunity to decide what a Thing-finder might do with various treasures; on page 73 they must visualize the situations described and infer what action is taking place.

evaluate Pippi's motives . . .

make inference . . .

WHOLE STORY

Point up the element of surprise that contributes to the humor of the story by asking how Tommy and Annika felt before Pippi appeared on the scene. When pupils recall the children's boredom and their wish for a playmate, call attention to Tommy's last remark on page 231. Do youngsters think Tommy and Annika will ever have a dull moment with Pippi around? Why not? Why might it be fun to have someone like Pippi for a neighbor? When pupils note that she always manages to do the unexpected, let them tell which of her actions particularly surprised and amused them.

analyze Pippi's appeal . . .

Conclude by pointing out that perhaps Pippi is fun to read about because she does some of the things that children themselves would like to be able to do. Which of those things would boys and girls most enjoy doing?

and consider reason.for it . . .

ORAL INTERPRETATION

The encounter between Pippi and the five bullies is a tall tale that children will enjoy reading aloud. To help readers sense the humor of the extraordinary character and her actions, suggest that as children read and listen, they visualize what the characters are doing. Begin with the last paragraph on page 225 and the first two on page 226.

visualize characters in action . . .

When oral reading reflects the tension and speed of the scene, comment that while Willie was being badgered, each onlooker had different thoughts and feelings. Encourage children to imagine they are each character in turn as they read silently the last paragraph on page 225 and all of the following page. Then assign groups to read as narrator, Bengt, Annika, Tommy, and Pippi. After giving each reader a few moments to find his specific part and to concentrate on his character's feelings, let the group read aloud.

interpret pace and mood of scene . . .

identify with thoughts and feelings of each character . . .

Many children have tasted enough teasing that they can make Bengt the true-to-life bully who tries to reduce Pippi to tears. Both boys and girls will read with relish the gibes that incite his followers to scream *Redhead! Redhead!*

suggest character of bully with his dialogue . . .

The essence of this tall tale is in Pippi's reactions. Challenge oral readers to make the amazing tall-tale justice dispensed by this "helpless" little girl seem believable. If narrators fail to visualize and consequently read monotonously, or if those who do visualize cannot resist giggling, have them

identify with Pippi's problem and solution . . .

imagine that they are surrounded by the bullies and that they are handling each as quickly and calmly as a lion tamer.

As pupils continue, help them note that once victory is won, Pippi calmly resumes her conversation, kindly reassures Willie, seals Bengt's lips with a final taunt, and continues on her way as a Thing-finder.

reflect relationships between characters in oral reading.

Extending competence

● Continue a review of spelling patterns that are clues to vowel sounds in accented syllables by writing these lists of known words and having them pronounced:

whisper	alphabet
lady	holiday
honor	history
balance	terrible
merry	radio

Then ask: "In which list are all the words two-syllable words? three-syllable words? Which syllable is accented in all the words? [the first one]"

Have the word *whisper* pronounced again, and ask whether the vowel sound in the accented syllable is short or long. How many consonant letters follow the letter *i* in *whisper?* In which three-syllable word (indicate the second list) do pupils hear the short *i* sound in the accented syllable? How many consonant letters follow the letter *i* in *history?*

Starting with the next two-syllable word (*lady*), use similar procedures to review the following understandings about clues to vowel sounds in accented syllables:

Pupils review clues to vowel sounds in two- and three-syllable words.

(1) A single vowel letter followed by one consonant letter may be a clue to a long vowel sound, as in *lady* and *radio*, or it may be a clue to a short vowel sound, as in *honest* and *holiday*.

(2) The letter *a* followed by *l* is more likely to represent the vowel of *hat* than the vowel of *salt*, as in *balance* and *alphabet*.

(3) The letter *e* followed by two *r*'s usually represents the vowel of *let*, as in *merry* and *terrible*.

Extending interests

Boys as well as girls will want to read the rest of *Pippi Long-stocking*, by Astrid Lindgren. Later, as pupils discuss elements of the story's tall-tale humor, be sure they include the matter-of-fact way Pippi's antics are related and the contributing rôle of the illustrations. (Children may also note that the illustrations for *Pippi Longstocking* and those for "Pippi Is a Thing-Finder" are very similar in style. This similarity is intended so that the mental images pupils form while reading the story are in accord with the illustrations they will see in the books about Pippi.) If time permits, let children tell which of Pippi's adventures they enjoyed most, and why.

Children read more about the redoubtable Pippi . . .

Acquaint youngsters with Pippi's realistic counterpart by reading at least the first chapter or two of Astrid Lindgren's *Mischievous Meg*. Afterwards invite pupils to compare Meg and Pippi. Does the word *mischievous* also describe Pippi?

compare realistic and fanciful characters in stories by the same author.

Anticipating the next story

Silent reading of the story "Pooh Goes Visiting" (pages 238-250 in *More Roads to Follow*) will be enhanced if pupils first hear a selection from A. A. Milne's *Winnie-the-Pooh*. Youngsters find the Pooh stories inexhaustibly funny once they catch the pattern of the author's subtleties of characterization, humor, and style. To insure enjoyment of these stories, therefore, take time now to introduce children to the world of Pooh.

Explain that you are about to read a story written by A. A. Milne for his son Christopher Robin and that in it pupils will meet Christopher and his best friend, a bear named Winnie-the-Pooh. Then read the first chapter of *Winnie-the-Pooh*. (This selection is also in *The Arbuthnot Anthology of Children's Literature*, where it has the title "*That* Is Why He Was Always Called Pooh.") Afterwards invite comments on Pooh and his project. When did he decide that he had found "the wrong sort of bees"? Then tell children they will soon read about what happens when Pooh goes underground to visit a friend.

With these poems boys and girls enter a hilarious world of improbabilities where an elephant is bullied by a grasshopper, an ostrich runs away from himself, and a glowworm is very fussy about how he is addressed.

Establishing background

To help youngsters anticipate the nonsensical character of the poetry on these pages, call attention to the title on page 232 and ask what other title it reminds them of. (It should bring to mind "Ridiculous People.") What kinds of poems were in that group? Do children recall the names of any of the poets who wrote those nonsense verses?

Make the observation: "Some very old and well-known poems and stories have this word printed where you might expect to see the writer's name. [Write *anonymous* as you say the word.] Does anyone know what the word *anonymous* means? Why do you suppose it is often the very old poems and stories whose writers are unknown?"

Guiding interpretation

PAGE 232

Lead children into a discussion of the illustration for Zhenya Gay's poem. What animals do pupils see? (Make sure the moose is properly identified.) What is ridiculous about these animals? (Verify the idea that the goose, the mouse, and the moose are drinking tea.)

Then suggest that pupils read the poem to themselves to see whether it brings to mind a scene something like the one the artist drew. Afterwards invite youngsters to describe what they saw. As they imagined it, what was different?

Pupils recall
earlier reading of
nonsense verse...

learn what
anonymous means...

note artist's image...

and contrast it
with their own...

Since most children will be able to identify the word *bananas,* let youngsters read the second poem independently to discover what is ridiculous about it. When the silliness of the elephant's complaint has been enjoyed, ask pupils whether the writer of this verse is known.

enjoy humor of ridiculous idea . . .

Children may listen to the last poem to decide what makes it especially amusing. Pupils have encountered alliteration in poems before, and in this one the sounds of the words should be cited as a source of amusement. Can children pick out the many words beginning with the consonant blend *fl* that make this verse a tongue twister? Meanings of *flaw* and *flue* (as distinguished from *flew*) may need to be explained.

and of alliteration . . .

Then let boys and girls read aloud any of these three poems that particularly appeals to them.

read poems aloud . . .

PAGE 233

To make use of the illustration in introducing "The Ostrich Is a Silly Bird," invite children to comment on the bird's appearance. Then ask: "Why do you suppose the ostrich looks so disgusted? Let's find out." Pupils may read silently for the answer.

observe comical quality of picture . . .

read poem silently . . .

After they have explained the reason for the ostrich's bored disgust, ask youngsters whether they think the poem's title is an appropriate one, and request reasons for their answer. If children want to read this poem aloud, remind them to keep its units of thought intact, drawing particular attention to the first two lines of the second stanza.

consider title's appropriateness . . .

PAGES 234-235

With the first two poems on these pages amusement is derived chiefly from the imagery invoked; with the latter two, the humor depends more upon recognition of the facetious quality of the ideas presented.

As you introduce each rhyme, use the illustration that accompanies it, and provide any assistance children may need to appreciate the humor.

discuss illustrations and poems . . .

Before children hear "A Centipede Was Happy Quite," ask them to tell what they know about a centipede's appearance. Then, after they have heard the verse, let them explain the centipede's dilemma and its cause. (Note pupils' comprehension of the word *distracted*.) Have children ever been able to do something perfectly until someone asked how they did it? You might comment, "Think of the poor centipede, trying to manage all those legs!"

In shifting attention to "Only My Opinion," lead boys and girls to contrast the centipede's expression with that of the happy little fellow at the bottom of the page. Do children have any ideas about why the caterpillar looks so jolly? Such discussion should prime youngsters to hear or read the poem. (Since most pupils should be able to identify the words *ticklish* and *belief* through context and spelling clues, you might suggest that they read the poem to themselves.) Children who have ever been tickled by a caterpillar's crawling across their palms should chuckle sympathetically at the thought of the caterpillar's own reaction to a fuzzy surface.

An invitation to pupils to describe the black animal at the top of page 235 and to decide whether they think it is a house cat will serve to create the mood for Ogden Nash's "The Panther." After hearing it, youngsters might talk about what makes Nash's poem so silly and amusing. During the discussion be sure to bring out the meaning of the second line, *Except it hasn't been peppered,* and the humor of the rhyming words, *panther* and *anther,* in the last two lines. Perhaps pupils may recall how they talked when they lost their two front teeth.

Elicit comments from children on the drawing that accompanies "Glowworm." Can youngsters guess what shining thing the boy is looking at? Do they know what a glowworm changes into when it grows up? (Pupils may know the adult form as a lightning bug or a firefly.) After "Glowworm" has been heard, make sure children have grasped its full meaning. Much of the poem's humor depends upon understanding the idiom *talk down,* for example.

enjoy the humor of centipede's distraction ...

the caterpillar's ticklishness ...

the sage advice about panthers ...

and the proper etiquette with glowworms ...

Before youngsters read the poem aloud, ask them why they think the words *knowworm, belowworm, slowworm,* and *helloworm* are each printed as one word. To provide fun for both readers and listeners and to emphasize the meaning of the poem, let groups of four read "Glowworm" aloud. One child may take the part of the narrator, reading the portions of the poem that are in roman type; three others may take turns reading the italicized parts in a line-a-child manner.

PAGES 236-237

read "Glowworm" aloud...

First ask pupils whether they know what a *duel* is. If necessary, clarify the definition by saying that it can be any type of contest or fight between two opponents. Then read aloud Eugene Field's "The Duel," being careful to say all the asides in a contrasting tone of voice and in a different pace. The shift in the train of thought will thus become obvious, and the effect should be similar to a refrain repeated in variations at the end of each stanza.

listen to "The Duel"...

When children have heard the poem, let them think about what their reactions would be should one of their classmates tell such a tale as this. Would they believe it? How does the teller of this tall tale shift responsibility for the story?

consider poem's exaggeration...

Then draw youngsters' attention to the lines printed in italic type and enclosed in parentheses. Why are parts of the poem in parentheses? See whether pupils can deduce that these words are not part of the story of the duel itself.

note purpose of parenthetic lines...

"The Duel" has such dramatic quality that youngsters should have the fun of interpreting it orally. After children have heard it once or twice, they may be invited to join in on the speeches of the dog, the cat, and the plate. Pupils attuned to the rhythm of the verses will sense the even beat of the *bow-wow-wow!* and will prolong the *mee-* of the cat's exclamation, ending it with an emphatic *-ow!* They will also be prompt in picking up their cue to the wail of the Chinese plate.

express rhythm...

As children listened, they heard the changes in pace and mood of the reader's voice when the refrains were read. With the next reading let a different child join in with each refrain.

distinguish refrains from narration...

When they are ready to read the entire poem with ease and enjoyment, help oral readers in advance by pointing out long sentences so that the continuity of thought will not be broken by falling inflections or meaningless pauses at the ends of lines. For example, refer to lines 5, 6, and 7 of the first stanza, and ask: "What did the clock and plate appear to know? Now read the lines that tell this."

sustain continuity of thought . . .

Because the humor and suspense of the climax will be heightened if the words *they ate each other up!* are preceded by a pause, remind pupils that storytellers often give listeners a moment to wonder before they tell the exciting end of a story.

point up humor and suspense with pause.

Extending interests

Youngsters who liked the zany humor of "Ridiculous Animals" will enjoy Ogden Nash's *Custard the Dragon*. When they have listened to this ridiculous adventure, pupils might point out which members of Belinda's household were considered brave and which stood the test of bravery. Why was Custard's courage so unexpected? The illustrations for this tale about a "realio, trulio, little pet dragon" will attract children to the library table, especially when they know that the artist is Ogden Nash's daughter, Linell. (If the book is not available, you can find the poem in *Time for Poetry,* where it has the title "The Tale of Custard the Dragon.")

Children are introduced to "Custard the Dragon."

Pooh's love for honey (which youngsters may know about by now) is a major cause of his problem in this story. Typically, much of Milne's humor is deftly delivered by implication, which pupils can enjoy interpreting.

An exercise on the use of context clues in determining word meaning insures more complete understanding of several words used in the story and serves to strengthen one of children's most useful reading skills.

New words: **Christopher*** (Pooh*, Edward*, Winnie-the-Pooh*, humming*, stoutness*, scuffling*, *mugs**, *condensed**, *directly**, *good-bye**, carelessly*, robin*, deal*, sustaining*, tightness*, north*, slenderer*, cork*)

Think-and-Do Book: **Pages 74, 75, and 76**

Establishing background

If, in anticipation of this story, a selection from *Winnie-the-Pooh* has been read aloud, as suggested on page 194 of this *Guidebook*, or if pupils have heard or read other Pooh stories, you will be able to trade on children's past experiences in introducing today's story. Invite boys and girls to open their books to the picture on pages 238-239, and ask whether they know this fat little bear's name. Other questions that you could use to draw out helpful information are these:

—Is this the sort of bear you might expect to meet in the woods? What kind of bear is he?

—Do you know his owner's name?

—Do you have a good idea about why Pooh is so stout? What is it?

—What does Pooh seem to be doing in this picture?

Children identify main character and anticipate story's whimsicality...

—What do you think he is about to do? [The story title should provide a basis for inference.]

Add the double entry word *condensed milk* to the glossary words that you list on the board for children's reference.

make inference . . .

Interpreting the story

To establish the appropriate tenor of light-hearted humor, you might read page 238 aloud to pupils. Then suggest that boys and girls finish the story independently to find out what happens during Pooh's visit.

When silent reading is completed, let youngsters follow their own inclinations in what is to be discussed, much as you would if they were talking about their personal reading. If they need help in getting started, you could ask why Pooh decided to call on Rabbit, what sort of conversation was carried on after he had made the decision, or what took place immediately after a situation shown in one of the illustrations.

discuss high points of story . . .

With most stories children read in their texts, discussions are guided to insure maximum enjoyment of each story and to develop specific interpretive skills. With stories like this one, however, it is perhaps preferable to let spontaneity alone be the guide. In the realm of fanciful tales those about Christopher Robin, Winnie-the-Pooh, and the other toys and animals of the make-believe forest appeal to readers of an unusually broad age span. Children who enjoy these fantasies at eight years of age may very well continue to be amused by them at ten and twelve years of age and even as adults. The subtleties they may miss when they hear or read the stories at this level can be reserved for enjoyment during a future reading when insights are more mature.

For many youngsters it is only through listening to a Winnie-the-Pooh story read by an adult that many of the nuances of Milne's humor become apparent. Therefore, after they have made observations about Pooh's adventure, suggest that pupils listen as you read aloud the entire story. Children's respon-

listen to oral interpretation of entire story.

siveness (their anticipation of and reaction to various passages) as you read will indicate their appreciation of amusing situations, funny or touching revelations of character, and the author's overall tone of gentle, disarming humor.

Extending competence

● To strengthen ability in recognizing character traits and in forming sensory images, use pages 74 and 75 of the *Think-and-Do Book*. On page 74 pupils identify personal traits revealed by passages from "Pooh Goes Visiting," and on page 75 they decide which descriptive phrases would help set a specified tone for a story.

In Think-and-Do Book pupils note clues to character traits and to mood.

● To refresh pupils' understanding of ways in which word meaning may be arrived at through context clues, take a few minutes to talk about how a reader can derive the meanings of words that he meets in reading. Although glossaries and dictionaries should be used in many instances, alert readers, like good detectives, search first for clues on the spot.

Begin by having a child read aloud the second sentence on page 241, and ask, "What helped you know what the word *scuffling* means in this sentence?" When children point out that the word *noise* amplifies the meaning, ask them what probably made the noise and how they think a scuffling noise would sound.

Pupils deduce word meaning from another word in same sentence . . .

Comment that sometimes the story itself—the way the character feels or the situation in which he finds himself—is a clue to the meaning of a word. To illustrate, have the last sentence on page 248 read aloud, and let youngsters explain possible clues to the meaning of *Sustaining*. What sort of book would Pooh be most interested in at this time? Perceptive pupils may infer such suitable words as *comforting, morale-building, helpful,* or *encouraging.*

consider character and story situation as clues to word meaning . . .

Although deriving meanings of words from context eventually becomes a process that is done almost unconsciously, at this level youngsters often need to stop and ponder the meanings of some words as they read. See whether pupils remember their thoughts regarding specific words. What one child has done may help point the way for others. Ask: "Do you recall figuring out the meaning of a word in this story by some detective work such as we've been talking about? What word was it? How did you arrive at its meaning?"

cite ways used in deriving word meanings in story...

If the following words are not brought up for discussion, you may want to supplement children's offerings by asking about clues to the meanings of these words. Sentences using the words can be found on the pages indicated.

> *Stoutness* (second sentence, page 238)
>
> *mugs* and *condensed milk* (first sentence, page 243)
>
> *deal* (third sentence in fourth paragraph, page 248)
>
> *North* and *slenderer* (page 249)
>
> *cork* (third paragraph, page 250)

Additional practice in deriving word meaning from context is given in an exercise on page 76 of the *Think-and-Do Book*.

use context clues in Think-and-Do Book.

Extending interests

Invite youngsters to listen to other make-believe adventures of Christopher Robin and his friends in A. A. Milne's *Winnie-the-Pooh*. If children did not hear the Pooh selection mentioned earlier, take time now to read the first chapter, "*In Which* We Are Introduced to Winnie-the-Pooh and Some Bees, and the Stories Begin." Afterwards you might guide boys and girls in a brief discussion of Pooh and his project, using the suggestions on page 194 of this *Guidebook*.

Children share Christopher Robin's world of make-believe.

The remaining chapters of this book are equally delightful, and they are made to order for reading aloud. If time does not permit you to read them all, however, you might select Chapter III, "*In Which* Pooh and Piglet Go Hunting and Nearly Catch a Woozle," or Chapter VI, "*In Which* Eeyore Has a Birthday and Gets Two Presents." Then make the book available so children can read for themselves the further adventures of Christopher Robin and his companions.

In describing the good times of Christopher Robin and Winnie-the-Pooh, the poet gives a moving picture of love and devotion. By reading between the lines boys and girls can glean the poem's complete story.

Establishing background

Link the inspirational basis of the Pooh stories to children's own experience by asking: "Was there ever one particular toy that you loved more than any other? What was it?" When several pupils have recalled such possessions, continue with the observation: "That is the way Christopher Robin felt about Winnie-the-Pooh, and that is why he asked his father to make up some stories about Pooh. In these stories how did Christopher Robin act toward Winnie-the-Pooh? How did Pooh feel about Christopher Robin?"

Even though some youngsters may be able to base their inferences only on the story they have just read, they should nevertheless be able to contribute to this discussion. You might suggest that they reread page 246 or the last paragraph of "Pooh Goes Visiting" before they reply. Comment that the answers to these questions will become clearer when they have heard a poem called "Us Two," also by A. A. Milne.

Guiding interpretation

When you invite pupils to listen to the poem "Us Two," explain that Christopher Robin is telling them about himself and Pooh. Perhaps children will be able to notice how Christopher and Pooh feel about each other from the things he says. Then read the poem in an easy, conversational manner.

Children think about their favorite toys ...

consider relationship of Christopher Robin and Pooh ...

listen to poem ....

While this poem has typical Winnie-the-Pooh humor in its droll dialogue, its basic appeal is emotional. So that they may not miss the full impact, help youngsters interpret the implied message of "Us Two" by asking:

—Do you understand now why Christopher Robin went to so much trouble to help Pooh get unstuck from Rabbit's doorway?

—How does the poem let us know Christopher and Pooh enjoyed being together?

—What were some of the good times they had together?

—How did Pooh show that he loved and admired Christopher Robin?

discuss attitudes and feelings that the poem reveals . . .

In conclusion lead children to associate the narrative portion of this poem with their own experiences. Have they, too, enjoyed discussions and make-believe games with their best friends? They may not have fought dragons, but they may have taken on a "bad guy" or two—or "lassoed horses"—or stalked animals in a "jungle."

tell about their own make-believe games.

Extending interests

This might be a good time to acquaint youngsters further with A. A. Milne's poetry. "Puppy and I" is written in the same conversational style as "Us Two," and Christopher Robin (or a child very like him) again addresses the reader or listener in "At the Zoo." "The Four Friends" is a whimsical description of four unlikely animal companions. Children will enjoy hearing these or other Milne poems which can be found in *Time for Poetry*.

Pupils listen to other Milne poems.

A fearsome fog poses quite a problem for a gentle scarecrow charged with protecting a rice paddy, but with the help of his crow friends Joji achieves success and fame as a scarefog. This charming Japanese fantasy will delight youngsters and increase their appreciation for skillful writing.

New words: **Joji, kimono*** (fog*, worms*, *paddy**, duty*, floated*, breathing*, *fumed**, *swirled**, tea*, steaming*, bath*, *swashed**, oozed*, spin*, collided*, guide*, slid*, blankets*, worst*, chilled*, roots*, droop*, cawed*, causing*, smooth*, painful*, tickle*, sank*, plug*, hips*, fluttered*, flurry*, tenderly*, flapped*, feebly*, peeked*, joyously*, winking*)

Think-and-Do Book: **Pages 77, 78, and 79**

Establishing background

Discussion of the title, the illustration, and the first paragraph on page 253 will establish the setting for the story and help youngsters set purposes for reading. After calling attention to the title, have pupils find the pronunciation of Joji (jō′jē) in the glossary. Then ask: "What clues does the picture give about the story? Who do you think Joji is? What is the scarecrow wearing? [If children do not know, write *kimono* and ask them to pronounce the word and find its meaning in the glossary.] What does this tell about where the story takes place? Are there other things in the picture or title that make you think of Japan? Why might people in Japan be familiar with fog?" If necessary, locate Japan on a map.

Continue: "What do you think Joji's job is? Does he seem to be succeeding in keeping the crows out of the rice field, or

Pupils identify new words ...

note setting of story ...

paddy? [You may wish to have children turn to the entry *paddy* in the glossary, read the definition, and study the illustration.] What do the picture and title make you want to find out as you read? I think you'll also be interested in discovering how Joji, the scarecrow, won the title of scarefog."

Fearsome and *dove* should be included in the list of words pupils can find in the glossary.

establish purposes for reading . . .

Interpreting the story

Immediately after silent reading focus discussion on the reason for Joji's fame as a scarefog. Read aloud the fourth paragraph on page 265, and ask pupils to explain how Joji won this reputation. Then let boys and girls discuss the questions they raised before reading which were answered by the story. During the conversation encourage them to tell which parts of the story they especially enjoyed and which parts they thought most humorous. If it is not mentioned, you might call attention to the double meaning of *foggiest* on page 258.

discuss story in light of purposes for reading . . .

To emphasize the contrast between the gentle Joji and the fearsome fog, first write on the board the following adjectives: *gentle, determined, greedy, gloomy, friendly, polite, selfish, troublesome, thoughtful, brave, frightful, thoughtless, helpful, unpleasant.* Then ask:

—Was Joji the type of character you'd expect a scarecrow to be? Why not? Which of the words on the board describe him? How do you know that he was both gentle and brave? In what ways did he show that he wanted to be friendly and polite, even to the fog?

identify traits of main characters . . .

—Which words in the list might be used to describe the fog as he was personified in the story? [Pupils should cite evidence to justify each response.] How did the author create the impression of the fog as a fearsome creature?

note personification of fog . . .

—Have you read or heard any other story or poem in which fog is personified in a different way? [Children who have heard or read Carl Sandburg's poem "Fog" might like to tell about this poet's description of fog.]

To point up the author's style and skill, call attention to the alliteration, witty wordplay, and vivid imagery of this story. First have pupils listen as you read aloud the second paragraph on page 254. With what one consonant sound do many of the words begin? Invite children to find similar phrases that appealed to them. (A few of the many examples that boys and girls might mention are *steaming on the stove* [page 255], *bath boiling and bubbling* [page 255], *swished and swashed* [page 256], *storming off into steaming space* [page 263], *fluttered about in a frightened flurry* [page 264].) During the discussion you might casually remark again that this repetition of beginning sounds in words is called alliteration. Bring out that this alliteration was not accidental, that the author planned it to help make the story fun to read and hear.

Then, after asking how it feels to be outside on a foggy day, encourage pupils to find phrases the author used to suggest dampness or moisture in personifying the fog. Make sure they do not overlook the more subtle references—for example, *thundered the fog, his face clouding up* (page 255); *foggy breath . . . oozed right through the farmhouse* (page 256); *It keeps me all steamed up* (page 259); *let off so much steam laughing* (page 260); *went storming off into steaming space* (page 263).

Lead children to observe the artist's contribution to the story's charm as they discuss these questions:
—How did the illustrations help you understand and enjoy this story? [You might point out that the style of the illustrations resembles that of Japanese art.]
—How do the pictures show the changing moods of the story? [Bring out the contrast between Joji's happy expression in the first and last pictures and his dismay in the ones on pages 254 and 259.]
—Why do you suppose the artist made the fog's face blue? [Some pupils may associate this color with the gloomy, depressive nature of the fog in the story, with the tendency of a foggy day to make one feel "blue," or with water.]

Finally encourage boys and girls to use the pictures in summarizing the main ideas of the story. Suggest that they look at

observe alliteration as element of author's style . . .

locate descriptive phrases used to create imagery . . .

note how pictures help create mood . . .

the first picture and think about the story episode it illustrates.
Next guide them in formulating a brief caption for it. When
the group has agreed on a concise, descriptive heading, write
it on the board. Continue in a similar manner with the other
illustrations. Then let youngsters use the captions on the
board as a basis for retelling the story. The completed list
may resemble the following:

associate main events
with pictures . . .

summarize and
retell the story . . .

Joji on Guard
A Fearsome Fog Arrives
The Fog Finds Water
The Farmer Returns
Joji Has a Plan
A Committee Meeting
Fooling the Fog
Rescue of the Hero

Extending competence

● As you guide pupils in comparing and contrasting this story
with others in the unit, lead them to recognize that "Joji and the
Fog" takes place in a specific country.
—In what way is this story like others in this part of the book?
—How does it differ from the other stories?
—What things would need to be changed if this story were set
in the United States instead of in Japan? [During the discussion you may wish to clarify the Japanese custom of washing
before getting into the tub (pages 262 and 265) and point up
the fog's breach of etiquette in this respect.]
—Do any of the other make-believe stories show the influence
of a particular time and place? Which ones show this? In
what way?
—Would a story written about a real or make-believe event in
our country today be concerned with princes, dukes, and
empires? Why not?

Pupils note relation
between settings and
specific aspects
of stories.

If there are pupils from varied cultural backgrounds in the
group, you might suggest that they share tales which originated
in other countries or cultures and which have been kept alive
in their own families or communities.

Extending interests

What do pupils think Joji might have said if he had been asked how he felt about crows? Read David McCord's "Crows" (in *Time for Poetry*), and ask whether Joji would have agreed with this poet's thoughts about crows.

Children hear a poet's thoughts about crows...

Boys and girls who enjoyed the oriental flavor of today's story will want to read Betty Jean Lifton's *Joji and the Dragon* and *The Very Special Badgers: A Tale of Magic from Japan,* retold by Claus Stamm. The illustrations might be used later by children in retelling both stories—how the crows rewarded Joji's friendship by helping their favorite scarecrow become a dragon-scarer, and how each of two tribes of badgers try to outcheat, outguess, and outmagic the other.

read two stories from Japan...

and use pictures in retelling them.

Evaluating progress

WORD ANALYSIS AND INTERPRETATION

The responses on page 77 of the *Think-and-Do Book* will help you in evaluating each child's ability to apply the word-analysis skills emphasized at this level. To complete the exercise, youngsters must apply what they have learned about affixes, spelling changes in root words when endings and suffixes are added, visual clues to vowel sounds in words of more than one syllable, and context clues as aids in identifying printed words.

Pupils take informal tests in Think-and-Do Book.

On pages 78-79 of the *Think-and-Do Book* children read statements that might have been made by story characters in *More Roads to Follow* and associate each statement with the character who made it. Responses will help you determine pupils' competence in grasping main ideas, making judgments, noting elements of style, perceiving relationships, using visual imagery and association of ideas as aids to memory.

PERSONAL READING

Because "the best evidence of a successful reading program is in the quantity and quality of reading that children do on their own," as A. Sterl Artley asserts in his special article in the *Guidebook* for *More Friends Old and New* (Book Two, Part

Two), you might look for assurance that pupils have been delving into a variety of reading materials that meets their different interests and reading levels. As you lead youngsters to recall and talk about examples of the many kinds of books and stories they have chosen to read on their own, it will become apparent that the rewards and pleasures reaped from reading increased as the scope of children's interests widened. A discussion of this sort will motivate boys and girls to explore further the world of reading during the summer months even as it helps you evaluate progress in personal reading.

The *Basic Reading Test* to accompany *More Roads to Follow* is to be given when pupils have finished reading the book. This test is designed to measure children's mastery of the skills, understandings, and vocabulary introduced at this level. The test results coupled with your personal evaluations should indicate which children can be expected to progress easily through the next reading level and which ones will probably need some special guidance.

Children take
Basic Reading Test.

Youngsters will be eager to read the new *Tall Tales, Part Two,* Revised Edition, the last of the five Reading for Independence books that accompany The New Basic Readers. The many new words in this book can be read without difficulty by youngsters who have mastered the sight vocabulary and word-analysis skills taught and reviewed in *More Roads to Follow.*

The central aim of the Reading for Independence books is to strengthen ability to read independently material that contains new words. Each book recognizes and deals constructively with conditions long familiar to the teacher: (1) if a child is to develop independence in the interpretation of written language, he must have material that interests him and is within the range of his ability; (2) if he is to establish the habit of identifying new words on his own initiative, he must encounter unfamiliar printed words that he can identify through the methods of word analysis he has learned to use; (3) if he is to master the skills of word analysis, he must apply them repeatedly.

Looking Back

Give pupils an opportunity to savor the pleasure they found in reading the selections in this book. First let youngsters tell whether they think *More Roads to Follow* is a good title for the book and why they think as they do. Then, as they look at the table of contents, encourage them to recall and share with one another their personal preferences. Ask:

—Which road led to the most exciting adventure?
—Which ones led to the discovery of new facts or information?
—Who was the most interesting person you met from the past?
—Who is your favorite of the friends along today's roads?
—Who is the most fascinating make-believe character?
—Which poem did you enjoy most?
—Along which roads did you see the most beautiful scenery? [Both word descriptions and illustrations should be recalled.]

Use the last question as a lead into a discussion of the contribution the pictures in this book made to children's enjoyment and learning. Which illustrations piqued their curiosity and made them want to read a selection? Which helped them sense the mood of a story or poem? Which increased their understanding of characters' feelings? In what other ways did pictures prove helpful? (Youngsters may find examples of illustrations that clarified the time and setting of stories, that helped them form mental images of characters, that explained action in a story, or that helped define an unfamiliar word or expression.) Which pictures did pupils enjoy most? Which did they think most amusing?

Children will be eager to take their books home if this is a pattern that has been followed in your school upon the completion of each book. Each child should be encouraged to select a favorite passage or story, review it carefully, and plan how he can bring the characters to life for listeners at home. Many youngsters, of course, will want to read several stories to various members of the family.

Pupils relate book title to contents ...

discuss contents from various points of view ...

recall favorite illustrations and consider their function.

Special Articles and Reference Materials

A Firm Foundation
for Middle Grades
by Helen M. Robinson

Bibliography

Methods of Analysis
Used to Identify Starred Words

Index of Skills, Abilities,
and Understandings

Cumulative Word List

A Firm Foundation
for Middle Grades

As boys and girls have progressed through the primary levels of The New Basic Reading Program, they have gradually acquired the basic word-perception and interpretive skills that make reading an enjoyable and purposeful activity. Not all pupils will have achieved the same degree of proficiency in every area. However, an overview of some of the major skills, abilities, and understandings that have been emphasized will give the teacher a general picture of the foundation that has been laid for successful and continued growth at middle-grade levels.

Word-perception skills and abilities

Although not an end in itself, word perception is fundamental to the reading process. One cannot comprehend, react to, or be influenced by the ideas of an author unless he can identify the printed words used to convey these ideas. One of the major goals of The New Basic Reading Program, therefore, is to teach children to respond to printed language as easily as they do to spoken language. Competent word perception rests on a foundation of efficiency in understanding relationships between spoken and written language, in using context clues, word analysis, and the dictionary.

Perceiving relationships between spoken and written language

The child who is ready to read uses and responds to hundreds of words in the flow of spoken language. His first reading experiences help him associate these familiar pronunciations and meanings with unfamiliar printed forms of words in context. In this way he builds up a stock of sight words on which he can base generalizations about the relationship between spellings and sounds (phonetic analysis) and about the function of root words and affixes (structural analysis).

When the pupil begins to read, he learns that printed words are separated by spaces and that he must look at a word from left to right. As he encounters words that are similar in appearance, he is led to note how words like *then* and *than* are different and to observe carefully the serial order of letters in words like *from* and *form*. Later his scrutiny of word forms reveals relationships in both form and meaning between such words as *friend, unfriendly,* and *friendship.*

Each time the child sees and hears a word in various contexts ("he left the yard," "his left hand"), he associates a different meaning with it and strengthens his memory of the word form. When he hears words that are not in his speaking vocabulary or when he uses the dictionary to find the meaning of unfamiliar printed words, he increases both his reading and his speaking vocabulary. At the same time he may be learning new meanings of familiar word forms.

Using context clues

Context clues are perhaps the most important single aid to word perception. Whether a youngster identifies a printed word quickly or whether he stops to analyze it, he must be sure it makes sense in the sentence. The use of context clues is based on two understandings of language: (1) a word may have more than one meaning (and pronunciation) and (2) meaning (and sometimes pronunciation) depends on context.

At early levels the child relies on pictures and sentence context for meaning clues. For example, if a picture of a horse accompanies the text in which the word *horse* is used, he is not likely to think that the word is *house*. Classification of words according to function is stressed too. When he reads "Tom has a pet cat," he anticipates that the last word in the sentence will name an animal; he is not likely to mistake the word *cat* for the word *eat*.

As the youngster learns to associate sounds with letters, he uses context clues to check words identified through phonetic analysis. For example, he can determine the sound that the letters *oo* stand for in such words as *cook* or *swoop* only by deciding which sound produces a word that makes sense in the sentence.

Later a child learns to use context clues to check appropriate meaning of prefixes and suffixes—for example, the prefix *un-* in *unhappy* and in *untie.* He develops skill in discriminating between various meanings and uses of words like *crowd* and *bark* and between meanings and pronunciations of words like *wind* and *row* in light of context.

As the pupil begins to use a glossary and a dictionary, he learns that he must always use context clues to choose the appropriate defined meaning. He also learns to use context clues to determine the accent as well as the meaning of words like *per fect'* and *per'fect.*

Gradually the child becomes aware that an unfamiliar word may be defined or its meaning explained in subsequent sentences or paragraphs. He discovers, too, that general context or the subject matter of a selection is a clue to the meaning of words. For example, the words *pitcher, batter,* and *plate* in an article about baseball have meanings different from those they have in an article about cooking.

In the middle and upper grades—indeed, throughout life—the reader will continue to use context clues, pictorial and verbal, to check word analysis, to discriminate between similar word forms, and to derive new meanings independently.

Analyzing words

To identify unfamiliar printed words that are already in his speaking-meaning vocabulary, the young reader must develop understandings of word analysis that he can use independently. Skill in associating sounds with the letters that commonly stand for them in groups of printed words which represent common spelling patterns, together with the habit of noting the structure of words, will enable the child to identify such words quickly and easily as he reads.

Phonetic analysis: Phonetic analysis is a means by which a reader determines the pronunciation of an unfamiliar printed word. It requires the ability (1) to hear and identify consonant sounds, vowel sounds, syllables, and accent; (2) to associate vowel and consonant sounds with the appropriate letters of the alphabet; and (3) to use spelling patterns as clues to vowel sounds in one-syllable words or in the accented syllables of words containing more than one syllable.

216

The child first learns to associate consonant sounds with the letters that commonly represent them in printed words. He then applies this knowledge in identifying one-syllable words. For example, he learns to identify such unfamiliar printed words as *make, hand, all* by substituting, adding, or dropping initial consonant letters in the known words *take, and, ball.*

As he learns to associate vowel sounds with the letters that commonly represent them in printed words, he begins to use these spelling patterns as clues to vowel sounds in one-syllable words:

—A single vowel letter followed by one or more consonant letters usually stands for a short vowel sound (*at, met, it, top, much*).

—Two vowel letters together in certain spelling patterns often stand for the long vowel sound that the first letter represents (*train, play, eat, need, tie, boat, toe*).

—A single vowel letter followed by one consonant letter and final *e* usually stands for a long vowel sound (*cake, Pete, fine, note, use*).

—A single vowel letter followed by two consonant letters and final *e* usually stands for a short vowel sound (*else, bridge*).

—A vowel letter followed by the letter *r* in certain spelling patterns usually represents an *r*-controlled vowel sound (*far, care, chair, store, deer, roar, large*).

—A single vowel letter at the end of a word usually stands for a long vowel sound (*he, so, my*).

—The letter *a* followed by *l, u,* or *w* usually stands for the vowel of *all* or *saw.*

—The letter *i* followed by the letters *gh* usually stands for the long *i* sound and the letters *gh* are silent (*night*).

—The letter *a* followed by one or more consonant letters and preceded by the letter *w* does not usually stand for the short *a* sound (*want, wash, watch, swan*).

As the next step in phonetic analysis, the child learns to hear syllables and accent and notes how accent affects vowel sounds. Drawing on what he has learned about vowel sounds in one-syllable words, he learns to use the following spelling patterns that function as clues to vowel sound in the accented syllable of two-syllable words:

—Two consonant letters following the first vowel letter are a clue to a short vowel sound (*jacket, silver*).

—A single vowel letter followed by one consonant letter may be a clue to a long or a short vowel sound (*silent, honor*).

217

—One consonant letter between a single vowel letter and *le* is a clue to a long vowel sound (*able*); two consonant letters are a clue to a short vowel sound (*bubble*).

—Spelling patterns that are clues to vowel sounds in one-syllable words apply in the accented syllable of many two-syllable words (*rain-raisin, point-poison, now-towel*).

—The vowel letter *a* or *e* followed by two *r*'s or a single *r* and a vowel letter does not represent the vowel of *car* or the vowel of *her* (*carrot, parent; errand, very*).

—The letter *a* followed by *l* is more likely to represent the vowel of *hat* than the vowel of *all* (*valley, palace*).

—A single vowel letter followed by a consonant blend often stands for a long vowel sound (*apron*).

—Two vowel letters together may represent two syllables, the first vowel letter usually representing a long vowel sound in an accented syllable (*science, lion, poet*).

As the young reader studies words containing more than two syllables, he discovers that the first or second syllable of a multisyllabic word is accented and that many words have two accents, primary and secondary. He also learns that clues to vowel sounds in two-syllable words apply to accented syllables in words of three or more syllables.

Structural analysis: Structural analysis is the means by which a pupil identifies meaningful parts of words—roots, endings, suffixes, prefixes.

The first step a pupil takes in structural analysis is that of noting root words and simple endings—*s, es, 's, ing, ed, er, est.* He also learns to recognize compounds made up of two known roots and contractions with one letter omitted.

At Book Two level the child learns to identify contractions with two or more letters omitted. He develops the understanding that prefixes and suffixes are meaningful parts of words; he learns the meaning of the prefix *un-* and the suffixes *-er, -y, -ly, -ful, -en, -ish;* and he begins to identify words with more than one affix (prefix, suffix, or ending). He notes that a suffix may change the function of the word to which it is added (for example, *I was happy; I played happily*). He learns that the spelling of a root word may change before an ending is added—final *y* changed to *i,* final *e* dropped, final consonant doubled.

Continuing his study of affixes at Book Three level, the youngster becomes acquainted with more prefixes (*im-, dis-, un-, a-, fore-, re-*) and

218

suffixes (*-ment, -ness, -less, -ous, -able, -ship, -teen, -th, -ty, -ward*). He notes the spelling change that occurs before *s* is added to form the plural of some words ending in *f* or *fe,* as in *halves* and *knives.* Through practice he reinforces two basic understandings: (1) endings, suffixes, and prefixes are meaningful parts of words, and (2) a root word retains one of its basic meanings in inflected and derived forms.

Using the dictionary

The dictionary is an indispensable tool for deriving the meaning and pronunciation of unfamiliar printed words that are not in the reader's vocabulary and for checking the accuracy of meanings and pronunciations derived through the use of context clues and word analysis.

Development of understandings that are basic to using a dictionary begins at an early level in The New Basic Reading Program. Before the dictionary is introduced, the pupil has acquired understandings about root words in inflected and derived forms. He has learned to recognize alphabetical sequence and general alphabetical position. He has had practice in selecting an appropriate definition to fit a specific context. He has learned to associate consonant and vowel sounds with the letters that represent them in printed words and to associate each vowel sound with the vowel sound in a key word.

Building on this knowledge, the child learns to use a glossary and dictionary. In learning to locate entries, he discovers the function of guide words and the need for identifying the root words in inflected forms. He learns about entries consisting of more than one word, abbreviations, special meanings, and homographs. He also becomes acquainted with the convention of cross reference.

He learns to use a pronunciation key and to interpret primary and secondary accent marks. He notes that for some words a dictionary gives more than one pronunciation. These pronunciations may be regional variations (*route*), or they may depend on the function of a word in context (*the rebel; they rebel*).

At the same time, the pupil discovers the ways in which a dictionary clarifies definitions of words—pictures and illustrative sentences, for example. He gains experience in choosing the correct meaning for a given context and in adapting definitions to fit that context.

By the end of third grade the child is prepared to use the dictionary efficiently to derive pronunciation and/or meaning of printed words he cannot identify through the use of context clues and word analysis.

Interpretive skills and abilities

Interpretation of written material calls a variety of skills into play. The flow of ideas on the page arouses a reaction on the part of the reader, and he in turn organizes these ideas into new patterns of thought. For the child who organizes, evaluates, and assimilates the insights gained, reading is a meaningful, rewarding experience.

In general there are two levels of interpretation, the experience level and the creative level. The first stories a youngster reads are largely within the realm of his experience. Because the people and the settings are familiar, he can interpret these stories in terms of what he knows about his own world. As the scope of his reading broadens, however, he learns to interpret at the creative level—to form and react to ideas and images that are beyond his immediate experience. To understand selections that deal with times, places, and cultures unlike his own, he must be able to visualize and evaluate the actions of the characters in terms of the circumstances that surround them.

As the pupil learns to interpret on each of these two levels, he is also learning to read critically. From the beginning he is encouraged to develop sound criteria or standards for judging the validity or worth of what he reads and for forming opinions about it. In considering differences between realistic and fanciful writing, between fact and opinion, between prose and verse, he learns to recognize types of material and what he can expect from each. He learns, for example, to test the validity of the statements or generalizations he makes by pointing out facts in the selection that support his assertions. When he reads historical fiction, he is encouraged to distinguish the factual basis from the fictional details added by the author. He begins to use information gained from reading one selection to aid him in interpreting another.

As reading demands more of the child, it is both important and logical that he demand more of reading. The interpretive skills discussed below are developed at the primary level in The New Basic Reading Program. At succeeding levels they will be refined and extended to help the young reader interpret more difficult material and to strengthen the habit of thorough and thoughtful interpretation of what he reads.

Comprehending phrase and sentence meaning

To comprehend what he reads, a youngster must understand the meanings of words in the context in which they appear.

The child's first experience with reading provides a transition from the picture book to the printed word. Illustrations carry the burden of the plot, while printed words indicate what the characters are saying and how they react. To comprehend the printed text, he must relate this conversation to the total action. The use of pronouns (*who, which, that*) and of words that indicate other relationships (*here, but*) provides an opportunity for the young reader to determine specific word meanings in relation to story context.

With the introduction of narrative text the reader assumes added responsibility for discovering what is happening in a story. He is called upon increasingly to visualize situations that are not pictured and to note relationships of place, time, and ideas indicated by the text. He learns that an idea may be expressed in different ways and that words used to express an idea, like *big* and *huge,* may convey different shades of meaning.

As interpretive ability grows, the child becomes aware that language is often idiomatic or figurative, that some expressions cannot be interpreted by determining word meanings alone. From familiar idiomatic phrases like *take time* and *catch cold* he progresses to similes, metaphors, personification, and other more complex figurative language encountered in poetry and fables.

Grasping the main idea

Fundamental to the interpretation of a selection is comprehension of the main idea. A pupil's ability to understand what happened in a story is dependent on his ability to understand how incidents or details are related to the whole.

Even at early levels, where the plot is carried by the illustrations, the young reader is encouraged to state in his own words the main idea of the pictured action. As he learns to summarize the action, he comes to view the story as a whole rather than as a series of isolated episodes.

At later levels the child begins to think beyond the story events to a central theme or a problem. He notes that this theme is often reflected in the story title or in expressions and sayings with which he may be familiar. And he is further encouraged to relate this central idea to the larger theme of a unit or a book. As ideas become more subtle, he is called upon to recognize main ideas that are centered in a character's attitudes and reactions rather than in a story situation.

Noting details and perceiving their relationship

A vital part of interpretation is the reader's perception of meaningful relationships in the text or in the illustrations. Even at early levels the child is encouraged to note clues to the story problem in text and pictures. He learns to anticipate plot development and to infer possible actions of the characters. On the basis of these relationships he begins to compare stories and story characters.

As the young reader gains skill in perceiving such relationships, he more easily grasps ideas that are implied rather than specifically stated in the text. He notes, for example, that the repetition of words may indicate the degree of a condition, as in *I see cars and cars and cars* and *The red boat was drifting, drifting,* and that descriptive details like *uneasy voice* and *sheepish grin* often indicate a character's reactions.

The child is encouraged to form opinions, make judgments, and make generalizations, defending his statements with details from the story and testing the validity of other statements.

Sensing emotional reactions and evaluating actions

Personal growth through reading depends largely on the ability to assimilate and evaluate the actions of story characters. When the child can recognize their reactions and evaluate their actions and ideas, he is on his way to making reading a living experience.

The first story characters a young reader meets are those with whom he can most easily identify. He considers the reactions of boys and girls his own age to situations like those that he is apt to meet. In evaluating the actions of these characters and relating their experiences to his own, he is establishing criteria for desirable standards of behavior.

As a pupil's reading experience broadens, he considers the characters' reactions in a variety of situations that may be unfamiliar to him. Some of these characters may be fanciful and the situations those that he would not expect to find in real life. Other situations deal with problems that he has yet to encounter in his own world. Eventually he learns to identify with reactions of characters in the remote past and to evaluate their actions in relation to circumstances in which they lived.

Forming sensory images

To participate in story events with the characters, the child must form images as he reads. When he visualizes the circumstances confronting the characters, he finds it easier to understand their reactions.

222

At first the images the youngster forms are of the types of people, places, and activities with which he is acquainted. Pictures help him visualize what may be unfamiliar. Gradually he becomes adept in recalling sights, sounds, and sensations that lie within his own experience and in associating them with story events. He then is led to form images that are delineated by words alone and to visualize intervening action that is not specifically mentioned.

A broader scope of subjects soon requires the young reader to visualize situations that are outside the realm of his own experience. To image places unlike his own surroundings, people unlike those he knows, and a past that is remote from his experience, he builds on familiar elements in his own experience. He modifies images as details are added until his mental picture brings the story to life and the clarity of his imagery aids him in its interpretation.

Perceiving relationships

The ability to relate ideas gained from reading and from everyday life will help the pupil evaluate and integrate new understandings as his reading experience grows.

When the child begins to read, he compares story events with experiences in his own life and notes clues to sequence, time, place, and cause-effect relationships.

A new step in interpretation is taken when he is required to keep several relationships in mind as he reads. In some stories, for example, he must visualize the simultaneous actions of several characters, and in others he must follow story events through a long time span or through several settings.

The young reader also begins to note relationships between stories. Beginning with realistic and fanciful material, he groups stories by type. Later experience with factual articles, poetry, historical fiction, and biography adds to his understanding of purposes and styles in writing. He also notes ways in which a group of stories are related to each other or to the central theme of a unit or a book.

With the introduction of historical fiction and biography the child is led to perceive relationships based on circumstances that are peculiar to a given place and time. Keeping the background in mind and adding whatever pertinent details he discovers as he reads will help him understand the characters and evaluate their reactions to the circumstances in which they lived.

Recognizing plot structure

Learning to recognize plot structure enables the pupil to see the relationships between the parts of a story, thereby increasing his understanding and appreciation of what he reads.

At the early levels each story usually presents a single brief episode. As the youngster progresses in reading, stories become longer and often cover several related incidents within the plot, which he learns to interpret sequentially. He also begins to pick up clues to story problems and their solutions.

Next the child becomes acquainted with introductory background material and its purpose and notes the starting point of the main action. He recognizes suspense as an element of plot interest. As he observes the repetitive pattern of folk tales, he begins to realize that different forms of writing have characteristic plot structures.

As the youngster's reading fare becomes more varied, there is greater opportunity for him to identify differences in story structure. He is led to note the distinguishing features of nonfictional writing, historical and biographical fiction, and the fable. In addition he is introduced to the flashback technique and is led to understand why an author uses this story-telling device.

Identifying author's or illustrator's purpose

Fiction and fantasy, biography and poetry are all written with different purposes in mind. When the child recognizes the author's and illustrator's purposes in choosing specific modes of presentation, he is clued to the way he is expected to interpret the material.

At early levels when the young reader distinguishes between realistic and fanciful elements in stories, he is acquiring skills necessary for making finer distinctions about more complex materials. After spotting clues to the fanciful nature of certain stories (the words *once upon a time* and *happily ever after* and the traditional three wishes), he notes that exaggeration may also be a key to fantasy—that although some things in a story or picture may be realistic, the absurd or extreme combination of these elements would hardly be found in real life.

In the course of story interpretation the child also discovers that the author or illustrator may choose and organize details with a specific effect in mind. He notes that details in text or pictures may be presented to help him visualize a situation, to create a specific mood, or to provide an adequate background for understanding events.

As the young reader interprets selections that are informative rather than imaginative, he learns to consider differences between fact and fiction in light of the author's purpose. He notes, for example, that some selections are written to impart information. When he reads historical fiction, he is encouraged to distinguish the factual basis from fictional details and to consider why the author added these details.

Identifying elements of style

When a child can identify the elements of style in prose and poetry, his appreciation of effective writing grows and he has made a start toward developing a discriminating taste in literature. Groundwork is laid at the earliest level to help him recognize elements of good writing.

The initial step is taken as the youngster learns to react to content, usually by forming associations with his own experiences and later by relating past and present reading in shaping his reactions. Through discussion of the words and phrases in a story he strengthens his ability to form sensory images, and by the time he has completed Book One he is beginning to note clues to pace and mood.

This foundation continues to be built upon at later levels as the child learns to interpret figurative, idiomatic, and picturesque language and to recognize exaggeration as an element of humor. At Book Two, Part Two level he takes the step from interpreting the author's words to identifying how the author achieves the effects he desires. He considers why certain figurative, idiomatic, and picturesque language has been used, and he looks for other image-forming and mood-creating expressions in the text. He begins to note distinctive story styles as he finds that folk tales are often repetitive and contain refrains with marked rhythm and rhyme.

At succeeding levels more and more emphasis is placed upon making the youngster aware of the power of expression in an author's or a poet's choice of words, particularly in creating imagery and establishing mood. While noting the impact of many literary tools, he also adds to his rhetorical terminology—*personification, alliteration, limerick,* and *nonsense verse,* for example, become a working part of his vocabulary.

Organizing or summarizing ideas

The child who summarizes and organizes ideas gained through reading remembers them more easily than he remembers isolated facts or incidents, and he finds it easier to utilize these ideas.

At early levels the young reader is encouraged to summarize the action on each page of a story or to state briefly the main idea of the entire story. While he is learning to spot important elements, he is also led to consider ways in which these elements may be organized. He notes, for example, the relationship between the theme of a book, the themes of its units, and the themes of stories in the units.

When the child has learned to summarize ideas and has noted that these ideas may be subdivided, he is ready to use a simple outline as a guide to remembering major points or for retelling a story. He begins to think in terms of important relationships and to subordinate detailed points to the main themes. These skills stand him in good stead when he begins to read factual material and to integrate and systematize information from several sources.

Reading aloud

Because reading is speech written down, the reader "hears" the natural cadences and intonations of speech as he follows the ideas on the printed page. If he understands what he reads, his auditory image of the written words will be accurate. The child who can reproduce this image as he reads aloud is demonstrating his understanding of the selection.

When the pupil begins to read and interpret stories, dramatic play helps him understand the feelings and actions of story characters. He then adds dialogue, using the natural intonations of speech to convey what the character feels.

Longer and more complex stories make heavier demands on the young reader. Longer sentences require him to read for continuity of thought without stopping at the end of a printed line. He must also be alert to changes in speakers, to transitions between narrative and dialogue, and to place relationships in the story, and he must cue his listeners to them by adjusting the pace and volume of his reading. If characters are talking at a distance, for example, he will "hear" them raise their voices, and he will raise his voice accordingly to help the audience visualize the scene.

Oral reading of nonfictional material requires even greater awareness of the way ideas are conveyed by natural intonations of speech. To hold the interest of listeners, the child must make these ideas understandable by reading in the same easy manner in which he would explain the matter to a friend. Assuming responsibility for communicating with his listeners sets him well on the road toward effective oral reading.

Bibliography

Books and stories

ROADS HERE AND THERE

Anderson, C. W. *Blaze and the Forest Fire*. Macmillan.
————. *Blaze Finds the Trail*. Macmillan.
Arbuthnot, May Hill, comp. *The Arbuthnot Anthology of Children's Literature**
  "The Doughnuts," by Robert McCloskey
  The Hundred Dresses, by Eleanor Estes
  Justin Morgan Had a Horse, by Marguerite Henry (selection)
Carroll, Ruth and Latrobe. *Beanie*. Walck.
————. *Tough Enough and Sassy*. Walck.
Chandler, Edna Walker. *Charley Brave*. Whitman.
Ciardi, John. *The Reason for the Pelican*. Lippincott.

An asterisk (*) following the title of a book indicates that complete bibliographical information for the book is given under the heading "Collections of stories and poems, reference books."

227

DeJong, Meindert. *The Last Little Cat.* Harper.
———. *The Singing Hill.* Harper.
Haywood, Carolyn. *Eddie and Gardenia.* Morrow.
———. *Eddie and Louella.* Morrow.
———. *Penny and Peter.* Harcourt.
Henry, Marguerite. *All about Horses.* Random House.
———. *Justin Morgan Had a Horse.* Rand.
Lenski, Lois. *Little Sioux Girl.* Lippincott.
Nordstrom, Ursula. *The Secret Language.* Harper.
Schweitzer, Byrd Baylor. *Amigo.* Macmillan.
Thompson, Vivian L. *Faraway Friends.* Holiday.

INTERESTING PEOPLE ALONG THE WAY

Arbuthnot, May Hill, comp. *The Arbuthnot Anthology of Children's Literature**
        Martin and Abraham Lincoln, by Catherine Cate Coblentz
        Pierre Pidgeon, by Lee Kingman
        The Wright Brothers, by Quentin Reynolds (selection)
Aulaire, Ingri and Edgar Parin d'. *Abraham Lincoln.* Doubleday.
Cavanah, Frances. *Abe Lincoln Gets His Chance.* Rand.
Coblentz, Catherine Cate. *Martin and Abraham Lincoln.* Childrens Press.
Gage, Wilson. *A Wild Goose Tale.* World.
Kingman, Lee. *Pierre Pidgeon.* Houghton.
Kuskin, Karla. *In the Middle of the Trees.* Harper.
Leaf, Munro. *Wee Gillis.* Viking.
Le Grand. *How Space Rockets Began.* Abingdon.
Rose, Mary Catherine. *Clara Barton, Soldier of Mercy.* Garrard.
Stevenson, Augusta. *Daniel Boone, Boy Hunter.* Bobbs.
Van Riper, Guernsey, Jr. *Babe Ruth, Baseball Boy.* Bobbs.

ROADS TO MAKE-BELIEVE

Arbuthnot, May Hill, comp. *The Arbuthnot Anthology of Children's Literature**
        "The Crow and the Pitcher" (fable from Aesop)
        "The Master Cat" (French folk tale)
        "The Shepherd's Boy" (fable from Aesop)
        "That Is Why He Was Always Called Pooh," by A. A. Milne.

Artzybasheff, Boris, ed. *Aesop's Fables*. Viking.
Ciardi, John. *John J. Plenty and Fiddler Dan*. Lippincott.
Corbett, Scott. *The Limerick Trick*. Little.
Dickens, Charles. *The Magic Fishbone*. Vanguard.
Evans, Katherine. *A Camel in the Tent*. Whitman.
————. *The Man, the Boy, and the Donkey*. Whitman.
Haviland, Virginia, ed. *Favorite Fairy Tales Told in France*. Little.
Johnson, Elizabeth. *The Three-in-One Prince*. Little.
Lifton, Betty Jean. *Joji and the Dragon*. Morrow.
Lindgren, Astrid. *Mischievous Meg*. Viking.
————. *Pippi Longstocking*. Viking.
Milne, A. A. *Winnie-the-Pooh*. Dutton.
Nash, Ogden. *Custard the Dragon*. Little.
Stamm, Claus. *The Very Special Badgers: A Tale of Magic from Japan*. Viking.

Collections of stories and poems, reference books

Arbuthnot, May Hill, comp. *The Arbuthnot Anthology of Children's Literature*, Revised Edition. Scott, Foresman.
————. *Time for Poetry*, General Edition, Revised. Scott, Foresman.
Audubon, John James. *The Birds of America*. Macmillan.
Childcraft: The How and Why *Library*. Field.
Huber, Miriam Blanton, comp. *Story and Verse for Children*, Revised Edition. Macmillan.
Johnson, Edna; Scott, Carrie E.; and Sickels, Evelyn R.; comps. *Anthology of Children's Literature*, Third Edition. Houghton.

Books for the teacher

Arbuthnot, May Hill. *Children and Books*, Third Edition. Scott, Foresman.
Eakin, Mary K., comp. *Good Books for Children*, Revised and Enlarged. University of Chicago.
Gray, William S. *On Their Own in Reading*, Revised Edition. Scott, Foresman.
Huck, Charlotte S., and Young, Doris A. *Children's Literature in the Elementary School*. Holt.

Jenkins, Gladys Gardner, and others. *These Are Your Children,* Expanded Edition. Scott, Foresman.

Larrick, Nancy. *A Teacher's Guide to Children's Books.* Merrill.

Directory of publishers

ABINGDON. Abingdon Press, New York, New York.

BOBBS. The Bobbs-Merrill Company, Inc., New York, New York.

CHILDRENS PRESS. Childrens Press, Inc., Chicago, Illinois.

DOUBLEDAY. Doubleday & Company, Inc., Garden City, New York.

DUTTON. E. P. Dutton & Company, Inc., New York, New York.

FIELD. Field Enterprises Educational Corporation, Chicago, Illinois.

GARRARD. Garrard Publishing Company, Scarsdale, New York.

HARCOURT. Harcourt, Brace & World, Inc., New York, New York.

HARPER. Harper & Row, Publishers, New York, New York.

HOLIDAY. Holiday House, New York, New York.

HOLT. Holt, Rinehart and Winston, Inc., New York, New York.

HOUGHTON. Houghton Mifflin Company, Boston, Massachusetts.

LIPPINCOTT. J. B. Lippincott Company, Philadelphia, Pennsylvania.

LITTLE. Little, Brown and Company, Boston, Massachusetts.

MACMILLAN. The Macmillan Company, New York, New York.

MERRILL. Charles E. Merrill Books, Inc., Columbus, Ohio.

MORROW. William Morrow and Company, Inc., New York, New York.

RAND. Rand McNally & Company, Skokie, Illinois.

RANDOM HOUSE. Random House, New York, New York.

SCOTT, FORESMAN. Scott, Foresman and Company, Chicago, Illinois.

UNIVERSITY OF CHICAGO. University of Chicago Press, Chicago, Illinois.

VANGUARD. The Vanguard Press, Inc., New York, New York.

VIKING. The Viking Press, Inc., New York, New York.

WALCK. Henry Z. Walck, Inc., New York, New York.

WHITMAN. Albert Whitman & Company, Chicago, Illinois.

WORLD. The World Publishing Company, Cleveland, Ohio.

Methods of Analysis Used
to Identify Starred Words

As children read *More Roads to Follow* they can be expected to identify independently the 625 words in the following list. Of this number, 591 are words that pupils should identify by combining context clues with methods of word analysis developed at preceding levels; these words are printed in blue and include 561 new root words and forms of new root words as well as 30 new forms of known words (including words made by adding or dropping the prefixes *a-, dis-, im-;* the suffixes *-less, -ment, -ness, -ous;* and plurals of words that end in *f* or *fe*). The 34 words that are printed in black are words that youngsters should identify by combining context clues with word-analysis skills that have been taught at this level.

The method of word analysis pupils may use is indicated following each word or grouping of words. Since the pronunciation of words like *bade, class, dew, costs, syrup,* and *neither* varies in different parts of the country, accept whichever pronunciation children are accustomed to using.

Roads Here and There
Billy and Thunderbolt, pages 9-17
Thunderbolt*, bareback* —compound (bolt—visual clue to long vowel sound; bare—visual clue to *r*-controlled vowel sound)
ranch*, west*, stretch*, ledge*, buck*—visual clue to short vowel sound
bought*—visual clue to vowel sound

trailer*—root plus suffix (trail—visual clue to long vowel sound)
enjoyed*, trusted*—root plus ending (enjoy—visual clue to vowel sound in accented syllable; trust—visual clue to short vowel sound)
cattle*, saddle*, except*, distance*, bother*, gentle*, unless*—visual clue to short vowel sound in accented syllable

arrived*, trembled*—root with final *e* dropped plus ending (arrive—visual clue to long vowel sound in accented syllable; tremble—visual clue to short vowel sound in accented syllable)

bridle*, eager*, advice*, became*—visual clue to long vowel sound in accented syllable

wore*, herd*, harm*—visual clue to *r*-controlled vowel sound

gaily*—root with final *y* changed to *i* plus suffix (gay—visual clue to long vowel sound)

twice*, shade*, mine*—visual clue to long vowel sound

whinnied*—root with final *y* changed to *i* plus ending (whinny—visual clue to short vowel sound in accented syllable)

moment*—context to determine vowel sound in accented syllable

lonely*—base of known form *alone* plus suffix

rear*—context to determine vowel sound

When Is a Horse a Pony? pages 18-19

breeds*, size*—visual clue to long vowel sound

less*—visual clue to short vowel sound

inches*—root plus ending (inch—visual clue to short vowel sound)

measured*—root with final *e* dropped plus ending (measure—context to determine vowel sound in accented syllable)

twenty*, Shetland*—visual clue to short vowel sound in accented syllable

world* (word, work)—consonant substitution

Out of Her Shell, pages 20-26

shell*, desk*, sell*, punch*—visual clue to short vowel sound

groups*(soup)—consonant substitution

Denmark*, extra*, giggle*, costumes*, envy*—visual clue to short vowel sound in accented syllable

classes*, gasped*, insisted*, frowned*, sandwiches*, added*—root plus ending (class, gasp, add—visual clue to short vowel sound; insist, sandwich—visual clue to short vowel sound in accented syllable; frown—context to determine vowel sound)

divided*—root with final *e* dropped plus ending (divide—visual clue to long vowel sound in accented syllable)

booth*, heart*—context to determine vowel sound

Larsen*—visual clue to *r*-controlled vowel sound in accented syllable

shyly*—root plus suffix (shy—visual clue to long vowel sound)

sort*—visual clue to *r*-controlled vowel sound

hastily*—root plus suffixes and spelling changes (haste—visual clue to long vowel sound)

pity*, manage*, stupid*—context to determine vowel sound in accented syllable

excuse*—visual clue to long vowel sound in accented syllable

joy*—visual clue to vowel sound

The World of Hogback Mountain, pages 27-34

precious*, figure*, present*—context to determine vowel sound in accented syllable mountain*—visual clue to vowel sound in accented syllable

Rufe*—visual clue to vowel of *boot*

doctor*, dollars*, fellow* — visual clue to short vowel sound in accented syllable

sighed*, wandered*, snatched*, swallowed*—root plus ending (sigh—visual clue to long vowel sound; wander, swallow—visual clue to vowel sound in accented syllable; snatch—visual clue to short vowel sound)

costs*, cliff*, rod*, stuck*—visual clue to short vowel sound

chairbound*, halfway*—compound (bound—visual clue to vowel sound; half—visual clue to short vowel sound)

leafy*—root of known form *leaves* plus suffix

whittling*, carved*, startled*, stared*, ruffling*—root with final *e* dropped plus ending (whittle, ruffle—visual clue to short vowel sound in accented syllable; carve, stare—visual clue to *r*-controlled vowel sound; startle—visual clue to *r*-controlled vowel sound in accented syllable)

sharp*, worth*— visual clue to *r*-controlled vowel sound

sea*, mind*, smoke*, pines*, trade* —visual clue to long vowel sound

forty*, forward*—visual clue to *r*-controlled vowel sound in accented syllable

breath*, moon*, tears*—context to determine vowel sound

speechless*—base word plus suffix (speech—visual clue to long vowel sound)

Charley Brave, pages 37-45

impatiently*—base word plus prefix and suffix (patient—context to determine vowel sound in accented syllable)

Charley*—visual clue to *r*-controlled vowel sound in accented syllable

dust*, mad*, dumb*, cloth*, song*, stuff*, fact*—visual clue to short vowel sound

Jean*, drove*, pay*—visual clue to long vowel sound

nurse*—visual clue to *r*-controlled vowel sound

Jerome*—visual clue to long vowel sound in accented syllable

panting*, suggested*—root plus ending (pant—visual clue to short vowel sound; suggest—visual clue to short vowel sound in accented syllable)

boiling-hot*—compound (boiling—root plus ending; boil—visual clue to vowel sound)

mistaken*—root with final *e* dropped plus ending (mistake—visual clue to long vowel sound in accented syllable)

lawn*—visual clue to vowel sound

mower*—root plus suffix (mow—context to determine vowel sound)

cocoa*, Friday*—context to determine vowel sound in accented syllable

granny*—visual clue to short vowel sound in accented syllable

aloud*—known root plus prefix

meant*—context to determine vowel sound

honey* (money)—consonant substitution

Louella, pages 48-57

shrieked*, allowed*, sputtered*, wailed*, loaned*, spilled*—root plus ending (shriek—visual clue to vowel of *eat;* allow—context to determine vowel sound in accented syllable; sputter—visual clue to short vowel sound in accented syllable; wail, loan—visual clue to long vowel sound; spill—visual clue to short vowel sound)

stray*, scream*, paid*—visual clue to long vowel sound

rewards*—visual clue to vowel sound in accented syllable

changed*, hated*, revolving*, refused*, declared*—root with final *e* dropped plus ending (change—visual clue to vowel sound; hate—visual clue to long vowel sound; revolve—visual clue to short vowel sound in accented syllable; refuse—visual clue to long vowel sound in accented syllable; declare—visual clue to *r*-controlled vowel sound in accented syllable)

parrot* (carrot)—consonant substitution

jealous*, Texas*, hotel*, lady*—context to determine vowel sound in accented syllable

themselves*—compound (selves—known root plus ending and spelling change)

appeared*—root of known form *disappeared* plus ending

dance*, tag*—visual clue to short vowel sound

borrow*, pardon*—visual clue to *r*-controlled vowel sound in accented syllable

south*—visual clue to vowel sound

drew*—visual clue to vowel of *boot*

enter*, written*, collar*—visual clue to short vowel sound in accented syllable

wagging*—root with final consonant doubled plus ending (wag—visual clue to short vowel sound)

Soo-Pung Measures Up, pages 58-65

Chinese*—visual clue to long vowel sound in accented syllable

excitement*, eagerness*, goodness*, measurement*—known root plus suffix

awakened*, dissatisfied*—known word (wakened, satisfied) plus prefix

Chinatown*—compound (China—context to determine vowel sound in accented syllable)

rice*, soles*, beans*, teeth*—visual clue to long vowel sound

dragon*—context to determine vowel sound in accented syllable

sprouts*, pound*, wall*—visual clue to vowel sound

silk*, Ping*, Lin*, ills*, thick*, wedges*, swung*, mid*—visual clue to short vowel sound

burst*, pairs*—visual clue to *r*-controlled vowel sound

trousers*—visual clue to vowel sound in accented syllable

shiny*—root with final *e* dropped plus suffix (shine—visual clue to long vowel sound)

marked*, switching*—root plus ending (mark—visual clue to *r*-controlled vowel sound; switch—visual clue to short vowel sound)

despair*, person*—visual clue to *r*-controlled vowel sound in accented syllable

234

possibly*—root of known form *impossible* with final *e* dropped plus suffix

shaped*—root with final *e* dropped plus ending (shape—visual clue to long vowel sound)

wisdom*—visual clue to short vowel sound in accented syllable

It's a Wolf, pages 66-74

backwards*—known root plus suffix and ending

vicious*—context to determine vowel sound in accented syllable

cautiously*—base word plus suffix (cautious—visual clue to vowel sound in accented syllable)

relieved*, lying*—root plus ending and spelling change (relief—visual clue to vowel of *eat* in accented syllable; lie—visual clue to long vowel sound)

delighted*, sniffing*, peered*—root plus ending (delight—visual clue to long vowel sound in accented syllable; sniff—visual clue to short vowel sound; peer—visual clue to *r*-controlled vowel sound)

bunk*, spent*, mist*, stag*, bent*, lump*, gun*, lick*, chops*, scamp*—visual clue to short vowel sound

shone*, doe*—visual clue to long vowel sound

antlers*—visual clue to short vowel sound in accented syllable

plainly*, stiffly*, fearfully*, toasty*—root plus one or more suffixes (plain, toast—visual clue to long vowel sound; stiff—visual clue to short vowel sound; fear—context to determine vowel sound)

paused*, choked*, chuckled*—root with final *e* dropped plus ending (pause—visual clue to vowel sound; choke—visual clue to long vowel sound; chuckle—visual clue to short vowel sound in accented syllable)

ceiling*—visual clue to long vowel sound in accented syllable

fairy*—visual clue to *r*-controlled vowel sound in accented syllable

growl*—context to determine vowel sound

apart*—known root plus prefix

fur*—visual clue to *r*-controlled vowel sound

rubbed*—root with final consonant doubled plus ending (rub—visual clue to short vowel sound)

May Day and Lei Day, pages 77-79

states*—visual clue to long vowel sound

united*—root with final *e* dropped plus ending (unite—visual clue to long vowel sound in accented syllable)

Maile's Lei, pages 80-87

giant*, beneath*, needle*—visual clue to long vowel sound in accented syllable

mention*,blossoms*,contest*,Japan*, ribbon*—visual clue to short vowel sound in accented syllable

alive*, aboard*—known root plus prefix

two-toned*—compound with final *e* dropped plus ending (tone—visual clue to long vowel sound)

win*, nets*, mix*—visual clue to short vowel sound

235

prize*—visual clue to long vowel sound

dead*, thread*—context to determine vowel sound

shaved*, glanced*, grumbled*, judging*—root with final e dropped plus ending (shave—visual clue to long vowel sound; glance, judge—visual clue to short vowel sound; grumble—visual clue to short vowel sound in accented syllable)

syrup*—visual clue to r-controlled vowel sound in accented syllable

coconut*—compound (coco—context to determine vowel sound in accented syllable)

disappointment*—root of known form disappointed plus suffix

dew*—visual clue to long vowel sound or vowel of boot

reminded*—root plus ending (remind—visual clue to long vowel sound in accented syllable)

mayor*—visual clue to long vowel sound in accented syllable

Manaluk's Gold Rush, pages 88-99

gold*, post*, lie*, weeds*, sky*, waist*—visual clue to long vowel sound

crayons*—visual clue to long vowel sound in accented syllable

peaches*, loaded*, flushed*, melted*, scooped*—root plus ending (peach, load—visual clue to long vowel sound; flush, melt—visual clue to short vowel sound; scoop—context to determine vowel sound)

sled*, pack*, hid*, mud*, rich*, till*, sick*—visual clue to short vowel sound

rescued*, striking*—root with final e dropped plus ending (rescue—visual clue to short vowel sound in accented syllable; strike—visual clue to long vowel sound)

whiskers*, pencil*, pebbles*, single*, castor*, bottle*—visual clue to short vowel sound in accented syllable

chores*—visual clue to r-controlled vowel sound

sickness*—known root plus suffix

threw*—visual clue to vowel of boot

squishy*—word plus suffix (squish—visual clue to short vowel sound)

Interesting People along the Way

The Babe, pages 102-110

babe*, ache*—visual clue to long vowel sound

Herman*, aware*—visual clue to r-controlled vowel sound in accented syllable

New York*—compound (York—visual clue to r-controlled vowel sound)

Yankees*, mischief*, problems*, fifteen*, hundred*, mustard*—visual clue to short vowel sound in accented syllable

fan*, chant*, tip*—visual clue to short vowel sound

bleachers*, tailor*—visual clue to long vowel sound in accented syllable

earn*—context to determine vowel sound

lanky*—root plus suffix (lank—visual clue to short vowel sound)

famous*—root with final e dropped plus suffix (fame—visual clue to long vowel sound)

236

lathered*—root plus ending (lather —visual clue to short vowel sound in accented syllable)

happiness*—known root with final *y* changed to *i* plus suffix

illness*—known root plus suffix

Get 'Em While They're Hot, pages 111-114

heat*, laid*, queen*—visual clue to long vowel sound

Coney*—context to determine vowel sound in accented syllable

Charlie*—visual clue to *r*-controlled vowel sound in accented syllable

inns*—visual clue to short vowel sound

obliged*, served*—root with final *e* dropped plus ending (oblige— visual clue to long vowel sound in accented syllable; serve—visual clue to *r*-controlled vowel sound)

sausage*, royal*—visual clue to vowel sound in accented syllable

wrapping*—root with final conso- nant doubled plus ending (wrap— visual clue to short vowel sound)

picnics*—visual clue to short vowel sound in accented syllable

Audubon's Birds, pages 117-126

upward*—known root plus suffix

marry*—visual clue to vowel sound in accented syllable

Frenchman*, underbrush*—com- pound (french, brush—visual clue to short vowel sound)

Lucy*—context to determine vowel sound in accented syllable

cave*, James*, fate*—visual clue to long vowel sound

nest*, rust*—visual clue to short vowel sound

graceful*, healthy*—root plus suffix (grace—visual clue to long vowel sound; health—context to deter- mine vowel sound)

gazed*, urged*, wasting*—root with final *e* dropped plus ending (gaze, waste—visual clue to long vowel sound; urge—visual clue to *r*-controlled sound)

dipped*—root with final consonant doubled plus ending (dip—visual clue to short vowel sound)

distant*—visual clue to short vowel sound in accented syllable

protested*, discussing*—root plus ending (protest, discuss—visual clue to short vowel sound in ac- cented syllable)

born*—visual clue to *r*-controlled vowel sound

bracelet*—context to determine vowel sound in accented syllable

indeed*—visual clue to long vowel sound in accented syllable

Sequoyah's Talking Leaves, pages 128-135

brief*—visual clue to vowel of *eat*

lame*, sheets*, tribe*, peace*—vis- ual clue to long vowel sound

magic*, honors*—context to deter- mine vowel sound in accented syl- lable

destroy*, daughter*—visual clue to vowel sound in accented syllable

spelling*, leaking*, printed*—root plus ending (spell, print—visual clue to short vowel sound; leak— visual clue to long vowel sound)

threatened*—root plus suffix and ending (threat—context to deter- mine vowel sound) foolishness*—known word *foolish* plus suffix

anger*—visual clue to short vowel sound in accented syllable

hut*—visual clue to short vowel sound

speech*—base of known form *speechless*

arranged*—root with final *e* dropped plus ending (arrange—visual clue to long vowel sound in accented syllable)

Sequoyah's Honors, pages 136-139

statue*—context to determine vowel sound in accented syllable

amazing*—root with final *e* dropped plus ending (amaze—visual clue to long vowel sound in accented syllable)

Abe Lincoln, pages 140-153

truth*—known root with final *e* dropped plus suffix

apron*—context to determine vowel sound in accented syllable

Abe*, Thee*, cheeks*, mite*—visual clue to long vowel sound

Lincoln*, Johnston*, bonnet*, Dennis*, wicked*, reckon*, dander*—visual clue to short vowel sound in accented syllable

Crawford*—visual clue to vowel sound in accented syllable

loft*, rinse*, damp*, tub*, hug*—visual clue to short vowel sound

ain't*—contraction

meekly*, sternly*—root plus suffix (meek—visual clue to long vowel sound; stern—visual clue to *r*-controlled vowel sound)

wiped*—root with final *e* dropped plus ending (wipe—visual clue to long vowel sound)

blessing*, spanked*, towering*—root plus ending (bless, spank—visual clue to short vowel sound; tower—context to determine vowel sound in accented syllable)

Lord*—visual clue to *r*-controlled vowel sound

stool*—context to determine vowel sound

didos*—context to determine vowel sound in accented syllable

breathlessly*—known root plus suffixes

Captain Smith of Jamestown, pages 157-162

terror*—visual clue to vowel sound in accented syllable

captured*—root with final *e* dropped plus ending (capture—visual clue to short vowel sound in accented syllable)

Smith*, tents*, clubs*—visual clue to short vowel sound

protected*—root plus ending (protect—visual clue to short vowel sound in accented syllable)

beads*, pale*—visual clue to long vowel sound

prisoner*—root plus suffix (prison—context to determine vowel sound in accented syllable)

spared*—root with final *e* dropped plus ending (spare—visual clue to r-controlled vowel sound)

The Girl with Three Names, pages 163-171

palace*, Thomas*—context to determine vowel sound in accented syllable

meal*, scrape*, Dale*—**visual clue to long vowel sound**

arguing*— root with final *e* dropped plus ending (argue—visual clue to *r*-controlled vowel sound in accented syllable)

argument*—root of known form *arguing* with final *e* dropped plus suffix

church*—visual clue to *r*-controlled vowel sound

Rolfe*—visual clue to short vowel sound

princess*—visual clue to short vowel sound in accented syllable

Roads to Make-Believe

Puss-in-Boots, pages 175-186

salad*, majesty*, cruel* tiger*, favor*—context to determine vowel sound in accented syllable

puss-in-boots*—compound (puss—context to determine vowel sound)

jacket*, master*, butler*, accept*, alas*, castle*, handsome*—visual clue to short vowel sound in accented syllable

sack*, wits*, split*, clap*—visual clue to short vowel sound

duke*—visual clue to long vowel sound or vowel of *boot*

poked*, rumbling*—root with final *e* dropped plus ending (poke—visual clue to long vowel sound; rumble—visual clue to short vowel sound in accented syllable)

throne*, dine*, coach*, cape*—visual clue to long vowel sound

drowning*, shivering*—root plus ending (drown—context to determine vowel sound; shiver—context to determine vowel sound in accented syllable)

guard*—visual clue to *r*-controlled vowel sound

barley*, larder*—visual clue to *r*-controlled vowel sound in accented syllable

hallo*—visual clue to long vowel sound in accented syllable

greedy*, faithful*—root plus suffix (greed, faith—visual clue to long vowel sound)

cloud*—visual clue to vowel sound

The Three Wishes, pages 187-192

fortunate*, prefer*—visual clue to *r*-controlled vowel sound in accented syllable

diamonds*—visual clue to long vowel sound in accented syllable

humble*, cottage*, empire*, instant*, rather*—visual clue to short vowel sound in accented syllable

granted*, complaining*, slightest*—root plus ending (grant—visual clue to short vowel sound; complain—visual clue to long vowel sound in accented syllable; slight—visual clue to long vowel sound)

pearls*—context to determine vowel sound

fault*—visual clue to vowel sound

towel*—context to determine vowel sound in accented syllable

Rapunzel, pages 193-201

Rapunzel*, rampion*, content*, thicket*, kingdom*—visual clue to short vowel sound in accented syllable

comfort*, proper*—context to determine vowel sound in accented syllable remarkable*—root plus suffix (re-mark—visual clue to r-controlled vowel sound in accented syllable)

terrified*—word with final y changed to i plus ending (terrify—visual clue to vowel sound in accented syllable)

surrounded*, enchanted*, blinded* —root plus ending (surround—visual clue to vowel sound in accented syllable; enchant—visual clue to short vowel sound in accented syllable; blind—visual clue to long vowel sound)

dared*, siezed*—root with final e dropped plus ending (dare—visual clue to r-controlled vowel sound; seize—visual clue to long vowel sound)

witch*, dusk*, fetch*, scratch*, crept*, snip*, wept*—visual clue to short vowel sound

slipped*, sobbing*—root with final consonant doubled plus ending (slip, sob—visual clue to short vowel sound)

neither*, deceive*—visual clue to long vowel sound in accented syllable

nor*, thorn*—visual clue to r-controlled vowel sound

child*, bade*, braids*, rage*—visual clue to long vowel sound

sweetly*—root plus suffix (sweet—visual clue to long vowel sound)

learnt*—context to determine vowel sound

sadness*—known root plus suffix

The Dog in the Manger, page 202

ox*, nap*—visual clue to short vowel sound

muttering*—root plus ending (mut-ter—visual clue to short vowel sound in accented syllable)

The Ant and the Grasshopper, page 203

ant*, chat*—visual clue to short vowel sound

The Dove and the Ant, page 204

stream*—visual clue to long vowel sound

helplessly*—known root plus suffixes

fowler*—root plus suffix (fowl—context to determine vowel sound)

deserves*—visual clue to r-controlled vowel sound in accented syllable

The Plate of Pancakes, pages 207-213

astonished*, frying*, selected*, crisp-est*, lingered*, hindered*—root plus ending (astonish, select—context to determine vowel sound in accented syllable; fry—visual clue to long vowel sound; crisp—visual clue to short vowel sound; linger, hinder—visual clue to short vowel sound in accented syllable)

fourteenth*—known root plus suf-fixes

fifteenth*—known word *fifteen* plus suffix

sawmill*—compound (mill—visual clue to short vowel sound)

Karl*—visual clue to r-controlled vowel sound

napkin*, goblins*—visual clue to short vowel sound in accented syl-lable

ripe*—visual clue to long vowel sound

disagreed*—known word *agreed* plus prefix

bid*, tempt*—visual clue to short vowel sound

count*—visual clue to vowel sound

Pippi Is a Thing-Finder, pages 217-231

absolutely*, utterly*—root plus suffix (absolute, utter—visual clue to short vowel sound in accented syllable)

Pippi*, villa*, gutter*, candy*, pickets*, hubbles*, necklace*, Willie*, hollow*, pillow*—visual clue to short vowel sound in accented syllable

Longstocking*, playmate*—compound (stocking—visual clue to short vowel sound in accented syllable; mate—visual clue to long vowel sound)

cradle*—visual clue to long vowel sound in accented syllable

dull*, thin*, rats*, hutch*, tin*, Bengt*, hash*, stump*, tuck*, slept*, quilt*—visual clue to short vowel sound

silence*, lazy*, cowards*—context to determine vowel sound in accented syllable

screws*—visual clue to vowel of *boot*

knees*, heels*, fight*—visual clue to long vowel sound

jar*, birch*—visual clue to r-controlled vowel sound

spool*, loop*—context to determine vowel sound

astonishment*—root of known form *astonished* plus suffix

coral*—visual clue to r-controlled vowel sound in accented syllable

Pooh Goes Visiting, pages 238-250

Christopher*, Edward*—visual clue to short vowel sound in accented syllable

Pooh*—context to determine vowel sound

Winnie-the-Pooh*, good-bye*—compound (Winnie—visual clue to short vowel sound in accented syllable; bye—visual clue to long vowel sound)

humming*—root with final consonant doubled plus ending (hum—visual clue to short vowel sound)

stoutness*, directly*—root plus suffix (stout—visual clue to vowel sound; direct—visual clue to short vowel sound in accented syllable)

scuffling*, condensed*—root with final e dropped plus ending (scuffle, condense—visual clue to short vowel sound in accented syllable)

mugs*—visual clue to short vowel sound

carelessly*, tightness*—known root plus one or more suffixes

robin*—context to determine vowel sound in accented syllable

deal*—visual clue to long vowel sound

sustaining*, slenderer*—root plus ending (sustain—visual clue to long vowel sound in accented syllable; slender—visual clue to short vowel sound in accented syllable)

north*, cork*—visual clue to r-controlled vowel sound

Joji and the Fog, pages 253-265

kimono*, duty*—context to determine vowel sound in accented syllable fog*, bath*, spin*, slid*, sank*, plug*, hips*—visual clue to short vowel sound

worms* (word, work, worth), worst* (word, work, worth)—consonant substitution

paddy*, blankets*, tickle*—visual clue to short vowel sound in accented syllable

floated*, swirled*, steaming*, swashed*, chilled*, cawed*, fluttered*, peeked*, winking*—root plus ending (float, steam, peek—visual clue to long vowel sound; swirl—visual clue to r-controlled vowel sound; swash, caw—visual clue to vowel sound; chill, wink—visual clue to short vowel sound; flutter—visual clue to short vowel sound in accented syllable)

breathing*—base word with final e dropped plus ending (breathe—visual clue to long vowel sound)

fumed*, oozed*, collided*, causing* —root with final e dropped plus ending (fume—visual clue to long vowel sound; ooze—context to determine vowel sound; collide—visual clue to long vowel sound in accented syllable; cause—visual clue to vowel sound)

tea*, guide*—visual clue to long vowel sound

roots*, droop*, smooth*—context to determine vowel sound

painful*, tenderly*—root plus suffix (pain—visual clue to long vowel sound; tender—visual clue to short vowel sound in accented syllable)

flurry*—visual clue to r-controlled vowel sound in accented syllable

flapped*—root with final consonant doubled plus ending (flap—visual clue to short vowel sound)

feebly*—root with final e dropped plus suffix (feeble—visual clue to long vowel sound in accented syllable)

joyously*—known root plus suffixes

Index of Skills, Abilities, and Understandings

Interpretation

Grasping main idea, pages 28, 28-29, 75, 84, 89, 111, 125, 134, 165, 179, 180, 201, 208-209. See also the "Guiding interpretation" section of all other lesson plans. (*Think-and-Do*, pages 21, 30, 40-41, 46-47, 50-51, 55, 66)

Noting or recalling details and perceiving their relationship for the purpose of
    Identifying story problem and/or solution, pages 34, 41, 53, 68, 89, 111, 128, 147, 183-184 (*Think-and-Do*, pages 1, 8-9, 13, 58-59)
    Making or checking inferences, pages 22, 23, 41, 55, 68, 75, 80, 88, 89, 98, 119, 122-123, 140, 148, 152, 191, 201 (*Think-and-Do*, pages 2-3, 11, 19, 73)

Page numbers that are underlined refer to exercises in the "Whole Story," "Oral Interpretation," or "Extending Competence" sections of the lesson plans.

243

Grasping ideas implied but not directly stated, pages 41, 42, 59, 62, 69, 96, 120, 135, 143, 166, 205. See also the "Guiding interpretation" section of all other lesson plans. (*Think-and-Do*, pages 2-3, 4, 7, 18, 19, 20)

Anticipating action or outcome, pages 33-34, 42, 53, 75, 96, 105, 191 (*Think-and-Do*, page 13)

Making judgments or drawing conclusions, pages 23, 24, 28-29, 35, 42, 84, 89, 90, 97, 112-113, 122-123, 125 (*Think-and-Do*, pages 1, 27-28, 38, 43, 64-65, 69, 70)

Comparing and contrasting, pages 28, 30, 39, 47, 54, 59, 69, 77-78, 84, 97, 98, 121, 125, 129, 148-149, 150, 152-153, 154, 160, 160-161, 170, 173, 188, 194, 195, 197, 207, 209 (*Think-and-Do*, pages 5-6, 14-16, 21, 22-23, 25, 42, 46-47, 49, 50-51, 67, 70)

Locating specific information, forming or verifying an opinion, or proving a point, pages 22, 27, 28-29, 43, 67, 69, 83, 96, 111, 112-113, 122-123, 128, 134, 147, 153-154, 207 (*Think-and-Do*, pages 2-3, 5-6, 11, 40-41, 61)

Generalizing, pages 69, 84, 166, 181, 184 (*Think-and-Do*, pages 21, 66)

Sensing emotional reactions and inferring motives of story characters, pages 22, 32, 34, 36-37, 39, 41, 42, 47, 63-65, 76, 77-78, 80, 119, 121-122, 128, 129, 141-142, 152, 160, 162-163, 172, 191, 192-193 (*Think-and-Do*, pages 4, 8-9, 55, 61, 62-63)

Evaluating actions and personal traits of story characters, pages 23, 34, 42, 47, 54, 58, 62, 63, 69, 73, 80, 90, 97, 99, 106, 120, 130, 139-140, 152, 162-163, 165, 183-184, 191, 192, 207 (*Think-and-Do*, pages 1, 7, 35-36, 48, 61, 74)

Comprehending phrase and sentence meaning, pages 29, 37, 44. See also the "Guiding interpretation" section of all lesson plans. (*Think-and-Do*, pages 37, 57, 70)

Using punctuation as an aid to comprehension, pages 29, 37-38, 50, 63, 126, 173, 198

Identifying the meaning of a word or phrase in specific context, pages 40, 128 (*Think-and-Do*, pages 26, 57). See also all exercises and *Think-and-Do Book* pages listed under the headings "Using context clues" and "Using context to select appropriate defined meaning."

244

Forming sensory images (visual, auditory, kinesthetic, tactile), pages 22, 24, 48, 59, 62-63, 63-65, 75, 76-77, 77-78, 81-82, 85, 89, 91, 115, 121-122, 125, 173-174, 192-193, 195, 197, 208 (*Think-and-Do*, pages 11, 19, 58-59, 73, 75)

Perceiving relationships
  Analogous, pages 39, 54, 69, 129, 148-149, 166, 184, 209 (*Think-and-Do*, pages 8-9, 22-23, 50-51, 72)

  Cause-effect, pages 35, 42, 53, 62, 89, 96, 97, 105-106, 119, 129, 147, 148-149, 152, 152-153, 153-154, 166, 172, 207. See also the "Guiding interpretation" section of all other lesson plans. (*Think-and-Do*, pages 4, 14-16, 18, 40-41, 46-47, 55, 58-59, 62-63, 67)

  General-specific, pages 90, 112-113, 122-123, 161-162, 172-173, 179, 209 (*Think-and-Do*, pages 8-9, 30, 66)

  Sequence, pages 106-107 (*Think-and-Do*, page 56)

  Class (*Think-and-Do*, pages 5-6, 43)

  Time, pages 24, 76-77, 146, 153-154 (*Think-and-Do*, pages 2-3, 49)

  Place or space, pages 76-77 (*Think-and-Do*, page 11)

  Size, page 123 (*Think-and-Do*, pages 5-6, 42)

Using aids to memory
  Association (*Think-and-Do*, pages 33-34, 71, 78-79)

  Sensory imagery, pages 85, 91 (*Think-and-Do*, pages 14-16, 71)

  Sequence, page 91

  Cause-effect relationships (*Think-and-Do*, pages 14-16, 55)

Reacting to content and linking it to personal experience, pages 23, 35-36, 49, 68, 82, 89, 97, 166, 179, 184, 205 (*Think-and-Do*, pages 22-23)

Recognizing clues to pace and mood, pages 50, 60, 75, 208 (*Think-and-Do*, pages 62-63, 75)

Recognizing plot structure, pages 106-107, 160-161, 172-173, 184 (*Think-and-Do*, pages 35-36)

Identifying author's or illustrator's purpose or point of view, pages 24, 30, 70, 75, 76, 84, 106-107, 116-117, 121, 135, 152-153 (*Think-and-Do*, pages 20, 27-28)

Evaluating and reacting to ideas in light of author's or illustrator's purpose, pages <u>43,</u> 50, <u>65,</u> 76, 106, 140, 182, 208

Interpreting figurative, idiomatic, and picturesque language, pages <u>37,</u> 49-50, <u>65,</u> 69, <u>76-77,</u> 82, <u>90,</u> 116-117, 125, 172, <u>173-174,</u> 198, 208 (*Think-and-Do*, pages 25, 30, 38, 57, 66)

Identifying elements of style
  Figurative, idiomatic, or picturesque language, pages 49-50, <u>65,</u> 82, 161-162, 207, 208 (*Think-and-Do*, pages 25, 38, 69)
  Refrain, repetition, rhythm, or rhyme, pages 49-50, 172-173, 180, <u>189,</u> 196, 208

Achieving effective oral interpretation
  Re-creating action and mood through dramatization, pages <u>36-37,</u> <u>63-65,</u> <u>121-122,</u> <u>141-142</u>
  Sensing need for changes in pace or volume, pages 50, <u>121-122,</u> <u>162-163,</u> <u>192-193</u>
  Projecting meaning, mood, and emotion through intonation, pages <u>36-37,</u> <u>43-44,</u> 50, 60, <u>63-65,</u> <u>77-78,</u> <u>107,</u> 117, <u>121-122,</u> <u>141-142,</u> 145, <u>162-163,</u> <u>166-167,</u> <u>180,</u> <u>184-185,</u> 187-188, <u>192-193,</u> 196, 198, 198-199

Organizing or summarizing ideas, pages 28-29, 75, <u>91,</u> 106, <u>107,</u> 111, 147, <u>153-154,</u> <u>181,</u> 208-209 (*Think-and-Do*, pages 14-16, 22-23, 35-36, 40-41, 46-47, 50-51, 55, 56)

Word perception

Perceiving relationships between spoken and written language
  Associating printed forms with the sounds and meanings of spoken words, pages 20-21, 22, 22-23, 27, 33-34, 41, 52-53, 61-62, 62-63, 67-68, 74-75, 83, 88, 89, 95, 96, 104-105, 110, 118-119, 127, 133, 135, 138-139, 146, 151, 159, 171, 178, 190, 206
  Classifying words by sound and form, pages <u>38,</u> <u>45-47,</u> <u>56-57,</u> <u>71-72,</u> <u>85-87,</u> <u>92-94,</u> <u>108-109,</u> <u>113-115,</u> <u>131-132,</u> <u>168-170,</u> <u>174-175,</u> <u>186,</u> <u>193</u> (*Think-and-Do*, pages 10, 12, 17, 24, 32, 39, 45)

Strengthening memory of word forms based on

Associating sound and meaning with printed words, pages 25-26, 55, 78-79, 107-108, 130-131, 155, 163-164, 167-168, 181-182, 202-203 (*Think-and-Do*, pages 60, 71. All pages of the *Think-and-Do Book* reinforce the association of meaning with printed words.)

Carefully observing visual details, pages 26, 38-39, 45-47, 56-57, 71-72, 79-80, 92-94, 108-109, 186, 193 (*Think-and-Do*, pages 10, 71)

Using clues to meanings of printed words

Understanding meaning and function of words and affixes, pages 30-32, 55, 65-66, 91-92, 98-99, 124, 130-131, 149, 167-168, 202-203 (*Think-and-Do*, pages 31, 77)

Using context clues, pages 107-108, 163-164, 202-203 (*Think-and-Do*, pages 37, 71, 76). See also all exercises and *Think-and-Do Book* pages listed under the heading "Using context to select appropriate defined meaning."

Developing ability in phonetic analysis

Associating consonant sounds and vowel sounds with the letters that commonly represent them, pages 38-39, 45-47, 56-57, 85-87, 113-115 (*Think-and-Do*, pages 10, 12, 17, 39). See also all exercises and *Think-and-Do Book* pages listed under the heading "Using spelling patterns as clues to vowel sounds in one-syllable words or accented syllables."

Perceiving syllables in spoken words, pages 71-72, 79-80, 85-87, 108-109, 113-115, 131-132, 168-170, 174-176, 186, 193 (*Think-and-Do*, page 39)

Perceiving accent in spoken words, pages 71-72, 79-80, 85-87, 108-109, 113-115, 131-132, 168-170, 174-176, 186, 193 (*Think-and-Do*, page 39)

Using spelling patterns as clues to vowel sounds in one-syllable words or accented syllables

A single vowel letter followed by one or more consonant letters in a one-syllable word or accented final syllable (*set, send, pretend, represent*), pages 45-47, 56-57, 168-170, 186 (*Think-and-Do*, page 12)

Two vowel letters together (*rain, raisin, afraid, entertain; lion, violin*), pages 45-47, 56-57, 86, 168-170, 186 (*Think-and-Do*, pages 12, 17)

A single vowel letter followed by one consonant letter and final *e* in a one-syllable word or accented final syllable (*ice, excite*), pages 45-47, 56-57, 186 (*Think-and-Do*, page 12)

A single vowel letter followed by two consonant letters and final *e* (*fence, bridge*), pages 45-47, 56-57 (*Think-and-Do,* pages 12, 17)

The letter *r* in a spelling pattern that is a clue to vowel sound (*art, party, alarm; pair, dairy, repair; care, parent, prepare; carpenter, barrier, character*), pages 45-47, 56-57, 71-72, 92-94, 131-132, 168-170, 186, 193 (*Think-and-Do,* pages 12, 17, 45)

A single vowel letter at the end of a one-syllable word or accented final syllable (*fly, reply*), pages 45-47, 56-57, 186 (*Think-and-Do,* pages 12, 17)

The letter *a* followed by *l, u,* or *w* in a one-syllable word or an accented syllable (*all, almost, Baltimore; balance, valley, alphabet; caught, author; saw, awning*), pages 56-57, 93-94, 131-132, 186, 193 (*Think-and-Do,* pages 17, 45)

The letter *i* followed by *gh* (*night, delight*), pages 56-57, 186 (*Think-and-Do,* page 17)

Two consonant letters following the vowel letter in an initial or medial accented syllable (*happen, battery, molasses, center, yesterday, electric*), pages 71-72, 85-86, 113-115, 168-170, 193 (*Think-and-Do,* pages 24, 39)

One consonant letter following the vowel letter in an initial or medial accented syllable (*paper, favorite, potato; cabin, amateur, examine*), pages 71-72, 113-115, 168-170, 193 (*Think-and-Do,* pages 24, 39)

One consonant letter or two consonant letters between a single vowel letter and final *le* in a two-syllable word (*apple, able*), pages 71-72 (*Think-and-Do,* page 24)

Using spelling patterns as clues to the number of syllables in words, pages 108-109

Using context clues to determine vowel sounds in words or accented syllables, pages 71-72, 79-80 (*Think-and-Do,* pages 24, 29)

Using context and phonetic analysis to identify printed words, pages 45-47, 57, 71-72, 79-80, 85-87, 92-94, 113-115, 131-132, 168-170, 174-176 (*Think-and-Do,* pages 12, 17, 24, 29, 37, 39, 45, 64-65, 76. See also all other *Think-and-Do Book* pages.)

Developing phonetic understandings

A consonant letter (or a two-letter consonant symbol) may represent more than one sound, pages 38-39 (*Think-and-Do,* page 10).

The same consonant sound may be represented by more than one letter, pages 38-39, 87 (*Think-and-Do,* page 10).

A vowel letter represents more than one sound.

The understanding immediately above and the two given on the preceding page are reinforced by all exercises and Think-and-Do Book *pages listed under the headings "Associating consonant sounds and vowel sounds with the letters that commonly represent them" and "Using spelling patterns as clues to vowel sounds in one-syllable words or accented syllables."*

A letter may represent no sound in a word. (See all exercises and *Think-and-Do Book* pages listed under the heading "Using spelling patterns as clues to vowel sounds in one-syllable words or accented syllables.")

Different spelling patterns may represent the same vowel sound, pages 45-47, 56-57, 79-80, 108-109, 131-132, 186, 193 (*Think-and-Do,* pages 12, 17, 39, 45)

The same spelling pattern may represent more than one vowel sound, pages 71-72, 79-80, 85-87, 92-94, 113-115, 131-132, 174-176, 193 (*Think-and-Do,* pages 24, 29, 39, 45)

A syllable is a word or part of a word in which a vowel sound is heard, pages 71-72, 79-80, 85-87, 108-109, 113-115, 131-132, 168-170, 174-176, 186, 193 (*Think-and-Do,* pages 24, 39, 45)

In words of two or more syllables, one syllable is accented more than the other or others, pages 71-72, 79-80, 85-87, 108-109, 113-115, 131-132, 168-170, 174-176, 186, 193 (*Think-and-Do,* pages 24, 39, 45)

In multisyllabic words both a primary and secondary accent may be heard, pages 168-170, 174-176

In multisyllabic words an accent (primary or secondary) is heard on one of the first two syllables, pages 108-109, 168-170, 174-176

Spelling patterns that function as clues to vowel sounds in one-syllable words may also function as clues to vowel sounds in the accented syllables of two-syllable words, pages 71-72, 79-80, 186 (*Think-and-Do,* pages 24, 29, 39, 45)

Spelling patterns that function as clues to vowel sounds in accented syllables of two-syllable words also function as clues to vowel sounds in accented syllables of multisyllabic words, pages 113-115, 131-132, 168-170, 174-176, 193 (*Think-and-Do,* pages 39, 45)

Spelling patterns that function as clues to vowel sounds in syllables with a primary accent also function in syllables with a secondary accent, pages 168-170, 174-176

Developing ability in structural analysis

Understanding structural changes made by adding endings, prefixes, and suffixes to known root words, pages 30-32 (*-teen, -ty, -th*), 65-66 (*-ward*), 91-92 (*fore-*), 98-99 (*-able*), 124 (*-ship*), 149 (*re-*) (*Think-and-Do,* pages 31 [*-teen, -ty, -th, -ward, fore-*], 77 [*-able, -ship, re-*])

Identifying root words in inflected, derived, or compounded forms, pages 30-32, 65-66

Identifying inflected or derived forms in which a spelling change occurs in the root before an ending or a suffix, pages 30-32

Using context and structural analysis to identify printed words, pages 31-32, 65-66, 91-92, 149 (*Think-and-Do,* page 31)

Combining structural and phonetic analysis

Identifying unfamiliar root words in inflected, derived, and compounded forms, page 124

Using context and combined structural and phonetic analysis to identify unfamiliar printed words, pages 98-99, 124 (*Think-and-Do,* pages 31, 37, 64-65, 76. See also all other *Think-and-Do Book* pages.)

Developing dictionary skills and understandings

Locating entries

Recognizing alphabetical sequence or general alphabetical position, pages 25-26, 155

Using guide words, pages 25-26, 155

Identifying root words in inflected or derived forms, pages 25-26. See also all exercises listed under this heading in the section "Developing ability in structural analysis."

Deriving meanings

Comprehending definitions, pages 25-26, 70-71, 78-79, 91-92, 98-99, 124, 130-131, 155, 163-164, 167-168, 181-182 (*Think-and-Do,* pages 26, 42, 44, 48, 60, 68, 74)

Using aids to understanding defined meanings (pictures and captions, illustrative sentences, cross references, etc.), pages 25-26, 70-71, 123, 142, 155 (*Think-and-Do,* page 42)

Understanding that a word or affix may represent more than one meaning, pages 25-26, 30-32, 55, 70-71, 78-79, 91-92, 98-99, 124, 130-131, 155, 163-164, 167-168, 181-182 (*Think-and-Do,* pages 26, 44, 60, 68)

Using context to select appropriate defined meaning, pages 25-26, 55, 70-71, 78-79, 91-92, 98-99, 130-131, 167-168, 181-182 (*Think-and-Do,* pages 26, 44, 60, 68)

250

Adapting definitions to context, pages <u>78-79</u>, 130-131, <u>155</u>, 181-182 (*Think-and-Do,* pages 26, 44, 68)

Deriving pronunciations

Using a pronunciation key to interpret dictionary symbols, pages <u>45, 136-137</u>, <u>155</u> (*Think-and-Do,* pages 8-9, 54)

Understanding the function of accent marks, pages <u>45, 55</u> (*Think-and-Do,* pages 8-9, 54)

Understanding that the pronunciation of a word may depend on its function in a sentence, page <u>55</u>

Understanding that a word may have more than one acceptable pronunciation, pages <u>136-137, 155</u>

As they use the exercises listed under the headings "Using a pronunciation key to interpret dictionary symbols" and "Understanding the function of accent marks," pupils develop the understanding that in dictionary pronunciations, unlike spellings, each symbol represents a sound and the same symbol always represents the same sound.

<u>Understanding language growth and change,</u> pages 135-136, 140

Competence in using interpretive and word-analysis skills is tested on pages 32, 33-34, 52-53, 54, 77, 78-79 of the Think-and-Do Book. *Suggestions for testing and evaluating pupils' progress are given in the* Guidebook *on pages 100, 156, 210-211.*

Cumulative Word List

In The New Basic Readers through Book Three, Part One, children identified by combining context clues with phonetic or structural analysis the 590 starred words in this list. The 385 new forms of known words that children identified by combining context clues with structural analysis are not included.

a	also	asked	baseball*	best*	boat*
able*	Alvin's	asleep*	basket	Betsy	Bob
about	always	at	battery	better	book
above	am	ate*	batting*	between*	Boots
accident	amateur	attacked*	be*	big	both
across	America	aunt	beach*	bigger*	bottom
act*	Amy*	autograph	beam*	biggest	bow*
aerial	an*	away	bears	bikes*	bowstring*
afraid	and	awful	beat*	Bill*	box
after	angry		beautiful	Billy	boys
afternoon	animals	baby	because	bird	Bradford*
again	ankle*	back	beds*	birthday	branch*
against*	Ann*	bad*	bee*	bit*	brass*
ago	answered	bag*	been	bite*	brave*
agree*	any	bait*	before	black	breakfast
ahead	apartment	bake*	began	blades*	breaks
aimed*	apple	balance	begged*	blazed*	bricks*
airplanes*	approaching*	ball	beginning*	blew*	bridge*
alarm*	are	bang	behind	block*	bright*
all*	arms*	bank*	believe	blow*	bring*
Allerton	around	barked	bell*	blue	broken*
almost	arrows	barn	belonged	blueberries	brother*
alone	as*	bars*	below	board	brought*
along	ashore	Barth*	beside	boast*	brown*

252

bucket*	chief	crows*	down	face*	forget
build	children	cruelty	draw*	faint*	forgot
built*	chimney	cry*	dressed*	fair*	fort*
bulb*	chin*	cupcakes	drifting*	fall*	forth*
bump*	chose*	curb*	drink*	family	found
bundles*	Christmas	curly*	drive*	fancy*	four
bunny*	churn*	cut*	drop*	far*	fox*
burning*	circle*		dry*	farm	free*
bus*	city	dad*	dryer	farmer*	fresh*
bushes*	clean	Dan*	duck	farther*	friend
busy	clearing*	danger	dug*	fast	friendly
but	clever*	dangerous	during*	fastened*	frightened
buttered	climb	Daphne		faster	from
button*	clip*	dark*		fat*	front
buy	clock*	darkness	each*	father	fruit
buzz*	close*	dashed*	ear*	feast*	full*
by*	closet	David	early	feathers	fun
	clothes	day	earth*	feed	funny
cabin	clothespins*	daydreaming*	easily*	feel*	
cage*	clowns	dear	easy	feet*	galloping
cake*	coats	Debbie	eat	fell*	games*
called	coax*	decided	eaten	felt*	garage
calm	code*	deck*	Eddie	fence	garden
came	cold*	deep*	edge*	few	gardenia
camping*	color	deer*	eggs*	field	gate*
can	come	deerskin*	eight	fierce	gather
candles*	coming*	defrost*	either*	filled*	gave
can't	common*	deliver	electric	finally	geese*
cap*	company	dial	electricity	find	George
captain*	connect*	Dick	elephant	fine	get
car	Constance*	did	Ellen	fingers*	getting
cards*	cook*	didn't*	else	finished	gift*
care*	cookies	died*	empty	fire	Giles
carefully	cool*	different	end	first	gingerbread
carolers	copper*	dig*	engine	fish*	girl
carry	corn*	dime*	engineer	five	give*
cart*	corner	dinner	enough	fix*	glad*
Carver*	could	diplomacy	envelope	flag*	glass*
case*	country	directions	even	flashlight	gloomy*
cat*	covered	dirty*	evening	flat*	gloves
catch*	cows*	disappeared	ever	flew*	go
caught	cracking*	dishes*	every	floor*	goat*
certainly	crash*	do	everybody	flowers	gobble
chair	crawl*	does	exactly	fly*	goes
chance	cream*	dog	excited	following	gone
Charles*	creek*	dolls*	exclaimed*	food	good
chasing*	cried*	done	expected*	foolish	good-by
check*	crops*	don't	explained*	foot	goose
cheered*	crossing	door	exploring*	for	got*
chickens	crowded	doubt*	eye	forest	governor

grabbed* grain* grandfather grandmother grass* gray* great green grew* grin* ground* grow* gruff* grunting* guess guests*

had hair* Hall* Halloween hand* handkerchief handle handy hang* happened happy harbor* hard* hardly hare* has hat have he* head hear* heard heavy hedgehog held* helicopter hello help helpful hens her here herself

hi* hide* high hill* him* himself his* history hit* ho* hobble* hold* hole* home honk* hook* hop* hoped* Hopkins* horns* horse hose* hot* hours* house how* howl* huff* huge* hung* hungry hunt* hurried hurry hurt* husband

I ice* I'd idea if* I'll I'm impolite important in Indians instead interesting

invented* invention inventor* invited iron is it it's* itself I've*

Jack* Jane Jeff* jerked* Jerry* Jill* Jim* job* John joined* joke* jolly jump just

katydids keep* kept* kettle key* kicked* kill* Kilpatrick kind* king* kitchen kite* kitten knew* knife* knob* knocked* know

lad* ladder lake landed* lanes*

language lantern large lass* last* late laughed lay* lead* leaned* leap* learned* least* leather* leave led* left legs let* let's letter* levers library life* lifted* lightning like Linda line* lion list* listen little live locked* logs* long look looked loose* lost lots* loud* love low* lucky* lunch*

machine made

magnet* mailbox* make* making man* many* march market Mary Massachusetts matter may* maybe me mean* meat* meeting* men* merry-go-round message* met* metal middle might* Miles* milk* million minute mirror Miss model money monkey more morning most mother motions motorboat* mouse* mouth* move moving* Mr. Mrs. much* music must* my

myself

nails* name* Nancy near* neck* need* neighborhood neighbor's never* new next nice nicer* nickel* night* nine* no nodded* noise nose* not note* nothing noticed now number

oak* obey ocean o'clock of off offer often oh oil OK* old old-fashioned on once one only opened or* orders* other*

254

ought
our
out
outfits*
oven
over
owl*
owns

pail*
paint
painter
pan*
paper
parade
parents
park
part*
party
passed*
past*
pasture
pat*
path*
Patty
paw*
peanut
pedal
pen*
penny
people
perfectly*
perfume
perhaps
pet*
Pete
Peter*
pick*
picture
pie*
pieces
pig*
pile*
Pilgrim*
pilot*
pink*
pioneers
pitching*
place
plane*

planning*
plants*
plates*
play
pleasant
please
plenty
plunged*
Plymouth
pockets
pointing
pole*
police
polite
pond*
pony
pool*
poor*
popped*
porch*
position
pot*
power*
practice
prepared*
pretending
pretty
prevention
prince*
probably
promise
proud*
Puff
pull*
pulleys*
pumpkin
puppy
purple*
push*
put
puzzled*

quarrel
queer*
quick
quickly*
quiet
quite*

rabbit

raccoon
race*
radio
rags*
rain
raise*
ran*
rang*
reach*
reads
ready
real*
really
red
reel*
refrigerator
release*
remembered
reply
rest*
returned
rid*
ride
right
ring*
river
road
roared*
roast*
rock*
rode*
Roger
roll
roof*
room
rope*
round*
row*
rug*
ruler*
run
running
rushing*

sad*
safe*
said
sailing*
sale*
Sally

salty*
Sam*
same*
Samoset
Sandy*
sang*
sat*
Saturday
save*
saw
say*
scare
scattered*
school
science
scolding*
scrubbed*
seat*
second
secret
see
seeds*
seemed*
seen*
semaphore
send*
sent*
seriously
set*
settlement
settlers*
seven
several
shake*
shall
she
sheep*
ship*
shirt*
shoes
Shoie
shook*
shoot*
shop*
shores*
short*
shot*
should*
shout*
shoved*

shovel
show
shut*
side*
sight*
sign
silently*
silly*
silver
since
sing*
sister
sit*
six
skipped*
sleep
sleepy
slides*
slinger*
slow
slower
slowly*
sly*
small*
smell*
smiled*
snapped*
snow*
snowstorm*
so
soap*
society
soft*
something
sons
soon
sore*
sorry
S O S*
sound*
soup
space*
speak*
special
spend*
splash
spoke*
Spot
spread*
spring

Squanto
squawking
squeaky*
squealing
squirrel
stamping*
stand*
Standish*
star*
start*
station
stay*
steady*
steel*
steer*
Stephen
steps*
Steve*
stew*
sticks
still*
sting*
stones
stood*
stop*
stopped
store*
story
stove*
straight*
strange
straw*
street
strips*
stronger*
struck*
Stuey
stumbled*
such*
sudden*
suddenly
suit*
summer
sunny*
supermarket
supper
supposed
sure
surely*
surprise

Susan	they	track*	use	well*	woke*
swan	think	traffic	useful	went	wolf
swiftly*	third*	train	useless	were	wolves
swim*	thirsty*	transom*		wet*	woman
swish	this	trap*	vacation	what	women
swooped*	those	tree	vacuum	wheels	wonder
	thought	trick*	valentines	when*	wonderful
table	three	tried	very	where	won't
tails	through	trip*	village*	whether	wooden
take	throwing*	troll*	violin	which	woods*
taken	thunder*	trotted*	visit	while*	word*
talk*	tick*	trouble	visitor*	whirling*	work*
tall*	tie	truck*	voice	whispering	worried
tape*	tight*	truly*		whistle	worse
tastes*	Tim	trunks*	wagon	white	worship
taught*	time	try	wait	who	would*
taxicabs	tiny	tube*	wake*	whole*	wound*
teacher*	tired	tune*	walk*	why	writes*
team*	to	turkeys*	walkie-talkie*	wide*	wrong*
telephone	today	turned	want	wife*	wrote
telescope	toe*	turnips	wanted*	wiggle	
tell	together	turtle	warmer	wild	yard
ten*	told*	TV	warned*	will	year*
tension	Tom	twelve*	was	William*	yell*
terrible	Tommy	twinkling	wash	Willing*	yellow
test*	tomorrow	two	watch	Wilson's	yes
than*	tongue		water	wind	yesterday
thank	tonight	ugly	waved*	window	yet*
that	too	uncle	way*	windy	you
thatch*	took*	under	we	wings*	you'll
the	tools	understood	wear*	winter	young
their	toot*	unhappy	weather*	wire*	your
them	top*	until	Weber	wise	yourself
then	toward	up	week*	wish*	
there	town*	upstairs*	weight*	with	zoo
these*	toy*	us	welcomes*	without	

MORE ROADS
TO FOLLOW

Helen M. Robinson
Marion Monroe
A. Sterl Artley
Charlotte S. Huck

Linguistic Advisor, W. Cabell Greet

Illustrators, Richard E. Loehle
Al Stine and Rod Ruth

Scott, Foresman and Company
Chicago   Atlanta   Dallas   Palo Alto   Fair Lawn, N. J.

Contents

Roads Here and There

Open Range 6
by Kathryn and Byron Jackson

Billy and Thunderbolt 9
by C. W. Anderson

When Is a Horse a Pony? 18

Out of Her Shell 20
by Lorrie McLaughlin

The World of Hogback Mountain. . 27
by Jeanne Hines

Green Hill Neighbors 35
by Frances Frost

How to Tell the Top of a Hill. . . 36
by John Ciardi

Charley Brave 37
by Edna Walker Chandler

New Mexico 47
by Polly Chase Boyden

Louella 48
by Carolyn Haywood

Soo-Pung Measures Up 58
by Shirlee P. Newman

It's a Wolf 66
by Carolyn Haywood

Horse-Chestnut Time 75
by Kaye Starbird

May Day and Lei Day 77
by Sandra Million Stephens

Maile's Lei 80
by Mary Dana Rodriguez

Manaluk's Gold Rush 88
by Marion Holland

Interesting People along the Way

Greatness 100
by Phillips Brooks

"The Babe" 102
by M. G. Bonner

Get 'Em While They're Hot . . . 111
by Martin Abramson

Wilbur Wright and Orville Wright . 115
by Stephen Vincent Benét

Audubon's Birds 117
by Janet Marshall

Spring Song 127
by Aileen Fisher

Sequoyah's Talking Leaves 128
by Janet Marshall

Sequoyah's Honors 136
  by Janet Marshall

Abe Lincoln 140
  by Frances Cavanah

Nancy Hanks 154
  by Rosemary Carr Benét

A Reply to Nancy Hanks 156
  by Julius Silberger

Captain Smith of Jamestown . . . 157
  by K. B. Frost

The Girl with Three Names . . . 163
  by K. B. Frost

Roads to Make-Believe

Roads 172
  by Rachel Field

Puss-in-Boots 175
  retold by Elizabeth Abell

The Three Wishes 187
  a Swedish Tale

Rapunzel 193
  retold by Virginia Haviland

The Dog in the Manger 202

The Ant and the Grasshopper . . . 203

The Dove and the Ant 204

The Boy and the Wolf 205
  adapted by Louis Untermeyer

The Plate of Pancakes 207
  by Maud Lindsay

4

Ridiculous People 214

There was an Old Man with a beard . . . 214
by Edward Lear

A tutor who tooted a flute 214
by Carolyn Wells

There was a Young Lady whose chin . . . 214
by Edward Lear

Mrs. Snipkin and Mrs. Wobblechin 215
by Laura E. Richards

Pippi Is a Thing-Finder 217
by Astrid Lindgren

Ridiculous Animals 232

When a goose meets a moose 232
by Zhena Gay

Way down South where bananas grow . . . 232
anonymous

A fly and a flea flew up in a flue 232
anonymous

The Ostrich Is a Silly Bird 233
by Mary E. Wilkins Freeman

A Centipede Was Happy Quite 234
anonymous

Only My Opinion 234
by Monica Shannon

The Panther 235
by Ogden Nash

Glowworm 235
by David McCord

The Duel 236
by Eugene Field

Pooh Goes Visiting 238
by A. A. Milne

Us Two 251
by A. A. Milne

Joji and the Fog 253
by Betty Jean Lifton

Open Range

by KATHRYN and BYRON JACKSON

Prairie goes to the mountain,
  Mountain goes to the sky.
The sky sweeps across to the distant hills
And here, in the middle,
  Am I.

Hills crowd down to the river,
  River runs by the tree.
Tree throws its shadow on sunburnt grass
And here, in the shadow,
  Is me.

Shadows creep up the mountain,
  Mountain goes black on the sky,
The sky bursts out with a million stars
And here, by the campfire,
  Am I.

Reprinted from Tenggren's *Cowboys and Indians* by Kathryn and Byron Jackson.
Copyright 1948 by Golden Press, Inc.

ROADS
HERE
AND
THERE

Billy and Thunderbolt

Billy was a boy who had a pony named Blaze that he loved very much.

One year when his parents decided to spend the summer on a ranch in the West, they bought a trailer so that Blaze could go along. Billy enjoyed the trip very much. Perhaps Blaze did not enjoy it so much, but he gave no trouble.

Billy had read many cowboy stories. He was excited to see the West. He was even more excited when he saw his first real cowboy.

9

Adapted with permission of the author and publisher from *Blaze and Thunderbolt* by C. W. Anderson. Copyright 1955 by The Macmillan Company.

The cowboy was very friendly. He talked to the family and said that the cattle ranch they were going to was only a few miles farther on. Billy liked the cowboy very much and hoped to see him again.

When the family arrived at the ranch, Billy led Blaze to a corral. Blaze seemed happy when he found that he was going to have such a nice big pasture. It had been a long ride for Blaze in the horse trailer. It felt good to stretch his legs.

Bright and early the next day Billy put a saddle and bridle on Blaze. Billy wore the new cowboy outfit his father had bought for him. As he started out on horseback to explore the ranch, he felt like a real cowboy. The pony seemed eager to explore, too, for he galloped gaily toward the blue hills a few miles away.

About an hour later Billy came to a herd of cattle and some cowboys. One was Jim, the cowboy Billy had seen yesterday. Jim offered to ride with Billy and show him the ranch.

They had almost reached the hills when they heard shouts and galloping horses. A beautiful black horse was running like the wind, with three cowboys chasing him.

"That's Thunderbolt!" cried Jim. "He is the last of the wild horses around here. Everybody has tried to catch him, but he's too fast for them. Isn't he a beauty?"

Billy was glad to see that the cowboys were falling farther and farther behind in the chase. He did not want them to catch that beautiful horse.

The next morning Billy and Blaze started again for the hills. "We're going to look for Thunderbolt," Billy said to the pony. "I'd like to see him close, wouldn't you?"

It seemed that Blaze understood Billy's words, for he began to gallop.

After riding for many miles, Billy came to Jim's herd of cattle. Billy told Jim he wanted to ride up into the hills to look for Thunderbolt.

Jim pointed out a place in the hills where the wild horse might be seen.

"I saw him there twice," Jim said. "You may catch sight of him if you keep your pony very quiet."

Billy and Blaze had climbed many of the smaller hills and were going through some scrub bushes when Blaze stopped suddenly. There just ahead on a flat, rocky ledge was Thunderbolt! He looked so wild and proud that Billy was sure he had never seen anything so beautiful.

Thunderbolt did not notice the boy and the pony until Blaze whinnied. Then the wild horse turned.

Thunderbolt did not seem frightened. He
seemed to know that the boy and his pony
did not mean to harm him. He looked at
them for a moment before he galloped away.

After that Billy rode out to the hills every
day. Often he brought his lunch and ate in
the shade of the scrub bushes by the ledge.
He took the saddle and bridle off Blaze and
let the pony crop grass where he liked.

Billy always brought enough carrots and
sugar for both Blaze and Thunderbolt. He
left the food for Thunderbolt on the ledge.
It was usually gone the next day. So Billy
felt sure the wild horse had been there.

13

One day after his lunch Billy fell asleep in the shade. When he woke up, he saw his pony and Thunderbolt side by side on the ledge, eating carrots and sugar. The boy watched them finish eating and walk off together. Billy called Blaze. He came at once, but Thunderbolt was not with him.

On the way home Billy met Jim and told him what had happened.

"Thunderbolt must be lonely," Jim said. "He never sees another horse except those that chase him. Your pony is friendly, and Thunderbolt likes him. Just keep watching. Thunderbolt may get to know you, too."

Billy dreamed about Thunderbolt for many nights afterwards. Once he even dreamed he was riding the black horse. The next day he started out earlier than ever. The nearer Billy and Blaze came to the hills, the faster the pony went. Billy knew that Blaze was eager to see his new friend.

When they reached the flat, rocky ledge, Thunderbolt was waiting for them. He did not run. He stood and whinnied to Blaze. Blaze whinnied back.

As fast as he could, Billy took the saddle and bridle off Blaze and turned him loose. The pony trotted over to the horse. Billy followed Jim's advice and just watched the two as they walked off together.

When it was time to go home, Thunderbolt started to follow the pony and the boy. But soon he saw some cowboys in the distance and galloped back to the hills. Billy and Blaze were both disappointed. Blaze walked slower than usual, for he did not like to leave his friend.

Early the next morning when Billy came to the corral to feed Blaze, he thought he must be dreaming. There was Thunderbolt with Blaze! The horse had come down from the hills during the night and jumped into the corral to be with his friend.

"If only I can make him want to stay, he will be mine," Billy said to himself as he hurried to get feed for Thunderbolt.

Thunderbolt soon found out that no one was going to harm or bother him. Then he became very friendly and seemed happy in his new home.

Billy was always quiet and gentle with Thunderbolt. Before long the horse would eat carrots and sugar from his hand. Billy often rode Blaze in the corral. Thunderbolt walked beside them. Billy was anxious for the horse to understand that having someone on his back wouldn't hurt him. Billy was sure no one would ride Thunderbolt unless the horse wanted him to.

One day Jim offered to try to ride the black horse. But Thunderbolt began to buck and rear when he saw Jim with a rope.

"He thinks you're one of the cowboys that chased him!" cried Billy. "He knows me. Let me try to ride him."

Billy called Blaze over to stand beside Thunderbolt. He patted the black horse and talked quietly to him. Then very gently Billy climbed onto the horse. Thunderbolt trembled a little but did not kick or buck, not one little buck. Soon he was walking around the corral with Billy on his back. Blaze walked beside them.

Billy rode Thunderbolt bareback in the corral for many days before he put a saddle on him. By that time the horse trusted Billy. With Blaze beside him, Thunderbolt felt that everything was all right. Soon he knew exactly what he was supposed to do as well as Blaze did.

Blaze and Thunderbolt became such good friends that they always had to be together.

When Billy went for a ride on Blaze, the black horse went along. When Billy rode Thunderbolt, Blaze galloped beside them.

Jim was very proud of the way Billy had trained Thunderbolt. He told Billy that he had the finest horse and the finest pony in that part of the country. Billy was proud and happy, for he felt sure that it was true.

When Is a Horse a Pony?

A horse is a pony when it belongs to one of the breeds of horses that average less than 58 inches in height when they are fully grown.

The height of a horse or a pony is not measured from the top of the head to the ground, as the height of a boy or girl is. Horses and ponies are measured from the highest part of the back, just behind the neck, to the ground.

Horses and ponies are not measured in feet and inches, either, as boys and girls are. Horses and ponies are measured in hands and inches. A foot is twelve inches. A hand is four inches.

4 feet

16 hands

You speak of a horse 58 inches tall as being fourteen hands and two inches. You say fourteen hands and two inches, but you write 14:2 hands. Breeds of horses that average less than 14:2 hands are ponies.

There are more than twenty breeds of ponies in the world. The best known are the Shetland ponies. Shetlands are the smallest of all breeds of ponies and average 9:3 hands (39 inches). These strong little ponies were first used as work animals in mines. Today many Shetland ponies are pets. They make good pets because they are very gentle.

Here are three breeds of ponies, standing beside a horse of average size.

HACKNEY

WELSH

SHETLAND

19

Out of Her Shell

Kirsten walked slowly into the schoolyard. Little groups of girls were standing around, laughing and talking. Kirsten wished she felt free to join one of the groups. But she didn't.

School in this new country was all right inside the schoolroom. She didn't feel left out of things when she sat at her desk with her head behind a book. "If only we had stayed in Denmark," she thought. There she had been part of a friendly group of girls and hadn't had to learn new ways.

Kirsten was glad when it was time to go into the school building.

Just before school ended that day, the teacher said, "I have a special surprise. Our school is having a fun fair to raise money to buy things for the playground. The classes are being divided into small groups that will do something for the fair. Each group in our class is to have a booth, any kind of booth you can think of."

Soon Kirsten heard the teacher read off the names Debbie Kilpatrick, Amy Lacour, and Kirsten Larsen.

Holding her handkerchief tightly and trembling a little, Kirsten went to the front row of desks where Amy and Debbie sat. "I am with you?" Kirsten asked shyly.

"I guess so," Debbie said and turned to Amy. "We have to think of something that will be the best booth at the fun fair."

In a puzzled voice Kirsten said, "I want to help, but what is a fun fair?"

"It's—it's a sort of sale," Amy explained. "There are games, and people sell things like pumpkin pie or white elephants."

Kirsten gasped. "White elephants! Now you are joking, Amy Lacour."

"No, I'm not," laughed Amy. "A white elephant is something you don't want any more—maybe a doll you don't play with."

"Kirsten won't be much help since she doesn't know anything about a fair," said Debbie Kilpatrick impolitely.

Hastily Kirsten offered to withdraw from the group.

"No," Amy insisted. "You're part of the class, and you're going to be in this group."

"I'm not," said Debbie. "I'm going to join the K group." Then she walked away.

"What a pity, Amy!" said Kirsten. "You just have me. I am next to no good at all."

"We'll get along OK," said Amy.

But at the end of the week the girls had no plan. "It's harder than I thought," Amy said to Kirsten as they walked home from school. "The difficulty is that every time we get an idea, we find out another group had the idea first."

"There is still time for you to join some other group," Kirsten said.

Amy shook her head. "You and I will manage to think of something. We'll just have to put on our thinking caps."

Kirsten frowned. "You have such strange words. Thinking cap—what is that?"

Amy laughed. "Oh, Kirsten, how hard a new language must be! A thinking cap isn't a real cap. It means we'll have to think extra hard."

When the girls reached the corner where they usually parted, Kirsten said shyly, "My mother said I should ask you to come home with me for milk and cookies. But if it is not convenient, we will understand."

"Of course, it's convenient!" Amy said happily. "I'd love to. And tomorrow you must come to my house."

Kirsten took Amy straight to the sunny, pleasant kitchen of the Larsen apartment to meet her mother.

"I am happy to know Amy Lacour, the friend of Kirsten," said Mrs. Larsen.

Then Mrs. Larsen started hurrying from the refrigerator to the table and back to the refrigerator as she put out milk and cookies and open-faced sandwiches for the girls.

Amy ate several of the tiny sandwiches. "I've never tasted anything like these," she said. "They're very good!"

"They are great favorites in Denmark," Kirsten said. "The cookies are a favorite kind made in Denmark, too."

Amy bit into a cookie. "M-m! It must be hard to cook like this," she said.

"It's easy. Even I can do it," Kirsten answered with a giggle. Then she added, "And you know how stupid I am."

"Not when you come out of your shell."

"Out of my shell—what is that?"

"When you stop being so shy," said Amy. She looked at the sandwiches and cookies. "Are they really easy to make?"

Kirsten's eyes widened. "Oh, Amy!" she cried. "We are both putting on our thinking caps at once!"

Amy said eagerly, "We can sell cookies and sandwiches like these in our booth, and we'll call it A Bit of Denmark."

"Excuse me!" shouted Kirsten as she dashed out of the room.

She came running back with two dresses and two caps. "I brought these costumes from Denmark," she said. "Of course, I wore them there only on holidays, but we can wear them in our booth!"

The day of the fair the two girls filled their booth with sandwiches, cookies, and cups of fruit punch and milk. They were ready for customers when Debbie came up.

"Yours is the best booth here," she said. There was envy in her voice but a kind look in her eyes. She smiled at Kirsten. "I'm sorry I was mean the other day," she said.

Kirsten offered some cookies to Debbie.

"They're on the house," said Amy with a laugh. Then she explained to Kirsten. "That means Debbie gets cookies free."

There was a smile on Kirsten's face and joy in her heart. For the first time since she had left Denmark, she felt that she was really among friends.

The World of Hogback Mountain

Rufe Kaller anxiously watched the doctor examine his friend Dan Steel.

Mary Kate Steel's eyes were as worried as Rufe's. "Anything new about my boy, Doctor?" she asked.

The doctor sighed and shook his head. Dan had been hurt in an accident when he was a baby. He'd never been able to walk. Probably never would, the doctor thought.

In a kind voice he asked, "Are you wishing for something you don't have, lad?"

Dan said, "Just a telescope to see birds and things over on Hogback Mountain."

The doctor said, "A good telescope costs a lot. Twenty, maybe twenty-five dollars."

Dan sighed. He wanted a telescope, even though he knew it was as far out of reach of his mother's pocketbook as the paths of Hogback were out of reach of his legs.

Rufe understood Dan's sigh and his wish. Rufe could climb to the top of the mountain and spend hours there. But chairbound Dan could only sit and look. The mountain was close, but not close enough for Dan to see things clearly. A telescope would help. But twenty dollars!

Rufe's eyes were stinging. He jumped off the shady porch and ran as fast as a hare through the rows of pumpkins growing near the house. On he ran to a rock cliff that faced Hogback. Rufe dropped down on the rocks and looked steadily at the green-covered mountain.

Within its leafy covering were birds and rabbits and squirrels and raccoons. Rufe couldn't see them at this distance, but he knew they were there because his legs had often taken him up the mountain.

When at last Rufe went home, he found his uncle sitting outside whittling as usual. Uncle Case Kaller was very old, but his eyes were still sharp and bright.

Rufe asked, "You know where I can get a telescope?"

Uncle Case looked at Rufe as if he could hardly believe he'd heard right. But all he said was "Can't say as I do."

"What're you whittling?" asked Rufe.

The old man held out a tiny figure. "It's Mary Kate hanging out her wash. You know that funny way she stands."

Rufe laughed. It was Mary Kate to the life. He went inside and got the ship he'd been whittling on for months and came and sat by his uncle. "Tell me about the sea again," he said.

"Forty years I sailed the seas!" began Uncle Case. He went on to tell about faraway places he had seen. Suddenly he said, "Don't be whittling that way, boy! This way, like I told you."

Rufe held up the ship. "I've finished!"

Uncle Case said, "Get the book."

Rufe got his uncle's book of ships, and Uncle Case leafed through it until he came to the right picture. Nodding, he looked from the book to Rufe's ship. "Good! It's real good, young fellow. Now take the book back. Mind you, be careful with it."

Feeling proud, Rufe put the precious book away. It was more than a book of ships to the old man. It was his life at sea.

To Rufe, it seemed that everyone wanted something. Uncle Case longed for the sea. He, Rufe, wanted book learning. He walked six miles to catch the bus to school, a place filled with books that he liked and children he was too shy to make friends with. Dan wanted a telescope. Yes, everybody wanted something.

Rufe started walking up the mountain to get away from his thoughts. Halfway up, he saw smoke and frowned. Moments later he saw that the smoke came from a campfire. Beside it were a woman and a man and a boy about his own size.

Rufe caught his breath sharply. The boy was looking through a telescope!

Rufe watched, hiding like a wild thing among the pines. The boy left the telescope and began fooling with the fanciest fishing rod and reel Rufe had ever seen. At times the whole family wandered off, leaving the telescope by the fire.

How easy to take it! But Rufe couldn't face his uncle if he did, and Mary Kate would throw such a present back at him.

Suddenly an idea struck him. He raced back home, snatched up his ship and the last little figure Uncle Case had carved, and dashed back up the mountain.

Rufe was winded when he got back to the campfire. He saw that the man and woman were taking a camping outfit from a trailer some distance from the fire. The boy was standing by the telescope.

"Hi," said Rufe, approaching the boy.

The boy looked startled. "Where did you come from?"

"Down the mountain. I live down there."

"You do? What's your name?"

"Rufe Kaller."

The boy stuck out his hand. "Mine is George Williams. Dad couldn't get away from his business for a vacation last summer. So we came camping this fall. I hope the weather stays good while we're here."

Rufe stuck out his hand, too. The little ship was in his hand.

"Let's see that!" George exclaimed. "It's perfect! Did you make it?"

"Watch out! Don't harm it," cried Rufe. "Took me six months to make it. But I'd trade it for your telescope." He looked at George. Surely he'd laugh at the idea of trading the costly telescope for the ship.

But George pushed the telescope toward Rufe. "I'll trade!" George cried.

Rufe was speechless as he took the telescope and started away with it.

A man's voice stopped Rufe. "Where are you going with the telescope, sonny?"

Rufe whirled. George pushed forward eagerly. "I traded it for this ship, Dad. He carved it. Took him six months."

The man examined the tiny ship carefully. "It's good work for a boy. But I don't——"

Rufe just had to have the telescope for Dan. He pulled from his pocket his knife and the figure of Mary Kate.

The man stared. "You didn't make that figure, did you?"

"My uncle did. He's made lots of them. I live with him at the foot of the mountain."

The man examined the figure. At last he said, "Keep the telescope. Tell your uncle that in my gift shop at home I can sell all the figures he can carve."

"You mean they're worth something?"

"Yes," said the man, ruffling Rufe's hair. "And I'll come to see your uncle tonight."

George said, "I'll come along with Dad. I'll show you how to use the telescope. We can look at the moon and the stars."

Rufe was very close to tears again. So he swallowed hard and gave a quick nod of thanks. Then he hurried away.

It was like a dream, a wonderful dream. Uncle Case could sell his wood carvings, and there would be money for school. Dan would have his telescope—and the world of Hogback Mountain would open up before him. Holding the precious telescope, Rufe went faster and faster down the mountain.

Green Hill Neighbors

by FRANCES FROST

When I look at our green hill,
I think of all the wild
Small hearts that live inside it:
The woodchuck's chubby child,

Rabbits with busy whiskered faces
Peering out of rocks,
The big-eared meadow mouse, the dainty
Gold-eyed baby fox.

When I look at our green hill
Beneath the sunny sky,
I'm pleased to have such friends inside—
And glad I live nearby!

35

With permission of McGraw-Hill Book Co., Inc./Whittlesey House from *The Little Naturalist* by Frances Frost. Copyright © 1959 by the Estate of Frances Frost and Kurt Werth.

How to Tell the Top of a Hill

by JOHN CIARDI

The top of a hill
Is not until
The bottom is below.
And you have to stop
When you reach the top
For there's no more UP to go.

To make it plain
Let me explain:
The one *most* reason why
You have to stop
When you reach the top—is:
The next step up is sky.

From *The Reason for the Pelican* by John Ciardi. Copyright © 1959 by John Ciardi.
Published by J. B. Lippincott Company.

Charley Brave

A boy sat on the top step of his new home and dug the toe of his shoe into the deep dust. He felt unhappy— and mad, too. Wasn't he, Charley Brave, an Indian? Then why were all the Indian boys on the reservation leaving him alone like this?

Charley thought of something his mother had said on the trip from California to the reservation. Mrs. Brave had warned him and his sister, Jean, "The Indians on the reservation will have ways you two won't understand. But remember, your dad and I grew up on reservations. I'm sure you can get along."

37

"I don't see any chance of getting along," thought Charley. "The boys don't even speak to me. I'll probably be here forty years before I make any friends."

He looked toward the new little hospital building. A sign in front read, "Winding Creek Hospital."

Charley thought with envy, "The rest of the family's lucky. Dad's a doctor. People need him. Mother's a nurse, and nurses are always needed. Jean has her friend Mary. Wouldn't you know the teacher's family would have a girl but no boy?"

Jean came outside just then. "Let's go see the goats," she said. That would be better than doing nothing, Charley decided. So the two started to the valley where the goats were kept.

Because the pasture was poor, there were no cows at the reservation. Mr. Jerome, the teacher, had bought milk goats for the school just before the Braves had arrived. The Indian boys would learn to care for the goats. The people at the reservation could have the milk, which they needed badly.

Just as Charley and Jean reached a spot from which they could see into the valley, two boys came racing along the path.

Mary Jerome was close behind the boys. "What's the matter, Billy?" she yelled.

The boys didn't stop. But the bigger one, Billy, yelled back impatiently, "Goats are out! Some dumb bunny opened the gate to the pen." Then Billy said the Sioux Indian words *hoksila cheecha*.

Panting, Mary gave up the chase. "Oh dear!" she said. "Now Dad and Billy will be late milking the goats tonight."

"What did he say?" asked Charley. "Not that dumb bunny part. I know that."

"Billy thinks that the open gate was no accident," said Mary. *"Hoksila cheecha* means bad boy. You say it like this: *hoke-she-la-chee-cha. Cheecha* is the Sioux word for bad."

"What's the word for good?" Jean asked.

"Wa-ste," replied Mary, saying *wash-tay.*

Charley said, "Things are *cheecha* enough. I'm going to try to make them *wa-ste.*"

Off he ran, calling, "I'll help, fellows!" As he ran, he thought, "White Indian, that's what they call me. They think I'm not much of an Indian because I lived in a city."

It is easier for three boys to round up a scattered herd and keep it from dividing than it is for two. The reservation boys were soon giving orders to Charley by motions and words—but only Indian words.

It was boiling-hot work. Finally the panting boys drove the goats through the gate and shoved it shut.

If Charley expected to be thanked, he was mistaken. He had to be satisfied with the girls' *wa-ste* and the exercise he'd had.

Charley went back home to work alone on the car he had brought from California. He and Doctor Brave had built it, using the engine from an old power lawn mower. The mower engine was always breaking down.

His parents came home together soon. His dad had needed a nurse at the hospital that day. They stopped to talk to Charley.

"Any of the boys drop around to work on our invention?" Doctor Brave questioned.

Charley shook his head.

"Just give them a little more time," was his mother's advice.

But as the days went by, Charley decided that time didn't help. So he worked on his car and tried not to think about the boys.

At supper one night Doctor Brave said, "You know, I've come to like goat's milk. It's a pity that the people here don't drink it. They won't even try it."

Charley could tell that Jean was thinking seriously about something. After a moment or two she said, "I think Mary and I should have a party for the children and give them cocoa made out of goat's milk."

After supper Jean talked more about the party to Charley.

"Nobody will come," her brother insisted. "At least none of the boys will. They act like they don't understand me when I say 'Hi.' They don't pay any attention to me." Charley was a friendly boy. So this whole business bothered him.

When Jean and Charley told Mary and her mother about the party idea, they thought it was wonderful. "Let's have the party in the school kitchen," said Mary. "The girls are used to it. They'll be less shy there."

Charley asked anxiously, "How about boys? I'm not going to any girl party."

Mrs. Jerome laughed. "All the children are curious about Doctor Brave's family. An excuse like a party is what they need to get to know you. Even if the boys don't like the party, they'll have a chance to see the car you brought from California. They are very curious about that."

Charley said, "They can ride it and work on the lawn mower engine all they like!" With that, he left the group to their plans.

Mary said, "Some of the girls may bring their Indian dolls. Granny Yellow Bird has made dolls for all the girls in the valley."

"Maybe we could sew," Jean suggested. "I can get some cloth from my mother."

Mary said, "I'll bring pieces of cloth, too. We'll ask Granny Yellow Bird to come and show us how to sew Indian things."

And so the plans were made.

Friday was the day of the party. Mary went by for three girls who had agreed to come if Mary would call for them. As soon as they saw the gay strips of cloth and the food ready for the party, they asked Mary a question.

She replied, "Yes, do that."

Jean looked surprised when she saw the first guests running off. Mary explained, "They're going to get others to come. We will have a real party yet."

Charley waited in front of the school in his car for the guests. When he caught sight of several boys coming to the party, he became excited and pulled too hard on a release lever. The car leaped forward.

When Charley finally got his car stopped, he called, "Hi! Anybody want to ride?"

The boys grinned and began talking in English without using any Indian words.

Charley couldn't help exclaiming aloud, "Say! You fellows speak English as well as I do! And Indian, too. That's great!"

To show Charley how well they spoke the Sioux language, the boys sang a rain song. Billy told Charley what the words meant.

What Billy really wanted to do was ask Charley about cars. "Do they cost much? Could I make one? Would you help me?"

"Sure, I'll help you," Charley told Billy. "And I'll help get the stuff to make it."

What a gay, friendly party it turned out to be! Twenty-six guests came—fourteen girls, eleven boys, and Granny Yellow Bird. The boys were so busy steering Charley's car that they didn't hear the first call to eat.

Everybody loved the little cakes topped with honey and brown sugar that Jean's mother had made. And they liked the cocoa made with goat's milk.

"*Wa-ste! Wa-ste!*" they said politely.

Afterwards the boys talked about cars, and the girls settled down to sew.

Later that evening Doctor Brave said to his children, "I understand the guests at the party liked the cocoa. They thought they had a feast. Billy fell in love with the car. He told me his friend Charley is going to help him make one. In fact, from what I hear, I guess the party made friends for the goats and for Charley, too."

New Mexico

by POLLY CHASE BOYDEN

Out West is windy
And Out West is wide.
I pass villages of prairie dogs
On every horseback ride.

    I pass jack rabbits and sunsets
    And Pueblo Indians,
    And Mexicans in great big hats,
    And they are all my friends.

But when the moon comes sliding
And sagebrush turns to foam,
Then outdoors is Out West,
But indoors is Home.

By permission of the author.

Louella

Eddie Wilson had had all kinds of animals ever since he was old enough to go around the block. He was always bringing stray dogs and stray cats home. Once he brought home a goat and put gardenia perfume on her to make her smell good.

Rewards for finding other people's pets had added much to the weight of Eddie's bank. What all this meant was that Eddie's pets changed often— all except Louella.

Louella was Eddie's parrot. She was a jealous bird. She was very jealous of other animals and called them all cats. When Eddie brought home a stray pup, she'd squawk, "Cats! Cats!"

48

From *Eddie and Louella* by Carolyn Haywood, copyright © 1959 by Carolyn Haywood, by permission of William Morrow and Company, Inc.

Even the birds that visited the bird feeder outside the window were cats to Louella. She'd scold at them and scream, "Cats!"

Cats themselves, Louella hated. If a cat appeared in the room, she closed her eyes and made believe it wasn't there. Every once in a while she'd open one eye. If the cat was still in sight, she'd ruffle up her feathers and pretend to be asleep.

Eddie had brought Louella home from Texas when he visited an aunt and uncle there. At first Louella had said over and over, "Texas is better! Texas is better!"

Eddie soon changed that. He taught her to say, "Eddie is best!" This made Eddie's brothers mad, and they called Louella "that dumb bird!" But Louella was far from dumb. She was not stupid at all.

One afternoon when Eddie came in from school, his mother said, "The committee that's planning the dance to raise money for the Old People's Home would like to borrow Louella."

"What do they want to borrow her for?" asked Eddie. "She can't dance."

"The committee wants to use Louella in the decorations," said Mrs. Wilson.

"In the decorations!" exclaimed Eddie. "Like a ball hanging on a Christmas tree? Like a star on the top?"

"Not exactly," laughed his mother. "You see the dance is to be a South Seas ball. So the committee decided to borrow some parrots for part of the decorations."

"They won't let Louella out of her cage, will they?" asked Eddie.

"Oh, no," said his mother. "They'll just have birds in cages in the hotel ballroom. They want Louella Friday afternoon."

"OK," said Eddie. "But I hope Louella doesn't squawk too much."

"If she squawks," laughed Mrs. Wilson, "everyone will know she is a live parrot, not a stuffed one."

On Friday afternoon Eddie cleaned the parrot's cage. "Listen, old girl!" he said. "You're going to a ball. See that you're good. No funny business."

"Yawk! No funny business!" shrieked Louella. "No funny business!"

At half-past four a taxicab with Eddie and Louella and Mrs. Wilson inside drew up in front of the hotel. Mrs. Wilson paid the cab driver. Then Eddie said, "Where do I take Louella?"

"Ask at the desk," answered his mother. "I'll wait here on the sidewalk for you."

As Eddie carried Louella to the hotel door, a barking dog rushed up to him.

"Yawk!" screamed Louella. "Cats!"

The dog jumped at the cage. Eddie held it high. "Hey! Go away!" he said to the dog.

The hotel had a revolving door. As Eddie stepped in, the dog pushed in with him.

Eddie lifted the cage and held it in front of him. There was a brass rod on the door to push against. Eddie pushed. The door revolved, and in a moment it was time to step into the hotel. But the dog was in the way. And someone was pushing the door from the rear. So Eddie and the parrot and the dog went around again.

When they all reached the outside, Eddie said, "Get out, dog! Get out!" But the dog refused to move.

Louella shrieked, "Cats! Cats!"

The dog barked.

Eddie yelled, "Mother! Come here!"

Before Mrs. Wilson could reach Eddie, a man who wanted to enter the hotel stepped into the door. So Eddie and Louella and the dog started around again.

When they reached the inside of the hotel, the doorman was there. He said, "Take that dog out! No dogs allowed in this hotel."

The doorman gave the door a shove, and Eddie and the parrot and the dog were again on their way out. When they reached the outside, Eddie said, "Mother! I can't get rid of this dog!"

Eddie's mother called the dog.

The dog sat at Eddie's feet.

A man with a suitcase came up and said, "Pardon me. I want to go into this hotel."

The man stepped in behind Eddie. The dog stood up. Eddie pushed on the brass rod. And around they went to the inside.

The doorman shouted, "I told you dogs aren't allowed in here! Now don't try to bring him in again."

"I'm not bringing the dog in!" Eddie declared. "I'm bringing Louella." That was as far as Eddie got. There was a shove from behind, and around he went again.

Outside, he said, "Here, Mother, you take Louella *in*, and I'll stay *out* with the dog."

He tried to hand the cage to his mother. But he discovered that was impossible. The cage was caught on the brass rod. He pulled at the cage, trying to get it loose.

Eddie's mother stepped into the revolving door to see if she could unfasten the cage.

"Pardon me! Pardon me, please," said a lady. "I'd like to enter the hotel."

"Oh, excuse me!" said Mrs. Wilson, and stepped out of the door.

Once again Eddie and Louella and the dog went around.

When the doorman saw them for the third time, he sputtered, "If you bring that dog in here again, I'll call the police!"

"I don't want to bring the dog in," said Eddie. "I want to bring my parrot."

"Well, then give me the parrot!" said the doorman.

"I can't," wailed Eddie. Before he could say why, there was a push from behind. Out went Eddie and the parrot and the dog once more.

Outside, his mother said, "Step out of the door, Eddie. The dog will follow you. I'll see if I can get the cage unhooked."

Eddie stepped out. So did the dog.

Before his mother could step into the door, someone inside the hotel gave the door an outward shove. Naturally, Louella went around all by herself.

Inside the hotel, the doorman stepped into the door to lift Louella's cage out.

"No funny business!" screamed Louella.

Once again the door was pushed. Now it was the doorman who went around with Louella. Outside, he saw Mrs. Wilson.

"What's going on here?" he asked.

"My son has loaned his parrot for the ball tonight," she said. "He's trying to deliver her. The cage is caught on the rod."

"I'll try to unfasten it," said the doorman.

Eddie and the dog watched the doorman.

"That dog has been around here for two days," said the man. "Is he your dog?"

"No, he's not mine," said Eddie. "But he's a nice dog," he added, patting the dog.

"Cats!" shrieked Louella jealously.

All of a sudden the cage came unhooked. "There!" said the doorman. "I'll take this parrot and deliver it to the ballroom. I see your name is written on the tag."

"Thanks a lot," said Eddie. "Her name is Louella. She has plenty of food. But maybe you'd better give her more water. Just in case some spilled out."

Mrs. Wilson started up the street. Eddie followed his mother. And the dog followed Eddie. The dog's tail was wagging.

Right then Eddie started to use diplomacy. "Just think!" he said. "This poor dog has been here two days. All alone! No food!"

"Now, Eddie!" said his mother. "Your father has said 'No more dogs.'"

"But this dog's my friend!" said Eddie.

"Your friend!" cried his mother. "When did he become your friend?"

"Why, on all those trips we had together. Going round and round," said Eddie.

His mother said, "He has no collar or tag."

"Maybe he lost them," said Eddie. "If we don't take him, somebody will call the dog catcher or that society. You know, the Society for the Prevention of Cruelty to Animals. He's an awful nice dog."

"Oh, bring him along," said Mrs. Wilson.

Eddie said, "I'll look in the paper at the Lost and Found. Maybe I'll find the owner."

"Maybe," said his mother.

Then Eddie said, "Mother, do I have to look hard, or can I look just a little bit?"

Soo-Pung Measures Up

The last day of the Chinese New Year was today. Soo-Pung was filled with excitement when he awakened.

His family had lived in San Francisco's Chinatown for years. But at the time of the Chinese New Year, Soo-Pung's family still did things the way they had done them in China. Many other Chinese families in San Francisco did, too.

At the start of the holidays Soo-Pung's family had fastened their house up tight to keep out bad spirits. During the days that followed they went from door to door, singing for rice cakes. Soo-Pung had joined his family in these things, but all through the holidays he had looked forward to tonight with the greatest eagerness.

"Tonight will be the best of all!" Soo-Pung said as he jumped out of bed. In his mind he pictured the Parade of Lanterns, led by the huge dragon that stood for goodness.

"I've never wanted anything so much as to be tall enough to help carry the dragon," he said to his brother Wei as they dressed.

Wei's dark eyes moved from the top of Soo-Pung's head to the soles of his shoes. "I don't know," Wei said doubtfully. "You have to be tall enough to keep your part of the dragon from touching the ground. But never mind. If you don't measure up, you can always carve a little dragon to carry."

Even though Soo-Pung liked to carve, he was dissatisfied with the idea. "I've done everything to make myself grow!" he said.

And he had. He'd done stretching exercises until he hurt all over. He'd always finished his milk and meat and rice and beans. He had eaten bean sprouts by the pound. He wondered sometimes how many pounds of bean sprouts he had eaten in the last year.

Soo-Pung went to look for his father. He found him stringing lanterns along the front of his shop. "Good morning, Father," said Soo-Pung. "Shall I get the yardstick?"

Mr. Li smiled. "I'll measure you later, my son. I have much to do now."

After breakfast Soo-Pung went to watch the men putting the finishing touches on the dragon. Its body was covered with more colors of silk than ever before. Its sharp teeth and horns looked more lifelike.

One of the men said to Soo-Pung, "Are you tall enough to help carry the dragon?"

Soo-Pung laughed and tried to pretend it didn't matter one way or the other.

Soo-Pung watched for a while and then went to the house of his friend Ping Lin.

"I wish you joy, Mrs. Lin," Soo-Pung said politely to Ping's mother when she opened the door.

"May joy be yours, Soo-Pung," replied Mrs. Lin. "Ping is upstairs in his room."

Soo-Pung bounded up the stairs and burst into his friend's room.

"What are you doing?" he asked. He had noticed at once that there were three pairs of brightly colored silk trousers on the bed.

"I'm trying to decide which trousers to wear," Ping answered. "My trousers may be all of me that shows tonight. So I want them to be just right."

"That means you're tall enough!" cried Soo-Pung. He looked with envy at the top of his friend's head, which was two or three inches above his own.

Ping said, "Just made it. How about you?"

Soo-Pung's heart pounded. If Ping was just right, then Soo-Pung was too small.

"Don't know yet," Soo-Pung said. "I'll go now and have my father measure me."

The bell on the shiny red door of Mr. Li's shop made a merry sound when Soo-Pung entered. Although there was a customer present, Mr. Li took up his yardstick.

Soo-Pung backed up to the wall, and his father marked the spot where the top of his head reached. Carefully his father checked the measurement to the floor.

Soo-Pung didn't have to ask. His father's serious face gave the answer. He was not tall enough!

"Two inches short," Mr. Li said softly.

Soo-Pung's brown eyes filled with tears. He swallowed hard.

Mr. Li said, "Remember what Confucius said. 'Despair only adds to man's ills.'"

As Soo-Pung left and ran up the stairs, he thought, "I wish Confucius had said how to manage to grow two inches in a day!"

When Soo-Pung's tears had stopped, he sat and thought more about Confucius and his father. Then he picked up a piece of wood and his knife. Despair really didn't help. Possibly if he carved something, he would feel better.

He had nothing special in mind. But as the blade of his knife cut the wood, an idea came to him. He worked quickly but carefully. At last he finished! He had made two blocks shaped exactly like the soles of his shoes. Each block was two inches thick, just what he needed to be a dragon-carrier.

He ran down the steps and burst into his father's shop. He set the blocks on the floor below the mark on the wall, then stepped up on the blocks.

"See! I'm tall enough!" he cried.

"By my ancestors!" exclaimed Mr. Li. "You begin to show wisdom, Soo-Pung!"

He helped the boy tape the wedges of wood to the soles of his shoes.

That evening the beautiful dragon swung through the streets of San Francisco mid the loud pop, pop, pop of firecrackers.

Not one person in all Chinatown noticed
the extra thick soles on the last pair of
shoes at the rear of the dragon. Under the
switching tail of the dragon was the smallest and proudest of the dragon-carriers.

Soo-Pung had measured up.

It's a Wolf

Peter and Penny were delighted with the cabin where their family was spending the weekend. There was a huge fireplace. A fire as bright as Penny's hair warmed the cabin. And there were bunk beds.

The boys were as hungry as bears and gobbled up the potato soup, chicken sandwiches, and hot cocoa their mother fixed for supper. They were so impatient to try out the bunks that they started to go to bed right after supper. They spent some time climbing up to the upper bunk and coming down again backwards. Their dad said that they were like monkeys on a stick.

Adapted from *Penny and Peter* by Carolyn Haywood, copyright, 1946, by Harcourt, Brace & World, Inc., and reprinted with their permission.

Both boys wanted to sleep in the upper bunk. It was settled that Peter would sleep in it on Friday night and Penny on Saturday. This satisfied both boys. Soon they were sound asleep.

In the middle of the night Penny woke up. He wondered where he was. He sat up in bed. Everything looked strange. There was a strange perfume of wood smoke and pine trees in the air. And things were so still that the tick-tick-tick of the clock sounded very loud.

Penny got up and looked out the window. Outside, things looked even more strange. A mist lay over everything, and moonlight was shining through the mist.

Penny felt certain that something was going to happen. Sure enough, in a moment a beautiful stag appeared in the clearing. The moonlight shone on his back and antlers as he moved silently toward the water. Penny could see the big antlers very plainly. He held his breath. In a minute he saw another deer. He knew that this one was a doe, for the deer had no antlers.

Penny watched the doe follow the stag to the water's edge. There they both paused. They bent their heads to drink. Then as quietly as they had come, they disappeared.

Penny turned away from the window. He knew where he was now. He was in a cabin in the Green Mountains, and the lump in the bunk up near the ceiling was Peter.

The next morning Penny told the family about the stag and the doe. "It was just like being in a fairy story," he said.

"Why didn't you call us?" asked Peter.

"I don't know," said Penny. "I guess I forgot you were here. I was afraid if I moved it would all disappear."

When breakfast was over, the boys went down to the lake. It was too cool to go swimming, so they took the rowboat out of the boathouse and rowed out to a little island in the lake.

From the island they could see a few other cabins along the edge of the lake. Faintly, they heard a dog barking far off. The boys explored the island and then rowed back to the boathouse.

At lunch Peter said, "Dad, is it OK for us to take a walk in the woods?"

"Certainly," said his father. "Just don't get so far into the woods that you lose sight of the lake. Keep it in sight, and you'll know how to get home."

The boys found a path that led around the lake and started walking. They were alone in what seemed to be a huge forest. Red and yellow leaves were thick on the ground. The boys kicked through piles of them. They heard the tiny crack of small branches breaking under their feet and the swish of squirrels in the trees overhead.

They stopped to pick up some nuts they found lying on the ground. And then all of a sudden they were startled by a sound. It was a low growl.

"What's that?" Penny whispered.

The boys looked around. About a foot away stood an animal. It was a peculiar gray color. Its eyes shone like big bright stones. Its pointed ears stood up stiffly. Its long tail switched back and forth. It growled again.

Peter gasped, "It's a wolf! Run, Penny!"

The boys started off as fast as their legs would go. The wolf bounded after them.

"Climb a tree!" cried Peter.

Penny ran to the pine tree nearest him. The branches were low enough to reach. He swung himself up. Peter did the same.

When they looked for each other, they had taken up positions out of danger in trees about ten feet apart. Penny was trembling so hard he shook the branches. Fearfully he looked for the wolf. There he was, sniffing at the tree.

"What shall we do?" asked Penny.

"I have a whistle in my pocket. I can blow an S O S on it," said Peter. "Maybe Dad will hear it and come."

"The wolf will get him!" cried Penny.

Peter said, "If he would just bring a gun! But if I blow S O S, he won't know he's to bring a gun. I guess I'd better not do it."

The wolf sat and looked up at the trees.

"He has a vicious face," said Penny. "His eyes are just like fire!"

"See him lick his chops with his tongue," said Peter. "See those enormous teeth!"

"We'll be here all night!" Penny cried.

Peter said, "Dad will come to find us."

"But I don't want him to be eaten by a wolf," said Penny in a choked voice.

Just then the wolf lifted his head, licked his chops with his red tongue, and showed his enormous teeth. Then he howled.

"He wants to eat us!" wailed Penny.

"Maybe Dad will hear that howl and bring his gun," said Peter.

"I hope so," said Penny. "That's a very vicious wolf. A dangerous, vicious wolf!"

The wolf, at this point, lay down on the ground. He put his head between his paws.

Balanced on their tree branches, the boys peered down at him.

"Maybe he's going to sleep," said Penny.

Peter said nothing. He just continued to peer at the animal. After a bit he said in a puzzled voice, "Hey, Penny! There's something shining on the wolf's neck. What do you suppose it is?"

"I guess it's just his fur," replied Penny.

Peter moved cautiously to a lower branch and looked. "It's a dog collar!" he cried.

"What's a wolf doing with a dog collar?" asked Penny.

"Maybe it isn't a wolf," said Peter. He climbed still lower and called, "Here, boy!"

The animal walked to Peter's tree. Then he wagged his tail and barked.

Peter dropped to the ground. "Come on down, Penny," he said in a relieved voice. "Were we stupid! This is only a dog. He has a tag on his collar, too."

The dog rubbed against Peter and wagged his tail while Peter patted his head.

Both boys were petting the dog when they saw a man approaching. The dog galloped off to meet him, barking happy barks.

The man cried, "Hey, Toasty, you scamp! I see you've been making new friends."

"Is that your dog?" Peter asked.

"Yes," the gentleman said. "This big scamp looks fierce, doesn't he? But he's as gentle as a kitten. I call him 'Toasty.'" Then he chuckled. "Short for Milk Toast. Some people think he looks like a wolf."

Peter's eyes twinkled as he said, "He does, a little. But nearly any-one would know that he is a dog. There's quite a difference."

Horse-Chestnut Time

by KAYE STARBIRD

When milkweed blows in the pasture
And winds start spinning the leaves,
And out by the wall the cornstalks
Are neatened in packs called sheaves;
When apples bump on the roadway
And over the road and higher
The last of the birds, like clothespins,
Are clipped to the telegraph wire . . .

75

I suddenly think, "Horse-chestnuts!"
And, singing a song, I go
And find a tree in the meadow
Where millions of chestnuts grow;
And underneath in the grasses
I gather the nuts, and then
As soon as I've filled my pockets,
I sing along home again.

And singing and scuffing homeward
Each year through the drying clover,
I feel like a king with treasure,
Though—now that I think it over—
I don't *do* much with horse-chestnuts
Except to make sure I've shined them.
It's just that fall
Isn't fall at all
Until I go out and find them.

May Day and Lei Day

In many states of the United States, the first day of May is celebrated by making and giving May baskets and by dancing around a Maypole. But in one state, Hawaii, May Day is called Lei Day. And it is celebrated differently.

On the day before Lei Day in Hawaii, children gather flowers and string them together in long strings called leis. The next day the children wear leis to school and take leis to their teachers.

Special dances in special costumes are a part of celebrating Lei Day at school.

In most schools in Hawaii there are many children whose parents came from different countries. On Lei Day the children wear costumes of the lands from which their parents came. They do the special dances of their parents' countries.

JAPAN

HAWAII

PHILIPPINES

SAMOA

CHINA

KOREA

TAHITI

The celebrating of Lei Day in Hawaii is a most beautiful sight. Anyone who can visit this part of the United States on the first of May is very lucky. He will see the gay costumes and the fancy dances of many countries.

79

Maile's Lei

"What a wonderful day for a fair! What a wonderful day to be alive!" thought Maile.

She was on her way to a waterfall high in the mountains. She was going there to get white ginger blossoms that grew beside the waterfall. She needed the flowers to make a lei. She was going to enter the lei-making contest at the fair.

This was the first year she had been old enough to enter the contest. For months she had planned the kind of lei she'd make.

The lei would be two colors. She would
make it of white ginger blossoms from the
mountains and yellow ginger flowers from
the valley. She would get the yellow blossoms from the yard of her old friend Tutu.

A two-toned lei should win at least third
prize, Maile thought. Although she knew
she shouldn't, she planned how she'd spend
the prize money. She'd buy a hat for her
aunt. She'd buy something her uncle could
use to fix his fishing nets. Maile and her
brothers lived with their aunt and uncle
because their own parents were dead.

As Maile gathered white flowers beneath the trees by the waterfall, she went on planning. She would take her little brother to the village and buy him a cup of shaved ice with fruit syrup poured over it. They'd each have a cup of shaved ice covered with the wonderful pink syrup!

Soon the paper bag was half filled with flowers. Then Maile hastened toward Tutu's house in the valley. Maile was alarmed when she reached Tutu's door. No singing came from the house, and there was no smell of baking cake. Tutu had entered the cake-baking contest each year the fair had been held. Each year her fresh coconut cake had been given first prize. Maile knew that Tutu needed the prize money very much this year. The crops that she raised to sell had not been good.

When Maile entered the house, she saw that the things to make the coconut cake were on the table. The oven was lighted. But Tutu was just sitting in her rocker with her hands over her face.

"Tutu, what's the matter?" cried Maile.

"For the first time I'll not have a cake to enter at the fair. I tried hard to mix the cake. But my hands are old and stiff."

Maile said, "Let me rub your hands with coconut oil. Then I'll help mix the cake."

Much later, as Maile was taking the cake out of the oven, she glanced at the clock. Tears of disappointment choked her for a second. The forenoon was gone! There was no time left to gather the yellow blossoms and make a lei. But Tutu looked so happy now that giving up the lei seemed worth while.

Tutu didn't feel strong enough to go to the fair. So she was trusting Maile to take the cake and enter it in the contest for her.

"There's a lunch in the bag by the door," Tutu said when Maile was ready to go.

Maile hurried to the bus stop, carrying the cake carefully. The bus drove up at the exact moment that Maile arrived at the corner. She climbed aboard and chose a seat. This was the first time since early morning that she'd had a chance to rest.

Maile sighed a big sigh.

Outside the bus there was a sigh much louder than Maile's.

"Flat tire! Everybody out!" called the driver.

Maile sat on a rock at the side of the road. She decided to eat the lunch that Tutu had sent along with her. How surprised she was when she opened the bag and found white ginger blossoms inside! Goodness! She'd picked up the wrong bag.

Her needle and thread were in the bag, too. So she began to fashion a lei. It could not be the two-toned one she had dreamed of making. But white ginger blossoms alone were very beautiful.

There was dew on the blossoms still. The flowers were as cool and fresh as the dew. Maile worked steadily. Her lei was nearly half done when the driver honked the horn and called, "All aboard!"

There was no use trying to string flowers on a moving bus, so Maile just held the cake. Before long she sighed again. And just then there was another giant sigh outside.

Another flat tire!

Other people grumbled. But Maile found a shady spot. She spent the tire-fixing time finishing her lei.

During the rest of the ride to the fair, Maile held both the cake and the lei very carefully. She entered Tutu's cake in the baking contest first. Then she found the flower booth where leis were to be kept until time for the judging. She entered hers in the contest. But she doubted that a lei made of plain white ginger would even win an honorable mention.

"Prize or no prize, there's fun to be had at a fair," Maile reminded herself.

Maile walked around and looked at all the other booths. In one booth an old man was bent over a log, carving a boat out of it. In another there were dolls from Japan for sale. In still others there were rows and rows of canned goods people had entered in contests.

Maile reached the baking booth again just in time to see the judges give first prize to Tutu's cake. Happily she took the blue ribbon and the money for her friend.

She had almost forgotten about her lei when she heard her name called over the loudspeaker. She was wanted at the flower booth. Her heart pounded with excitement as she raced to the booth.

There was her lei among the prize winners! On it was a white ribbon. And on the ribbon were the words *Honorable Mention*.

She noticed that first prize had gone to a two-toned lei of the kind she had planned to make. But Maile was not sad. She thought instead how pleased Tutu would be with her blue ribbon and the prize money that she needed so badly.

No money went with honorable mention. Even so, Maile was happy that her lei had pleased the judges. As she was taking it down, she heard a voice calling to her. It was a gentleman's voice, and it was both familiar and unfamiliar.

Maile turned around. It was the Mayor! The Mayor was speaking to her! She had often heard him on the radio and at a few meetings. That's why the jolly voice was familiar. But the Mayor had never spoken straight to her before!

"Young lady," the Mayor said, "white ginger is my wife's favorite flower. Your lei is fresh and very beautiful. I'd like to buy it for her."

He held out two dollars to Maile.

She thanked him. Then she reached up and placed the lei around his neck.

Maile was smiling. "Two dollars!" she thought happily. "Not enough money to buy all the presents—the hat and the shaved ice with pink syrup poured over it. But plenty of money to buy the family something very special for dinner!"

Manaluk's Gold Rush

During the long Alaska winters Manaluk's father set his traps in the snow. Manaluk helped him. In the spring they took a pile of skins to the trading post and traded the skins for the things they needed. But this had been a bad winter for trappers. Time after time many traps had been empty.

Manaluk thought about the things they needed—candles and salt and oil. He knew it was no use to hope for other things this year. But his mother wanted a real glass window for their cabin, and Manaluk wanted paper and crayons. He had gone to school one winter. Perhaps he would have learned to read better if he had not spent so much time drawing pictures of foxes and rabbits. Yes, Manaluk wanted paper and crayons and canned peaches. He had tasted canned peaches only once in his whole life.

Manaluk's father was checking the last trap. The bait was gone, but the trap was empty. While his father set the trap again, Manaluk looked at the ice-covered river.

89

There was a man down on the river, pulling a loaded sled. As Manaluk watched, the man stumbled and fell. He did not get up again. He lay very still on the ice. Manaluk pulled at his father's arm and pointed.

It is dangerous to lie still for long in Alaska in winter. A person has to keep moving to keep warm. This man must be rescued. Manaluk's father started quickly down the hill on his snowshoes. He called back to Manaluk, "Bring the sled!"

The man on the ice was a stranger to them, an old man with whiskers. He was dressed in fur and skin clothes.

Manaluk's father helped him to his feet, but the man could not stand by himself.

"He has hurt his ankle," said Manaluk's father. "Help me get him onto our sled."

They bundled the man onto the sled, and Manaluk's father pulled it toward home. Manaluk followed, pulling the stranger's loaded sled. When they reached the cabin, Manaluk's father carried the old man in. His mother helped get the man settled on a bunk and put a warm fur rug over him.

There was a kettle of meat stew on the little iron stove. Manaluk helped himself to a dish of hot stew. Then he was so warm and so comfortable that he curled up on his own bunk and went to sleep.

When Manaluk woke, the old man was still lying on a bunk, covered with the rug. The man opened his strange blue eyes and looked at Manaluk. Then he smiled. The boy smiled back. They were friends at once.

Before many days had passed, the old man could hobble around a little. But mostly he just rested and talked to Manaluk. He knew some of Manaluk's language. He got a pencil and notebook from his pack, and when he did not know the word for something, he drew a picture of it.

The old man's name was Jim. He had come to Alaska forty years ago to look for gold. Year after year he had panned for gold. Year after year he was sure that the next year would be the lucky one. Jim talked and talked. Manaluk listened, bright-eyed.

At last Jim did not have to hobble when he walked. His ankle was as good as new. It was time for him to be on his way.

He got his belongings together to load his sled. He took a flashlight from his pack and gave it to Manaluk's father. To Manaluk's mother he gave a little box of pins. He gave Manaluk the pencil and notebook to keep. Then he gave Manaluk something else from the pack. It was a shiny metal pan.

"Now you can pan for gold," the old man said, grinning.

Manaluk stood outside and waved good-by until Jim was out of sight. When he went back in, he found that his mother had put the pan with her cooking things.

"Jim made a mistake," she said. "Pans are for women."

Manaluk flushed. "This is a miner's pan," he said fiercely. "A man's pan! It is mine."

He took the shiny pan outside and hid it beneath the snow.

Soon after that, spring came on with a rush. Each day the sun shone for a longer time. The snow melted. Melting snow made mud everywhere.

Most years Manaluk could hardly wait for the snow to melt. But this year he day-dreamed around inside the cabin and forgot to do his chores. He asked his father, "Why do you never go looking for gold? That is the way to be rich."

His father grunted. "I have watched men run about foolishly," he said. "They go hungry with game all around them. I am not like them." Then he added proudly, "I am a hunter and a trapper."

At last the sun shone night and day. The mud dried, and Manaluk's mother planted a garden. One of Manaluk's chores was to keep the weeds out of the garden. But the weeds sprouted and grew merrily, while Manaluk disappeared day after day.

He took his fishing pole with him, but he brought back no fish. He took a basket, but he brought back no berries.

Manaluk was looking for gold. Day after day he explored the creeks, using the shiny pan he had hidden. He scooped pebbles and muddy water into the pan. He splashed the pan round and round till the heaviest bits were left in it.

He looked and looked and looked for the bright color of gold.

With all of his scooping and splashing, Manaluk did not find a single bit of gold.

When he was at home, he daydreamed more and more. His parents began to be worried. They thought he was sick.

Lying awake in his bunk, Manaluk overheard them talking about him.

"He looks and sees nothing. He listens and hears nothing," said his father. "Have you given him medicine?"

"Medicine will do him no good," said his mother. "It is sickness of the mind, not the body."

"Try the medicine anyway," his father said. "Try the castor oil from the store."

Just the thought of the awful-tasting castor oil made Manaluk choke. He lay awake for a long time, thinking. Before he went to sleep, he had almost decided to give up being a gold miner and become a mighty hunter and trapper instead.

When he woke in the morning, he ran to do his chores. He weeded the garden. Weeds flew in every direction. So did a few of his mother's vegetables.

Then Manaluk dashed to the cabin for his fishing pole. He grabbed it and ran outside before his mother could reach for the bottle of castor oil.

"I will bring some fine fish for dinner," he called back over his shoulder as he ran out the door.

Manaluk walked down to the river. The sky was blue. The sun was hot on his head. Small wild flowers blazed with color under his feet.

Most summers Manaluk could hardly look enough at the sun and the flowers before the long darkness came back. But this summer he had hardly noticed the sun over his head or the flowers under his feet. He had been too busy looking for gold.

Manaluk found a good place to fish and threw in his line. Before long he felt a jerk. He had hooked a big one!

Manaluk pulled hard on the line. Then the bank gave way, and he fell in with a splash.

He stood up in icy water to his waist. His hands were full of muddy pebbles from the river bottom. He threw the pebbles angrily. They landed on the bank, striking a rock and scattering in all directions.

The biggest pebble shone bright yellow in the sunlight. Manaluk climbed out and picked it up. Yes. This was it. A piece of gold! How cold it was and how heavy!

He had found gold at last. Should he go back to looking for gold day after day?

Manaluk thought hard for a long time. He thought about his father. His father could track game in the wildest country. He could steer his boat through the fiercest water. He could care for his sled dogs on the longest trip. What wonderful stories his father told during the long winter nights about trapping and hunting!

What if Manaluk spent his life scooping up squishy mud and splashing it around in a pan? What kind of wonderful stories would he be able to tell about that?

Manaluk decided, once and for all. He decided to grow up to be a great hunter and trapper like his father.

Pans are for women!

But even a great hunter can make use of a piece of gold if he finds one.

"I will take this to the man at the trading post," he thought. "The man will tell me how much it is worth, and I will tell him what I want.

"First, a fine knife for my father. Next, the piece of window glass for my mother. Then a whole pile of paper and a box of crayons, all colors.

"And last of all— no, first of all— a whole can of peaches. I will ask the store man to open it. And I will eat the peaches, every bite, myself!"

99

Greatness

"Greatness, after all, in spite of its name, appears to be not so much a certain size as a certain quality in human lives."

PHILLIPS BROOKS

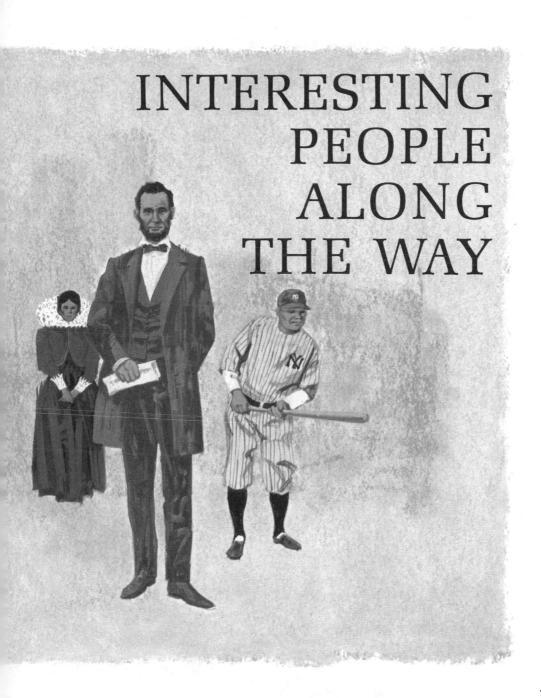

INTERESTING
PEOPLE
ALONG
THE WAY

"The Babe"

Among the baseball players of the past, there is one whose name is known by nearly everyone. His name is George Herman Ruth. But the name that people know him by is Babe Ruth, or just plain "the Babe." He played with the New York Yankees from 1920 to 1935.

103

During the years that Babe Ruth played with the New York Yankees, everyone was a friend and a fan of his. He was a favorite of all.

People came in such crowds just to see the Babe at Yankee Stadium in New York that the stadium itself was known as the "house that Ruth built."

The right-field bleachers at the stadium were called "Ruthville." They were given that name because Babe Ruth's noisiest and youngest fans were wedged into them.

All through game after game Babe's fans would chant, "We want a homer! We want a homer!"

Whenever the Babe trotted off the field after he had made one of his mighty hits, everyone in the Ruthville bleachers would leap to his feet and cheer long and loud. Quite often the hit was a homer.

Babe Ruth, the great baseball star, loved the game, and the whole world of baseball loved him. But George Herman Ruth had not always been loved as he was by his friends in Ruthville.

When George was a small boy, he lived in Baltimore, and almost no one loved him. He had no real home. So he spent his time on the streets. It was not often that he had all he needed or wanted to eat. He was nearly always hungry.

He found plenty of mischief to get into on the city streets. So he did not look upon the Baltimore policemen as his friends.

His only friends were other boys, as wild as he was, who sometimes played baseball with him.

When George Herman Ruth was seven years old, he was placed in an orphanage in Baltimore. The school at the orphanage was one in which trades were taught. Children were expected to learn a trade, or way of making a living. George began his schooling with the idea of learning to be a tailor. He would earn his living making suits and coats when he grew up.

Tailoring did not interest him much. He missed his old friends, and he didn't like the orphanage and its rules. But as soon as he began to play with the school baseball team, he did not mind the rules so much.

A teacher at the school, Brother Matthias, took a great interest in George Ruth and changed the boy's whole life.

Before George had come to the school, he had not been taught the difference between right and wrong. Brother Matthias was the kind of person who could teach him. Instead of yelling at the boys, he talked over their problems with them. He also helped with baseball practice. George thought he was everything that a man should be.

At baseball practice one day when George was almost fifteen, he was catching as usual. His team's pitcher was taking a terrific beating. George wasn't helping matters any. He was laughing at the pitcher.

Quietly Brother Matthias suggested that George should take over since he seemed to know so much about pitching.

George looked startled for a second and felt uncertain of himself. He was aware that Brother Matthias understood only too well that George knew nothing about pitching. This was just his way of teaching the boy something.

As George stood on the hill ready to pitch, he was relieved to find that he did not feel uncertain of himself any longer. For even though he was not quite fifteen, George had a wonderful throwing arm.

Soon it was clear to everyone that pitching was the place for this young left-hander. When neighboring teams came to play, it was not unusual for George to strike out ten, fifteen, or even twenty players before the game was over.

Ruth was given a chance to try out for the Baltimore Orioles a few years later. He did not look like a promising ballplayer. He was tall and lanky and walked in a funny way, with his toes pointed out. He walked this way because Brother Matthias did.

To George's surprise, after the tryout he was no longer an amateur baseball player. He was signed up to play with the Orioles.

His next surprise came when he learned that he was to be paid for playing baseball. He found it hard to believe that he could earn money doing what he liked best. Six hundred dollars! It sounded like all the money in the world! Now he would not have to be a tailor and work for a living. He would earn money having fun!

It was the first day of spring training with the Orioles that George Ruth got the name by which he was known for the rest of his life. The Orioles were famous for their young players. On that first day of training someone pointed out Ruth as the newest "babe." Before long everyone was calling him Babe. The name stuck.

Perhaps Babe Ruth's early life made him do some of the things that he did when he was a grown man and a famous ballplayer.

Possibly it was because he was so often hungry when he was a boy that Babe Ruth never missed a chance to make up for it when he was a man. He ate enormously. Three helpings of everything, topped off by a whole pie, were not too much for him.

One time he had so many bottles of pop and hot dogs lathered with mustard that the whole country was aware of his stomach ache. At first it was feared that he might be seriously ill. Then everyone found out that he just had a stomach ache from too many hot dogs and too much pop. Babe Ruth, the famous ballplayer, had broken training rules with a bang.

Babe loved children and was eager to bring them happiness. He gave out autographs to them by the hundreds.

If he heard of a boy who was kept in bed by a serious illness and discouraged because getting well was so slow, Babe Ruth would call on the lad.

Babe Ruth would promise to hit a homer for the sick boy. It was quite a promise to make, but Babe managed to keep it when it was most needed. It did wonders for any boy who had lost heart to have the Babe sit by his bed and then go and hit a special homer as they had agreed.

Babe liked hitting home runs as much as his fans liked to see him send them over the right-field bleachers. But he liked most of all to connect with the ball when there were lots of children in the stands. Then his face would break into a wider grin than usual. He'd tip his cap to the cheers of his young fans, the boys and girls of Ruthville.

Get 'Em While They're Hot

A heat wave came early in the summer in 1868. By mid-May the hot sun was beating down on the fine sand beach at the park known as Coney Island.

Charlie Feltman stood in his pie wagon, which he drove to the beach each day. He was worried and discouraged. Two new inns had just opened along the sea front. These inns had hot sandwiches for sale, along with fruit punch, other cold drinks, and cakes.

Charlie had nothing to sell but pies. He was afraid he would lose his Coney Island customers to the inns.

What to do? He felt obliged to sell hot sandwiches, too. But what kind?

The pie wagon was small. There was no room to do fancy cooking. Besides, he wasn't much of a cook—only an amateur one. Anything fancy he'd cook would be a failure. These were discouraging thoughts.

The pieman thought about his problem for weeks. Then one day he got an idea. Why not make a hot sandwich out of a sausage?

It wouldn't be very hard to put a small stove in the wagon and boil the sausages in a kettle. He'd put the hot meat between two pieces of bread. Better yet, in a roll. Yes, that was it! A nice, long roll would be the handiest wrapping for the tube-shaped meat. No mixing and salting to do either. The meat could be covered with mustard for extra taste.

The fact that nobody had ever put a sausage into a sandwich did not need to keep Charlie Feltman from doing it.

It was midsummer when Feltman was ready for business with his sausages and rolls. The first sausage was boiled and picked out of the kettle. It had mustard spilled over it and was placed in a roll. Then the very first hot dog was served to a customer at Charlie Feltman's pie wagon at Coney Island.

Just who that first customer was no one knows. But since that day frankfurters in rolls have become the most popular food in America. Hot dogs are eaten at home and at picnics. They are served on plates and without them. People find them handy to eat while watching a game at the ball park or walking around at the zoo.

If all the frankfurters eaten in America in a year were laid in a line, they'd reach to the moon and back.

In the summer of 1939 the President of the United States had a picnic for the King and Queen of England. The President might have served his royal guests turkey, since turkey was served on the first Thanksgiving.

Or he might have had fancy food cooked for them. But what the President did serve at the picnic was the most popular food in America—hot dogs.

The King was delighted. He asked for a second. The Queen asked for a second and a third. Hot dogs made headlines around the world.

When the Queen went home, she had frankfurters mailed to her. She served them to friends, and they sent for frankfurters. In this way America's most popular food began to be popular in England.

Wilbur Wright and Orville Wright
1867-1912   1871-1948
by STEPHEN VINCENT BENÉT

Said Orville Wright to Wilbur Wright,
"These birds are very trying.
I'm sick of hearing them cheep-cheep
About the fun of flying.
A bird has feathers, it is true.
That much I freely grant.
But, must that stop us, W?"
Said Wilbur Wright, "It shan't."

And so they built a glider, first,
And then they built another.
—There never were two brothers more
Devoted to each other.
They ran a dusty little shop
For bicycle-repairing,
And bought each other soda-pop
And praised each other's daring.

115

They glided here, they glided there,
They sometimes skinned their noses.
—For learning how to rule the air
Was not a bed of roses—
But each would murmur, afterward,
While patching up his bro.
"Are we discouraged, W?"
"Of course we are not, O!"

And finally, at Kitty Hawk
In Nineteen-Three (let's cheer it!),
The first real airplane really flew
With Orville there to steer it!
—And kingdoms may forget their kings
And dogs forget their bites,
But, not till Man forgets his wings,
Will men forget the Wrights.

Audubon's Birds

A young Frenchman had come to live across from the Bakewells. His queer ways were the talk of the Pennsylvania countryside. He wore his best clothes every day. He went hunting. But instead of having the game he shot cooked for his supper, he drew pictures of it.

After Tom Bakewell had paid a call on the new neighbor, he told his sister, "You must go there with me sometime, Lucy. The Frenchman's name is John Audubon. His house is like a museum. It is full of birds and animals he's stuffed. Birds are his favorites. He has one of every kind he has seen in our woods."

117

Lucy did go with Tom to call on the Frenchman, and friendship grew among the three. They took long walks together, looking for birds to add to the museum. Lucy helped John with his pictures. She would hold a bird in whatever position he wanted to show it in his drawing.

One spring Audubon found a cave in the cliff beside the creek. He took Tom and Lucy to see it. He pointed out an old nest that was still hanging from the roof of the cave. The nest was made of grasses held together with mud.

As they were examining the nest, Lucy gave a sudden cry. "Look, John! Did you see those birds? They wanted to come in the cave. They saw us and flew away!"

"Perhaps they built the nest," said John. "Let's give them a chance to come in."

The friends climbed out of the cave and hid in the underbrush near the opening. After a while the birds came back. They were small birds, brown and yellow and white. They had a peculiar way of flying that was very quick and graceful.

The birds lighted on a branch above the cave. As the young people gazed at them, the birds flew quickly upward, then dipped gracefully into the cave. They flew straight to the nest and hopped in and out. In a few minutes they came out of the cave and flew swiftly away.

"They will be back," John said. "They have come all the way from the South to Pennsylvania to find their old nest! What do you call those wonderful little birds?"

"Phoebes," said Lucy. "There are lots of them here every spring and summer. You haven't seen one before because they all left in the early fall before you arrived."

"That means they fly to some distant place in the South," said John. "Yet they find the way back to their old nest!"

"Now, John!" protested Tom. "You don't know that is their old nest. They may be looking around for just any old nest."

"No," John insisted. "They knew the nest was there. They flew right to it."

Tom was not satisfied with the answer. He had many questions. And he wanted answers that could be proved. If these were birds that were returning to an old nest, had they built the nest? Or were they the babies born in the nest last year? How did they find their way back?

John said seriously, "Those are all questions that I cannot answer. If only there were a book in my library that gave the answers! But I have found no book that tells about the birds of America."

"You should write one," Tom suggested.

Audubon sighed. "I'd like to. No! Not write. English is difficult for me. I'd like to draw the birds as I see them. Alive! Natural! Flying, nesting, feeding! Not dead, as they are in my museum."

"Do it, then," Lucy urged. "You could. You draw such wonderful pictures."

"I don't know enough yet to draw living birds," said John. "But I go on learning. I've decided to come here every day and try to learn all about these phoebes."

John did just that. Alone or with Lucy, who brought her needlework, John sat in the cave day after day. The phoebes soon became used to the silent watchers. They trusted them and went about their business, paying no attention to John and Lucy.

The phoebes put a new lining of down in the old nest. Then the mother bird, over several days' time, laid six eggs in the nest.

Two weeks later there were baby birds in the nest. John and Lucy peered at the babies. The parent birds did not seem to mind. So John lifted up one of the babies. It did not seem frightened.

John whispered, "Will you come back next year, little bird? Will I know you if you do? If only I could put a mark on you!"

"You could clip the wing feathers," Lucy said quietly. "But they'd grow back."

John went on discussing the problem in a low voice. "I can put nothing on the bird unless it is very light."

Pulling the thread from her needle, Lucy asked softly, "A bit of thread?"

"Yes," whispered John. Then Lucy tied a thread around the tiny leg of the bird.

When the baby birds were about ready to learn to use their wings, John looked for the one with the thread. He examined each baby. None was wearing a thread. "The mother bird must have pulled it off," he told Lucy. "I need something stronger than thread. Fine wire, perhaps."

"Wouldn't wire rust?" asked Lucy.

"Not gold or silver wire. But I have none. Before I could ride my horse to the city and get some, the baby birds would already have gone away."

Lucy was silent for a moment. Then she spoke. "I'll bring some silver wire to the cave this afternoon."

Just before the mother bird settled on the nest for the night, Lucy brought a piece of very fine silver wire. "I pulled it out of an old bracelet that belonged to my mother," she said. "I had to work slowly so as not to harm the bracelet. Is it enough?"

"Yes, indeed!" said John gratefully.

That night each of the young phoebes went to sleep with a bracelet of silver wire around one leg.

The phoebes and John James Audubon went away from Pennsylvania that winter. By the time spring came again, Audubon had already returned.

Lucy Bakewell had agreed to marry him. The young people were busy getting ready for the marriage, but they took time each day to go to the cave in the cliff to look for their phoebes. The nest was always empty. In fact, not a single phoebe was to be seen along the creek, although it was long past the time when they usually appeared.

"I'm sure our phoebes are dead," said Lucy sadly. "If they were alive, they'd be back."

"They may have been in a storm. Or maybe there was sickness," said John.

Tom said, "You two are wasting time being unhappy. I think your birds had a happier fate. They are probably quite healthy, making nests somewhere else."

Lucy and John were not cheered, as Tom had meant them to be. But they stopped going to the cave and began taking walks on the other side of the creek.

One day just a week before the marriage, John and Lucy paused to rest at a spot across the creek from the cave.

When John glanced across the creek, he cried, "There's a phoebe! I must see it up close. Wait for me here, Lucy."

Lucy was used to waiting. But even to her the time seemed long. The sun was low in the sky before John returned. He was holding a bird in the cup of his hand.

"It's one of ours!" he said to Lucy. "I looked until I found the nest."

"In the cave?" asked Lucy excitedly.

"No. In the underbrush near the cave. But there are phoebes in the old nest, too, Lucy. I believe they are the mother and father bird we watched. They were not afraid of me. They let me close enough to see they wore no silver bracelets."

"We should've put bracelets on the parent birds, too!" cried Lucy. "We could have put them on the right legs of the babies and the left legs of the older birds. That way we could have told which was which afterwards. Why didn't we do that?"

As he opened his hand, John said, "We can do it next time."

Lucy saw the tiny circle of silver wire flash in the sun as the bird spread its wings and flew.

"There are so many things to do," said Audubon. "But I have a whole lifetime in which to do them."

Spring Song

by AILEEN FISHER

A meadow lark came back one day
and searched beneath the faded hay
out in the rocks, beside a cleft,
to find a song that he had left.

He found it. And he tried it out.
He tossed the melody about,
and not a note was hurt a bit
by winter drifting over it.

127

Sequoyah's Talking Leaves

Sequoyah sat carving with his knife on piece after piece of tree bark. As he worked, he talked softly to himself.

Other Cherokee Indians peered at him from behind trees. They had fear and hate in their eyes. They believed that the lame man by the cabin was practicing bad magic. They believed he was calling on bad spirits to destroy the Cherokee people.

Even if Sequoyah had told the watchers what he was doing, they would not have understood. "I am trying to make talking leaves for the Cherokees," Sequoyah would have said. By this he would have meant he was trying to discover a way to write the language that the Cherokee Indians spoke.

Sequoyah had first seen writing on sheets of paper some years before. These sheets were letters that had come in the mail for white men. At that time Sequoyah thought these sheets of paper must be magic. They seemed to tell the men what had been said by people far away.

This talk on paper Sequoyah called "talking leaves." He decided to find a way to make talking leaves for the Cherokees. They should be able to send messages to distant friends and relations. More important, the wisdom of their ancestors should be kept. The history of the tribe should be written for the children to read.

Sequoyah first thought that Cherokee talk could be put on paper by making pictures of all Cherokee words.

Sequoyah made one picture for "horse," another for "run," a third for "shovel." Before very long he had hundreds of pictures. He decided no one could remember so many pictures. He must try something else.

He visited the white man's school. The teacher there drew pictures for Sequoyah. The teacher drew a horseshoe and said, "This is the letter *C*." A bow with a string he called *D*. Then the teacher put several pictures together to make just one word.

After a brief time the Indian shook his head sadly. There was more to remember with the white man's pictures than with his own. When Sequoyah left, the teacher gave him a "bundle of talking leaves." This was the name Sequoyah gave to the white man's spelling book.

Sequoyah thought long and hard about his problem. Finally he was sure he knew the secret of the talking leaves. Spoken words could be divided into parts. The same parts were in many words. There were fewer different parts than there were different words. He would make pictures of the parts.

Sequoyah felt that he had been wasting his time. To make up for it he must work every day on the new pictures. He became so busy shaping the pictures that he paid no attention to the Indians who stared at him and threatened to do him harm. He didn't hear the old men say that he was a bad spirit. He didn't hear them say that he meant trouble for the tribe.

Sequoyah paid no attention when his wife insisted that he give up this foolishness and work in the fields as other men did. And when she grumbled that the cabin roof was leaking, he did nothing about it.

The lame Cherokee worked for weeks and months on his new pictures. Then one day all Cherokee tribesmen were called together for an important meeting. Sequoyah went. When he returned home, he discovered that his wife had destroyed his work! In her anger, she had burned all his pictures and the white man's spelling book, too.

So Sequoyah built a hut deep in the woods where he could work in peace. There, he thought, his work would be safe.

Sequoyah left the lonely hut only to visit his little daughter. One evening he came back from visiting her to find that the hut in the woods had been burned! Twice his precious work had been destroyed—this time by the old men of the tribe.

Broken-hearted, Sequoyah went to the Chief of the village. The Chief was his friend. He didn't consider Sequoyah dangerous. But he thought that the Lame One was foolish. He suggested that Sequoyah go away for a while.

Sequoyah joined a group of Cherokees who were moving to lands farther west. He planned to return with leaves that talked.

Three years later Sequoyah came back to the village with a letter for the Chief. The letter was written by the Chief's son, who had been with Sequoyah in the west. It was written in the Cherokee writing that Sequoyah himself had invented.

The Chief was doubtful of the invention. Others had tried to put Cherokee speech into writing. No one had been able to do it. The Chief would not look at the letter for weeks after Sequoyah returned.

But one day the Chief went to Sequoyah's cabin. He looked at the paper. He heard his friend read what was on it. He was still doubtful until Sequoyah's daughter read the same words.

No longer was the Chief in doubt. He was just as excited about the talking leaves as Sequoyah was. He asked and was told all about Sequoyah's work.

The Lame One had not made an alphabet of letters like that of the white man. He had made pictures of syllables. He had discovered there were eighty-six syllables in the Cherokee language. He had made a different picture or sign for each of the eighty-six syllables. These pictures of syllables could be fitted together to write all the words in the language. Anyone could learn the eighty-six signs, and in a short time, too.

The Chief was eager to prove to the old men that Sequoyah was not foolish or bad but very wise. He arranged for braves from all villages to come to Sequoyah to be taught to write and read the Cherokee language. Some of the braves who came could write and read English, but none had seen the Cherokee language written down.

At the end of a week they all could read and write in Cherokee. They were ready to prove that Sequoyah's magic was good.

The old men and chiefs for miles around gathered together. They heard the braves declare that Sequoyah's magic was good. He had found a way to put Cherokee talk on paper and had taught it to them.

The old men tested the magic in every way they could think of. At the end of the test a mighty cheer went up from both old and young. The cheer was not for Sequoyah alone. It was for all Cherokee Indians. The secret of the talking leaves was within reach of all of them!

The Cherokee people were eager to learn to read and write. Everywhere they practiced writing. They printed with a stick in the dust, with a knife on a tree trunk, with a stone on another stone, with a pen on paper. In a few months' time nearly all Cherokees could write and read.

Sequoyah felt rewarded for his work when he saw his people sending letters to friends and family and beginning to write down the wisdom of the tribe. His work had brought him happiness. He did not dream it would bring him honors in the years to come.

Sequoyah's Honors

Sequoyah's invention was a wonderful thing for the Cherokees, and an amazing thing for Sequoyah to have done.

He had never been to school. He could not read or write any language. Yet all alone he invented a way to write the language of his people.

Since he died, more than a hundred years ago, he has been honored and remembered in many ways and in many places.

The giant redwood trees of California were named for him.

In Washington, D.C., there is a statue of Sequoyah. It was put there by the state of Oklahoma. Once it was thought that the state would be named Sequoyah. It was not. So to honor him, the people of Oklahoma placed a statue of him in Washington, D.C. It stands with statues of other great men of our country.

There is a figure of Sequoyah on a door of a library building in Washington, D.C. It is there among other great alphabet makers of the world.

Sequoyah's home in Oklahoma has been kept for people to visit.

"Sequoyah" by Vinnie Ream Hoxie.
Photo from Oklahoma Historical Society.

It is fitting that the last sad news about Sequoyah was written using the signs that he had invented.

When Sequoyah was quite old, he went to Mexico. He was looking for part of the Cherokee tribe that had moved there. He died somewhere in Mexico. After he had been away from home for some time, his friends became worried and started for Mexico to look for him. They sent back the letter that is shown on 138. Part of what the letter said is given below.

Where I was traveling, we met Cherokees who had been in Mexico—Jesse, the leader, Worm, Spider, Standing Man, and Standing Rock. Standing Rock had looked after Sequoyah all the time he was sick, and saw them bury him. It is evident that Over-There-He-Holds-His-Hand-Up, the son of the late Sequoyah, is now searching for him, and he feels sad that his father lies so far away. He does not want to return to the Cherokee Nation. He is staying here at Red-place, and here we saw each other. The Indians told me that he died, and that is the way it is.

. . . .

I, Wind, just wrote this.

May 15, 1845

Translated by Jack Frederick Kilpatrick and Anna Gritts Kilpatrick, who is the great-great-granddaughter of Sequoyah.

Abe Lincoln

Abe Lincoln went home early from work at the Crawford place. Mr. Crawford had loaned him a new book to read.

When Abe reached the Lincoln cabin, he found his stepsisters, Betsy and Mathilda Johnston, waiting outside for their mother. She was inside the cabin, putting on her best bonnet.

140

From *Abe Lincoln Gets His Chance*, by Frances Cavanah, copyright © 1959 by Rand McNally & Company, publishers.

Abe entered the cabin and saw his step-mother before the mirror putting on her bonnet. "Your pa and Dennis have gone squirrel hunting," she said as she tied the bonnet strings in a bow beneath her chin. "The girls and I are going to visit a new neighbor. You keep an eye on Johnny and put some potatoes on to boil for supper."

"Oh, Ma, not potatoes again?"

"Now they'll be right tasty with squirrel. Before you put the potatoes on——"

Abe patted Mr. Crawford's book inside his shirt front. "I can read?" he asked.

"You can after you go down to the horse trough and wash your head."

"Wash my head! How come?" Abe wailed.

"Take a look at the ceiling, and you'll know how come. See that dark spot on the ceiling below the loft? Your head made that. You're getting so tall you bump into the ceiling every night when you climb up to the loft to go to bed."

Abe rolled his eyes upward. "If some of the learning I've got in my head starts leaking out, how can I help it?"

Sarah Lincoln refused to be put off by any of Abe's foolishness. "When you track dirt into the house, I can wash the floor," she said. "I can't get to the ceiling so easy. It needs a coat of whitewash, but there's no use in doing it if your head ain't clean."

"All right," said Abe meekly.

"Take a gourdful of soap with you," said Sarah. "And mind you, no reading till you finish washing your hair."

Abe grumbled under his breath as he carried a gourd filled with soft soap to the trough. With a book to be read, washing his hair seemed like a waste of time. But if that was what his stepmother wanted, he would do it. He lathered his head with soap and ducked into the water. He lathered and ducked again. Soap got into his eyes, and he began to sputter. He heard a giggle.

"Hey, Johnny, is that you?" Abe asked. "Get a bucket of water. Quick!"

Johnny, the eight-year-old stepbrother, was glad to oblige. He poured pail after pail of water over Abe's head to rinse it. Finally all the soap was rinsed away.

Abe took the tail of his shirt and wiped the soap out of his eyes. Both boys were covered with water. The once dusty ground around the horse trough was now a sea of mud. Johnny was delighted. He liked to feel the mud squish up between his toes.

"Look at me, Abe!" he shouted. "Look at me in this squishy mud. Ain't we having fun?"

Abe took his stepbrother by the hand. His eyes were twinkling. "I've thought of something else that's fun. Come on, we're going to play a joke on Mamma."

When Sarah returned to the cabin late that day, she noticed that Abe's hair was still damp. He was very quiet as he stood by the fireplace, swung the kettle outward, and dipped out the potatoes. Tom Lincoln and Dennis had come in grumbling. They had not brought back a single squirrel.

Only Johnny seemed in good spirits. He whispered in Mathilda's ear. They both began to giggle. By the time the family had gathered around the table, Betsy and Dennis had been let in on the secret, whatever it was. They were red in the face from trying not to laugh.

"Quiet!" said Abe's father. "Quiet now, while I say the blessing."

"Oh, Lord, we thank Thee," Tom Lincoln began. He usually gave thanks for each kind of food. But today the only food was potatoes. "We thank Thee, Lord," he said. "We thank Thee for all these blessings."

"Mighty poor blessings," chuckled Abe.

The girls giggled. Dennis threw back his head and roared. Johnny was laughing so hard that he fell off his stool backwards. He lay on the floor, rolling and shrieking.

"I wish you young ones would stop carrying on," said Sarah, "and tell me what you are carrying on about."

"Oh, Ma, can't you see? Look up there!" said Betsy.

Sarah gasped. Marching across the ceiling were the marks of two bare feet.

"Don't they look like Johnny's bare feet?" Mathilda asked.

"Johnny Johnston, you come right here," said Sarah sternly.

Johnny picked himself up from the rag rug before the fireplace. He went and stood by his mother. His blue eyes danced. This was a scolding he looked forward to.

"Now tell me the truth, Johnny Johnston! What do you mean by——"

Sarah paused. She could hardly scold her son for walking on the ceiling.

Johnny had been told exactly what to say.

"I got my feet all muddy down at the horse trough," Johnny explained. "Then I walked on the ceiling."

"Walked on the ceiling! Johnny Johnston, you know it's wicked to lie!"

"That's the truth! I'm telling the truth! Those are my footprints clear across the ceiling under the loft."

Sarah gazed upward.

The footprints were too small to belong
to anyone but Johnny. Sarah looked at Abe.
He seemed to have taken a sudden liking
for boiled potatoes and kept his eyes on
his plate.

"Abe Lincoln, is this some of your foolishness?" said Sarah. "Is this one of your didos?"

"I—I reckon so."

"But how——"

"It was easy," Johnny interrupted. "I held my legs stiff, and Abe held me upside down, and I walked."

Abe stood up, tipping over his stool. He glanced toward the door.

Sarah was not often angry. When she was, she reminded her children of a mother hen ruffling its feathers. "Well, Abe, have you got anything to say for yourself?"

Abe flushed and shook his head. Suddenly his joke did not seem quite so funny.

"I declare!" said Sarah. "A big boy like you! You ought to be spanked."

The children looked at tall, lanky Abe towering over their mother. They burst out laughing again. "Mamma's going to spank Abe!" they chanted. "Mamma's going to spank Abe for cutting up didos."

Dennis hit the table with a bang. "That's a good one, that is!" he roared.

Sarah threw her apron over her head. The children watched the peculiar way the apron began to shake. When she took it down, they saw that she was laughing. She laughed so hard that tears ran down her cheeks.

"I reckon I'll have to let you off, Abe," she said, wiping away the tears. "You'd be a mite too big for me to handle."

Tom Lincoln jumped up. "He ain't a mite too big for me! He ain't a mite too big for a good-sized switch."

Sarah's brief anger was forgotten. "Now, Tom," she protested.

"You'll not talk me out of it!"

Abe said, "I was aiming to whitewash the ceiling, Pa. Ma said it needs a fresh coat."

Sarah looked relieved. "That's exactly what he can do—whitewash the ceiling."

"He can after I give him a licking."

Sarah put out her hand. "Sit down, Tom, and eat your potatoes. I figure it this way. Before Abe starts reading that new book Mr. Crawford loaned him, he can whitewash the ceiling. The walls, too. That ought to learn him not to cut up any more didos."

Sarah pulled down the corners of her mouth, trying to look stern. Tom sat down and started to eat his potatoes.

"You're a good one, Sarah," he chuckled. "You know how to get work out of him."

Abe looked at his stepmother gratefully. At the same time he was disappointed. He had been thinking about that book all day.

The next forenoon Sarah sent everyone out of the cabin. Abe was down by the horse trough mixing whitewash in a big tub. By the time he returned, she had a bucket of hot water and a gourdful of soft soap ready.

After he washed the walls of the cabin, Abe got busy with the whitewash. When he finished the walls, he started on the ceiling. He gazed upward at the muddy footprints.

"They make a right pretty picture. Shall I leave them on for decoration?"

Sarah, seated on a stool by the fireplace, looked up from her sewing. "Abe, you big scamp! You get that ceiling nice and white, or I'll be carrying out my threat."

Her eyes were laughing. Abe grinned, glad to be at peace with her again.

"After I finish here," Abe asked, "do you have any more chores?"

"No. I reckon there'll be time then for you to do some reading. But first you finish your whitewashing. Then there is something I want to talk to you about."

Abe dipped his brush into the whitewash again and again until he had covered up the last mark of Johnny's feet.

The cabin was bright and shining when Abe finished. He pulled another stool up to the fireplace and sat facing Sarah.

"I wasn't meaning to tell you just yet," she said. "Leastways till I had a chance to talk to your pa when his dander ain't up."

"What is it, Mamma?"

"There's a new neighbor. He's farming now, but he's fixing to keep a school next winter."

Abe jumped up and stood looking down at her. "Do you reckon that Pa——"

"Your pa is worried," Sarah interrupted. "Money worried. He may have to sell some of his land. That's why he gets his dander up so easy—like yesterday."

Abe flushed.

"I want you to be careful!" said Sarah. "Try not to get his dander up."

"I'll try not to," Abe said meekly.

"Maybe you remember what I promised you when I first came. I said I'd ask your pa to let you go to school again. Now I'm a body that believes in keeping promises. I just want to wait till he feels good."

Sarah's sewing basket spilled to the floor as tall, lanky Abe pulled her to her feet. He put his long arms around her waist and gave her a hug—a good big bear hug.

"Abe Lincoln, you're choking me," said Sarah breathlessly. "Here I was thinking how grown-up you were getting to be. Now you be acting like a young one again."

Nancy Hanks
1784-1818

by ROSEMARY CARR BENÉT

If Nancy Hanks
Came back as a ghost,
Seeking news
Of what she loved most,
She'd ask first
"Where's my son?
What's happened to Abe?
What's he done?

"Poor little Abe,
Left all alone
Except for Tom,
Who's a rolling stone;
He was only nine
The year I died.
I remember still
How hard he cried.

"Scraping along
In a little shack,
With hardly a shirt
To cover his back,
And a prairie wind
To blow him down,
Or pinching times
If he went to town.

"You wouldn't know
About my son?
Did he grow tall?
Did he have fun?
Did he learn to read?
Did he get to town?
Do you know his name?
Did he get on?"

A Reply to Nancy Hanks

by JULIUS SILBERGER

Yes, Nancy Hanks,
The news we will tell
Of your Abe
Whom you loved so well.
You asked first,
"Where's my son?"
He lives in the heart
Of everyone.

In *Children and Books,* published by Scott, Foresman and Company, Chicago, 1947.

Captain Smith of Jamestown

More than ten years before the *Mayflower* set out to cross the ocean, three English ships sailed to America. Only men and boys were on these ships. They had not come to find new homes in a new land. They were looking for riches. Many of them hoped to find gold.

On a spring day in 1607, the ships sailed up a river into what is now Virginia. The men named the river the James after the King of England. They went ashore and pitched their tents on a low point of land that was almost an island. The water along the shore was so deep that the ships were tied to trees at the river's edge.

The settlement was named Jamestown. One of the leaders of these settlers was Captain John Smith. He knew the men were not used to hard work but must learn to do it. Land had to be cleared for tents and gardens, and gardens had to be planted.

John Smith knew, also, that a settlement in a strange land should be protected. He urged that a fort be built. But the other men thought there was little danger of being attacked. They saw no need to waste their time building a fort. When space was cleared for tents and gardens, most of the men and boys started hunting for riches.

Captain Smith feared that the Jamestown settlers would not raise enough food to last through the winter. They would need to get food from the Indians. So he set out to visit Indian villages, taking cloth and tools and beads with him. He hoped to trade cloth, beads, or tools for Indian corn.

Some Indians were friendly and willing to trade. Others were afraid of these men with pale faces. The guns the men carried filled the Indians with terror.

Before long the fearful Indians attacked the settlement at Jamestown. Only then did the men stop hunting for gold long enough to build the fort that John Smith had urged them to build. And just as he had feared, the settlers' gardens were a failure.

The summer heat was terrific. Many men became ill. Captain Smith urged those who were well to build houses. But winter came, and the houses were not built. The cold was more uncomfortable than the heat had been. The men ached with cold.

John Smith spent most of his time trading for food to keep the settlers alive. On one trip he was captured by Indian warriors. They took their prisoner to the great chief of all tribes in that part of Virginia.

Many years later Captain Smith told the story. He said that Chief Powhatan was seated at one end of a large room. The warriors stood around the walls. Women stood behind the men. John Smith noticed a young girl seated near Chief Powhatan. She looked at Captain Smith with bright black eyes.

Powhatan questioned the prisoner. Then
he turned to talk with some of the Indians.

John Smith understood little that was said.
But soon a large rock was brought into the
room. Warriors made him lie down and
put his head on the rock. When he had laid
it there, the Indians raised heavy clubs.

Captain Smith thought for a brief moment
that it was his fate to be killed by a club.
But just as the clubs were about to strike,
the girl with black eyes ran forward. She
put her arms around the prisoner.

Again there was talk among the Indians. John Smith understood little of it. But soon Powhatan waved his men away. He told the prisoner to stand.

Captain Smith learned later that the girl who had protected him was Powhatan's daughter. She had begged that his life be spared. Powhatan could not refuse anything that his favorite daughter asked.

Friendship grew between the Indian girl and the English captain. She visited Jamestown often. Because she was friendly with the settlers, the Indians gave them food. It is doubtful that many of the people at Jamestown would have lived through the first hard winter without the food.

The next year more men and boys came to Jamestown. After a while women and children joined the men to make homes.

Families continued to live at Jamestown until a fire destroyed most of the houses. By that time other settlements had been built in Virginia. So Jamestown was not rebuilt. Instead, the Jamestown people went to live in other places.

If you should go to Jamestown, Virginia, today, you would see a statue of Captain John Smith, the man who played so large a part in the history of Jamestown.

You would see a fort just like the one that Captain Smith helped build. It has been rebuilt for visitors to see.

You would see some houses that have been rebuilt to look just like the ones that were burned long, long ago.

Jamestown Foundation Photo

The Girl with Three Names

She was called Matoaka when she was a baby. When she grew up, she chose the name Rebecca. But everyone remembers her by her third name, Pocahontas. In the Indian language spoken by her people, a *pocahontas* was a little girl who liked to run and jump and play. Matoaka could turn handsprings, and she could run faster than most boys. She was full of mischief and fun. Her father, Powhatan, watched Matoaka at play. He called her Pocahontas.

Pocahontas learned from her mother how to pound Indian corn into meal. She helped in the garden in summer.

She learned how to scrape deerskins and get them ready to make clothes for the family. All the hair had to be scraped from a skin. Then the scraped hide had to be softened before clothes could be made from it.

But what Pocahontas liked best was to play. She liked to swim in the river. She liked to visit other villages. She knew how to find her way in the woods, and she was never afraid.

When Pocahontas was about twelve, a frightening message came to her village. Her father was the leader of all Indians in that part of the country. A runner brought word to him that men with queer pale faces had come to live nearby. The strangers, the runner said, were friendly most of the time. But when they were angry, they used sticks that shot fire. Several Indians had been killed by the fire sticks.

Pocahontas listened to all that was said. She wished that she could see one of these strangers with the pale faces.

It was not very long until news came that a chief of the strangers had been captured. The braves who had captured him were bringing him to Powhatan.

Pocahontas looked with interest at the stranger when he stood before her father. She had never seen a person who looked like this one. His skin was pale. He had reddish hair and whiskers. His eyes were blue. He was not tall, but he looked strong. Outwardly at least, he did not seem to be afraid when Powhatan said he must die.

When the stranger was about to be killed, Pocahontas ran to him to protect him. She begged her father to spare his life.

Powhatan made a sign for the warriors to stand back. Pocahontas could have her wish. The stranger would be spared.

Pocahontas learned later that his name was John Smith. He gave her presents of beads. She told him what *pocahontas* meant and taught him words of her language.

Pocahontas and John Smith became good friends. The young Indian girl often went to Jamestown, taking presents of food.

Once when the Indians and whites were arguing, Powhatan sent Pocahontas to settle the argument. Another time she hurried through the dark woods at night to warn her friend at Jamestown that some Indians were threatening to attack.

As long as Captain Smith stayed in Jamestown, Pocahontas went there often. But one day he was badly hurt in an accident. He was sent to England immediately and did not come back to Virginia. Pocahontas stopped visiting the settlement.

A few years later another English captain found Pocahontas a prisoner in an Indian village far from her home. He took her to Jamestown. He sent word to Powhatan that she was safe but would be kept until some English prisoners were set free by the Indians.

Jamestown seemed strange to Pocahontas without her old friend. Women and girls had come to the settlement. Pocahontas learned to speak and dress as they did. She went with them to church, wearing a bonnet and gloves. When she decided to join the church, she took Rebecca as her name.

A young man named John Rolfe fell in love
with Pocahontas. He asked Governor Dale
if they could marry. Governor Dale agreed
to the marriage. So one spring day they
were married in the church at Jamestown.

Powhatan did not come to see Pocahontas
married. But he sent her uncle and two of
her brothers. Powhatan said the marriage
was a sign of peace and friendship between
the Indian people and the white people.

A son was born to Pocahontas and her
husband. They named him Thomas. When
the boy was about a year old, Governor Dale
made a visit to England. He arranged for
the Rolfe family to go with him.

John Smith was in England. He came to see Pocahontas. The graceful young woman dressed in beautiful silks looked more like a Rebecca than a little Pocahontas. But Captain Smith looked at her bright black eyes and knew she had not changed much. As they talked about Virginia, he could tell she was a happy young woman.

The English people heard about the Indian girl whose father was a chief. They called her a princess. Everyone wanted to see the Indian princess.

Pocahontas saw new places and met many new people in England. She was invited to the palace to meet the royal family.

Soon it was time for the Rolfes to go home, and they boarded their ship. Before it left the harbor, Pocahontas fell sick. She was taken ashore. A doctor was called, but he could not save her. The light-hearted girl from the forest of Virginia died in a strange land. She was about twenty-two years old.

John Rolfe went back to America. But he was afraid to take his baby son with him on the long trip to the distant land.

Thomas stayed in England with an uncle until he was a young man. Then he went to America. His grandfather Powhatan had kept peace with the settlers as long as he lived. By the time Thomas went to Virginia, many English people were living there.

Thomas Rolfe stayed in Virginia. He had children, and they had children. Even today some people living in America can say that they have a famous ancestor—Pocahontas, the little Indian girl who saved the life of a stranger.

Roads

by RACHEL FIELD

A road might lead to anywhere—
  To harbor towns and quays,
Or to a witch's pointed house
  Hidden by bristly trees.
It might lead past the tailor's door,
  Where he sews with needle and thread,
Or by Miss Pim the milliner's,
  With her hats for every head.
It might be a road to a great, dark cave
  With treasure and gold piled high,
Or a road with a mountain tied to its end,
  Blue-humped against the sky.
Oh, a road might lead you anywhere—
  To Mexico or Maine.
But then, it might just fool you, and—
  Lead you back home again!

ROADS
TO
MAKE-BELIEVE

174

Puss-in-Boots

Long ago a man died and left three sons. To one he left his house, to another his fields. To the youngest he left only his cat.

Jack, the youngest son, could think of no way to make a living with a cat. "I could kill it," he said, "and use its fur for a jacket. But it wouldn't cover much of me."

"Oh, Master! Don't kill me," said the cat to Jack. "Give me a jacket and boots like a man's, and you'll not be sorry."

Jack knew he had little to lose. So he gave the cat a jacket and boots and a hat. The cat put them on, picked up an empty sack, and set off down the road.

The cat had not gone far when he saw a house and behind it a garden of fresh salad greens. He knocked at the door. When the housewife opened it, he said, "My master, the Duke of Willowonder, wants a salad for his lunch. If you'll give me a handful of greens, he'll reward you well someday."

The woman was happy to give the cat what he asked for. The cat quickly stuffed his sack with the salad greens and set off once more down the road.

Soon the cat came to a field full of rabbit holes. He chose the largest hole and put the open sack beside it. Before very long a fat rabbit came out of the hole and poked his nose into the sack to sniff the greens. Next he poked his head in. Presently the rabbit was inside the sack eating away at the salad greens.

Then the cat grabbed the sack and set off down the road. He walked until he came to the last hill but one. There stood the King's palace.

"Hear! Hear!" called the cat. "There is a cat come to see the King!"

The King's butler stuck his head out a
window and saw a cat dressed like a man
in the courtyard. The butler was scared
out of his wits. He pulled in his head and
ran to the King.

"Your Majesty, Your Majesty!" he cried.
"There's a puss-in-boots in the courtyard!"

"Now that's a sight I've never seen,"
said the King. "And I'd like to. Take the
key, unlock the door, and let the cat in."

So the butler brought
the cat to the King, who
sat on his tallest throne
and looked at the cat.

He sat on the throne,
and he looked the cat up
and looked him down.

At last the King said, "This is indeed an amazing sight! What is that kicking in the sack on your shoulder, Puss?"

The cat said, "A fine rabbit. My master begs you to accept it for your dinner."

"Who is the master of puss-in-boots?" asked the King.

"Why, he is the Duke of Willowonder, of course," said the cat.

"Of course," said the King. "Of course. He must dine with me sometime."

The next day the cat brought two ducks to the palace. Once more he stood in the courtyard and shouted, "Hear! Hear!—— There is a cat come to see the King!"

The butler ran to the King, calling, "Your Majesty, that puss-in-boots is back again!"

"Show him in," said the King.

The butler took the cat to the King, who sat on his throne and asked, "What's that kicking in the sack on your shoulder today?"

"Two fat ducks," answered the cat. "My master begs you to accept them."

"I'd like to meet your master," said the King. "Ask him to dine with me one day."

The cat raced home and told Jack, "The King will pass by here tomorrow. Then you must do just as I say. Remember! You are no longer Jack. You are the Duke of Willowonder."

The next forenoon the cat heard the King's coach rumbling along the road and called, "Run, Jack! Run and jump in the river! But leave your clothes under a stone."

Jack did as he was told, and the cat stood by the road. When the coach came in sight, he cried, "Help! My master is drowning! The Duke of Willowonder is drowning!"

The King said to the coachman, "I've seen that puss before. Go and save his master."

Then he turned to the cat and said, "Bring your master to me when he is rescued."

"Alas, I cannot," said the cat. "He has no clothes. They drowned before he did."

"That's easy to fix," said the King, and sent his guard to the palace for clothes.

Meanwhile, Jack, who had been rescued from the river, stood shivering behind a bush. Presently the cat brought him the clothes. Jack put them on.

When Jack had put on the blue hose and
the fine blue cape and had buttoned all the
gold buttons and tied all the gold tapes, he
presented himself to the King. Jack felt as
grand as a duke and even grander.

The King invited Jack to ride in the coach
with him and his daughter. The coachman
asked the cat to ride beside him, but the
cat said he would run ahead.

The cat ran like the wind till he was out of sight of the coach. Soon he came to a fine field of barley, where two men were standing guard. The cat called to them, "The King is coming along the road. He will ask whose field this is. If you don't say it belongs to the Duke of Willowonder, I'll come back and chop you to bits."

Then the cat ran on until he came to a herd of fat cattle. Two herdsmen were watching the cattle. The cat called to the herdsmen, "Hallo there! The King will be coming along soon. He will ask whose cattle these are. If you don't say they belong to the Duke of Willowonder, I'll come back and bite you into pieces."

Now the fine barley and the fat cattle really belonged to a cruel ogre who lived over the hill. But the guards and herdsmen were used to obeying orders, so they agreed to do what the cat asked.

The cat ran on over the hill to the castle of the cruel ogre. From the courtyard he called, "Hallo there! Here is a cat come to see the master of this castle."

Immediately the ogre opened the door and growled, "Where did you get those boots?"

"They were given to me by my master, the Duke of Willowonder," said the cat.

A cat wearing boots like a man's caught the fancy of the greedy ogre. He invited the cat to walk into the castle.

The ogre turned the key in the lock, and then he led the cat into a great hall filled with beautiful things. The cat sat by the fire and wrapped his tail around himself.

"I have heard," said the cat, "that you are a most wonderful fellow. Is it true that you are able to change yourself into any animal you wish?"

"I can do that," said the ogre gruffly.

"I should have to see it to believe it," said the cat.

"Aha! Believe it, then!" roared the ogre, changing himself into a tiger.

The cat was so frightened at the sight of the fierce tiger that he leaped right through a window and onto a tree branch.

The ogre laughed until he split his tiger skin. Then he was an ogre again.

The cat came down out of the tree and said, "It can't be too hard for a big fellow like you to change himself into a tiger. If you had changed yourself into something small, like a bird or mouse, I should really have been surprised."

"Be surprised, then!" cried the ogre as he changed himself into a tiny gray mouse.

That was just what the sly cat had been waiting for. With one leap he fell on the mouse and gobbled him up.

All this while the King and Jack and the Princess were rolling along the road in the King's coach. When they came to the field of barley, the King asked the guards who owned the barley.

"The Duke of Willowonder," replied the men in one voice.

When the coach came to the herd of fat cattle, the King called to the herdsmen, "Whose cattle are those?"

The herdsmen called back, "They belong to the Duke of Willowonder."

As the coach neared the ogre's castle, the cat came bounding out of the courtyard.

"Welcome to the castle of the Duke of Willowonder," he called. "Do step down from your coach and come in."

Inside the castle a great feast from the ogre's larder was spread and waiting.

After the guests had dined, the King said to Jack, "My dear Duke, I don't know what plans you may have. But I'd be happy to have you marry my daughter."

That was exactly what Jack had hoped for since he had first seen the lass.

The Princess said she would like nothing better. So it was agreed that Jack and the Princess should marry the very next day. Then the King drove off with his daughter.

As soon as they had gone, Jack turned to the cat. "Faithful friend!" he said. "To think I considered killing you and using your fur for a jacket! When I've married the Princess, I'll make you a lord. You shall be known as His Honor the Lord High Cat."

The cat said, "No, now you must kill me. Take a silver knife and cut off my head."

"That I'll never do!" cried Jack.

The cat said, "You will be doing me the greatest favor." And he begged until Jack finally agreed to do what the cat asked.

No sooner had the knife touched the cat's neck than there was a loud clap of thunder. The cat disappeared in a cloud of smoke. In his place stood a handsome prince.

"You have freed me from a spell put on me long ago by the ogre," said the Prince. "This castle and these lands are mine. I gladly give them to you, Jack. Now I am off to my other lands across the sea that are richer by far than these."

With that, the Prince set off down the road, carrying the small boots with him.

The Three Wishes

There was once a man who was very poor. He and his wife lived in a humble cottage. Every day the man went into the forest to chop wood.

One day in the forest he said to himself, "Oh dear! I am so unhappy! I am poor, and I have to work hard all day long.

"My wife is often hungry. And I am hungry, too. We never have honey to put on our bread. We don't have meat to eat, not even a good, thick stew. Oh, I am unhappy! I am unhappy indeed!"

At that moment a beautiful fairy appeared before the man. She said to him, "I heard everything that you have been saying. I am sorry for you and would like to help you. Ask for whatever you like. Your first three wishes shall be granted."

Then the fairy disappeared just as suddenly as she had come.

The man felt grateful to the fairy and very much excited. "I'll hurry home and tell my wife about the wishes!" he cried.

The man ran to his home. "Wife! Wife!" he called. "We are very fortunate! I saw a fairy in the forest who granted me three wishes. 'Ask for whatever you like,' she said. 'Your wishes shall be granted.' Oh, Wife! How fortunate we are!"

"We are fortunate indeed," declared the woman. "And I am so happy! Let's go into the house and discuss what to wish for."

The pair went into their humble cottage.

"I'm hungry, Wife," said the man. "I'd like some dinner. We can talk about the three wishes while we eat."

The man and his wife sat at the table to eat their meal and discuss the wishes.

"We might ask for great riches," the man said. "Or we might——"

The wife interrupted. "We might ask for a fine house to live in."

"Ho, ho! That's little enough!" cried the man. "We can ask for a whole empire!"

The wife said, "We can ask for pearls and diamonds! Hundreds of diamond rings and pins and fine purple clothes to wear the pins on! Purple coats for you, dresses for me!"

"We can ask for diamonds and pearls," the man agreed. "And we can ask for a big family—five boys and five girls."

"I'd prefer six boys and four girls," said the wife.

The pair went on talking, but they could not decide what three wishes would be best.

The man ate his watery soup and looked at his piece of dry bread. "I wish I had a great big sausage for dinner," he said.

At that very instant a sausage of enormous size appeared on the table.

Naturally the man was surprised to see the giant sausage on the tiny table, and so was his wife.

"Oh, Husband!" she cried. "That was a terrible mistake! You asked for a silly old sausage. So one of the wishes has been wasted. Now there are only two wishes left. You've been very, very foolish."

"Yes," said the man meekly. "I've been foolish. I made a mistake, but we still have the two wishes. We can ask for great riches and for an empire."

"We can ask for riches and an empire, but we can't ask for ten children," grumbled the wife. "And it's all your fault. It's your fault for asking for a sausage. You chose to have a sausage. You'd rather have a big sausage than a big family."

The woman went on complaining. Over and over she sputtered, "It's your fault. It's all your fault for being so foolish."

Finally the man became impatient. He spoke to his wife in anger. "I am tired of your complaining! I wish that sausage were hanging on the end of your nose!"

The next second the man was aware that the sausage was hanging on the end of his wife's nose. Naturally the poor woman was greatly surprised, and so was her husband.

The wife began complaining more loudly than before. "Husband, you have been very, very, very foolish! First you asked for a sausage. Then you wished that the sausage were hanging on my nose. That makes two wishes. Two foolish wishes! May I remind you that we now have only one wish left!"

"But we can still ask for riches with the one wish," the man protested.

"What good are riches to me," the woman complained, "if I have a sausage hanging on my nose? Why, I look silly! And it is all your fault. I'll be obliged to throw my apron over my head or wrap a towel around my face every time I go out of the house. How can I spend a lifetime in this fashion? This is a terrible fate!"

The woman began to cry. This made the man feel uncomfortable. He said, "Oh, I wish that sausage were not here at all!"

Instantly the sausage disappeared. The man and the woman were sitting at the table in their humble cottage, as poor as ever. They both grumbled and quarreled and complained and argued, but it didn't do them the slightest bit of good, for they had used up the wishes.

The three wishes had been granted, and still the man and his wife had no riches, no empire, no pearls and diamonds, no little boys, and no little girls. They didn't even have a sausage to eat for their dinner.

Rapunzel

Once upon a time a man and his wife lived in a house with a window in back. The window looked into a garden full of the finest flowers and vegetables. A wall surrounded the garden. No one dared to enter the garden because it belonged to a witch who was feared by all the world.

One day the wife stood looking down at the vegetables. She saw a bed of the finest rampion. The leaves looked so fresh and green that she longed to eat them.

From *Favorite Fairy Tales Told in Germany* by Virginia Haviland. Text copyright © 1959 by Virginia Haviland, by permission of Little, Brown and Co.

Just because the wife knew she couldn't get the rampion, her wish for it grew day by day. She pined away and became pale and ill. This alarmed her husband. He asked her what was wrong.

"Alas!" she replied. "I know I shall die unless I get some rampion to eat from that garden. I can never be content without it."

The man, who loved his wife dearly, said to himself, "Rather than lose her, I'll get some rampion, no matter what the cost."

So at dusk he climbed cautiously over the wall and slipped into the witch's garden. Hastily he pulled some rampion and took it back to his wife. She made it into a salad. The salad tasted so good that her longing for rampion was greater than ever.

Nothing would do but that her husband should climb over the wall and fetch her some more. So at dusk, over he went.

He was ready to climb out again when he saw the wicked witch standing before him. The man drew back in terror.

"How dare you take my rampion?" said the witch. "You shall pay dearly for this!"

"I had to do it," the man said. "Neither witch nor dragon could have kept me away. My wife longed so much for your rampion that she'd certainly have died without it."

At this, the witch's anger grew less. "I am not greedy," she said. "If things are as you say, you may take all the rampion you like. But it is only proper that you should give me something in return.

"You must give me the child that will soon be born to your wife. The child will be a comfort to me. And I will look after it like a mother."

In his great fear, the man agreed.

A daughter was born to the man's wife, and then the witch appeared at once. She gave the baby the name Rapunzel, which means "rampion," and carried her away. The baby was fine and healthy and grew to be the most beautiful child in the world.

When Rapunzel was fourteen, the witch shut her in a tower in the middle of a wood. The tower had neither stairs nor doors. It had only one window, high up. It was surrounded by a thicket of thorn bushes. The thorns could scratch mightily.

Each morning the witch came and stood at the foot of the tower and cried out:

Rapunzel! Rapunzel!
Let down your golden hair.

Rapunzel immediately did as the witch bade her. She unloosed her braids and let them fall down from the window so that the witch could climb up. Soon after, the witch would leave in the same way.

It happened that a handsome prince was riding one day near the thorny thicket. He heard someone singing so sweetly that he stopped, spellbound.

It was Rapunzel. The lovely music of her voice filled the wood. The Prince longed to see the person who sang so sweetly. He crept through the thicket. But he could find no door in the tower. Disappointed, he went away, but he was so enchanted by the song that he returned each day to listen.

One morning as he stood in the thicket listening, he saw the witch come to the tower. He heard her call:

Rapunzel! Rapunzel!
Let down your golden hair.

Then the Prince saw Rapunzel let down her braids and the witch begin to climb up.

"What a remarkable ladder!" thought the Prince. "I, too, will climb it!" On the following day he waited till dusk to go to the foot of the tower. Then he cried out:

Rapunzel! Rapunzel!
Let down your golden hair.

When Rapunzel let down her braids, the Prince climbed up to the window. Rapunzel was terrified. She shivered with fright till the Prince spoke to her kindly. He told her his heart had been so touched by her songs that he knew he would have no peace of mind till he had spoken to her.

Rapunzel had lost all fear by the time the Prince asked her to marry him. "He is young and handsome," she thought. "I'd be happier with him than I am here."

So she said, "I will gladly marry you and go with you to your kingdom. But we must think of a way for me to get down from this tower."

She thought a moment, then added, "You must come every evening and bring a skein of silk, each day another skein of silk. I shall braid it into a ladder. When you've brought enough skeins, and the ladder is ready, I'll climb down. Then you shall take me away."

And so it was arranged.

The witch, of course, knew nothing of what was going on. But a day came when Rapunzel said, without thinking, "Why do you climb up so much more slowly than the Prince? It takes him only a minute."

"Oh, you wicked girl!" cried the witch. "What is this I've learnt! I thought I had you put safely away from the world! Yet you've managed to deceive me."

In her rage, the witch seized Rapunzel's beautiful hair. She wound it around her hand. Then snip—off came the braids.

The witch fastened them on a hook by the window. She took Rapunzel away from the tower to a hut in a wild and lonely spot at the very heart of the forest.

The witch then returned to the tower. She climbed up the braids and pulled them up after her.

At dusk the Prince came and called:

> *Rapunzel! Rapunzel!*
> *Let down your golden hair.*

The witch let the braids down, and the Prince climbed up.

The cruel witch looked at the Prince with angry eyes. "Aha, my grand fellow!" she cried. "You came to fetch your ladylove, but the pretty bird is no longer singing in her nest. A cat has snatched her away. And the cat is waiting to scratch out your eyes. Rapunzel is lost to you forever!"

The Prince was filled with sadness. In his despair, he jumped from the window and fell into the thicket that surrounded the tower. He was not killed but was blinded by the thorns. Thereafter he wandered sadly in the wood and wept for his precious Rapunzel.

At last one day the Prince wandered near the hut where Rapunzel was. He heard a song and knew it was hers. He walked toward the lovely sound. When Rapunzel saw the Prince, she fell sobbing into his arms for comfort. As she wept, two of her tears touched his poor blind eyes, and he was no longer blind.

The Prince took the beautiful Rapunzel to his kingdom. They were welcomed with great joy in the kingdom, and there they lived happily ever after.

The Dog in the Manger

A Dog jumped into the manger of an Ox to take an afternoon nap. It lay sleeping on the straw when the Ox returned from its work. The Ox came up to the manger and wanted to eat some of the straw.

The Dog was in a rage at being wakened from its nap. It stood up and barked at the Ox. Whenever the Ox came near, the Dog tried to bite it.

At last the Ox gave up hope of getting the straw. It went away muttering:

People often don't want others to have what they themselves cannot enjoy.

The Ant and the Grasshopper

In a field one pleasant summer's day, a Grasshopper was singing to its heart's content. An Ant passed by, carrying a grain of corn.

"Instead of working, why not stop and chat with me?" asked the Grasshopper.

The Ant said, "I am laying up food for the winter. I suggest you do the same."

"Why bother about winter?" asked the Grasshopper. "There is plenty of food at present." But the Ant continued to work.

When winter came, the Grasshopper no longer sang. It had nothing to eat and was about to die. The hungry Grasshopper watched the ants eating grain from the stores they had gathered in the summer. Then the Grasshopper knew:

It is best to prepare in good times for
bad times ahead.

The Dove and the Ant

An Ant was very thirsty and went to drink from a stream. The water snatched up the Ant and carried her down the stream. A Dove saw the Ant drifting helplessly along and took pity on her. The Dove broke a branch from a tree and dropped it into the water. The Ant used the branch to save herself.

Not long after, a Fowler wanted to catch the Dove. He placed his nets without letting the Dove see him. The Ant saw the Dove about to be caught in the nets. The Ant bit the Fowler on the foot. He gave so sudden a start that the Dove took alarm and flew away.

One good turn
deserves another.

The Boy and the Wolf

adapted from THE GREEK OF AESOP
by LOUIS UNTERMEYER

A boy employed to guard the sheep
Despised his work. He liked to sleep.
And when a lamb was lost, he'd shout,
"Wolf! Wolf! The wolves are all about!"

The neighbors searched from noon till nine,
But of the beast there was no sign.
Yet "Wolf!" he cried next morning when
The villagers came out again.

205

One evening around six o'clock
A real wolf fell upon the flock.
"Wolf!" yelled the boy. "A wolf indeed!"
But no one paid him any heed.

Although he screamed to wake the dead,
"He's fooled us every time," they said,
And let the hungry wolf enjoy
His feast of mutton, lamb—and boy.

The Moral's this: *The man who's wise*
Does not defend himself with lies.
Liars are not believed, forsooth,
Even when liars tell the truth.

The Plate of Pancakes

Once upon a time a woman was frying some pancakes. As she turned a cake in the pan, she said to her little boy, "If you were a bit older, I would send you to the sawmill with some of these cakes for your father's dinner. But as it is, he must wait till supper for them."

"Oh, do let me take them," said the boy, whose name was Karl. "Do let me go." And he begged and begged, till at last his mother selected the brownest and crispest pancakes. She put them on a plate with a napkin over them and bade her son take them to the mill.

It was a lovely day with not a cloud in the sky. Karl set out just after eleven o'clock. The path that led to the mill where Karl's father worked was straight enough, and plain enough, but it ran through the wood that was called Enchanted. Fairies lived there, so some people thought, and goblins that liked to do mischief. Never before had Karl been allowed to go there alone.

As he hurried along with the pancakes, he glanced into every leafy thicket. He was half fearful and half hopeful that he'd see a fairy or a goblin hidden among the leaves. But not one fairy or goblin did he see.

When Karl came to some bushes where sweet berries were growing, a remarkable thing happened. A voice seemed to whisper to him, "Stop! Stop! Stop and eat."

Karl was far from terrified by the sound. But he was astonished. He said aloud, "I am taking pancakes for my father's dinner."

"A minute or two will make no difference. You can run fast," came the whisper again.

"Yes, I can," said Karl. And he put the plate down and began to pick berries.

The berries were as ripe and sweet as
they looked. Every one that the boy put
into his mouth made him wish for another.
Each time he turned from the bushes, he
heard a whisper, "One more and then go."

The pancakes grew cold on the plate, and
the sun slipped farther and farther into the
west. Still Karl lingered, till suddenly he
noticed that night was approaching.

"Why, it is time for my father to come
home!" he cried. "Dear me! Dear me!
What shall I do?"

There was nothing for Karl to do but go home. So home he went with the plate of cold pancakes in his hand and tears rolling down his cheeks. When he told his mother and grandmother what had happened, they looked at each other knowingly as if they thought something they would not say.

They bade him wipe away his tears. His mother said, "You will be more careful another time." And so the matter ended.

But Karl did not forget it. It was many a month before his mother fried pancakes again. But no sooner did he see her doing so than he said, "I wish my father had some cakes for dinner, don't you, Mother?"

She said, "Indeed I do. He deserves a hot meal. I'll trust you to take it to him."

When the cakes were done, she selected the brownest and crispest and put them on a plate with a napkin over them.

"I'll get to the mill in time for Father's dinner today," said Karl as he started out.

But in a short while he was back with an empty plate in his hand and tears rolling down his cheeks.

"I put the plate down for a minute," Karl sobbed. "I was curious about a rabbit that said, 'Catch me, and you may have me.' I chased after the rabbit but didn't catch it. When I went back to get the pancakes, none of the cakes were left."

"It's just as I thought the first time," said his mother. "Without the slightest doubt, the goblins are at work in the wood. Karl must never go there again."

Karl's grandmother disagreed. "The boy deserves another chance," she said. "And I know the proper thing to do."

The next day she fried pancakes. She selected the brownest and crispest and put them on a plate with a napkin over them. She bade Karl take them to his father.

Karl's grandmother said, "Here is a bit of advice. If any bid you stop or stay or turn your feet from out your way, say the word that is spelled with the fourteenth and fifteenth letters of the alphabet. Say it three times in a loud voice, and all will be well with you."

Karl nodded proudly, for he had learnt all his letters and could spell hard words like *c-a-t, cat*. But he was in a hurry to be off and did not stop to count the letters.

There was no whispering voice that day and no talking rabbit to tempt Karl to a chase. But when his path crossed another, a bird called from the heart of the wood, "Quick, quick! Come here, here, here——"

"Where, where?" cried Karl. He was about to go looking for the bird when he remembered his grandmother's advice: "If any bid you stop or stay or turn your feet from out your way, say the word that is spelled with the fourteenth and fifteenth letters of the alphabet."

"*A, B, C, D, E, F, G,*" he chanted, counting the letters. "*H, I, J, K, L, M, N, O.*"

N was the fourteenth letter. *O* was the fifteenth. *N-O*. That was easy.

"No! No! NO!" shouted Karl in a very loud voice.

And then things did go very well for Karl. In less time than it takes to tell it, he was at the mill door with the plate of pancakes. Every pancake was safe and hot.

Although Karl came and went through the Enchanted Wood all the days of his life, he was never again hindered by anything. And he never did see a goblin though he lived to be as old as his grandmother.

RIDICULOUS PEOPLE

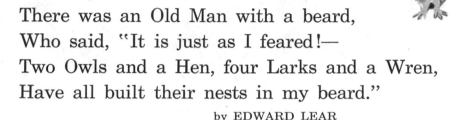

There was an Old Man with a beard,
Who said, "It is just as I feared!—
Two Owls and a Hen, four Larks and a Wren,
Have all built their nests in my beard."

by EDWARD LEAR

A tutor who tooted a flute
Tried to teach two young tutors to toot.
  Said the two to the tutor,
  "Is it harder to toot, or
To tutor two tutors to toot?"

by CAROLYN WELLS

There was a Young Lady whose chin
Resembled the point of a pin;
So she had it made sharp, and purchased a harp,
And played several tunes with her chin.

by EDWARD LEAR

Mrs. Snipkin and Mrs. Wobblechin

by LAURA E. RICHARDS

Skinny Mrs. Snipkin,
With her little pipkin,
Sat by the fireside a-warming of her toes.
Fat Mrs. Wobblechin,
With her little doublechin,
Sat by the window a-cooling of her nose.

215

From *Tirra Lirra* by Laura E. Richards, published by Little, Brown & Company.

Says this one to that one,
"Oh! you silly fat one,
Will you shut the window down? You're
    freezing me to death!"
Says that one to t'other one,
"Good gracious, how you bother one!
There isn't air enough for me to draw my
    precious breath!"

Skinny Mrs. Snipkin,
Took her little pipkin,
Threw it straight across the room as hard
    as she could throw;
Hit Mrs. Wobblechin
On her little doublechin,
And out of the window a-tumble she did go.

Pippi Is a Thing-Finder

Way out at the end of
a tiny little town was an
old overgrown garden,
and in the garden was
an old house, and in the
house lived Pippi Longstocking. She was
nine years old, and she lived there all alone.
She had no mother and no father, and that
was, of course, very nice, because there was
no one to tell her to go to bed just when she
was having the most fun.

Once upon a time Pippi had had a father.
Naturally she had had a mother, too, but
that was so long ago Pippi didn't remember her at all. Her mother had died when
Pippi was just a tiny baby and lay in a
cradle and howled all the time.

Her father Pippi had not forgotten. He
was a sea captain who sailed on the great
ocean, and Pippi had sailed with him until
one day her father blew overboard in a storm
and disappeared. But Pippi was absolutely
certain he would come back sometime.

Adapted from *Pippi Longstocking* by Astrid Lindgren. Translated by Florence Lamborn.
Copyright 1950 by The Viking Press, Inc., and reprinted by their permission, and the
permission of Oxford University Press.

Many years ago Pippi's father had bought the old house to live in someday. So while Pippi was waiting for him to come back, she went straight to Villa Villekulla. That was the name of the house.

Beside Villa Villekulla was another garden and another house. In that house lived a father and mother and two children, a boy and a girl. The boy's name was Tommy and the girl's Annika. They had often wished for a playmate. Before Pippi came, they often used to hang over the fence and say, "Isn't it silly that nobody ever moves into that house? Somebody ought to live there— somebody with children."

On the summer day when Pippi moved into Villa Villekulla, Tommy and Annika were not at home. They had gone to visit their grandmother for a week. On the first day after they came home again, they stood by the gate, looking out onto the street, and even then they didn't know that there was a playmate so near. As they were standing there, considering what to do and wondering whether it was going to be one of those dull days when they couldn't think of anything to play—just then the gate of Villa Villekulla opened, and a little girl stepped out.

She was the most remarkable looking girl Tommy and Annika had ever seen. She wore an unusual dress, blue with red on it. On her long, thin legs she wore a pair of long stockings, one brown and the other black. She had on a pair of black shoes that were exactly twice as long as her feet.

The thing that made Tommy and Annika open their eyes widest of all was the monkey sitting on the strange girl's shoulders. It was a little monkey, dressed in blue pants, yellow jacket, and a white straw hat.

Pippi walked along the street with one foot on the sidewalk and the other in the gutter. Tommy and Annika watched as long as they could see her. In a little while she came back, and now she was walking backward.

When she reached Tommy and Annika's gate, she stopped. The children looked at each other in silence. At last Tommy spoke. "Why did you walk backward?"

"Why did I walk backward?" said Pippi. "Isn't this a free country? Can't a person walk any way he wants to?"

And that's how Tommy and Annika met Pippi Longstocking.

The very next day Pippi said to her new friends, "I don't know what you're going to do today, but I can't be lazy. I am a Thing-finder, and I haven't a minute to spare."

"What's a Thing-finder?" asked Tommy.

"Somebody who hunts for things, naturally," said Pippi. "What else could it be? The whole world is full of things, and somebody has to look for them. And that's just what a Thing-finder does."

"What kind of things?" asked Annika.

"Oh, all kinds," said Pippi. "Lumps of gold, dead rats, candy snapcrackers, little tiny screws, and things like that."

Tommy and Annika wanted very much to be Thing-finders, too, although Tommy did say he hoped he'd find a lump of gold and not a little tiny screw.

All three Thing-finders set out. They decided it would be best to hunt around the houses in the neighborhood, because Pippi said that although it could perfectly well happen that one might find a little screw deep in the woods, still the very best things were usually found where people lived.

Tommy and Annika watched Pippi to see just how a Thing-finder acted. Pippi ran from one side of the road to the other side, shaded her eyes with her hand, and hunted and hunted. Sometimes she crawled about on her hands and knees, stuck her hands in between the pickets of a fence, and then said in a disappointed tone, "Oh dear! I was sure I saw a lump of gold."

"May we take everything we find?" asked Annika.

"Yes," said Pippi, "everything that is lying on the ground."

Presently they came to an old man lying asleep on the lawn outside his cottage.

"There!" said Pippi. "That man is lying on the ground, and we have found him. We will take him!"

Tommy and Annika were utterly terrified. "No, Pippi, we can't take an old gentleman. We couldn't possibly," said Tommy. "Anyway, whatever would we do with him?"

"What would we do with him? Oh, there are plenty of things we could do with him. We could keep him in a little rabbit hutch instead of a rabbit. But if you don't want to, I don't care. Though it does bother me to think that some other Thing-finder may come along and grab him."

They walked on. Suddenly Pippi gave a terrific yell. "Well, I never saw the like!" she cried, and picked up a rusty old tin can. "What a find! Cans—that's something you can never have too many of."

Tommy looked at the rusty can doubtfully. "What can you use it for?"

"Oh, you can use it in all sorts of ways," said Pippi. "One way is to put cookies in it. Then it becomes a delightful Jar with Cookies. Another way is not to put cookies in it. And then it becomes a Jar without Cookies. That certainly isn't so delightful, but still that's good, too."

She examined the can, which was indeed rusty and had a hole in the bottom. "It looks almost as if this were a Jar without Cookies," she said thoughtfully. "But you can put it over your head and pretend that it is midnight."

And that is just what she did. With the can on her head she wandered around the block like a little metal tower. She didn't stop till she stumbled over a low wire fence and fell flat on her stomach. There was a big crash when the tin can hit the ground.

"Now, see that!" said Pippi, and took off the can. "If I hadn't had this thing on me, I would have fallen flat on my face and hurt myself terribly."

Annika said, "Yes, but if you hadn't had the can on your head, you wouldn't have tripped on the fence in the first place."

Before she finished speaking, there was another cry from Pippi, who was holding up an empty spool. "This seems to be my lucky day! Such a sweet little spool to blow soap bubbles with or to hang around my neck for a necklace!"

Just at that moment the gate of a cottage nearby opened, and a boy came rushing out. He looked scared, but that was no wonder, because head over heels after him came five other boys.

They soon caught him, and all five began to punch and hit him. He cried and held his arms in front of his face to protect himself.

"Give it to him! Give it to him!" cried the oldest and strongest of the boys.

"Oh!" said Annika. "It's Willie they're hurting. Oh, how can they be so mean?"

"It's that awful Bengt. He's always in a fight," said Tommy. "And five against one —what cowards!"

Pippi went up to Bengt, the largest of the boys, and spoke. "Hello there!" she said. "What's the idea? Are you trying to make hash out of little Willie with all five of you jumping on him at once?"

Bengt turned and saw a little girl that he had never seen before, a wild-looking little stranger. For a while he stared at her in astonishment. Then a grin spread over his face. "Boys," he said, "let Willie alone and take a look at this girl!"

The boys all gathered around Pippi, all except Willie. He wiped away his tears and walked cautiously over to stand beside Tommy.

"Have you ever seen hair like hers? Red as fire! And such shoes," Bengt continued. "Can't I borrow one! I'd like to go rowing. And I haven't any boat." He took hold of one of Pippi's braids but dropped it instantly and cried, "I burned myself!"

Then all five boys joined hands around Pippi, jumping up and down and screaming, "Redhead! Redhead!"

Pippi stood in the middle of the ring and smiled in the friendliest way. Bengt had hoped she would get mad and begin to cry. At least she ought to have looked scared. When nothing happened, he pushed her.

"I don't think you have a very nice way with ladies," said Pippi. And she lifted him in her strong arms, which were very strong indeed, and carried him to a birch tree and hung him over a branch. Then she took the next fighter and hung him over another branch. The next one she set on a gatepost outside a cottage, and the next she threw right over a fence so that he landed in a flower bed. The last of the fighters she put in a toy cart that stood by the road.

Then Pippi, Tommy, Annika, and Willie stood and stared at the five boys for a long while. The boys were absolutely speechless with fright.

Pippi said, "You are cowards. Five of you attack one boy. That's cowardly. Then you begin to push a helpless little girl around. Oh, how mean!"

Pippi said to Tommy and Annika, "Come now, we'll go home." And to Willie, "If they try to hurt you again, you come and tell me." And to Bengt, who sat up in the tree, she said, "Is there anything else you have to say about my hair or my shoes? If so, you'd better say it before I go."

But Bengt had nothing more to say. So Pippi took her tin can in one hand and her spool in the other and went away, followed by Tommy and Annika.

When they were back in Pippi's garden, Pippi said, "Dear me, how awful! Here I found two beautiful things, and you didn't get a thing. Tommy, why don't you look in that hollow tree? Hollow trees are about the best places of all for Thing-finders."

Tommy was absolutely sure that he and Annika would never find anything, but just to please Pippi he put his hand slowly down into the hollow tree trunk.

"Goodness!" he cried, utterly amazed, and pulled out his hand. In it he held a little notebook with a leather cover. In a special loop there was a little silver pencil.

"Now, see that!" said Pippi. "There's nothing so nice as being a Thing-finder!"

And then she said to Annika, "Why don't you feel in that old tree stump? One nearly always finds things in old tree stumps."

Annika stuck her hand down in the stump and almost immediately got hold of a coral necklace, a red coral necklace. She and Tommy were so astonished they stood open-mouthed for a long time.

Pippi had been up half the night before, playing ball, and now she suddenly felt very sleepy. "I think I'll have to go and take a nap," she said. "Can't you come with me and tuck me in?"

When Pippi was sitting on the edge of the bed, taking off her shoes, Tommy asked, "Why do you wear such big shoes, Pippi?"

"So I can wiggle my toes, of course," was the answer Pippi gave to Tommy's question.

Then she crept into bed. She always slept with her feet on the pillow and her head way down under the quilt. "It's the only way to sleep," she said. "I can wiggle my toes when I'm sleeping, too."

As Tommy and Annika tiptoed quietly and cautiously away from the bed, they could see nothing of Pippi except her feet resting on the pillow.   There she lay, wiggling her toes.

Tommy and Annika ran home.   Annika held her coral necklace tightly in her hand. "That certainly was queer," she said.   "You don't suppose—do you suppose Pippi had put these things in place beforehand?"

"You never can tell," said Tommy.   "You just never can tell about anything when it comes to Pippi Longstocking."

RIDICULOUS ANIMALS

When a goose meets a moose
At the house of a mouse
I wonder if all three
Sit down and drink tea.

by ZHENYA GAY

Way down South where bananas grow,
A grasshopper stepped on an elephant's toe.
The elephant said, with tears in his eyes,
"Pick on somebody your own size."

ANONYMOUS

A fly and a flea flew up in a flue
Said the fly to the flea, "What shall we do?"
"Let's fly," said the flea.
"Let's flee," said the fly.
So they fluttered and flew up a flaw in the flue.

ANONYMOUS

The first poem from *Jingle Jangle* by Zhenya Gay. Copyright 1953 by Zhenya Gay. Reprinted by permission of The Viking Press, Inc.
The second and third poems from *A Rocket in My Pocket* compiled by Carl Withers. Copyright 1948 by Carl Withers. Reprinted by permission of Holt, Rinehart and Winston, Inc. and Carl Withers.

The Ostrich Is a Silly Bird

by MARY E. WILKINS FREEMAN

The ostrich is a silly bird,
  With scarcely any mind.
He often runs so very fast,
  He leaves himself behind.

And when he gets there, has to stand
  And hang about till night,
Without a blessed thing to do
  Until he comes in sight.

This poem first appeared in *Harper's Magazine* in August, 1905.

A Centipede Was Happy Quite

A centipede was happy quite,
Until a frog in fun
Said, "Pray, which leg comes after which?"
This raised her mind to such a pitch,
She lay distracted in the ditch
Considering how to run.

ANONYMOUS

Only My Opinion

by MONICA SHANNON

Is a caterpillar ticklish?
  Well, it's always my belief
That he giggles, as he wiggles
  Across a hairy leaf.

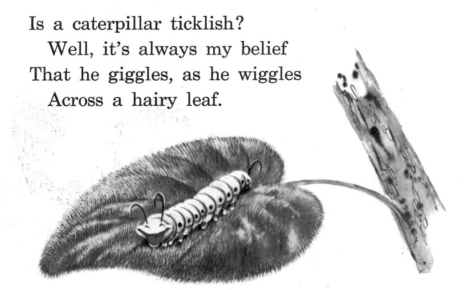

The Panther
by OGDEN NASH

The panther is like a leopard,
Except it hasn't been peppered.
Should you behold a panther crouch,
Prepare to say Ouch.
Better yet, if called by a panther,
Don't anther.

Glowworm
by DAVID McCORD

Never talk down to a glowworm—
Such as *What do you knowworm?*
How's it down belowworm?
Guess you're quite a slowworm.
No. Just say

Helloworm!

235

The Duel

by EUGENE FIELD

The gingham dog and the calico cat
Side by side on the table sat;
'T was half-past twelve, and (what do you think!)
Nor one nor t' other had slept a wink!
  The old Dutch clock and the Chinese plate
  Appeared to know as sure as fate
There was going to be a terrible spat.
    (I was n't there; I simply state
    What was told to me by the Chinese plate!)

The gingham dog went, "bow-wow-wow!"
And the calico cat replied, "mee-ow!"
The air was littered, an hour or so,
With bits of gingham and calico,
  While the old Dutch clock in the chimney-place
  Up with its hands before its face,
For it always dreaded a family row!
    (Now mind: I'm only telling you
    What the old Dutch clock declares is true!)

The Chinese plate looked very blue,
And wailed, "Oh, dear! what shall we do!"
But the gingham dog and the calico cat
Wallowed this way and tumbled that,
  Employing every tooth and claw
  In the awfullest way you ever saw—
And, oh! how the gingham and calico flew!
  (*Don't fancy I exaggerate—*
  I got my news from the Chinese plate!)

Next morning, where the two had sat
They found no trace of dog or cat;
And some folks think unto this day
That burglars stole that pair away!
  But the truth about the cat and pup
  Is this: they ate each other up!
Now what do you really think of that!
  (*The old Dutch clock it told me so,*
  And that is how I came to know.)

Pooh Goes Visiting

Edward Bear, known to his friends as Winnie-the-Pooh, or Pooh for short, was walking through the forest one day, humming proudly to himself. He had made up a little hum that very morning, as he was doing his Stoutness Exercises in front of the glass.

Tra-la-la, tra-la-la, as he stretched up as high as he could go, and then *Tra-la-la, tra-la —oh, help!—la,* as he tried to reach his toes.

After breakfast he had said it over and over to himself until he had learnt it off by heart, and now he was humming it right through, properly. It went like this:

> *Tra-la-la, tra-la-la,*
> *Tra-la-la, tra-la-la,*
> *Rum-tum-tiddle-um-tum.*
> *Tiddle-iddle, tiddle-iddle,*
> *Tiddle-iddle, tiddle-iddle,*
> *Rum-tum-tum-tiddle-um.*

Well, he was humming this hum to himself, and walking along gaily, wondering what everybody else was doing, and what it felt like being somebody else, when suddenly he came to a sandy bank, and in the bank was a large hole.

"Aha!" said Pooh. *Rum-tum-tiddle-um-tum.* "If I know anything about anything, that hole means Rabbit," he said, "and Rabbit means Company," he said, "and Company means Food and Listening-to-Me-Humming and such like. *Rum-tum-tum-tiddle-um.*"

So he bent down, put his head into the hole, and called out, "Is anybody at home?"

There was a sudden scuffling noise from inside the hole, and then silence.

"What I said was, 'Is anybody at home?'" called out Pooh very loudly.

"No!" said a voice, and then added, "You needn't shout so loud. I heard you quite well the first time."

"Bother!" said Pooh. "Isn't there anybody here at all?"

"Nobody."

Winnie-the-Pooh took his head out of the hole and thought for a little, and he thought to himself, "There must be somebody there, because somebody must have *said* 'Nobody.'" So he put his head back in the hole and said, "Hallo, Rabbit, isn't that you?"

"No," said Rabbit, in a different sort of voice this time.

"But isn't that Rabbit's voice?"

"I don't *think* so," said Rabbit. "It isn't *meant* to be."

"Oh!" said Pooh.

He took his head out of the hole and had another think, and then he put it back and said, "Well, could you very kindly tell me where Rabbit is?"

"He has gone to see his friend Pooh Bear, who is a great friend of his."

"But this *is* Me!" said Bear, very much surprised.

"What sort of Me?"

"Pooh Bear."

"Are you sure?" said Rabbit, still more surprised.

"Quite, quite sure," said Pooh.

"Oh, well, then, come in."

So Pooh pushed and pushed and pushed his way through the hole, and at last he got in.

"You were quite right," said Rabbit, looking at him all over. "It *is* you. Glad to see you."

"Who did you think it was?"

"Well, I wasn't sure. You know how it is in the Forest. One can't have *anybody* coming into one's house. One has to be *careful*. What about a mouthful of something?"

Pooh always liked a little something at eleven o'clock in the morning, and he was very glad to see Rabbit getting out the plates and mugs; and when Rabbit said, "Honey or condensed milk with your bread?" he was so excited that he said, "Both," and then, so as not to seem greedy, he added, "But don't bother about the bread, please." And for a long time after that he said nothing . . . until at last, humming to himself in a rather sticky voice, he got up, shook Rabbit lovingly by the paw, and said that he must be going on.

"Must you?" said Rabbit politely.

"Well," said Pooh, "I could stay a little longer if it—if you——" and he tried very hard to look in the direction of the larder.

"As a matter of fact," said Rabbit, "I was going out myself directly."

"Oh, well, then, I'll be going on. Good-bye."

"Well, good-bye, if you're sure you won't have any more."

"*Is* there any more?" asked Pooh quickly.

Rabbit took the covers off the dishes and said, "No, there wasn't."

"I thought not," said Pooh, nodding to himself. "Well, good-bye. I must be going on."

So he started to climb out of the hole. He pulled with his front paws and pushed with his back paws, and in a little while his nose was out in the open again . . . and then his ears . . . and then his front paws . . . and then his shoulders . . . and then——

"Oh, help!" said Pooh. "I'd better go back."

"Oh, bother!" said Pooh. "I shall have to go on."

"I can't do either!" said Pooh. "Oh, help *and* bother!"

Now by this time Rabbit wanted to go for a walk, too, and finding the front door full, he went out by the back door and came round to Pooh and looked at him.

"Hallo, are you stuck?" he asked.

"N-n-no," said Pooh carelessly. "Just resting and thinking and humming to myself."

"Here, give us a paw."

Pooh Bear stretched out a paw, and Rabbit pulled and pulled and pulled. . . .

"*Ow!*" cried Pooh. "You're hurting!"

"The fact is," said Rabbit. "You are stuck."

"It all comes," said Pooh crossly, "of not having front doors big enough."

"It all comes," said Rabbit sternly, "of eating too much. I thought at the time," said Rabbit, "only I didn't like to say anything," said Rabbit, "that one of us was eating too much," said Rabbit, "and I knew it wasn't *me*," he said. "Well, well, I shall go and fetch Christopher Robin."

Christopher Robin lived at the other end of the Forest, and when he came back with Rabbit and saw the front half of Pooh, he said, "Silly old Bear," in such a loving voice that everybody felt quite hopeful again.

"I was just beginning to think," said Bear, sniffing slightly, "that Rabbit might never be able to use his front door again. And I should *hate* that," he said.

"So should I," said Rabbit.

"Use his front door again!" said Christopher Robin. "Of course he'll use his front door again."

"Good," said Rabbit.

"If we can't pull you out, Pooh, we might push you back."

Rabbit scratched his whiskers thoughtfully and pointed out that, when Pooh was pushed back, he was back, and of course nobody was more glad to see Pooh than *he* was, still there it was, some lived in trees and some lived underground, and——

"You mean I'd *never* get out?" said Pooh.

"I mean," said Rabbit, "that having got *so* far, it seems a pity to waste it."

Christopher Robin nodded. "Then there's only one thing to be done," he said. "We shall have to wait for you to get thin again."

"How long does getting thin take?" asked Pooh anxiously.

"About a week, I should think."

"But I can't stay here for a *week!*"

"You can *stay* here all right, silly old Bear. It's getting you out which is so difficult."

"We'll read to you," said Rabbit cheerfully. "And I hope it won't snow," he added. "And I say, old fellow, you're taking up a good deal of room in my house —*do* you mind if I use your back legs as a towel-horse? Because, I mean, there they are—doing nothing—and it would be very convenient just to hang the towels on them."

"A week!" said Pooh gloomily. "*What about meals?*"

"I'm afraid no meals," said Christopher Robin, "because of getting thin quicker. But we *will* read to you."

Bear began to sigh, and then found he couldn't because he was so tightly stuck; and a tear rolled down his eye as he said, "Then would you read a Sustaining Book, such as would help and comfort a Wedged Bear in Great Tightness?"

So for a week Christopher Robin read that sort of book at the North end of Pooh, and Rabbit hung his washing on the South end . . . and in between Bear felt himself getting slenderer and slenderer.

And at the end of the week, Christopher Robin said, "*Now!*" So he took hold of Pooh's front paws, and Rabbit took hold of Christopher Robin, and all Rabbit's friends and relations took hold of Rabbit, and they all pulled together. . . .

And for a long time Pooh only said "*Ow!*" . . . And "*Oh!*"

And then, all of a sudden, he said "*Pop!*" just as if a cork were coming out of a bottle.

And Christopher Robin and Rabbit and all Rabbit's friends and relations went head-over-heels backwards . . . and on the top of them came Winnie-the-Pooh—free!

So, with a nod of thanks to his friends, he went on with his walk through the forest, humming proudly to himself. But Christopher Robin looked after him lovingly, and said to himself, "Silly old Bear!"

Us Two

by A. A. MILNE

Wherever I am, there's always Pooh,
There's always Pooh and Me.
Whatever I do, he wants to do,
"Where are you going to-day?" says Pooh:
"Well, that's very odd 'cos I was too.
Let's go together," says Pooh, says he.
"Let's go together," says Pooh.

"What's twice eleven?" I said to Pooh.
("Twice what?" said Pooh to Me.)
"I *think* it ought to be twenty-two."
"Just what I think myself," said Pooh.
"It wasn't an easy sum to do,
But that's what it is," said Pooh, said he.
"That's what it is," said Pooh.

"Let's look for dragons," I said to Pooh.
"Yes, let's," said Pooh to Me.
We crossed the river and found a few—
"Yes, those are dragons all right," said Pooh.
"As soon as I saw their beaks I knew.
That's what they are," said Pooh, said he.
"That's what they are," said Pooh.

"Let's frighten the dragons," I said to Pooh.
"That's right," said Pooh to Me.
"*I'm* not afraid," I said to Pooh,
And I held his paw and I shouted "Shoo!
Silly old dragons!"—and off they flew.
"I wasn't afraid," said Pooh, said he,
"I'm *never* afraid with you."

So wherever I am, there's always Pooh,
There's always Pooh and Me.
"What would I do?" I said to Pooh,
"If it wasn't for you," and Pooh said: "True,
It isn't much fun for One, but Two
Can stick together," says Pooh, says he.
"That's how it is," says Pooh.

Joji and the Fog

There was no scarecrow in all Japan more famous than Joji—even though he didn't scare anyone, and his best friends were crows.

The crows loved Joji so much that they ate worms instead of rice and helped him guard the paddy. Sometimes there were so many crows in the field protecting the rice plants it was hard to tell if crows or rice were growing there.

253

Each week when the farmer went to market, he boasted to his friends, "Nothing can happen to my rice paddy as long as Joji and the crows are on duty."

But one day while the farmer was gone, a fearsome fog floated over the farmyard, breathing his foggy breath on Joji and the crows and all the young rice plants. From his long foggy nose to his long foggy toes, he was the most frightful fog that Joji had ever met.

"I have just blown in from the sea," the fog called down to Joji. "I thought I would visit the countryside, but I'm becoming dried out. Can I get some wet water in your farmhouse?"

"The farmer is at market now," said Joji, shivering from the fog's damp breath. "And since it is my duty as a scarecrow to guard his house and fields, I cannot let you in."

"Then I will let myself in," fumed the fog. And he whirled open the farmhouse door and swirled inside.

He swallowed all the tea he found steaming on the stove, but he still felt thirsty and dry.

Then he saw the farmer's bath boiling and bubbling. "Just what I need!" cried the fog, and not even taking off his kimono, he plunged into it.

"Stop, you can't do that," called the crows, who were watching from a window.

"F-a-aah," thundered the fog, his face clouding up. "Neither crow nor scarecrow can get me out of this tub!"

The fog swished and swashed in the bath until his foggy breath became so strong it oozed right through the farmhouse and spread for miles around.

Joji and the crows could hardly see each other. Two crows who were coming home from a spin into town collided in mid-air and almost crashed to the ground.

The farmer could not see anyone at the market place. Buses could not see to move on the road. Ships could not see to sail up the river. And the sun could not see its way down to shine on the rice plants.

Joji sent one of the crows to market to guide the farmer home. But when the farmer slid the door open and saw what was inside, he shook with fear and cried, "Help, there's a fog in my bath!"

And he dove into the closet under all the blankets.

"Oh, if only I had a scarefog instead of a useless old scarecrow," wept the poor farmer. But even his tears turned to fog.

The fearsome fog was having such a fine time that he stayed and stayed and stayed in the bath.

The farmer stayed in the closet.

And the village nearby stayed in damp and darkness.

But worst of all, the sun stayed away from the rice paddies, and the young rice plants became chilled to the roots and began to droop.

Joji knew he had to do something to save the rice plants. "Even though I am just a scarecrow and not a scarefog, I must scare the fog out of the tub," he said to the crows.

"But how!" cawed the crows, for they knew Joji was much too gentle to scare anyone.

"I haven't the foggiest idea," sighed Joji. "Not the foggiest. But maybe if I go and tell him all the trouble he is causing, he will agree to go back to sea."

The crows were willing to try anything. Two of them with the best eyesight flew Joji through the foggy farmyard and made a smooth landing right in front of the farmhouse door.

They found the fog in his hot bath. He was so foggy that all they could see was his long nose. "Come in," said the fog, "and have a bath with me."

"I am sorry," replied Joji, "but water is not good for my straw."

"It is good for me," said the fog. "It keeps me all steamed up. I feel so healthy here I may stay forever."

Joji cried, "I came to ask you to leave tonight! You're keeping the sun from shining on the rice, the traffic from moving in the village, the people from working in the fields, and my farmer from taking a bath."

"F-a-a-aah to all that," growled the fog. "What do people ever do for me except toot loud foghorns in my ears or shine bright fog lights in my eyes! Why should I care if their rice plants die as long as I am happy here in this tub!"

"But wouldn't you be much happier back at sea?" asked Joji.

"Not any more," said the fog. "I have decided it's too large for me. I'd rather be a big fog in this small tub than a small fog in the big sea. And so, Mr. Scarecrow, you'd better start scaring crows, for you will not scare me out of this bath. But if you ever get tired of being a scarecrow and want a new job, I'd be glad to give you one rubbing my foggy back."

And then the fog let off so much steam laughing that the crows could hardly see to fly Joji home.

"I am a failure," Joji sobbed, "both as a scarecrow and a scarefog. Because of me, the rice plants will die. The farmer must spend his life in the closet, and we must spend ours in a fog."

Later that same night the crows flew off and held a meeting to decide what they could do to help Joji become a scarefog. A few hours later they told Joji their plan.

"I'll do it," cried Joji.

"But it may be painful for you," cawed the crows.

"I don't care," said Joji, "not even if it takes my last straw."

Then the two crows with the best eyesight flew Joji to the farmhouse again.

"What do you want now?" frowned the fog when he saw them.

Joji said, "Oh, Mr. Fog, I'm already tired of being a scarecrow. I would like to accept the job of rubbing your back."

"That is very wise of you," said the fog. "Come right in with me."

The crows helped Joji take off his kimono. They soaped and rinsed him with a small bucket of water, and when he was clean, they put him into the tub.

"Be careful not to tickle," warned the fog.

Poor Joji! The bath was so deep he sank up to his chin.

Joji thought he would go to pieces from the hot water rushing through his straw. Still, very bravely, he settled into the bath.

Then with one hand he began rubbing the fog's back. But with the other hand he felt carefully around to the corner of the tub and pulled out the plug!

In a few seconds the fog noticed that the water was dropping down to his foggy waist, his foggy hips, until he jumped up in terror, screaming, "Water! Water! What happened to the water?"

"There will be no more water here!" gasped Joji. "So you'd better look somewhere else!"

Then the crows grabbed the fog by his long nose so that he jumped through the window in pain.

"I'm going back to the sea!" shouted the fog. "It may be too large, but at least it doesn't leak like that old tub!"

And the fog went storming off into steaming space.

But alas, poor Joji did not hear the fog's words. He had fainted in the tub.

The crows fluttered about in a frightened flurry. "Joji, Joji," they cawed, and their tears fell like dewdrops in the misty room.

Very tenderly they lifted Joji from the bath and spread him out on the floor. Then they flapped their wings wildly to dry him off, cawing, "Joji, Joji, the fog is gone! You are a scarefog at last!"

Joji opened his eyes and smiled at them. "Dear feathered friends," he whispered feebly. "You're the most faithful friends a scarefog ever had."

Then Joji asked the crows to stuff him back into his kimono and fly him home to his old post in the rice paddy.

The next morning when the farmer peeked through the closet door, he was surprised to see that Joji had scared away the fog. He was so happy he ran to the rice fields and hugged Joji in front of all the crows. Then he ran back to the farmhouse, heated some more bath water, washed himself off, and jumped joyously into the tub.

The buses began moving along the road again, the ships sailed up the river, and the sun shone brightly on the young rice plants. The farmer's friends were so grateful to Joji they brought fresh straw for his body. They even brought worms for the crows.

Proudly they said, "Joji is the greatest scarefog in all Japan."

Joji smiled happily up at the sun and then down at the young rice plants. "I am also the cleanest scarefog in all Japan," he said, winking at the crows. "But I don't think I'll take another bath ever again!"

Glossary

Full Pronunciation Key

The pronunciation of each word is shown just after the word, in this way: **ab bre vi ate** (ə brē′vē āt). The letters and signs used are pronounced as in the words below. The mark ′ is placed after a syllable with primary or heavy accent, as in the example above. The mark ′ after a syllable shows a secondary or lighter accent, as in **ab bre vi a tion** (ə brē′vē ā′shən).

a	hat, cap	j	jam, enjoy	u	cup, butter
ā	age, face	k	kind, seek	u̇	full, put
ã	care, air	l	land, coal	ü	rule, move
ä	father, far	m	me, am	ū	use, music
		n	no, in		
b	bad, rob	ng	long, bring		
ch	child, much				
d	did, red	o	hot, rock	v	very, save
		ō	open, go	w	will, woman
		ô	order, all	y	young, yet
e	let, best	oi	oil, voice	z	zero, breeze
ē	equal, be	ou	house, out	zh	measure, seizure
ėr	term, learn				
		p	paper, cup		
f	fat, if	r	run, try	ə	represents:
g	go, bag	s	say, yes		a in about
h	he, how	sh	she, rush		e in taken
		t	tell, it		i in April
i	it, pin	th	thin, both		o in lemon
ī	ice, five	ᵺH	then, smooth		u in circus

This pronunciation key is from the *Thorndike-Barnhart Beginning Dictionary*, Fifth Edition. Special acknowledgment is made to Clarence L. Barnhart, editor of the Thorndike-Barnhart Dictionaries, for his assistance in the preparation of this glossary.

-able, suffix meaning **1** that can be ____ed: Enjoy*able* means *that can be* enjoy*ed*. **2** adapted for or suitable to ____: Comfort*able* means *adapted for* comfort. **3** inclined to ____: Peace*able* means *inclined to* peace.

ain't (ānt), **1** am not; are not; is not. **2** have not; has not. Careful speakers do not use *ain't*.

Alas ka (ə las′kə), the largest state of the United States, in the northwestern part of North America. Alaska is the 49th state of the United States.

al pha bet (al′fə bet), the letters of a language arranged in a certain order, not as they are in words.

amid (ə mid′), in the middle of; among: *The church stood unharmed amid the ruins of the bombed town.*

an ces tor (an′ses tər), person from whom you are directly descended. Your father, your mother, your grandfathers, your grandmothers, and so on back, are your ancestors.

An ni ka (än′i kä).

ant ler (ant′lər), **1** horn of a deer, elk, moose, etc. **2** branch of such a horn.

anx ious (angk′shəs), **1** uneasy because of thoughts or fears about what may happen; troubled; worried: *The week of the flood was an anxious time for all of us.* **2** wishing very much; eager: *She was anxious to please her mother.*

as ton ish (əs ton′ish), surprise greatly; amaze: *The gift of ten dollars astonished me.*

Au du bon (ô′də bon), **John James** (1785-1851), an American painter who made a study of birds.

av er age (av′ər ij), **1** the average of several quantities is found by dividing the sum of all the quantities by the number of quantities: *The average of 3 and 10 and 5 is 6.* **2** obtained by averaging: *The average temperature for the week was 82.* **3** have as an average; be on the average: *The cost of our lunches at school averaged two dollars a week.* **av er aged, av er ag ing.**

bade (bad or bād), **1** commanded: *The captain bade the soldiers go on.* **2** invited. **3** told: *She bade us good-by.*

Bal ti more (bôl′tə môr), a city in northern Maryland.

bar ley (bär′lē), a grasslike plant or its grain. Barley will grow in cool climates. It is used for food.

hat, āge, cãre, fär;
let, bē, tėrm; it, īce;
hot, gō, ôrder;
oil, out;
cup, pút, rüle, ūse;
ch, child; ng, long;
th, thin; ₮H, then;
zh, measure;

ə represents *a* in about, *e* in taken, *i* in April, *o* in lemon, *u* in circus

antlers (definition 1)

white birch

bridle (definition 1)

castle (definition 1)

bid (bid), **1** command: *Do as I bid you.* **2** invite: *The King bade the nobles stay for the feast.* **3** say; tell: *His friends came to bid him good-by.*
bade or **bid, bid den** or **bid, bid ding.**

birch (bėrch), a slender tree with smooth bark and hard wood, used in making furniture.

bleach ers (blēch′ərz), seats, often roofless, at a baseball game or other outdoor sport.

bless ing (bles′ing), **1** a prayer asking God to show His favor. **2** anything that makes people happy and contented: *Good health is a great blessing.* **3** a short prayer of thanks before or after a meal; grace: *We asked Mr. Hall to say the blessing.*

body (bod′ē), **1** the whole material part of a man or animal: *This boy has a strong, healthy body.* **2** the main part of anything, such as the hull of a ship. **3** person. **bod ies.**

booth (būth), place where goods are sold or shown at a fair, market, etc. **booths** (būŦHz or būths).

breed (brēd), **1** produce young: *Rabbits breed rapidly.* **2** race; stock: *Terriers and spaniels are breeds of dogs.* **bred, breed ing.**

bri dle (brī′dl), **1** the head part of a horse's harness, used to hold back or control a horse. **2** put a bridle on. **bri dled, bri dling.**

brief (brēf), **1** short: *a brief meeting, a brief letter.* **2** give detailed information to: *The officer briefed the pilots just before they took off.*

buck (buk), **1** male deer, goat, hare, or rabbit. **2** jump into the air with back curved and come down with the front legs stiff: *The horse began to buck, but the cowboy stayed on.*

busi ness (biz′nis), **1** thing one is busy at; work; occupation: *A carpenter's business is building.* **2** matter; affair: *Mind your own business.* **3** trade; buying and selling: *The store does a big business.*

but ler (but′lər), male servant in charge of pantry and table service in a household; head servant.

cas tle (kas′l), **1** a large building or group of buildings with thick walls, towers, and other defenses against attack. **2** a palace that once had defenses against attack. **3** large and stately residence.

cau tious (kô′shəs), very careful; never taking chances: *a cautious driver.*

chant (chant), **1** song. **2** to sing. **3** a singsong way of talking. **4** say over and over.

Cher o kee (cher′ə kē), **1** member of a tribe of American Indians, now living mostly in Oklahoma. **2** their language. **Cher o kees** or **Cher o kee.**

Chi na town (chī′nə toun′), section of a city where Chinese people live.

chop[1] (chop), **1** cut by hitting with something sharp: *You can chop wood with an ax.* **2** cut into small pieces: *to chop up cabbage.* **3** slice of meat, especially of lamb, veal, or pork with a piece of rib. **chopped, chop ping.**

chop[2] (chop), jaw: *The dog licked his chops.*

chore (chôr), odd job; small task: *Feeding the chickens is a chore on the farm.*

cliff (klif), a very steep slope of rock, etc.

coach (kōch), **1** a large, old-fashioned, closed carriage with seats inside. **2** a passenger car of a railroad train. **3** a bus. **4** a person who teaches or trains athletic teams: *a football coach.* **5** train or teach.

com fort (kum′fərt), **1** ease the grief or sorrow of: *The mother's words comforted the sobbing child.* **2** anything that makes trouble or sorrow easier to bear: *His kind words brought comfort to the suffering family.* **3** person or thing that makes life easier or takes away hardships.

com fort a ble (kum′fər tə bl), **1** giving comfort: *A soft, warm bed is comfortable.* **2** in comfort; at ease; free from pain or hardship: *The warm fire made him feel comfortable.*

com mit tee (kə mit′ē), group of persons appointed or elected to do some special thing.

con densed milk (kən denst′), a thick, sweetened milk prepared by evaporating some of the water from sweetened milk.

Co ney Is land (kō′nē), an amusement park on a beach at the southwest end of Long Island, New York.

Con fu cius (kən fū′shəs), (551?-478 B.C.), a famous Chinese philosopher and moral teacher.

con tent[1] (kon′tent), **1** what is contained in anything; all things inside: *the contents of the room, the contents of a container or holder of any kind.* **2** what is written in a book; what is said in a speech: *I agreed with the content of the speech.*

con tent[2] (kən tent′), **1** satisfy; please. **2** satisfied; contented: *Are you content to wait till tomorrow?* **3** contentment; satisfaction: *The cat lay beside the fireplace in sleepy content.*

hat, āge, cãre, fär;
let, bē, tėrm; it, īce;
hot, gō, ôrder;
oil, out;
cup, pùt, rüle, ūse;
ch, child; ng, long;
th, thin; ᴛʜ, then;
zh, measure;

ə represents *a* in about,
e in taken, *i* in April,
o in lemon, *u* in circus

coach (definition 2)

269

coral

corral (definition 1)
horses in a corral

doe of the Virginia deer
(about 2¾ feet high
at the shoulder)

con test (kon′test for 1, kən test′ for 2), **1** a trial of skill to see who will win. A game or race is a contest. **2** dispute; struggle; fight.

cor al (kôr′əl), a hard red, pink, or white substance. Coral is made up of the skeletons of tiny sea animals. Coral is often used for jewelry.

cor ral (kə ral′), **1** pen for horses, cattle, etc. **2** drive into or keep in a corral. **cor ralled, cor ral ling.**

court yard (kôrt′yärd′), space enclosed by walls, in or near a large building: *Two big buses stood in the courtyard of the hotel.*

crop (krop), **1** plants grown or gathered by people for their use: *Wheat, corn, and cotton are three main crops of the United States.* **2** cut or bite off the top of: *Sheep had cropped the grass very short.* **cropped, crop ping.**

dan der (dan′dər), **1** temper; anger. **2 Get one's dander up** means get angry; lose one's temper.

D.C., District of Columbia.

Den mark (den′märk), a small country in northern Europe.

de spair (di spãr′), **1** loss of hope; a being without hope; a dreadful feeling that nothing good can happen to you: *Despair seized us as we felt the boat sinking under us.* **2** lose hope; be without hope: *The doctors despaired of saving the child's life.*

di do (dī′dō), prank; trick; mischievous or disorderly action. **di dos** or **di does.**

dif fi cul ty (dif′ə kul′tē), **1** a thing that is hard to do or understand. **2** something which stands in the way of getting things done. **3** trouble: *What is your difficulty?* **dif fi cul ties.**

dine (dīn), **1** eat dinner. **2** give dinner to; give a dinner for. **dined, din ing.**

di rect ly (də rekt′lē), **1** in a direct line or manner; straight: *This road runs directly north.* **2** exactly; absolutely: *directly opposite.* **3** immediately; at once: *Come home directly.*

District of Columbia, district in the eastern United States belonging to the United States government. It is entirely occupied by the capital, Washington.

dive (dīv), **1** plunge headfirst into water. **2** act of diving. **3** plunge (the body, the hand, or the mind) suddenly into anything: *The child dived into bed.* **dived** or **dove, dived, div ing.**

doe (dō), a female deer, goat, rabbit, or hare.

dove[1] (duv), bird with a thick body, short legs, and a beak enlarged at the tip; pigeon. The dove is often a symbol of peace.

dove[2] (dōv), dived: *The diver dove deep into the water after the sunken treasure.* See **dive.**

dusk (dusk), **1** the time just before dark. **2** shade; gloom.

em pire (em′pīr), **1** a group of nations or states under one ruler or government. **2** a country ruled by an emperor. **3** power; rule.

en chant (en chant′), **1** use magic on; put under a spell: *The witch had enchanted the princess.* **2** delight greatly; charm: *The music enchanted us.*

Eng land (ing′glənd), the largest division of Great Britain, in the southern part.

Eng lish (ing′glish), **1** of or having to do with England, its people, or their language. **2** the people of England. **3** the language of England. English is spoken also in Canada, the United States, New Zealand, Australia, and in many other places.

en vy (en′vē), **1** discontent or ill will at another's good fortune because one wishes it had been his; dislike for a person who has what one wants: *The boys were filled with envy when they saw Ed's bicycle.* **2** feel envy toward: *Some people envy the rich.* **3** the object of such feeling; person who is envied: *She was the envy of the girls in school.* **en vies, en vied, en vy ing.**

ex am ine (eg zam′ən), **1** look at closely and carefully: *The doctor examined the wound.* **2** test; test the knowledge or ability of; ask questions of. **ex am ined, ex am in ing.**

ex cuse (eks kūz′ for 1, 2, and 3, eks kūs′ for 4 and 5), **1** offer an apology for; try to remove the blame of: *She excused her own faults by blaming others.* **Excuse oneself** means ask to be pardoned: *He excused himself for bumping into me by saying that he was in a hurry.* **2** pardon; forgive: *Excuse me; I have to go now.* **3** free from duty; let off: *You are excused from spelling today.* **4** a reason, real or pretended, that is given; explanation: *He had many excuses for coming late to the party.* **5** act of excusing. **ex cused, ex cus ing.**

ex tra (eks′trə), **1** beyond what is usual, expected, or needed: *extra pay, extra fine quality, extra fare.* **2** anything that is extra: *Her bill for extras was $30.* **3** special edition of a newspaper.

dove

extra

hat, āge, cãre, fär;
let, bē, tėrm; it, īce;
hot, gō, ôrder;
oil, out;
cup, pùt, rüle, ūse;
ch, child; ng, long;
th, thin; ᵺ, then;
zh, measure;

ə represents *a* in about, *e* in taken, *i* in April, *o* in lemon, *u* in circus

dove[1]
(about 1 foot long)

271

faith ful (fāth′fəl), **1** worthy of trust; loyal:
a faithful friend. **2** true to fact; accurate.

fash ion (fash′ən), **1** the way a thing is shaped or
made or done: *He walks in a peculiar fashion.*
2 current custom in dress, manners, speech, etc.;
style: *She likes to read about the latest fashions.*
3 to make, shape, or form: *He fashioned a whistle
out of a piece of wood.*

fate (fāt), **1** a power that is believed to fix what
is to happen. Fate is beyond any person's control:
He does not believe in fate. **2** one's lot or fortune;
what happens to a person, group, etc.: *In every game
it was her fate to get caught.*

fear some (fir′səm), causing fear; frightful:
a fearsome sight.

fetch (fech), **1** go and get; bring: *Please fetch
me my glasses.* **2** be sold for: *I think these eggs
will fetch a good price.*

fit ting (fit′ing), right; proper; suitable.

flush (flush), **1** blush; glow: *The girl flushed when
they laughed at her.* **2** cause to blush or glow:
Exercise flushed his face.

fore-, prefix meaning **1** front: *Fore*foot means the
front foot. **2** before; beforehand: *Fore*see means
see *beforehand.*

for tu nate (fôr′chə nit), **1** having good luck;
lucky. **2** bringing good luck; having favorable results.

fowl er (foul′ər), person who hunts or traps
wild birds.

France (frans), a country in western Europe.

French man (french′mən), man born in France,
living there, or having French parents. **French men.**

friend ship (frend′ship), **1** state of being friends.
2 a liking between friends. **3** friendly feeling or
behavior.

fume (fūm), **1** vapor, gas, or smoke, especially if
harmful or strong: *The strong fumes of the acid nearly
choked him.* **2** give off vapor, gas, or smoke. **3** let
off one's rage in angry complaints: *He fumed about
the slowness of the train.* **fumed, fum ing.**

gasp (gasp), **1** a catching of the breath with open
mouth. **2** catch the breath with open mouth; breathe
with gasps. **3** utter with gasps: *"Help!"* he gasped.

gin ger (jin′jər), **1** spice made from the root of a
ginger plant. It is used for flavoring and in
medicine. **2** the root. Ginger is often preserved in
syrup or candied.

a ginger plant

good-by or **good-bye** (gud′bī′), farewell: *We said "Good-by" and went home.*

gourd (gôrd), **1** the fruit of certain vines whose hard, dried shell is used for cups, bottles, bowls, etc. **2** the plant itself. **3** a cup, bottle, bowl, etc., made from such a dried shell.

grate ful (grāt′fəl), thankful: *I am grateful for your help.*

hal lo (hə lō′), **1** call or shout to attract attention. **2** call of greeting or surprise. **3** shout; call. **hal los, hal loed, hal lo ing.**

has ten (hās′n), **1** hurry; cause to be quick; speed: *It's very late; hasten everyone off to bed.* **2** be quick; go fast: *hasten to explain.*

hast i ly (hās′tə lē), **1** in a hurried way; quickly and not very carefully. **2** rashly. **3** in a quick-tempered way.

Ha waii (hə wī′ē), island group in the Pacific Ocean. Hawaii is the 50th state of the United States.

height (hīt), how tall a person is; how high anything is; how far up a thing goes: *the height of a mountain.*

herd (hėrd), **1** a number of animals together: *a herd of cows, a herd of horses, a herd of elephants.* The animals in a herd are usually large and all of one kind. **2** form into a flock, herd, or group. **3** tend or take care of (cattle or sheep).

herds man (hėrdz′mən), man who tends a herd. **herds men.**

hin der (hin′dər), keep back; hold back; get in the way of; make hard to do: *Snow hinders travel.*

hon or (on′ər), **1** glory; fame: *The honor of inventing the electric light belongs to Thomas Edison.* **2** great respect; high regard. **Your Honor** is a title of respect used in speaking to a judge, mayor, etc. **3** respect highly; think highly of. **4** show respect to: *We honor our country's dead soldiers on Memorial Day.*

hon or a ble (on′ər ə bl), **1** having or showing a sense of what is right and proper; honest; upright: *It was not honorable for him to cheat.* **2** bringing honor or honors to somebody: *honorable mention.*

hum ble (hum′bl), **1** low in position or condition; not important; not grand: *We live in a humble cottage.* **2** modest; not proud. **3** make humble; make lower in position, condition, or pride. **hum bler, hum blest, hum bled, hum bling.**

hutch (huch), **1** a pen for rabbits. **2** hut. **3** box.

hat, āge, cãre, fär;
let, bē, tėrm; it, īce;
hot, gō, ôrder;
oil, out;
cup, pùt, rüle, ūse;
ch, child; ng, long;
th, thin; ᴛʜ, then;
zh, measure;

ə represents *a* in about, *e* in taken, *i* in April, *o* in lemon, *u* in circus

gourds (definition 1)

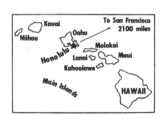

Hawaii

kimono (definition 1)
Japanese woman
wearing a kimono

girl wearing a lei

---

inn (in), a public house for lodging and caring for travelers. Hotels have largely taken the place of the old inns.

is land (ī′lənd), a body of land surrounded by water: *To reach the island, you go by boat or plane.*

James town (jāmz′toun), the first successful English settlement in the United States (1607), in Virginia. See the map under **Virginia.**

Ja pan (jə pan′), a country made up of several islands in the Pacific Ocean, along the eastern coast of Asia.

Jo ji (jō′jē).

ki mo no (kə mō′nə), **1** a loose outer garment held in place by a sash, worn by men and women in Japan. **2** a woman's loose dressing gown. **ki mo nos.**

king dom (king′dəm), a country that is governed by a king or a queen; the land or territory ruled by one king.

Kir sten (kir′stən).

La cour (lä kür′).

lar der (lär′dər), **1** pantry; place where food is kept. **2** stock of food: *The hunter's larder included flour, bacon, and what he had shot.*

lath er (laᴛH′ər), **1** foam made from soap and water. **2** put lather on: *He lathers his face before shaving.* **3** form a lather: *This soap lathers well.*

ledge (lej), **1** narrow shelf: *a window ledge.* **2** a shelf or ridge of rock.

lei (lā), wreath of flowers, leaves, etc. **leis.**

Li (lē).

Lin coln (ling′kən), **Abraham** (1809-1865), sixteenth President of the United States, 1861-1865.

lin ger (ling′gər), stay on; go slowly, as if unwilling to leave: *Daylight lingers long in the summertime.*

loft (lôft or loft), **1** space just below the roof in a cabin: *Abe Lincoln slept in a loft as a boy.* **2** the room under the roof of a barn.

Ma i le (mä′ē le).

maj es ty (maj′is tē), **1** stately appearance: *the majesty of the starry sky.* **2 Your Majesty, His Majesty,** or **Her Majesty** is a title given to kings, queens, and the like. **maj es ties.**

Man a luk (man′ə lük).

man ger (mān′jər), a box in a barn or stable built against the wall at the right height for horses and cows to eat from.

Mat o a ka (mat′ō ä′kə).

meal[1] (mēl), **1** breakfast, lunch, dinner, or supper. **2** the food eaten or served at any one time: *We enjoyed each meal at the hotel.*

meal[2] (mēl), **1** grain ground up: *corn meal.* **2** anything ground to a powder.

meek (mēk), **1** not easily angered; mild; patient. **2** submitting tamely when ordered about or injured by others: *The little boy was as meek as a lamb after he was punished.*

men tion (men′shən), **1** speak about: *Do not mention the accident to the children.* **2** a short statement (about): *There was mention of our school party in the newspaper.*

Mex i co (mek′sə kō), a country in North America, south of the United States.

mid[1] (mid), middle.

mid[2] or **'mid** (mid), amid.

mist (mist), **1** a cloud of very fine drops of water in the air; fog. **2** come down in mist; rain in very fine drops: *It is misting.*

mite (mīt), **1** anything very small; little bit: *Though poor, she gave her mite to charity.* **2** very small child: *What a little mite she is!* **3** a very tiny animal that lives in foods, on plants, or on other animals.

mug (mug), **1** a heavy china or metal drinking cup with a handle. **2** amount a mug holds.

mu se um (mū zē′əm), the building or rooms in which a collection of objects illustrating science, ancient life, art, or other subjects is kept.

nat u ral (nach′ə rəl), **1** produced by nature; coming in the ordinary course of events: *natural feelings, natural curls.* **2** belonging to the nature one is born with: *natural ability. It is natural for ducks to swim.* **3** in accordance with the facts of some special case: *a natural conclusion.* **4** like nature; true to life: *The picture looked natural.* **5** of or about nature: *natural history.*

nat u ral ly (nach′ə rəl ē), **1** in a natural way: *Speak naturally; don't try to imitate some actress.* **2** by nature: *a naturally obedient child.* **3** as might be expected; of course: *She offered me some candy; naturally, I took it.*

hat, āge, cãre, fär;
let, bē, tėrm; it, īce;
hot, gō, ôrder;
oil, out;
cup, pùt, rüle, ūse;
ch, child; ng, long;
th, thin; ᴛʜ, then;
zh, measure;

ə represents *a* in about, *e* in taken, *i* in April, *o* in lemon, *u* in circus

mite (definition 3)
(10 times actual length)

mug

275

na ture (nā′chər), **1** the world; all things except those made by man: *the wonders of nature.* **2** the regular ways in which things are and act: *It is against nature for a mother to hurt her child.* **3** life without artificial things: *Wild animals live in a state of nature.* **4** what a thing really is; quality; character: *It is the nature of robins to fly and to build nests.* **5** sort; kind: *books of a scientific nature.*

oblige (ə blīj′), **1** bind by a promise, contract, or duty; compel; force: *The law obliges parents to send their children to school. I am obliged to leave early to catch my train.* **2** bind by a favor or service; do a favor to: *Kindly oblige me by closing the door.* **obliged, oblig ing.**
ogre (ō′gər), in stories, a giant or monster that was supposed to eat people.
or phan age (ôr′fən ij), home for orphans.
over hear (ō′vər hir′), hear when one is not meant to hear: *I could not help overhearing what they said.* **over heard, over hear ing.**
ox (oks), **1** the full-grown male of domestic cattle when trained for farm work. **2** any of the group of animals, with horns and cloven hoofs, to which cattle, buffaloes, and bison belong. **ox en.**

pad dy (pad′ē), field of rice.
pal ace (pal′is), **1** a grand house for a king, a queen, or a bishop to live in. **2** a very fine house or building.
pan (pan), **1** a dish for cooking and other household uses, usually broad, shallow, and with no cover. **2** anything like this. Gold and other metals are sometimes obtained by washing ore in pans. **3** wash gravel in a pan to separate the gold. **4 Pan out** means turn out or work out: *His latest scheme panned out well.* **panned, pan ning.**
pause (pôz), stop for a time; wait: *He made a short pause and then went on reading. The dog paused when he heard me.* **paused, paus ing.**
phoe be (fē′bē), a small American bird.
pine[1] (pīn), **1** a tree with evergreen leaves shaped like needles. Many pines are of value for lumber, tar, turpentine, etc. **2** the wood of the pine.
pine[2] (pīn), **1** long eagerly; yearn: *The mother was pining to see her son.* **2** waste away with pain, hunger, grief, or desire. **pined, pin ing.**

rice paddy

phoebe
(about 7 inches long)

pine[1] (definition 1)
pine needles and cone

Po ca hon tas (pō′kə hon′təs), (1595?-1617), Indian girl who is said to have saved the life of Captain John Smith.

Pow ha tan (pou′ə tan′), (1550?-1618), Indian chief in Virginia.

pres ent ly (prez′nt lē), **1** before long; soon: *The clock will strike presently.* **2** at the present time; now: *Most nine-year-old children are presently in fourth grade.*

prom is ing (prom′is ing), likely to turn out well; hopeful: *a promising beginning, a bright, promising student.*

ram pi on (ram′pē ən), European plant whose root and leaves are used for salad.

re-, prefix meaning **1** again: *Reopen means open again.* **2** back: *Repay means pay back.*

rear[1] (rir), **1** back part; the back: *The kitchen is in the rear of the house.* **In the rear** often means behind. **2** back; at the back: *Leave by the rear door of the bus.*

rear[2] (rir), **1** make grow; help to grow; bring up: *The mother was very careful in rearing her children.* **2** set up; build: *The men of old reared altars to their gods.* **3** raise; lift up: *The snake reared its head.* **4** (of an animal) rise on the hind legs: *The horse reared as the fire engine sped past.*

reck on (rek′ən), **1** find the number or value of; count: *Reckon the cost before you decide.* **2** consider; judge: *He is reckoned a fine speller.* **3** depend; reply: *Can we reckon on your help?* **4** think; suppose.

red wood (red′wùd′), **1** a California evergreen tree, sometimes growing to a height of 300 feet. **2** the brownish-red wood of this tree.

re mark a ble (ri mär′kə bl), worthy of notice; unusual: *a remarkable memory.*

res er va tion (rez′ər vā′shən), **1** keeping back; hiding in part; something not expressed: *She outwardly approved of the plan with the mental reservation that she would change it to suit herself.* **2** land set aside for a special purpose: *The government has set apart Indian reservations.* **3** arrangement to keep a thing for a person; the securing of accommodations, etc., in advance: *Please make a reservation for a room at the hotel.*

Rolfe (rolf or rôlf), **John** (1585-1622), English colonist who was the husband of Pocahontas.

hat, āge, cãre, fär;
let, bē, tèrm; it, īce;
hot, gō, ôrder;
oil, out;
cup, pùt, rüle, ūse;
ch, child; ng, long;
th, thin; ᴛʜ, then;
zh, measure;

ə represents *a* in about,
e in taken, *i* in April,
o in lemon *u* in circus

rampion

scrub² (definition 1)

snowshoes

ruf fle (ruf′l), **1** make rough or uneven; to wrinkle: *A breeze ruffled the lake.* **2** a strip of cloth, ribbon, or lace gathered along one edge and used for trimming. **ruf fled, ruf fling.**

Ruth (rüth), **George Herman** (1895-1948), American baseball player whose nickname was Babe.

San Fran cis co (san frən sis′kō), large seaport city in California.

saw mill (sô′mil′), building where machines saw timber into planks, boards, etc.

scrub¹ (skrub), **1** rub hard; wash or clean by rubbing: *She scrubbed the floor with a brush and soapsuds.* **2** a scrubbing: *Give your face and hands a good scrub.* **scrubbed, scrub bing.**

scrub² (skrub), **1** low, stunted trees or shrubs. **2** small; poor; inferior: *scrub oak.*

Se quoy ah (si kwoi′ə), (1770?-1843), an Indian who invented a system of Cherokee writing.

shave (shāv), **1** cut hair from (the face, chin, etc.) with a razor. **2** cut off in thin slices: *She shaved the chocolate.* **shaved, shaved** or **shav en, shav ing.**

-ship, suffix meaning **1** office or rank of: Governor*ship* means the rank of *governor.* **2** state or condition of being: Partner*ship* means the condition of being a *partner.* **3** power or skill of ____: Workman*ship* means the skill of a *workman.* Dictator*ship* means the power of a *dictator.*

Sioux (sü), **1** member of a tribe of American Indians. **2** of this tribe. *pl.* **Sioux.**

skein (skān), small bundle of yarn or thread.

Smith (smith), Captain **John** (1580-1631), English explorer and early settler in Virginia.

snow shoe (snō′shü′), a light wooden frame with strips of leather stretched across it. Trappers in the far North wear snowshoes on their feet to keep from sinking in deep, soft snow.

Soo-Pung (sü′pùng′).

spare (spãr), **1** show mercy to; refrain from harming or destroying: *He spared his enemy.* **2** get along without; omit; do without: *Dad can't spare the car; so I have to walk.* **spared, spar ing.**

spell¹ (spel), **1** write or say the letters of (a word) in order: *We learn to spell in school.* **2** mean: *Those clouds spell a storm.* **spelled** or **spelt, spell ing.**

spell² (spel), **1** word or set of words supposed to have magic power. **2** fascination; charm: *We were under the spell of the beautiful music.*

spell bound (spel′bound′), too interested to move; fascinated; enchanted: *The children were spellbound by the circus performance.*

spir it (spir′it), **1** soul: *At death, the spirit leaves the body.* **2** supernatural being. God is a spirit. Ghosts and fairies are spirits. **3 Spirits** means state of mind; disposition; temper: *He is in good spirits.* **Out of spirits** means sad; gloomy.

sprout (sprout), **1** begin to grow; shoot forth: *Seeds sprout. Buds sprout in the spring.* **2** a shoot of a plant: *bean sprouts.*

sta di um (stā′dē əm), place shaped like an oval or a U, consisting of tiers of seats around an open field. **sta di ums, sta di a** (stā′dē ə).

stag (stag), **1** a full-grown male deer. **2** male: *A stag dinner is for men only.*

step broth er (step′bruᴛʜ′ər), a stepfather's or stepmother's son by a former marriage: *If John's father marries a widow with a little boy, this boy will be John's stepbrother.*

step fa ther (step′fä′ᴛʜər), man who has married one's mother after the death or divorce of one's real father.

step moth er (step′muᴛʜ′ər), woman who has married one's father after the death or divorce of one's real mother.

step sis ter (step′sis′tər), a stepfather's or stepmother's daughter by a former marriage.

swash (swosh), **1** dash (water, etc.) about; splash. **2** such action or sound: *the swash of waves against a boat.*

swirl (swėrl), **1** move or drive along with a twisting motion; whirl: *dust swirling in the air, a stream swirling over rocks.* **2** swirling movement; a whirl. **3** twist; curl: *a swirl of whipped cream.*

syl la ble (sil′ə bl), **1** a word or part of a word pronounced as a unit that usually consists of a vowel alone or a vowel with one or more consonants. There are three syllables, sil, ə, and bl, in the pronunciation of the word *syllable.* Certain consonant sounds may be used as a vowel sound in syllables, such as the (l) in *bottle* (bot′l) or the (n) in *hidden* (hid′n). **2** one or more letters in a printed or written word that may be separated from other syllables of the word by a space, hyphen, or other mark to show where the word may be divided at the end of a line. *Strength* has only one syllable; *ap prox i mate* has four.

hat, āge, cãre, fär;
let, bē, tėrm; it, īce;
hot, gō, ôrder;
oil, out;
cup, put, rüle, ūse;
ch, child; ng, long;
th, thin; ᴛʜ, then;
zh, measure;

ə represents *a* in about, *e* in taken, *i* in April, *o* in lemon, *u* in circus

stag (definition 1)
(about 4 feet high
at the shoulder)

279

syr up (sir′əp or sėr′əp), a sweet, thick liquid. Sugar boiled with water or fruit juices makes a syrup. A cough syrup contains medicine to relieve coughing. Maple syrup is made from the sap of maple trees. Also spelled **sirup.**

tai lor (tā′lər), **1** man whose business is making or repairing clothes. **2** make by tailor's work: *The suit was well tailored.*

-teen, suffix meaning ten more than ____: Seven*teen* means *ten more than* seven.

ter rif ic (tə rif′ik), **1** causing great fear; terrifying: *A terrific earthquake shook Japan.* **2** very great, severe, etc.: *A terrific hot spell ruined many of the crops.*

ter ri fy (ter′ə fī), fill with great fear; frighten very much: *He was terrified by the sight of the bear.* **ter ri fied, ter ri fy ing.**

ter ror (ter′ər), **1** great fear. **2** cause of great fear: *Pirates were once the terror of the sea.*

-th¹, suffix meaning **1** a being ____: Warm*th* means *a being* warm. **2** that which is ____: Tru*th* means *that which is* true.

-th², suffix meaning ____ in order or position in a series: Six*th* means six *in order or position in a series.*

thee (ᴛHē), an old word meaning **you.**

thick et (thik′it), shrubs, bushes, or small trees growing close together: *We crawled into the thicket and hid.*

threat (thret), **1** statement of what will be done to hurt or punish someone: *We stopped playing in the street because of the policeman's threats to arrest us.* **2** a sign or cause of possible evil or harm: *Those black clouds are a threat of rain.*

trail er (trāl′ər), **1** wagon or cart pulled by an automobile, truck, etc. **2** a vehicle fitted up for people to live in and pulled by an automobile; house on wheels.

trough (trôf or trof), **1** a long, narrow container for holding food or water: *He led the horses to the watering trough.* **2** something shaped like this: *The baker used a trough for kneading dough.*

Tu tu (tü′tü).

-ty¹, suffix meaning ____ tens: Six*ty* means six *tens.*

-ty², suffix meaning state or condition of being ____: Safe*ty* means *state of being* safe. *-ity* is often used instead of *-ty,* as in *timidity.*

trailer (definition 2)

un der brush (un′dər brush′), bushes, small trees, etc., growing under large trees in woods or forests.

ut ter ly (ut′ər lē), completely; totally; absolutely.

val ley (val′ē), **1** low land between hills or mountains: *Most large valleys have rivers running through them.* **2** wide region drained by a great river system: *the Mississippi valley.* **val leys.**

vi cious (vish′əs), **1** evil; wicked: *The criminal led a vicious life.* **2** having bad habits or a bad disposition: *a vicious horse.* **3** spiteful.

vil la (vil′ə), a house in the country or suburbs, sometimes at the seashore. A villa is usually a large or elegant residence.

Vil le kul la (vil′ə kûl′ä).

Vir gin ia (vər jin′yə), a southern state of the United States.

-ward suffix meaning toward ___: Back*ward* means *toward* the back. Home*ward* means *toward* home.

Wash ing ton (wosh′ing tən or wôsh′ing tən), **1** the capital of the United States. **2** a northwestern state of the United States, on the Pacific coast.

wedge (wej), **1** piece of wood or metal with a thin edge used in splitting, separating, etc. **2** something shaped like a wedge or used like a wedge: *Wild geese fly in a wedge.* **3** thrust or pack in tightly; squeeze: *The man's foot was wedged between the rocks.* **wedged, wedg ing.**

Wei (wā).

whin ny (hwin′ē), **1** the sound that a horse makes. **2** make this sound. **whin nies, whin nied, whin ny ing.**

white wash (hwīt′wosh′ or hwīt′wôsh′), **1** liquid for whitening walls, woodwork, etc. Whitewash is usually made of lime and water. **2** whiten with whitewash. **3** cover up the faults or mistakes of.

whit tle (hwit′l), **1** cut shavings or chips from (wood, etc.) with a knife, usually for fun. **2** cut or shape (wood) with a knife: *The old sailor was whittling a boat.* **whit tled, whit tling.**

wis dom (wiz′dəm), **1** being wise; knowledge and good judgment based on experience. **2** wise conduct; wise words: *His wisdom guided us.*

with draw (wiŦH drô′), **1** draw back; draw away: *The child quickly withdrew his hand from the fire.* **2** take back; remove. **3** go away: *She withdrew from the room.* **with drew, with drawn, with draw ing.**

hat, āge, cãre, fär;
let, bē, tèrm; it, īce;
hot, gō, ôrder;
oil, out;
cup, pùt, rüle, ūse;
ch, child; ng, long;
th, thin; ŦH, then;
zh, measure;

ə represents *a* in about, *e* in taken, *i* in April, *o* in lemon, *u* in circus

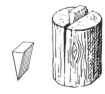

wedge (definition 1)
wedge splitting a log

About This Book

More Roads to Follow, Book Three, Part Two, of The New Basic Reading Program, readies children for moving successfully into the middle grades, where reading interests broaden along with expanding subject matter. The content of *More Roads to Follow*—stories, articles, biographical sketches, poems—is purposely varied to prepare children for this step. The independence in interpretation and word analysis that boys and girls must have to deal competently with the demands of the middle grades is the special object of the guidance suggested in the *Guidebook* and of the exercises in the *Think-and-Do Book*.

The stories in Unit I, "Roads Here and There," were selected for their intrinsic quality, their appeal for boys and girls, and the human values presented in them. At the same time the selections give young readers some impression of the variety in our nation, which now leaps half a continent to include Alaska and part of an ocean to embrace Hawaii. Unit II, "Interesting People along the Way," introduces biography into The New Basic Reading Program. Here the child, building on his introduction to the Pilgrims in Book Three, Part One, will continue to develop appreciation for the past and feelings of warm personal relationship with people and events that precede his own times. All stories and articles in this unit are in some way related to the content of earlier stories in The New Basic Reading Program (Babe Ruth with baseball, for example) or are concerned with familiar persons (Abe Lincoln) or everyday things (the origin of the hot dog). The third unit, "Roads to Make-Believe," includes new and old fanciful tales, fables in classic form, and narrative verse.

More Roads to Follow uses 735 words not previously used in The New Basic Readers. Some of these are introduced as root words, others as inflected or derived forms. The 561 new words that can be identified independently by pupils who have mastered the word-analysis program through the level of Book Three, Part One, are printed in blue and starred in the list below. Thirty new forms of known words are also printed in blue and starred. These forms, not counted as new, include words made by adding or dropping the prefixes *a-, dis-, im-;* the suffixes *-less, -ment, -ness, -ous;* and plurals of words that end in *f* or *fe.*

The 174 words printed in black are words that pupils cannot be expected to identify on the basis of skills learned through Book Three, Part One. Blue stars on 34 of these words indicate that children should be able to identify them by combining context clues with word-analysis skills that have already been taught at some point in *More Roads to Follow*, Book Three, Part Two.

A glossary is included in this book to encourage the habit of looking up the pronunciation and meaning of words. All words printed in italic type in the vocabulary list are in the Glossary, either in the form shown or the root form.

Vocabulary List

Roads Here and There

6. Poem
7. . . . .

---

8. . . . .
9. . . . .
   Thunderbolt*
   ranch*
   west*
   bought*
   *trailer**
   enjoyed*
10. *corral*
    cattle*
    arrived*
    stretch*.
11. . . . .
    *saddle**
    *bridle**
    *wore**
    eager*
    gaily*
    *herd**
12. . . . .
    twice*
    *ledge**
    *whinnied**
13. carrots
    sugar
    usually
    harm*
    moment*
    shade*
14. afterwards
    lonely*
    except*

15. disappointed
    advice*
    distance*
    mine*
    bother*
    became*
16. *anxious*
    understand
    gentle*
    unless*
    *buck**
    *rear**
17. . . . .
    trembled*
    *bareback**
    trusted*

---

18. *average*
    height
    *breeds**
    less*
    inches*
    measured*
19. fourteen
    twenty*
    world*
    Shetland*
    size*

---

20. *Kirsten*
    shell*
    groups*
    desk*
    *Denmark**

21. *Lacour*
    classes*
    divided*
    *booth**
    Larsen*
    shyly*
22. . . . .
    sort*
    sell*
    *gasped**
    *hastily**
    insisted*
    pity*
23. *difficulty*
    convenient
    course
    manage*
    frowned*
    *extra**
24. favorites
    sandwiches*
    giggle*
    added*
    stupid*
25. holidays
    *excuse**
    costumes*
26. customers
    among
    punch*
    *envy**
    *joy**
    heart*

---

27. Kaller
    examine

mountain*
Rufe*
doctor*
sighed*
28. though
    costs*
    dollars*
    chairbound*
    *cliff**
    leafy*
29. months
    *whittling**
    sharp*
    figure*
    sea*
    forty*
30. precious*
    fellow*
    mind*
    halfway*
    smoke*
    breath*
31. . . . .
    *pines**
    rod*
    wandered*
    present*
    snatched*
    carved*
32. *business*
    startled*
    stuck*
    trade*
33. . . . .
    speechless*

forward*
stared*
worth*
ruffling

34. . . . .
moon*
tears*
swallowed*

35-36. Poems

---

37. *reservation*
California
Charley*
dust*
mad*
Jean*
38. hospital
valley
nurse*
Jerome*
39. impatiently*
Sioux
dumb*
panting*
40. satisfied
exercise
boiling-hot*
drove*
mistaken*
41. questioned
lawn*
mower*
cocoa*
42. none
attention
curious
pay*
43. sew
granny*
suggested*
cloth*
Friday*
44. *English*
aloud*
song*
meant*
45. eleven
stuff*
honey*
fact*

46-47. Poem

---

48. Louella
stray*
rewards*
changed*
parrot*
jealous*
49. *committee*
scream*
themselves*
hated*
appeared*
Texas*
dance*
borrow*
50. decorations
shrieked*
south*
hotel*
51. hey
drew*
paid*
revolving*
refused*
52. . . . .
enter*
allowed*
pardon*
53. . . . .
54. discovered
impossible
declared*
lady*
sputtered*
55. outward
naturally
wailed*
56. . . . .
loaned*
written*
tag*
spilled*
57. become
wagging*
collar*

---

58. *Soo-Pung*
San Francisco's
spirits
Chinese*
excitement*
awakened*
Chinatown
rice*
eagerness*

---

59. *Wei*
touching
dragon*
goodness*
soles*
60. *Li*
dissatisfied*
beans*
sprouts
pound*
silk*
teeth*
61. . . . .
Ping*
Lin*
burst*
pairs*
trousers*
62. although
shiny*
wall*
marked*
measurement*
63. *Confucius*
despair
ills*
possibly*
shaped*
thick*
64. *ancestors*
wisdom
wedges
swung*
mid
65. . . . .
person*
switching*

---

66. potato
backwards*
delighted*
bunk*
spent*
67. . . . .
mist
stag
shone*
antlers
plainly*
doe
68. . . . .
69. *island*
paused
bent*

---

lump*
ceiling*
fairy*
70. lose
peculiar
lying*
growl*
stiffly*
71. . . . .
apart*
fearfully*
sniffing*
72. *vicious*
enormous
gun*
lick*
chops
choked*
73. continued
cautiously
relieved*
peered*
fur*
rubbed*
74. difference
toasty*
scamp*
chuckled*

75-76. Poem

---

77. *lei*
celebrated
Hawaii
states*
united*
78. whose
79. . . . .
80. *Maile's*
alive*
blossoms*
contest
81. *Tutu*
two-toned*
win*
prize*
nets*
dead*
82. poured
beneath*
shaved
syrup
coconut*

83. forenoon
   mix*
   glanced*
   disappoint-
      ment*
   aboard*
84. giant*
   needle*
   thread*
   dew*
85. honorable
   mention*
   grumbled*
   judging*
   reminded*
86. ....
   Japan*

87. ribbon*
   familiar
   mayor*
   _____
88. Manaluk's
   Alaska
   gold*
   post*
   crayons*
   peaches*
89. ....
90. ....
   loaded*
   sled*
   lie*
   rescued*
   whiskers*

91. comfortable
92. ....
   pencil*
   pack*
93. ....
   flushed*
   hid*
   melted*
   mud*
   chores*
   rich*
94. ....
   weeds*
   scooped*
   pebbles*
   till*

95. medicine
   vegetables
   single*
   sick*
   sickness*
   castor*
96. shoulder
   bottle*
   sky*
97. ....
   threw*
98. ....
   waist*
   striking*
   squishy*
99. ....
   _____

Interesting People along the Way

100. Quotation
101. ....
   _____
102. Ruth
   babe*
   Herman*
   New York*
   Yankees*
103. ....
104. stadium
   Ruthville
   fan*
   bleachers*
   chant*
105. Baltimore
   mischief*
106. orphanage
   Matthias
   tailor*
   earn*
   problems*
107. terrific
   fifteen*
   aware*
108. orioles
   lanky*
   hundred*
   famous*
109. stomach
   discouraged

lathered*
mustard*
ache*
happiness*
illness*
110. ....
   tip*
   _____
111. ....
   heat*
   Coney*
   Charlie*
   inns*
112. failure
   obliged*
   sausage*
   wrapping*
113. frankfurters
   popular
   served*
   picnics*
   laid*
114. president
   England
   queen*
   royal*
   _____
115-116. Poem

117. Audubon's
   Pennsyl-
      vania
   museum
   Frenchman*
   Lucy*
118. friendship
   cave*
   nest*
   underbrush*
   graceful*
119. upward*
   gazed*
   dipped*
120. phoebes
   proved
   distant*
   protested*
   born*
121. ....
   urged*
122. ....
   discussing*
123. already
   gratefully
   rust*
   bracelet*
   indeed*
124. marry*
   marriage

James*
   wasting*
   fate*
   healthy*
125. ....
126. ....
   _____
127. Poem
   _____
128. Sequoyah's
   Cherokee
   lame*
   magic*
   destroy*
129. relations
   sheets*
   tribe*
130. brief*
   spelling*
131. ....
   threatened*
   foolishness*
   leaking*
   anger*
   hut*
   peace*
132. consider
   daughter*

133. . . . .
speech*
134. *alphabet*
syllables
arranged*
135. . . . .
printed*
honors

___

136. . . . .
amazing*
137. *Washington,*
D.C.
statue*
Oklahoma
138. . . . .
139. *Mexico*

___

140. Mathilda
Abe*
*Lincoln**
*Crawford**
*Johnston**
bonnet*
141. pa
ma
trough

Dennis*
*loft**
142. Sarah
gourdful
*ain't**
*meekly**
rinse*
143. . . . .
wiped*
144. mamma
damp*
*blessing**
Lord*
*Thee**
145. truth*
stool*
sternly*
146. . . . .
wicked*
147. . . . .
148. interrupted
*didos**
*reckon**
spanked*
towering*
149. apron*

cheeks*
*mite**
150. . . . .
tub*
151. . . . .
152. . . . .
*dander**
153. . . . .
hug*
breathlessly*

___

154-156. Poems

___

157. *Virginia*
*Smith**
tents*
158. *terror**
protected*
beads*
pale*
159. captured*
warriors
Powhatan
prisoner*
160. . . . .
clubs*

161. rebuilt
*spared**
162. . . . .

___

163. *Matoaka*
Rebecca
Pocahontas
164. . . . .
*meal**
scrape*
165. . . . .
166. . . . .
167. immediately
arguing*
argument*
168. . . . .
church*
169. . . . .
*Rolfe**
Dale*
Thomas*
170. . . . .
princess*
171. *palace**

___

Roads to Make-Believe

172. Poem
173. . . . .

___

174. . . . .
175. . . . .
puss-in-boots*
jacket*
master*
sack*
176. salad*
Willowonder
duke*
poked*
177. *courtyard*
*majesty**
*butler**
wits*
throne*
178. . . . .
accept*
*dine**

179. . . . .
*coach**
rumbling*
drowning*
alas*
guard*
shivering*
180. . . . .
cape*
181. cruel*
ogre
*barley**
*hallo**
*castle**
182. . . . .
greedy*
183. aha
tiger*
split*

184. . . . .
*larder**
185. . . . .
*faithful**
186. . . . .
favor*
clap*
cloud*
handsome*

___

187. . . . .
*humble**
cottage*
granted*
188. *fortunate**
diamonds*
*empire**
pearls*
189. . . . .
prefer*
instant*

190. . . . .
fault*
rather*
complaining*
191. . . . .
192. . . . .
towel*
slightest*
193. Rapunzel*
*rampion**
surrounded*
dared*
witch*
194. . . . .
*content**
*dusk**
slipped*
*fetch**

195. *comfort**
neither*
nor*
proper*
child*
196. ....
*thicket**
thorn*
scratch*
*bade**
braids*
sweetly*
197. ....
crept*
*enchanted**
198. *remarkable**
*terrified**
199. *skein*
*kingdom**
learnt*
deceive*
200. ....
rage*
seized*
snip*
201. ....
sadness*
blinded*
wept*
sobbing*
202. *manger*
*ox**
nap*
*muttering**
203. ....
ant*
chat*
204. *dove*
stream*
helplessly*
*fowler**
deserves*
205-206. Poem
207. ....
frying*
*sawmill**
Karl*
selected*
crispest*
napkin*

208. *astonished**
goblins*
209. ....
ripe*
*lingered**
210. ....
211. ....
disagreed*
212. **fourteenth***
fifteenth*
*bid**
count*
tempt*
213. ....
*hindered**

214-216. Poems

217. **absolutely***
Pippi*
Longstocking*
cradle*
218. *Villekulla*
Annika
*villa**
playmate*
219. ....
dull*
thin*
220. ....
gutter*
silence*
221. ....
lazy*
rats*
candy*
screws*
222. ....
knees*
pickets*
223. ....
*utterly**
*hutch**
tin*
224. ....
jar*
225. ....
spool*
bubbles*
necklace*
heels*
226. ....
Willie*
Bengt*
fight*

cowards*
hash*
astonishment*
227. ....
*birch**
228. ....
229. ....
hollow*
loop*
230. ....
stump*
*coral**
tuck*
slept*
pillow*
quilt*
231. ....

232-237. Poems

238. ....
Pooh*
Edward*
Winnie-the-Pooh*
humming*
stoutness*
239. ....
240. ....
241. ....
scuffling*
242. ....
243. ....
*mugs**
*condensed**
244. ....
*directly**
*good-bye**
245. **Christopher***
carelessly*
robin*
246. ....
247. ....
248. ....
deal*
sustaining*
tightness*
249. ....
north*
slenderer*
250. ....
cork*

251-252. Poem

253. *Joji*
fog*
worms*
*paddy**
254. ....
duty*
floated*
breathing*
255. *kimono**
*fumed**
*swirled**
tea*
steaming*
bath*
256. ....
*swashed**
oozed*
spin*
collided*
257. ....
guide*
slid*
blankets*
258. ....
worst*
chilled*
roots*
droop*
cawed*
causing*
259. ....
smooth*
260. ....
261. ....
painful*
262. ....
tickle*
sank*
263. ....
plug*
hips*
264. ....
fluttered*
flurry*
tenderly*
flapped*
feebly*
265. ....
peeked*
joyously*
winking*

287

Acknowledgments

Grateful acknowledgment is hereby given for the right to adapt and use the following copyrighted material:

"When Is a Horse a Pony?" from *Fact and Fiction Book—Animals in Action* edited by George S. Amsbary. Copyright © 1958 by Spencer Press, Inc. By permission of American Peoples Press, Inc.

"Out of Her Shell" from "Kirsten Comes Out of Her Shell" by Lorrie McLaughlin in *Highlights for Children*, August-September, 1962. By permission of Highlights for Children, Inc., Columbus, Ohio. Copyright © 1962.

"The World of Hogback Mountain," by Jeanne Hines in *American Junior Red Cross News*, January, 1961. By permission of the author and publisher.

"Soo-Pung Measures Up" by Shirlee P. Newman. From *Child Life* Magazine (January), copyright 1958. By permission of the author and publisher.

"May Day and Lei Day" from "Lei Day in Hawaii" by Sandra Million Stephens in *Jack and Jill*, May, 1962. Reprinted by special permission from *Jack and Jill* 1962, The Curtis Publishing Company. By permission of the author and publisher.

"Maile's Lei" by Mary Dana Rodriguez in *American Junior Red Cross News*, April, 1957. By permission of the author and publisher.

"Manaluk's Gold Rush" by Marion Holland in *American Junior Red Cross News*, February, 1956. By permission of the author and publisher.

"Get 'Em While They're Hot" by Martin Abramson in *Boys' Life*, July, 1963. By permission of the author and *Boys' Life*, published by the Boy Scouts of America.

"Audubon's Birds" by Janet Marshall. By permission of the author.

"Sequoyah's Talking Leaves" by Janet Marshall. By permission of the author.

"Sequoyah's Honors" by Janet Marshall. By permission of the author.

"Captain Smith of Jamestown" by K. B. Frost. By permission of the author.

"The Girl with Three Names" by K. B. Frost. By permission of the author.

"Puss-in-Boots" from *The First Book of Fairy Tales* as retold by Elizabeth Abell. By permission of Franklin Watts, Inc.

"The Dog in the Manger" adapted with permission of the publisher from *The Fables of Aesop* by Joseph Jacobs. Copyright 1950 by The Macmillan Company.

"The Ant and the Grasshopper" adapted with permission of the publisher from *The Fables of Aesop* by Joseph Jacobs. Copyright 1950 by The Macmillan Company.

"The Plate of Pancakes" by permission of Lothrop, Lee & Shepard Co., Inc., from *The Story Teller* by Maud Lindsay.